Paul J. Murphy

BREZHNEV
SOVIET POLITICIAN

McFarland & Company, Inc.
Publishers
Jefferson, N.C., 1981

Also by Paul J. Murphy
Naval Power in Soviet Policy (ed.)

Frontispiece: relaxing during his smoking days.

947.085
30924
Mur

Library of Congress Cataloging in Publication Data

Murphy, Paul J
Brezhnev, Soviet politician.

Includes bibliographical references and index.
1. Brezhnev, Leonid Il'ich, 1906-
2. Russia — Presidents — Biography.
I. Title.
DK268.B69M87   947.085'3'0924 [B]   80-15901
ISBN 0-89950-002-1

Preface

This is a book about the political struggle and the rise to power of Leonid Ilyich Brezhnev.

On October 12, 1964, Brezhnev seized the reins in the Union of Soviet Socialist Republics, although Western diplomats had not regarded him as a serious contender for Nikita Khrushchev's throne. Brezhnev's health (he had a record of heart trouble), personality and background had seemed to disqualify him from the top job. His sudden ascendancy came as a surprise to many; his aggrandizement of power since then has surprised yet more. After more than 15 years at the top, Brezhnev still remains an enigma to the West.

The present work attempts to remove some of the confusion about the Soviet politician. It reaches as far back as the Bolshevik Revolution to focus on Brezhnev's political rise, beginning with Lenin, and the political, sometimes personal, conflicts experienced on the way to Moscow. Brezhnev is sketched as the young Stalinist, provincial official, Khrushchev client, political conspirator and, finally, Communist Party chief.

Since, as Erik Erikson stated (in his 1962 *Young Man Luther*), "We cannot lift a case history out of history" just as we cannot "separate the logic of the history event from that of life history," I have selected significant events from each period of Brezhnev's life to provide a full and systematic portrait of his political growth. The chronological approach is followed with little exception. Like his predecessors, Brezhnev has had to fight to preserve and enhance the power won in 1964, since his official position as Party chief does not automatically make him secure from threats and challenges to his leadership. The last chapters depart from chronology to show this methodical aggrandizement.

I have taken the view that conflict is the principal element of Soviet political life and that there are several sources of conflict, beginning with the Party itself, whose leaders have all had to fight their way to power using methods prescribed by the political system and prevailing circumstances. Brezhnev is an exemplary product of this process. Rivalry, struggle and intrigue over power and policy are the stuff of Soviet politics. In this regard, the book is also a study about the dynamics of Soviet politics, and should provide the general reader with an understanding of how Soviet politicians are made and how Soviet policy decisions are reached.

In the main, though, this is a political biography. The reader should keep in mind that political biography, like Kremlinology, is akin to the writing of fiction in that conclusions must necessarily be drawn from evidence that is complex, fragmentary and often imprecise; the role of personal judgment is high. Furthermore, the secrecy surrounding Brezhnev makes him difficult to know. Not all of his actions can be explained. For these and other reasons this biography of the Soviet Communist Party leader must remain tentative.

I am indebted to a number of people who provided aid, advice, criticism and encouragement since the work began in 1972. I owe a special debt to Carl Linden of the Institute for Sino-Soviet Studies at George Washington University for reading the original and complicated drafts. My thanks also go to John Armstrong, Paul Smith, Sidney Ploss, Harry Rigby and others whose discussions with me were invaluable. I am also grateful to my colleagues in the Department of Government, University of Queensland (Brisbane, Australia), for their encouragement and support during my tenure there.

Of course, this study would not have been possible without the help of Russian and Ukrainian émigrés who kindly consented to be interviewed. Nathan Kruglak, who was born in Brezhnev's hometown and shared many of the same growing-up experiences and emotions, and whom I interviewed in his home in Milwaukee in December 1973, was especially helpful. Others have asked not to be mentioned by name.

Finally, I must acknowledge the assistance of Margaret. Without her contributions, ranging from research to editing, this book would never have reached the publisher.

Paul J. Murphy

Washington, D.C.
Summer 1979 & Winter 1980

Table of Contents

List of Photographs

Accomplished leaders do not fall from the skies, they are raised up only in the course of the struggle. — Joseph Stalin.

Part I
The Formative Years

Ilya and Natalya Brezhnev early in the century.

I

Child of the "Meshokniki"

I had not yet reached the age of 11 when an historical event of immense significance, the revolution of October 25 [November 7], 1917, occurred in Russia. I witnessed the birth of a new era in modern history — although, naturally, I realized this only as I grew older. — L.I. Brezhnev, 1978.

LEONID ILYICH BREZHNEV was born into that generation of Russian children, the sons and daughters of the true Russian proletariat, who witnessed, and survived, the transfer of political power in czarist Russia during October (*i.e.*, November in the new style Julian Calendar) 1917. Lenin's October Revolution and the establishment of Soviet power in the Russian empire was especially complicated in Brezhnev's native Ukraine where a bloody civil war raged on for four years. The unprecedented suffering and deprivations of everyday existence in those years deeply affected the young Brezhnev. Indeed, he was lucky to survive.

Born on December 16, 1906, in what is today the industrial city of Dneprodzerzhinsk, Brezhnev was the first male child born in the Ukraine to the Brezhnevs. A Great Russian family, the Brezhnevs had migrated south with the metallurgical industry to the newly discovered rich mineral lands of the Ukraine during the Russian industrial boom of the 1880s and 90s. Two generations of Brezhnevs had labored in the steel mills of Kurskaya Province[1] in Russia before Yakov, Leonid's grandfather, his wife, and son Ilya resettled in their new home.

By the turn of the century this forbidding land had become a bustling industrial frontier. Here French and Belgian companies, attracted by the prospects of huge profits as well as by the cheap and abundant Russian labor force, and welcomed by Czar Alexander III, carved out a vast metallurgical empire whose blast furnaces supplied more than half the Czar's pig iron. In 1887, the South Russian Metallurgical Company built the "Dneprovskiy" factory in the village of Kamiansk on the Dneper River. It became the source of livelihood for three generations of the Brezhnev family.

5

In 1889, the Brezhnevs, uprooted and facing difficult conditions, began life anew in the squalid little industrial settlement in which the factory was located. Kamiansk, founded by and named after the Cossack settler Kamion in 1750, was later to be called Kamenskoye-Zaporozhye, and even later, simply Kamenskoye,[2] by its Russian occupants. A one-room house of crude slag bricks, the ready byproduct of factory waste, complete with an earthen floor, became home. Situated in the Dneprovskiy factory, which was to assume particular importance in Leonid Brezhnev's life, it was one of many such primitive dwellings lining the road down which Yakov and later Ilya trudged to the factory each morning.

The bustling settlement grew from 2000 to nearly 18,000 inhabitants by 1896. Great Russians predominated, but Bulgarians, Germans, Greeks, Moldavians, Serbs, Tartars and Ukrainians came to Kamiansk too. Disease accompanied the overcrowded and unsanitary conditions in the town and soon claimed Yakov's wife. Later, Ilya took his father's place at the factory when Yakov succumbed, not to disease, but to the 18-hour factory shifts and the poor working conditions.

There, Ilya met the daughter of a coworker. Natalya Brezhnev was barely 17 when she married Ilya. Being a robust, deeply religious and strong-willed woman she quickly assumed absolute command of the Brezhnev household.[3] Since Ilya's work allowed him little time with the family, left up to her were the guidance and character development of the children, Vera the first born, Leonid and a younger brother, Yakov, born in 1908 and named after his grandfather. She would become a dominant figure in Leonid's childhood, making exceptional demands for achievement on him because he was the eldest son. Until her death in 1975 at the age of 89, she remained a central figure in his life, sharing his Moscow apartment in her later years.

The Brezhnevs were truly a steelworking family. The traditional Russian proletarian values of thrift, hard work, humility, strict discipline, religious worship in the Russian Orthodox faith, and morals overseen by elders pervaded the atmosphere at home. Despite the harsh life, the family took pride in their traditional occupation, to which in turn Leonid came to aspire. "I take pride," Brezhnev has often said, "that I am the fifth generation of steel workers in my family."[4]

When Leonid Ilyich was born only two of his political precursors were then active. Lenin was already 36 yet the Bolshevik *apparat* he had founded was barely three years old and struggling for survival. Stalin, later to become absolute ruler, and hysterical executioner, was 27 and becoming well-known as an exponent of Lenin's doctrine in Georgia. Nikita Khrushchev, the patron on whose coattails Brezhnev would rise to political prominence, was 12 and helping his dirt-poor peasant father scratch out an existence in the village of Kalinovka near Kursk.

Brezhnev's father Ilya was a young man during these years when two prominent Marxist political parties, the Ukrainian Social Democratic Union and the Ukrainian Social Revolutionaries, organized and became active in the Ukraine. Soviet accounts of daring and heroic revolutionaries risking arrest, hard labor in Siberia and even death to "free" their homeland from czarist rule in those years are numerous and exciting. Soviet history books are filled with many such heroes. Ilya Brezhnev, however, was not one of them. Political radicalism did not appeal to him, not did it appeal to any member of the family before, during or immediately after the Bolshevik Revolution in 1917. For the Brezhnevs revolution, until 1917, was limited to those political radicals who would appear in Kamenskoye, organize strikes, spread propaganda and generally stir up trouble.

Yet in the main workers benefited from the revolutionary agitation. Harsh working conditions could be found in any factory in the Russian empire in the early 20th century and the Dneprovskiy factory was certainly no exception. But the worker's lot in Kamenskoye gradually improved. A strike organized at the factory in support of the All-Russian General Strike that spread across the country in October 1905 and trade union agitation at the factory in 1906 brought better wages, safer working conditions and free medical care for employees and their families.

Life for an adventurous boy growing up in this industrial frontier town was exciting. The cosmopolitan influence of the Franco-Belgian South Russian Metallurgical Company brought new people and interesting things to Kamenskoye daily. A Frenchman speaking broken Russian opened a shoe repair shop. Down the block a Greek named Manduduckis started a variety store which sold imported frying oil. Next door, a Russian named Volkov ran a grocery store. The "Magazin Volkov" offered the best French sardines, cheese from the Netherlands, herring from Riga and Russian hard sugar sold in cone-shaped chunks of five and ten pounds. Twice a week rich German and Ukrainian farmers, later liquidated by Stalin as capitalist landlords (*kulaks*), brought their chickens, geese and ducks to town to sell at the bazaar.

For amusement there were the silent movies, the *Yarmarka* (carnival), combining amusements and a flea market, and *kovinky*, a game that involved knocking out sticks with a heavy bat. The pre-World-War movies featuring a Russian comedian by the name of Gluspyshkin and the British movies starring Max Linder were the most popular. In the summer the Dneper River offered an inviting place to cool off.

The Russian Orthodox Church was the pillar of the community and an important feature in young Brezhnev's life before the Revolution. Colorful religious icons hung in the windows of his home and the family regularly attended church on the Sabbath. The priest, Father Konstantin, was an influential figure in Kamenskoye, particularly at the local boys school that Leonid attended.

Educating the children was Natalya's greatest concern in the prewar years. Ilya rose from a common laborer to a miller at the factory, allowing the family to put away a few kopecks each month toward the expensive school fees. In addition, the local trade union persuaded the company to provide a small education stipend to workers so there could be the hope of educating some of the children.

The Zhenskaya Gimnaziya "Moroza," the all-girls school on main street, would serve Vera's needs when she turned nine, the minimum age for entry. Next to it stood the Klassicheskaya Gimnaziya, a typical boys' school (or *gimnasium*) of czarist Russia, offering a rigorous classical curriculum to which Leonid and Yakov aspired. Both were exceptionally good schools but the cost of tuition frequently excluded many children.

Natalya had a grand vision of seeing her eldest son one day become an engineer and move to that part of Kamenskoye, the "Lower Colony," where workshop bosses, engineers, foremen and other highly paid members of the factory staff lived in separate and orderly houses with running water and electricity. She diligently saved for Leonid's tuition and for the tutor needed to prepare him for the difficult high school entrance exam.

Preparations for the exam to test Brezhnev's reading, writing and arithmetical skills and his potential in a variety of other school subjects began when he was six. There was no grade school, so a tutor, often a pupil in his last year of high school, or, when the family could afford it, a teacher, came to the house once a week. Brezhnev passed on what he learned to his sister and brother; both would have to wait until after the civil war to start school. All hope for the future was placed in Brezhnev.

In September 1915, a year after Germany declared war on Russia, Leonid entered the *prigotovitelnyy class* (preparatory class) at the boy's *gimnazium*. He would spend a year in the class before advancing to the first year of high school. It was an occasion for grand celebration in the Brezhnev household. Vera's ninth birthday had come and gone without her entry into the girls' school, nor had her family been able to save enough even to pay for Leonid's schooling. But Brezhnev scored exceptionally well on the exam, "a surprising and substantial achievement for a millhand's son," Nathan Kruglak, a classmate, recalls. That became Brezhnev's saving grace. The school agreed to take him on a provisional basis with the family paying as much as they could afford.

School nevertheless proved difficult for Brezhnev. The demands made on him in mathematics, world history, Russian and the Classical languages were unquestionably rigorous. Nathan Kruglak who sat three rows behind Brezhnev in the original class of 45, remembers that he held unswervingly to the path of mediocrity, very rarely speaking up in class and certainly never standing out in performance.

Today Brezhnev only remembers that in the years before World War I, "Talk [at home] was always about the mill, the owners, the hard work, the low wages, the daily frustrations and cares."[5] But compared to the turbulence of the war and the Russian Revolution, life was wholesome. On the eve of the war the factory was operating 15 furnaces, a Bessemer processor, and rail and rolling mills. It produced 14 percent of Russia's steel, cast iron and rolled iron and future prospects looked good.

However, outside Brezhnev's world of relative safety black clouds of war and revolution were building. Lenin wrote to Maksim Gorky in 1914, "War between Austria and Russia would be very useful to the cause of the revolution... But it is hard to believe that Franz Joseph and Nicholas will grant us this pleasure."

They did within the year. By 1914, the peace in Europe, dependent on a delicate balance of power between the Triple Entente nations of Russia, France and Britain, and the Triple Alliance of Germany, Austria-Hungary and Italy, had become strained to the

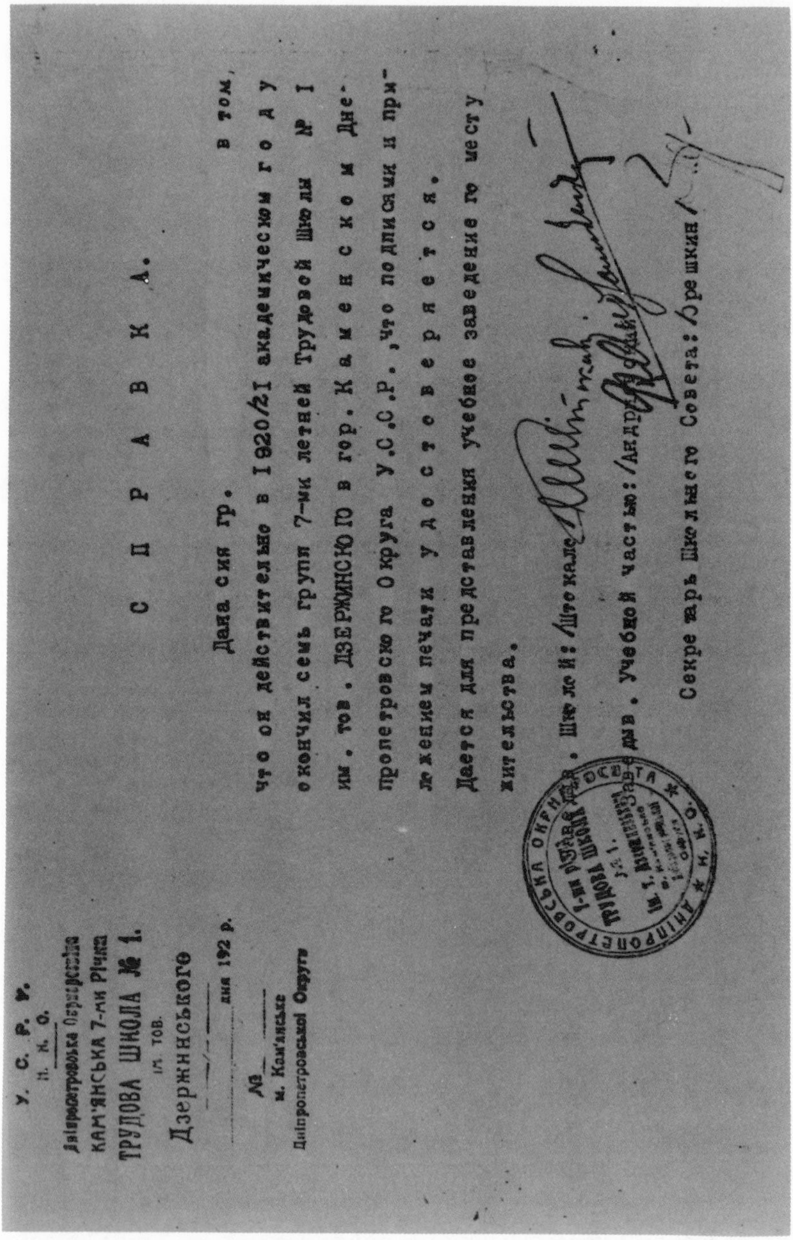

У. С. Р. Р.
Н. К. О.
Дніпропетровська Округова
КАМ'ЯНСЬКА 7-ми Річна
ТРУДОВА ШКОЛА № 1.
ім. тов.
Дзержинського
____ дня 192 р.
№ ___
м. Кам'янське
Дніпропетровської Округи

С П Р А В К А.

Дана сия гр. ___ в том, что он действительно в 1920/21 академическом г о д у окончил семь груп 7-ми летней Трудовой Школы № I им. тов. ДЗЕРЖИНСКОГО в гор. К а м е н с к о м Днепропетровского Округа У.С.С.Р., что подписями и приложением печати у д о с т о в е р я е т с я.

Дается для представления учебное заведение по месту жительства.

Зав. Школой: /Штокало/
Зав. учебной частью: /Андр...
Секретарь Школьного Совета: /Брешкин/

Kamenskoye High School diploma, 1921.

limit by conflicting nationalisms and dangerous imperialist schemes. In Eastern Europe and the Balkans insurgent nationalism, particularly the Serbian movement which had gained Russian support, threatened the dynastic Hapsburg power. Austria was obsessed with the idea of crushing Serbia and the murder of the Austrian Archduke Franz Ferdinand in the Balkan town of Sarajevo in June 1914 gave her the pretext to do so while thwarting Russia's Pan-Slav ambitions in the Balkans and Eastern Europe.

The mobilization notice nailed to a telegraph pole in the center of town brought Kamenskoye its first news of the war. Horses were immediately drafted. They were brought into town mainly by peasant farmers from surrounding villages. Russian army cavalry officers in full uniform, on horseback, spread out across the square and selected the best horses for the army.

In no time the drafting of men began. Ilya, however, was deferred and with few exceptions so were most factory workers. They were kept on at the factory to produce the arms needed to fight the war. So peasant farmers, strong physically, were sent to fill the army's ranks. Later on as war casualties mounted, factory employees were drafted. Fortunately for Ilya Brezhnev the younger workers were taken first.

The war quickly depleted the skilled labor forces at the factory. So much so that in the winter of 1915, the army brought in Kirghiz males to work the factory. While these men, wearing their colorful long robes and skull caps, added a dash of color to the war-weary scene, their unskilled hands did more harm than good as factory life was totally foreign to them.

Within a year the war began to seriously affect the Brezhnev family. Shortages of food and commodities became common. Farm production dropped and as a consequence the market had little to offer. At one time, refined salt was unobtainable. Large chunks of coarse salt appeared on the market as a substitute. Sugar and honey became scarce. A thick, black syrup, resembling maple syrup in taste, was sold by all grocers. There were no more imported sardines, no cheeses. Instead, barrels of salted fish from Siberia saw everyone through the winter of 1916. The flood of refugees from Warsaw to Kamenskoye, swelling the town's population to 63,000 by 1917, aggravated the food situation.

The deteriorating economic conditions brought on by the war sparked revolutionary outbreaks among the proletariat in Russia in 1915 and 1916. This naturally affected the industrial population of the Ukraine. In the nearby provincial capital of Yekaterinoslav, a volatile proletariat became engaged in strikes and clashes with the police and czarist military units. Difficulties caused by the war and the influx of political agitators in Kamenskoye also aroused revolutionary activity among workers at the Dneprovskiy factory.

The presses of Lenin's propaganda newspaper *Pravda*, which had begun circulating in Kamenskoye in 1910, now cranked out fiery antiwar, antigovernment propaganda. The agitation campaign was effective and so were the Kamenskoye Bolsheviks in organizing the work force at the factory. In July 1915, and in January 1916, factory workers went on strike, demanding higher wages to keep up with the spiraling cost of living.

In April 1916, Ilya and 10,000 other workers participated in yet a third strike which lasted 28 days, broken up only by the arrest and exile of strike leaders. "Sharp class battles unfolded before Leonid's eyes. Leonid and the other children waited with bated breath for the outcome of this grim drama of their fathers."[6]

The factory granted a 30 percent increase in wages; 200 strikers were sent to the front to fight as punishment. Ilya's role in the strike was either comparatively minor or he was lucky, for he was neither exiled nor drafted.

"The lessons of those years have never been forgotten," Brezhnev later wrote. "My own perception of life was shaped largely by factory life, by the thoughts and aspirations of the workingman, by his approach to life."[7]

The social, economic and political situations in Russia deteriorated as Brezhnev's tenth birthday approached. Demands for food and an end to the war intensified across the empire. All confidence was lost in the monarchy as Czar Nicholas, a weak and stubborn man, relied more and more on the high-strung Czarina Alexandra and the healer "monk" Grigoriy Rasputin to make decisions for him. In Petrograd (the former St. Petersburg) there were whispers that a coup d'état was necessary to save Russia from the weak Czar and a government whose only able personality, Protopopov, the Minister of Interior, customarily picked the day for convening the Duma (the Russian parliament) by consulting his horoscope.

Though 1916 passed with the monarchy intact, the respite for the Czar and his government was to be short. In the new year, new strikes, demonstrations, food riots, disorder and chaos rocked the foundations of his throne. The 300-year-old monarchy was finally toppled in February in one of the most spontaneous, unorganized and leaderless revolutions in history. March brought Nicholas II's abdication.

The Brezhnev family—indeed most if not all workingclass Russians in Kamenskoye—welcomed the events in Petrograd. They believed that it would mean an end to the war and in Leonid's case that his father would no longer face the possibility of being drafted.

In Kamenskoye the police became the first visible casualty of the February revolution. The police chief and his *gorodovoy* simply disappeared, opening the town up to crime. The factory director Makomatskiy and many top management personnel also took heed and fled with their families. Nowhere was it more evident to Brezhnev that the Romanov monarchy had fallen than at school where the portraits of the Czar and Czarina were removed from the walls. The religious icons, however, were untouched. They would remain and the daily opening and closing prayers in class would continue until 1919.

The following six months brought a great deal of joy and political activity to Kamenskoye. In the spring of 1917, the snow gone, a wooden platform was erected in the center of the church-yard, where the horse "cabbies" used to wait for customers going to the railroad station or to the steamer dock. Father Konstantin announced an official celebration and the entire town participated. With church bells ringing and the choir singing, he conducted a Russian mass, blessing the Provisional Government and its leader, Prince Georgiy Lvov.

The first known excitement of really free elections in Kamenskoye came in March. New words like Menshevik, Social Revolutionary, anarchist, and so on were on everyone's tongue, though it was impossible to distinguish a Bolshevik from a Menshevik. Both were elected to the local Soviet of Workers' and Soldiers' Deputies, but the Social Revolutionaries, professing a less radical political platform, were popular and won a majority. The local intelligentsia, the merchants and what was left of the factory administration organized a local executive committee of the Russian Provisional Government.

Those were inspiring days indeed. Everyone got caught up in the slogans of "Liberty, Equality, Fraternity," and Kamenskoye had all three for a time. However, the enthusiasm of the time turned to disillusionment and even bitterness when, instead of suing for peace, the Provisional Government declared new war aims. Despite the hopeless state of the army, the Provisional Government seemed fully committed to a policy of prosecuting the war – a policy foredoomed.

When the Russian Army collapsed in the summer and autumn of 1917, Kamenskoye became a halfway stop for deserters and thousands of destitute and crippled veterans. Carrying whatever they could, they would come to the market square and try to sell or barter an army jacket or a pair of boots.

As the year progressed extreme economic hardship befell the Brezhnev family. The factory had gone into full war production in 1914 to meet the needs of the ill-equipped Russian Army, but in the winter of 1917 could not keep going. Amazingly, with top management gone, some of the shops continued to operate for a short time. But the political upheaval, transportation difficulties and lack of coal and iron ore soon brought the factory to a complete standstill.

Having returned from his exile in Switzerland after the fall of the monarchy, Lenin now feverishly prepared to capture political power in Russia in the name of the "Soviets." Weak and disorganized, the Provisional Government in Petrograd fell on October 7. That morning Lenin's Military Revolutionary Committee, which had served as the executive council of the October Revolution, announced:

> "State power has passed into the hands of the organ of the Petrograd Soviet of Workers' and Soliders' Deputies – the Military Revolutionary Council which stands at the head of the Petrograd proletariat and garrison. The cause for which the people fought – immediate proposal of a democratic peace, abolition of landlords' property rights in land, workers' control over production, the creation of a Soviet Government – is assured."

Up North the Soviet regime was consolidated within a few months, but in the Ukraine, in Kamenskoye, a brutal and bloody civil war began. For the next three years, control over Brezhnev's destiny passed back and forth from one political group to another almost every month.

It is necessary to go back for a moment. Revolution in the Ukraine had assumed a largely national character in February 1917 and as a result the Ukrainian parliament, the Central Rada, contested the Provisional Government's political authority over the Ukraine. When the Provisional Government fell in October the Rada assumed full responsibility for the political administration of the Ukraine and on November 20, 1917, a national Republic of the Ukraine was declared.

The new Ukrainian government found no support in the Brezhnev household. In that period of the civil war when the Ukrainian nationalists, the Bolsheviks (Reds), and the anti-Communist Volunteer White Army were vying for power, the sentiment of the Russian community in the Ukraine generally rested with either the Reds or the Whites. When asked why he was on the side of the Bolsheviks, one worker simply explained, "I am working now ten and twelve hours a day and I am poor. When the Bolshevik Government comes, I will have to work six hours a day, or even less, and I will be rich."[8] Similarly, "The social and political sympathies of the Brezhnevs lay with the [Bolshevik] revolution."[9]

On December 27 Lenin established a Provisional Soviet Government of the Ukraine to represent Russian interests there. A few days later he declared war on the young Ukrainian Republic in the name of defending the provisional government, taking immediate possession of Yekaterinoslav and Kamenskoye. Brezhnev watched as the roundup and execution of the intelligentsia, priests and the bourgeoisie began. General Anton Denikin who commanded White forces in the region numbered the Bolshevik victims in 1918-1919 at 1,700,000.[10] The names of those executed were posted in the Kamenskoye market place daily.

The killings became a daily routine to the schoolboys and continued until Austrian forces occupied Kamenskoye three months later in accord with the agreement made between the Ukrainian national government and Germany and Austria at the Brest-Litovsk peace negotiations in February 1918. Early in April, a small German reconnaissance airplane, flying low and circling, appeared in the sky over Kamenskoye. The next day Austrian soldiers armed with rifles and bayonets marched into town. They took over the two-story police building, long the symbol of authority in Kamenskoye, a theatre which they used as barracks, and the factory hospital building. Their export of meat, flour, and other scarce commodities paid for in worthless marks further depleted the food available in Kamenskoye.

With the evacuation of occupation armies in the fall of 1918 as a result of the collapse of the German front and internal disorder in the Austrian empire, a new Soviet offensive was launched in the Ukraine. The struggle between the Red Army, the volunteer White Army, and the peasant guerrilla movements in 1919 was one of the most violent and tragic ordeals of the Civil War.

The second Bolshevik incursion in December 1918 went swiftly. Soviet troops succeeded in taking the left bank of the Ukraine and by January they had recaptured Kamenskoye. Soldiers of the newly formed Red Army in long grey coats and helmets decorated with the red star probably made a lasting impression on Brezhnev. Kamenskoye was now made part of the new Ukrainian Soviet Republic proclaimed on December 18, 1918, in a proclamation of the Military and Revolutionary Committee of the Red Southern Army signed by none other than Joseph Stalin.

Violence quickly engulfed the countryside. The fight for free land gave rise to roving peasant gangs, *povstantsy*, who after seizing land in the countryside, turned to pillaging and murdering unarmed civilians in Kamenskoye and in other cities. The Brezhnevs lived in constant fear of these gangs. When the *povstantsy* would approach town and shooting was heard, the church bells would ring the alarm. School would be dismissed. Until the raids became more frequent and dangerous the bell was popular with the schoolboys.

A gang led by the infamous anarchist Nestor Makhno occupied villages nearby. While not engaged in fighting the Reds or Whites, Makhno's expert cavalry would attack Kamenskoye with lightning speed, loot, kill and carry away the booty. The Volunteer Red Guard composed of untrained civilians could not cope with Makhno's "flying squads." Only the Red Army, after assigning the task to Semyon Budennyy's cavalry, a unit of crack Cossack and former Russian Army horsemen, could and did defeat these gangs.

For a brief time in 1918, the Bolsheviks fired up the blast furnaces at the factory and conscripted labor to build armored train cars for the Red Army. Brezhnev's father helped build two such cars, the *Sovetskaya Rossiya* and the *Sovetskaya Ukraina*, before the White Army appeared in Kamenskoye in the summer of 1919, dispersed the Reds, closed down the factory and carried out reprisals against those who had collaborated with the Bolsheviks. Caught in the crossfire between the Reds, the Whites, and the *povstantsy*, who would join the Reds one day and the Whites the next, the Brezhnevs lived through a hectic six months.

The Red Guard volunteers, armed with old-style army rifles, were no match for the cavalry of the White Army. The first wave of the Army consisted of Cossacks from the Caucasus, wild, cruel, swordsmen who chased and surrounded the Reds, killing great numbers and forcing others to flee in terror. Their orgy of pillaging, particularly of Jewish homes, lasted three days. When they left to rout the Reds near Kiev on June 28, 1919, the regular White Army under the command of General Denikin passed through Kamenskoye and established a government administration which only lasted fifteen days.

On July 13 units of the Soviet Crimean Division commanded by P.V. Kybenko delivered a devastating blow to the White Army near Sukhatchivka station. Kamenskoye was taken in fiery battle, only to be lost back to the Whites again on July 26.

One morning in early January 1919, new faces once more appeared in the windows of the police station. General Denikin's forces had deteriorated to such an extent that he could no longer hold the Ukraine. The defeat of his army on the Southern Front had allowed Kamenskoye once again to fall into Soviet hands. Detachment after detachment of the Red Army showed up in Kamenskoye. Weary, unshaven infantry would enter town, stay a few hours at the market place, and then leave for mopping-up operations against the Whites and the *povstantsy* who were still active.

By now one could sense that the Bolsheviks were taking over on a permanent basis. A group of 12 local men, all former coworkers of Ilya's, formed the first Soviet administration. The head of the Party organization in Kamenskoye was a Commissar Lichmanov, a handsome fellow of about 25 but illiterate. He married a graduate of the "Moroza" girls' school, who taught him to read and became his constant counselor. Young Brezhnev would see him parading around town carrying an impressive big black briefcase, wearing high leather boots, a black leather jacket and a revolver in a holster strapped over his shoulder.

Propaganda trains decorated with fancy artistic designs showing beautiful aspects of life under Communism soon began to arrive at the train station. These trains, with printing shop, library, a car for personnel and a private car for the VIP who was on tour made a beautiful sight. Important revolutionaries like Trotsky, Kamenev, Zinoviyev, Lunacharskiy, Radek and others all visited Kamenskoye in 1919 on such trains.

By 1920 the civil war was almost over and nominal peace came. But new enemies — famine and sickness — began to stalk the land. Years of political upheaval had disrupted the normal planting of crops and livestock had been decimated either by export or slaughter. What food reserves remained in the villages the Bolsheviks confiscated to feed the Red Army. These difficulties were compounded by a drought in the Ukraine, resulting in no crops at all in some planted areas.

The winter of 1920-1921 was unquestionably Brezhnev's most difficult. Hunger and disillusionment set in equally as Kamenskoye became one vast desperate slum. Professor Meredith Atkinson of Melbourne University saw "dead bodies piled up in the window sills of railroad stations" and "evidence of cannibalism" on his travel through the famine areas. "Bodies were thrown into the snow, left unburied, and stolen by night for food."[12] The dead were stripped of their clothing. So dire were the needs of families that they often had to share a pair of shoes. Brezhnev himself showed up at school with his feet wrapped in rags.[13]

That winter he also suffered several personal losses. Father Konstantin had been killed by the Bolsheviks in 1918. His replacement, a teacher Brezhnev had come to admire a great deal, was killed a few days before Christmas by a class dropout who had joined the Whites. Classmates also died from starvation and sickness. Only about 15 students continued to attend class.

In addition to those who had dropped out or died, several students with strong political convictions, some no more than 12 or 13 years old, further depleted the class by running off to join and fight with the Bolsheviks or the Whites. "So many of us became disillusioned and half caught up in the politics of the moment," Kruglak recalls. Politics, however, "simply did not interest Brezhnev."

The last year of school found the town stricken with black typhus, a deadly addition to the malnutrition, contaminated water, lack of sanitation and lice-infested dwellings that already characterized life in Kamenskoye. Brezhnev himself was one of the first to contract the sickness. Three million people died from this and other, related diseases in the Ukraine but Brezhnev was fortunate. After months, during which his mother nursed him, he recovered and returned to classes.

Earlier in the civil war, barter had been the only means of obtaining essentials. Cigarette lighters, kerosene lamps or crude stoves made from scrap metal had been traded to the peasants in the surrounding villages. The food was gone from the villages now. Ironically, Kiev had a reasonable amount of rain and was blessed with a harvest, but next to none of the grain reached Kamenskoye. Transportation difficulties were in part responsible. Available trains were in use transporting the Red Army.

Faced with dismal prospects for the survival of herself and her family, Natalya Brezhnev was forced to join the growing number of *Meshokniki* (bag people, as the Red Army called them). Taking an empty flour or potato bag and a few unneeded items, she would go to the railroad station to join other women who used the infrequent army train as a traveling barter line. They would wait until a train bound for Kiev would stop and the soldiers would let them on. They were often unloaded at a station enroute and forced to wait for another train which would take them to Kiev. There they would barter their items for flour or grain. Many had to spend weeks traveling in the freezing cold but the "bag people" saved their families.

Relief came in the spring as shipments of food and medical supplies from America under Herbert Hoover's Relief Administration began to trickle into Kamenskoye. Natalya's trips to Kiev now became less frequent and ceased that summer when the Bolsheviks issued ration coupons for food and clothing.

By 1921, Lenin's vision had become a reality. The Bolsheviks had succeeded in their enormous effort to reconquer the majority of multinational territories that had constituted the vast czarist Russian empire, but at a tremendous human, social and economic cost. For Brezhnev the disorder, danger and violence associated with four years of revolution and civil war in the Ukraine were now nearly a way of life. For him, and others, it had become a "routine" in which "We...studied, ate, slept, read, laughed..., made friendships and even planned for the future."[14]

Out of the turmoil of revolution and Civil War which surrounded him, Brezhnev developed a profound instinct for self preservation. It was during these difficult formative years of both the new Soviet socialist state and of Brezhnev's own personality and character that he assembled the two most basic and valuable tools of his political kit: the will to survive and the habit of survival. Armed with these, Leonid Brezhnev was prepared to take his place in the new political order when he graduated from high school in August 1921.

II
Commissar with a Whip

It was common talk in the countryside that the aim of the kolkhozy was "to put the peasants on rations and seize the surplus," that everyone would be made to live in barracks and that "the commissar with a whip" had taken the place of the old landowner. — An Observer.

IN 1921 LENIN'S NEW ECONOMIC POLICY (NEP) greatly lifted Brezhnev's spirits. Despite charges by the Party's Left Opposition that the NEP would reverse the course of socialism in Russia[1] — later, as a member of Komsomol, Brezhnev personally denounced its accusers — the economy began to show signs of recovery that winter as a result of the policy introduced in April. Convinced that the Dneprovskiy factory would soon resume operation and jobs would become available, Brezhnev set out to study engineering.

Kamenskoye's economic program under the NEP involved two features, recovery of local agricultural production and assurances that the factory would soon resume operation with local Party sponsorship of a short course in the basics of metallurgical engineering for the town's youth. Brezhnev enrolled in the weekly classes on the principles of metallurgical engineering and machinery operation.

Kruglak vividly remembers the classes: "There were no textbooks as all books, and paper for that matter, had been burned to keep from freezing in the winter. It was all very informal. Instruction was on a personal and practical basis with a former factory engineer by the name of Petrov running the class. We studied smelting temperatures, blast furnace operation, etc."

"It lifted us all," Kruglak recalls, "but Brezhnev thrived on it." Nonetheless, the next year and a half was spent agonizingly waiting for the factory to reopen. It seemed like an eternity. Kamenskoye responded slowly to the NEP. Out of town commissars arrived and made a clean sweep of local Party and Komsomol elements ideologically opposed to the policy. The market square once again became a busy place and trade picked up on the river. But the factory's blast furnaces remained silent.

It soon became painfully evident that the government was not going to reopen the factory. A mass exodus from Kamenskoye began in 1922, the government allowing the unemployed to go to other parts of the country, even abroad, to seek work. With the promise of work in Europe, particularly in France, many left Russia. The Brezhnevs though, still hopeful of prospering in the new Russia, headed north to the family's ancestral home.

Thus, in early January 1923 as Lenin lay gravely ill in Moscow, his "Political Testament" in which he undertook to evaluate the Bolshevik leaders capable of succeeding him now nearly complete, the Brezhnev family began making their way back to Kursk. It was a wearisome journey, complicated by the heavy winter snow and the endless police checks at train stations along the way. But the trip was for the best. Kamenskoye would never be forgotten. The family would return when times became better but for now the disillusionment and disappointments of the last few years were left behind. In Kursk Ilya found work in a wire factory, and Yakov and Vera entered school. As for Brezhnev, he took a gigantic step, the first in his climb to the pinnacle of the Party and leadership of the Soviet Union: he joined the Young Communist League, Komsomol.

An astute awareness of who possessed power, burning personal ambition and the promise of immediate success that Komsomol membership offered persuaded him in the early months of 1923, nearly six years after the Bolshevik Revolution, to cast his lot with the Communists. Ideology was not foremost in his mind. Komsomol members, after all, were the youth being selected by the regime for the best jobs and study courses at higher educational institutions.[2]

Brezhnev's motives, however, mattered little so long as he proved loyal to the new Komsomol, then emerging from a drastic purge of left-wing elements opposing the NEP. "I remember the year I entered Komsomol," Brezhnev told the Seventeenth Congress of the organization in 1974, "there were no more than 30,000 members in its ranks then ... [and] they constituted only a small handful of people."[3]

That year the Komsomol saw fit to recruit no less than 93,000 youths to strengthen its ranks, with recruitment preference being given to those from working-class backgrounds. Being of Great Russian stock and a high school graduate, Brezhnev, easily qualified for membership. The local Komsomol recruiters actively sought out youths possessing such high qualifications. But as a rule most of those recruited lacked political savvy.[4] Only through the political indoctrination of such "politically illiterate" raw recruits, whose loyalties the Party sought to capture after the purge, were the wounds caused by the purge able to be healed over time. In those early years of the NEP even the most basic of Marxist-Leninist concepts still remained to be integrated into Brezhnev's thinking and world view. The Komsomol undertook to carefully mold his thinking to conform to the Party's essential understanding of the Marxist-Leninist philosophy and the broad and strategic purpose of building socialism in NEP Russia. Only then, Brezhnev recalls, was "I able to grasp the complicated science of life, comprehend the class struggle, and the necessity for the construction of a new society."[5]

Whatever kind of Communist society Lenin ultimately envisaged for Russia, construction of Soviet society under the NEP in 1921 taught that, above all, the proprietary interest of the Russian peasant had to be accommodated. Quite simply, if Russia was going to increase its agricultural production to avert another famine or popular uprising—like the 1921 revolt at the Kronstadt garrison where sailors called for "Soviets without Communists"—the Party would have to bring together the peasant's diverse land holdings.

The search for appropriate measures led the Party to adopt an expanded policy of "land consolidation" designed to do away with strip farming. The traditional strip method of farming in Russia was not only unpopular with the peasant, it was inefficient and a major impediment to improving cultivation. Under the czar the function of "land consolidation" was to confirm existing titles to land and unravel some of the complexities of land tenure, but after the Revolution it was used to enforce equalization of peasant holdings. Now it became an exclusive function of agricultural cultivation. The Third Union Congress of Soviets, held in 1925, decided that all "principal regions" must be consolidated within ten years. Although the policy was clear enough, the regime faced innumerable difficulties in implementing it. Chief among them was the inadequacy of trained administrators. Even with the mobilization of all active and retired consolidators the regime still fell far short of the required numbers of officials needed for the task. Agricultural schools would have to turn to training qualified consolidators.

Komsomol provided a ready source of raw material and in 1923 the Party tapped its ranks for promising young administrators. Brezhnev was picked to study at the Kursk Land Teknikum. A four-year higher educational institution, the school specialized in training *zemleustroitelni* (land measurers and consolidators).

The allocation of land to the state farms (*sovkhozy*), the organization of land in the possession of "land communities," the rectification of boundaries, the mapping of roads and water courses, the planning of places of habitation, and the establishment of rural district boundaries, are among the multifarious duties of the consolidator listed in the Agricultural Code of 1922. Mastering its various components was a heady undertaking, complicated by the endless Komsomol meetings and hours Brezhnev had to devote first to reserve military training and then to part-time work taken out of economic necessity and because it was customary to combine employment with studies.

He endured and upon graduating in 1927 joined about 6000 other consolidators working in the field throughout Russia.[6] He was immediately assigned to the Land Department of the Kokhanovksiy *rayon* (district) *soviet* (government). The local *soviets* were the vehicle of the Party's new policy in the countryside.

By the time Brezhnev stepped off the train in the Kokhanovskiy *rayon*, the Party's concept of land consolidation had fundamentally changed. At school he had been taught that the essence of Party policy was to live at peace with the well-to-do peasant, the *kulak*. Kulak farms constituted only about 5 percent of all peasant farms in Russia in 1927, though they produced a fifth of the total marketable grain.[7] But in mid 1927 the emphasis began to shift from viewing land consolidation as an effective means of raising agricultural cultivation to viewing it as an instrument for eliminating "nests of kulak landlords" and collectivizing Russia's peasants by putting them on government-run farms to work the land in common.

In December 1927 Stalin declared that land consolidation would be the principal instrument for "organizing collective farms for production and for guaranteeing the interests of poor and middle peasants in the struggle with the kulak."[8] Although the use of land consolidation to facilitate the development of private farming was to continue for a time, the view that it should be "entirely subordinated to the task of collectivization" predominated by the spring of 1928.

With the NEP peasant becoming rich and increasingly independent, Lenin dead, and the power of his self-annointed successor Stalin dominant, the Party ultimately choose to coopt NEP with a policy of all-out socialization of Russian agriculture through the collectivization of peasant farms.

The mass collective farm movement involved millions of peasants. In just four years 7 million peasants were expropriated and deported to concentration camps in Siberia and elsewhere and an estimated 14 million more died from starvation. Stalin's collectivization drive became a human, social and economic catastrophe.

All official biographies of Brezhnev published in the Soviet Union completely skirt those years of his Komsomol youth zealously expended on collectivization, dismissing it (as one Soviet diplomat told me) as "unimportant because it happened before he joined the Party" or playing it down as much as possible by simply saying that he "worked for a short time in land surveying, but did not take this up as his profession."[9] Only one English-language official Soviet biography has been forthcoming in this regard, stating "The collectivization of farming ... proceeded in the face of fierce resistance on the part of the kulaks, the rural exploiters... Leonid Brezhnev was among those who, at the bidding of their hearts and conscience, *spared no efforts to accomplish* those tasks [collectivizing agriculture and liquidating the kulak], fully aware of the great responsibility they had undertaken."[10]

Collectivizing the peasants of the Kokhanovskiy *rayon* was no easy job. In 1928 Belorussia had 3.4 million hectares of land under cultivation, which was small compared to the Ukraine's 24.9 million hectares, but ranked about sixth in the total of 113 million hectares under cultivation for the whole of the U.S.S.R. that year. In that year 95,000 hectares in Belorussia were under winter wheat and 111,000 were under summer wheat.[11] The *rayon* was overwhelmingly agricultural, but the broken configuration of the land was better suited for livestock breeding than for grain farming. Peasant conservatism was strongly entrenched in the *rayon*. The structure of agriculture there, the predominance of the "individual farming household" as opposed to the traditional village community, the "mir," all made for determined opposition to the Party's efforts to promote collective forms of agriculture.

"No special prospects exist for the significant increase in the area of *sovkhozy* and *kolkhozy* ... [and] there are no special reasons to count in the immediate future on any significant transition to collective forms of cultivation."[12] Such was the official prospectus of the Belorussian S.S.R. on extending socialist means of agriculture to Belorussia.

Collectivization will result in mechanization, alleviation from toil, flowing streams of golden grain, bright comfortable dwellings, schools, hospitals and clubs," Brezhnev told the peasants. But stubborn farmers, some wealthy kulaks who had survived the Revolution in Belorussia where the establishment of Soviet power had been delayed by the Civil War, quickly dismissed this Communist's appeals.

Throughout 1928, the Party sought to neutralize and weaken the disruptive influence of the kulak. The noose was gradually tightened around his neck by sharply increasing his tax burden, denying him agricultural credit and equipment, depriving him of land which had allegedly been improperly distributed to him, and by prosecuting him for speculation in grain and concealment of grain surpluses. At the same time, an effort was made to acquire the support of poor peasants by freeing them from agricultural taxes and giving them agricultural credit and other assistance. Nevertheless, until the application of physical threat in 1929, collectivization was slow to take root in the *rayon*.

Chiefly with a view to solving the state's grain problem, Brezhnev undertook "extraordinary measures" in the winter of 1927-1928 to disgorge grain from the peasant in the *rayon*. That winter rumors of the possibility of another war and government stockpiling of grain for feeding the Red Army created panic in the countryside. Instead of selling his grain surpluses to the state, the peasant hoarded them. This, coupled with crop difficulties, caused a serious grain shortage. Attempts to draw on grain reserves around the country to feed the growing industrial cities and the Red Army proved useless.

During the December 1927 Party Congress the Kokhanovskiy *rayon* and other local Party and Soviet organizations were alerted as to the severity of the problem. In early January, Stalin threatened local officials with harsh penalties "in the event of their failure to bring about in the shortest possible time a revolution in grain collections."[13]

Collectors like Brezhnev, assisted by special Party emissaries, were empowered to administer "shock tactics" to obtain grain from the kulak. But as the distinction between the kulak and the middling and even poor peasant became blurred, terrible abuses of power by collectors became common. "Individual comrades have begun to slip into methods of war communism," Aleksey Rykov, then chairman of the U.S.S.R. Council of Peoples Commissars, later to be purged by Stalin as a rightward deviationist, wrote in *Pravda* on March 11, 1928. Peasants were beaten, jailed, and their homes ransacked in order to retrieve the grain. So effective were the collectors' methods that Red Army detachments (composed predominantly of peasants) stationed in Belorussia threatened revolt in sympathy with the victimized peasants.

By the spring the grain crisis was over. Now the Party hastened collectivization, partly out of fear that peasants would sow less grain in retaliation for the brutal collections and partly out of the Party's desire now to totally liquidate the kulak.

The Party insisted upon collectivization not merely because it wished to apply Marxist theories to the countryside, but because a majority of Party leaders seriously believed that large-scale collective farms would produce more. In July, Stalin presented figures to show that in 1926-1927, state and collective farms marketed 47 percent of their produce and kulaks, 20 percent, while poor peasants marketed only 11 percent. One official source estimated that collectivization and mechanization of small holdings could double the grain output.[14]

But coerced collectivization to achieve these ends had not begun in Belorussia before Brezhnev left for more schooling in Kursk and then on to a new assignment in the Bisertskiy *rayon* of the Urals.

He was to have a companion on this trip, a slim, raven-haired woman a year younger than himself. Her name was Viktoriya Petrovna and she was his wife of only a few weeks. She was probably born in Kursk, to Jewish parents according to highly placed sources in Moscow. They met during Brezhnev's last year at the Land Teknikum and married upon his return to Kursk in 1928. A daughter, Galina, was born in the Bisertskiy *rayon* in 1929.

The room housing the Bisertskiy Land Department was filled with tobacco smoke, a typewriter clattered, and several people hovered over the wood stove. It might have gone like this: Chief Vladimir Antonov was emersed in the work at his desk. He looked up.

"Good morning comrade. Brezhnev, isn't it? Yes, of course, I have your file right here. You're a day late. But it doesn't matter. We won't waste any time putting you to work.

"You will lead a land team in our collectivization.[15] Things here are well behind schedule. Less than fifteen percent of the farms in the *rayon* have been collectivized. The rich kulaks are still behind with their grain deliveries. So, you've got your work cut out.

"These are your orders: You're to set out for the northern part of the *rayon* with full power to carry through collectivization. Have you read Stalin's November nineteenth speech on the grain question?"

Brezhnev: "Yes, of course, and the [Five Year] Plan's figures on collectivization too."*

*At the November plenum of the Party's Central Committee Stalin had said that because the rate of development of grain production "is still excessively backward" compared to the rate of development and the needs of industry, grain production would be "accelerated" through a "great extension" of collectivization to a "level suf-

"Then you understand how important your job is. All the poorest and middling peasants must be brought into the farm. If you meet with any difficulty, come to the district office. Send us periodic reports. I'll have you supplied with horses, and the militia will be at your disposal. Remember, you'll be measured by the percentage of collectivization you achieve.

"Oh yes, one more thing. There is the kulak in our district who delivers the grain demanded of him, then there's the one who is obstinate. For the moment we overcome this by squeezing the kulak who conceals his grain through economic measures and by applying Article 107 of the People's Courts."

Such were presumably Brezhnev's instructions, more or less, upon arriving in the Bisertskiy *rayon*, a slightly larger, less remote, wheat and livestock area on the Asiatic side of the Ural mountains near the city of Sverdlovsk.

For the greater part of 1929 the *rayon* land department sought to collectivize largely through the policy's own merits, pointing out to the local peasants the advantages of joining the collective farm.

"The Party proposes collectivization so as to hitch each and every one of you to a tractor. We'll give you everything you want, you'll no longer have to depend upon the blood sucker kulak. Remember what Lenin said just before he passed away: 'Only in the collective farm can the peasant find salvation from his poverty, otherwise he is doomed,'" Brezhnev might have worded his message to the prospective collective farmer. But his appeals fell on many deaf ears.

When reason failed, more effective methods were tested. Those who failed to join the collective farm were subjected to relentless administrative measures and ultimately forced to capitulate by over-taxation and confiscation of their livestock and property. In Brezhnev's *rayon* the Party sanctioned open requisition of grain under the guise of self-taxation voted by the local Soviet. These "legal economic measures" yielded such positive results that Stalin was persuaded to personally praise the "Ural method of grain collections" as a way of "mobilizing the toiling strata of the countryside against the kulak."[17]

The year 1929 was a year of great change on all fronts of socialist construction in the Soviet Union. Labor productivity

ficient to guarantee the rapid progress of the national economy." *The area for collective farming was to increase from 2.3 million to 26 million dessiatines (1 dessiatine equals 2.7 acres) by 1933, of which 21 million were to be collective farms incorporating 20 million souls.*[16]

radically improved and in agriculture the Party succeeded in leading the bulk of the peasantry on the road to collective farming. One million peasant households were enrolled in collective farms in July through September alone, doubling the number of farms established since the October Revolution. In the second half of 1929, Stalin transformed the mass collectivization movement into a policy of "solid collectivization" which meant that all land in the village was to be brought into the collective and the kulak class was to be liquidated.

The year was also one in which the Party decisively split over the methods to resolve the regime's agricultural problems. The right wing of the Party, composed of Nikolay Bukharin and his followers, accused Stalin of leading the country into ruin, famine, and a police regime by exacting tribute from the peasant for forced industrialization. They preached caution in dealing with the peasants and they opposed Stalin's idea of wholesale collectivization. By appealing to the Party's practical politicians "like Ordzhonikidze, Kuibyshev, the Ukrainians Stanislav Kosior and Grigorii Petrovskiy, and the Leningrad Party chief Sergei Kirov," Stalin was able to defeat Bukharin in April 1929[18]; his victory manifested itself by a cleansing of Party and state organs.

It was precisely because of this "leftward turn" in Party policy that Brezhnev rose to replace his superior in the Bisertskiy Land Department. In the summer of 1929, he was informed by the chairman of the district soviet that Antonov had had a run-in with the *rayon* Party chief and that he (Brezhnev) had been chosen by the Party organization and district soviet executive committee to succeed him to head up the Department. Responsibility for compulsory collectivization, liquidation of the kulak, and the execution and administration of orders emanating from the district Party committee and soviet executive committee, of which he now became a proforma member, would now be his.

It is not difficult to understand why Brezhnev was picked for the job. Although he had limited administrative experience, the Party's decision was governed by more timely considerations. He had obviously displayed the necessary enthusiasm for Stalin's method and shown in his job as head of the collectivization team. There was also the need to fill the post as quickly as possible in order to get on with the pressing business of collectivization. This could best be done by selecting a candidate already working in the district. The choice was simplified by the small number of adequately trained personnel in the *rayon*. Brezhnev had been in the right place at the right time.

The purge of 1929 opened up possibilities for promotion of many lesser officials like Brezhnev, provided of course they had been recognized as active supporters of Stalin's policies. A significant result of this kind of identification was that it gave the apparatus the incentive to make its active supporters Party members so as to convert them into fully committed agents of mass collectivization.[19] Notably, Brezhnev entered the Party as a candidate member in 1929. That year, 300,000 candidates were admitted to the Party's ranks, all new, malleable members like Brezhnev, brought in to strengthen Stalin's majority.

Brezhnev's case was nevertheless special. He had been active in Komsomol since age 17. In December 1929, he would reach the upper age limit for Komsomol membership. He was a member of the technical *intelligentsia*, active in soviet work and obviously politically trustworthy. Why hadn't he joined the Party earlier?

The answer lies in the unfavorable position in which he found himself because of the Party's archaic recruitment policies. Many Komsomol members had reached the age of 25 and not attained Party status. They were generally students, peasants and "employees" who had difficulty gaining admission because of the priority being given to workers engaged in labor production jobs or transport. Brezhnev fell into the unfavorable "white collar" worker category whose rate of admission into the Party was extremely low. He was indeed fortunate to be admitted in 1929, since over 75 percent of such white collar or clerical workers who applied for membership that year were turned down.[20]

For Brezhnev 1930 was a time of genuine enthusiasm and feverish exertion. He was promoted again that year, this time to the position of first deputy chairman of the Land Management Board for the whole of the Urals region. He was fast moving up as an emissary of Stalin's collectivization.

For the majority of peasants though, 1930 was a time of extreme repression and misery. Collectivization had become a battle cry. In a *Pravda* article on November 7, 1929, Stalin asserted, contrary to the actual situation, that peasants were quitting their private plots and joining collective farms by "entire villages, groups of villages, *rayons*, and even *oblasts*." Speaking at a meeting of Marxist agrarians a month later, he dismissed the collectivization target of 75 percent of poor and middle peasants for 1930-1931 established by the Party's Central Committee. He now put pressure on local Party and state organs to achieve "total collectivization." The practice of "hunting for high percentages" was encouraged and "collectivization was artificially speeded up."[21]

Stalin dictated that collectivization in the Urals must be completed by the spring of 1932. Only 30 percent of the peasant households had been collectivized by 1930.[22] Under Brezhnev the tempo of collectivization in the Bisertskiy *rayon* mounted quickly in January and February 1930. Using every available resource and applying repressive measures, he unleashed a reign of terror against kulak and middle peasant alike to achieve collectivization by whatever means it took. In one area peasants were threatened at gunpoint. In another they were told that they would be branded as kulaks and sent off to Siberia if they did not join the collective farm. In March and April 1930, the pages of *Pravda* were filled with case after case of collectivizers using these and other coercive methods to meet collectivization quota.

Until now Brezhnev had been unable to understand the complexities of the class struggle in the countryside. Nor still could he understand the reasoning of the peasant who preferred to slaughter his own livestock rather than turn over his pigs, sheep and poultry to the collective farm for the common good. In the economic year of 1929-1930, the number of cattle in the country decreased by 14.6 million, pigs by one-third, sheep and goats by more than a quarter. Large numbers of livestock were slaughtered in February and March 1930 during the worst period of collectivization. It took the U.S.S.R. more than 15 years to recover from these enormous losses.

The battle for collectivization was worst on the kulak front. In areas where the foundation had not yet been knocked out from under them, kulaks declared war on the Communists and for a brief time triumphed. They carried on "malicious propaganda" against the collective farm movement, spread "provocative rumors," set fire to collective farm buildings, poisoned the livestock, damaged tractors and other machinery, assassinated rural Communists, chairmen of collective farms, rural newspaper correspondents and village activists. Just before seeding time they incited the poor peasants into withdrawing from collective farms, taking with them their seed grain, horses and machinery.

Withdrawals from the collectives became more numerous when Stalin published his article, "Dizzy with Success", in *Pravda* on March 2, 1930. In that article he called a temporary halt to the reign of terror and blamed local officials for the "excesses." Peasants,

Brezhnev the Loyal Stalinist, 1930.

however, were not allowed to remain outside the collective farm. Brezhnev could find no other solution to withdrawals in his district than to arrest and deport the farmers. The *rayon* prosecutor arraigned them before the People's Court and the *rayon* soviet quickly expelled them from the district.

Deportations numbered into the thousands as Brezhnev extirpated the "class enemy" from his district. *"Dekulakization"* began on orders received from *oblast* headquarters on February 5, 1930.[23] That day Brezhnev organized "general meetings" in the collective farms and resolutions to expell all kulak families were "unanimously adopted." Groups of activists accompanied by the militia moved to carry out the evictions and seize kulak property. Brezhnev's orders were very specific. "Counter revolutionary kulak activists" were to be promptly arrested, deprived of all voting rights and exiled to Siberia. "Second-class kulaks" were to be arrested and sent to out-of-the-way northern *rayons* and "third-class kulaks" were to be dispersed to "far away districts outside the *kolkhoz*.[24]

The Party estimated that between 10 and 15 thousand kulaks would be eliminated from the *oblast*, but this was a conservative figure excluding the number of middling and poor peasants who suffered the kulak's fate because they refused to join collective farms. By the end of the year the "first stage of dekulakization" in the Urals had been completed.

In the late spring of 1930, Brezhnev moved to the regional headquarters in Sverdlovsk to assume his new duties as deputy head of the Urals Land Management Board. He was a mere 23.

A new education plan had been introduced by the Party's Central Committee in January 1930. It provided for the restructuring of higher educational institutions to facilitate the training of mid and lower-level technical personnel and included a comprehensive program for training and upgrading of leadership cadres, particularly in agriculture.[25] Various governmental agencies were called upon to select their most promising personnel for full-time study.

Within weeks of arriving in Sverdlovsk, Brezhnev was sent to study at the Moscow Agricultural Academy, also known as the Timiryazev Academy, a higher agricultural school. This school was founded in 1865 and in 1930 was being used exclusively to train specialists in managerial and high administrative positions in agriculture. As the Industrial Academy, which Khrushchev attended in 1929, its students were handpicked for training as the new ruling elite in agriculture.

The prospective graduate could expect to be assigned to a high level position either in agricultural management or administration. For Brezhnev, the stay in Moscow would have other advantages too. He would be close to the center of power and would in all likelihood make valuable future contacts. It is possible, for example, that Brezhnev first met Khrushchev in Moscow since he was a student at the nearby Industrial Academy.

The future looked bright in late 1930; however, Brezhnev mysteriously dropped out of school. Khrushchev, for example had left the Industrial Academy to become the Party Secretary of the prestigious Bauman district of Moscow. Brezhnev left to return to Kamenskoye and go to work in a factory. What happened?

A variety of explanations, ranging from a bureaucratic mix-up to Brezhnev's dismissal for academic reasons, can be offered. Then again the change may have been engineered by an impersonal bureaucrat concerned with cadre requirements or program needs, or Brezhnev may have found himself on the losing side of a political debate. Or the move may simply have been of Brezhnev's own choosing because he recognized that life under collectivization might prove short and that industry was clearly the wave of the future.

Most of the explanations can be repudiated. The least plausible is that it was the result of a bureaucratic mix-up. No official selected for study and brought to Moscow would be permanently transferred by mistake. Nor was Brezhnev expelled from the Academy for academic reasons. Even if he had performed badly Soviet educational institutions were relatively lenient with their scholastically poorer students. Those who failed examinations could take them over and if after the second try they still failed one or two subjects, they could repeat them. Furthermore, students on Party scholarships such as Brezhnev almost never flunked out. They were assigned a tutor if they had difficulty and allowed to graduate regardless of their grades. Neither is it likely that Brezhnev made the move on his own. Despite the risks he might face in agriculture it is doubtful that he would have traded the opportunities Moscow afforded for the relative safety of a factory, and even if he had wanted to he could not have done so because trained cadres in agriculture were still in short supply.

Then what did happen? It seems Brezhnev got himself into political hot water. Discussion and grumbling over Stalin's policies was as widespread at the Academy as in the other schools in Moscow. If this school was anything like the Industrial Academy followers of the right dominated its Party Committee. Brezhnev could not have helped but become involved in the political discussions. After the Urals he may have had some reservations about Stalin's methods of collectivization and voiced them, but that is doubtful. If he had spoken out he would have been remembered and later purged from the Party; he gained full Party membership the next year instead and he escaped the massive Party purges two years later. What probably happened is that he found himself at odds with a Bukharinite at the Academy who was in a position to get him expelled.

Thus, Brezhnev's initial step into agriculture came to an abrupt end. But important gains had been made. Collectivization had been excellent schooling; he was now a knowledgeable organizer with expertise he would later put to good use as an *oblast* and republic Party secretary. More importantly, under Stalin Brezhnev went by the rules and developed his own personal method of coping and preserving his balance against anxiety and stress. He learned to observe carefully and to move cautiously and methodically. These attributes were not so much shrewd as essential for an ambitious young Communist on his way to the top.

III

Informer, Engineer, Soldier

That garden shall bloom
that city must arise
when Soviet Russia has such men
as those before my eyes. —Vladimir
    Mayakovskiy, on the Russian worker, 1929.

LATE 1930 SAW BREZHNEV retreat from Moscow to Kamenskoye to be with his family and friends in familiar surroundings. The family had returned home three years earlier. Felix Dzerzhinskiy, Lenin's onetime secret police chief made head of the Supreme Council of the National Economy (VSNkh), reopened the Dneprovskiy factory in 1925 and an appeal to Kamenskoye's displaced workers to return brought the family back. Ilya, Yakov and even Vera took jobs at the factory. They now lived in a modern apartment house in the "Lower Colony." Leonid, Viktoriya and baby Galina moved into a two-room apartment in a whitewashed two-story building on main street.

In nine years Kamenskoye had changed almost beyond recognition. Stalin's plunge into breakneck industrialization following the defeat of the right and his rise to the position of unchallenged dictator had totally altered the landscape. Indeed, the face of the Soviet Union changed radically in those years as Stalin strived to overcome the country's age-old industrial backwardness through a program of rapid industrialization under a series of five year plans.

Although Stalin set impossible industrial production targets in those plans, labor productivity for the whole of the Soviet Union in 1929 alone exceeded the prewar level by 30 percent. The best workers broke world production records. Giant factories came into being one after another and cities, long deserted, sprang to life again.

Kamenskoye was no longer the little town Lenin forgot to put back on the map after the Civil War, but a bustling industrial metropolis with over 100,000 inhabitants. New apartment buildings were going up daily to accommodate the growth of the population. A new hydroelectric dam and power station had been built on the Dneper. The factory, renamed the *Zavod imeni Dzerzhinksiy* in 1929 in honor of its hero, had even changed.

A chemical combine, a large cement works, a railway assembly line, an electrical equipment plant and a coke works had been added to the original plant. Stalin now depended on the factory's production of rolled steel, railroad stock, fertilizer and plastics to meet much of the country's industrial, agricultural and consumer demands. In 1930 he personally praised the factory as a "model enterprise."[1]

Kamenskoye offered ample opportunity now too. The factory needed skilled technicians and even unskilled laborers. Brezhnev had not progressed far enough in engineering classes in 1923 to qualify as an engineer, so he hired on as a boiler stoker.[2] Standing in front of the steaming boiler day after day was dirty work. It was a backbreaking job which left the hands calloused and the body nearly lifeless at the end of a shift. But there were rewards: the family was back together and prospering in their Kamenskoye. Brezhnev felt a deep sense of belonging and satisfaction. Days, weeks, sped by. The new year approached rapidly.

Stalin correctly foresaw difficulties in Russia's vast labor force acquiring the skills and mastering the new technologies required to rapidly modernize Russia. In 1930 the country desperately needed highly qualified engineers and technicians. A strong drive for technical knowledge was therefore launched; hundreds of new higher and secondary schools opened.

The M.I. Arsenichev Metallurgical Institute named after the founder of the Kamenskoye Bolshevik organization, opened in Kamenskoye in 1929. As an extension of the factory's training scheme, the Institute initially operated in the evenings with engineers from the factory instructing student workers. By 1931, it had an enrollment of nearly 600 students and was turning out "fully qualified engineer shock workers."[3]

Now that Brezhnev had returned home Natalya was after him constantly to complete his engineering studies. The factory and the Institute encouraged him too. The factory needed engineers and the Institute offered to grant him a semester of credit for the study in Petrov's class. But it was Brezhnev's personal determination to elevate himself, reinforced by the possibility of being drafted into the Red Army unless he could gain student deferment, that prompted him to enroll in the engineering curriculm at the Institute on the eve of the new year.

Brezhnev found studies at the Institute infinitely more demanding than at the Teknikum in Kursk. The abolition of the brigade system of collective study and examination in 1932 now meant that Brezhnev had to go it alone. The combination of work at the factory and study at night exhausted him.

He changed jobs twice in 1931, which helped him to cope. He became a machine oiler, then became skilled as a fitter. By the following summer he was working as a gas purificaiton machine operator. He also became politically active in his shop.

Nineteen thirty-two was a terrible year for the Russian factory worker as Stalin set higher and higher production goals. the quotas for the factory's gas shop were boosted dramatically that summer despite loud protests from the workers. Their complaint was legitimate. The existing equipment was too old and rundown to withstand the added work. Workers insisted that without new equipment production could not be increased. The matter was finally brought to a head at a meeting of the factory's Party committee.

According to the official account, "it was a stormy affair." Brezhnev took the floor in the name of Stalin. "The country," he told the besiged workers, was "in need of more pig iron, steel, and rolled stock, but it could spare no money now to renew the eqiupment." Some of the parts needed for the equipment could be made right at the factory. Others, he insisted, could be produced from scrapped equipment and restored to working order. The shop would have to make do with what it had at hand. As a loyal Stalin follower, he implored the workers to "sacrifice" for the sake of the "grand dream." Brezhnev reportedly turned the tide: "The meeting agreed with the young Communist" and the shop soon had higher production. [4]

Work and studies were going well for Brezhnev by 1932. He fit in both at the factory and at the Institute. He became chairman of the Trade Union Committee at the Institute and involved in its research effort to solve some of the factory's pressing production problems. In 1933 he was made director of the Institute's Workers' Faculty, designed for those who could not qualify for entry into a higher educational institution but were afforded an opportunity to gain needed technical skills through specialized training.

Brezhnev organized a volunteer student construction crew to work weekends and help with the addition of a new second story to the Institute. [5] He also became active in city affairs. He was elected head of the town's Emergency Flood Control Commission and directed emergency operations when the spring's melting snows flooded the Dneper. In 1933, an addition was also made to the family: a son, Yuriy, was born.

Brezhnev was busy constantly. There seemed to be no end to his energy. He was in his element, and he was obviously making a comeback. Whatever had occurred in Moscow was, or soon would be, past history. He became Party Secretary, that is *Partorg*, at the Institute.[6] In the eyes of the local Party organization he was a trusted worker and Party member, worthy and capable of the political leadership and oversight of a student body numbering over 600. His enthusiastic participation in the Party's special grain collection campaign in the *oblast* in 1933 reinforced this view.

Because of its geographic and strategic position, its rich economic resources and vast manpower, the Ukraine was destined to play a major role in the creation of Stalin's empire. It also suffered more than any other part of the Soviet Union from Stalin's policies. Peasant resistance to collectivization was stronger in the Ukraine and the repressive measures implemented and the economic exploitation of the countryside all brought the Republic to a state of ruin and revolt by 1933.

In January 1933, Stalin sent Pavel Postyshev, armed with dictatorial powers and a sizeable staff, to the Ukraine to conduct a ferocious purge of the Ukrainian Party and break once and for all the resistance of the peasantry. Postyshev was to "ensure the unconditional and immediate execution by the *kolkhozy* and their members of all their obligations to the state regarding grain quotas."

Terror was to characterize both Postyshev's rule and the rule of Nikita Khrushchev who followed Stanislav Kosior as head of the Communist Party of the Ukraine (bolshevik) in 1938. Their reigns of terror took an untold number of lives. The Dnepropetrovsk *oblast* was one of the regions suffering the most, with the highest death toll.

In 1932 the Party had become gravely concerned over the *oblast's* poor grain deliveries to the state. In December this prompted a halt in the supply of commercial products to district villages in an attempt to force an improvement in grain deliveries.[7] It did little good. Finally Mandel Khatayevich was installed as *oblast* Party secretary to deal with problems. Khatayevich, determined to correct the deficiencies, organized one no-holds-barred search and seizure campaign for grain. Brezhnev participated.[8]

A search brigade typically consisted of members of the local *soviet*, two or three Komsomol members, a Party member, a "specialist" equipped with an iron crow bar used for prodding for hidden grain, and student activists. As *Partorg* of the Institute,

Brezhnev organized one group of students to perform the task of preparing collective farmers in the surrounding villages for mass shock work in the field and another group to handle brigade grain collections. The ever-present danger of grain seizure compelled the ingenious peasants to conceal grain in a myriad of places. Collective farms and private houses were searched. Ceilings, attics, floors, cellars, pantries, sheds, barns, straw piles, pig pens, hollow logs, and empty granaries were ripped apart. Everything was searched and anything edible was seized.

Such searches were conducted in every *oblast* of the Ukraine in 1933. Famine followed. Signs of an approaching famine had been evident in the early autumn of 1932. By then the entire grain reserve and other crops that could have supported the population had been seized and shipped to the Russian Republic or sold on the foreign market.

Anna Kasha, then a student at the Dnepropetrovsk Medical Institute, vividly remembers visiting a village near Dnepropetrovsk in search of friends at the height of the famine:

> I did not see anyone in H's courtyard, no child was looking out through the window as they used to. On entering the room I heard groaning, and advancing in that direction, I saw two children lying on the bed. One of them tried to speak to me. I recognized her as the elder girl, one of my former pupils. 'I'm afraid of rats,' she said, 'they run all over me. Tania died a few days ago; the rats have eaten her eyes out, now they run over me. Mother and the children are on the oven; they stopped talking the day before yesterday.[9]

The *oblast's* official death registry records 11,680 deaths due to starvation out of a population of 60,000 in one village near Kamenskoye. Slaughterhouses for children were discovered in the *oblast*. Criminals lured small children, killed them, salted the meat in barrels and sold it. Mass suicides were reported in Shyroka Balka, Dnepropetrovsk oblast.[10] Even the most conservative estimates indicate that the famine death toll in the Ukraine was at least 4.5 million.

Brezhnev, as a participant in the grain seizures, was in part responsible. He, his family, local Party and state officials, and the militia were not at all affected by the famine. Special stores where they could buy food and other products in normal quantities at fixed government prices had been set up for them.

The tactics used against the peasant worked; 1933 was really the first year in which a decisive break in agriculture was made in the Ukraine. "We have sufficient grain deliveries and in such quantities that they surpass the previous year by 16.7 million cwts," the Ukrainian representative told the Seventeenth Congress of the All-Union Communist Party (b) in 1933.[11] "There can be no doubt, famine ... was an effective means of breaking any tendency on the part of the peasants to indulge in passive resistance or 'sabotage.'" Indeed, "work in the collective farms proceeded at a much faster pace in 1933 than in preceding years, even when the collective farm members were weakened by hunger."[12]

But Stalin's methods to achieve such victories were now being questioned by the most senior members of the Party and government, by those who had helped Stalin defeat first the Trotskyites and then the Bukharinites. They were "exchanging propaganda urging that the Central Committee should have the courage to vote Stalin out of office by constitutional means."[13] What followed, once Stalin found out about the "plot" was a largescale purge, sparked by the assassination of Sergey Kirov, the Leningrad Party boss, on December 1, 1934. Midnight arrests, gruelling cross examinations and torture by the secret police, banishment in forced labor camps and execution with and without trials descended with its full weight upon Soviet Russia.

There are few clear facts about Brezhnev's role in the Ukrainian version of the Great Purge. Brezhnev avoided it himself. "That fortunate circumstance," a former member of the Ukrainian Communist Party told me, "was because he was lucky and because he must have had a hand in it." An involvement is clear.

Allegations of "anti-Soviet centers," "blocs" and "plots" ran rampant throughout the country. They were no less muted at the Arsenichev Institute than at any other educational institution in 1934. As *Partorg*, Brezhnev was responsible for leadership of the Party group and Party activities at the Institute, but his chief responsibility during the purge rested in establishing close liaison with the local department of the Peoples Commissariat of Internal Affairs (the NKVD or secret police*) and maintaining political surveillance over his classmates and teachers. Under Stalin, thoroughness in political

*In the course of 60 years of Soviet history the name of the organization responsible for secret police activities has changed numerous times. After the October Revolution it was known as the Cheka and became the GPU, OGPU, and in the 1930's, the NKVD. It is known today as the KGB, the Komitet Gosudarstvennoy Bezopasnosti, or Committee for State Security.

vigilance was a measure of Party loyalty and hence self protection. Brezhnev was in no position to maintain either an invisible posture or neutrality in these matters.

Political paranoia spread like a plague across the country. The first large public trial of 16 accused principal conspirators, chief among them the prominent Party figures Grigoriy Zinoviyev and Lev Kamenev, was held in August 1936. Both were convicted and executed. Another 17, including Georgiy Pyatakov, along with Karl Radek, the former secretary of the Communist International, were convicted at a second trial in January 1937. In March 1938, Bukharin, Trotsky in absentia, and Rykov were tried and Bukharin and Rykov, executed (Trotsky was assassinated in Mexico City in 1940). These prominent Party leaders, excluding Radek and Rykov, had been listed as potential successors to Lenin in his "Testament."

At the lower levels, millions of local Party and government officials, technicians and specialists in industry, Komsomol members, students, and political suspects of all kinds fell victim to accusations and were arrested. Brezhnev was assuredly active, giving at the very least a few "annihilate the enemy" speeches and denouncing a suspect or two that would assure him of safety. The extent of his "activity" would further seem to be indicated in part by two facts: all "chance" and "passive" elements were expelled along with "aliens" during the verification and exchange of Party cards,[14] but Brezhnev retained his Party membership, and, at about the time Bukharin was tried in Moscow, Brezhnev was promoted. More will be said about the promotion later.

Despite the numerous diversions, or even because of them, Brezhnev graduated with honors from the Arsenichev Institute. He received high praise in the factory newspaper. Yevgeniy Tyazhelnikov, Komsomol First Secretary, extolling Brezhnev's leadership qualities at the Twenty-fifth Party Congress in February 1976, stood up and quoted this passage from a 1935 edition of the newspaper *Znamya Dzerzhinskogo*:

> I cannot imagine where this man gets so much energy and enthusiasm for his work. The son of a worker, he himself worked in the plant as a stoker and fitter for five years. He was sent from production to Party economic work, heavy burdensome work. He is studying in our Institute.... The young engineer promises a great deal in production and he will fulfill this promise because he is made of strong stuff.[15]

And so in the summer of 1935, Brezhnev was ready to put his new skills as an engineer to work and carve out a brand new career.

He took a job as a shift foreman in the shop where he had worked as a fitter. Here he immediately revealed himself to be a master of Stalin's "shock" style. This style presupposed that production could be increased through sheer physical exertion, mixed, in Brezhnev's case, with sweet reason: "He [Brezhnev] frequently *spoke* to the workers, *explaining* the policy of the party and the government to them."[16]

On August 30, 1935, a coal miner named Aleksey Stakhanov, in the presence of his manager, a Party secretary, and the local *Pravda* editor, cut a record of 192 tons of coal in only six hours. He earned 225 rubles for the shift, more than a month's wages. The miner's achievements were given intense publicity in the press and soon duplicated elsewhere.

Innovation in production came to the fore at the Dzerzhinskiy factory and in Brezhnev's shop. When Stalin launched a massive Stakhanovite competition campaign, offering bonuses to technical, engineering, trade and other personnel for exceeding planned output, Brezhnev worked his shop at a feverish tempo. Production figures soared as specialization was implemented, time and equipment were put to better use, and lagging workers were goaded to produce.

Workers won cash and valuable prizes. Automobiles, pianos and bicycles went to the top *Stakhanovites* (as super-achieving workers were soon dubbed). Between August 1935 and March 1936, the factory won three all-union competitions, entitling it to be billed as "one of the top metallurgical factories in the country."[17]

Using the records set at this and other factories Stalin ordered the production norms for all workers revised significantly upward in 1936. The age of superindustrialization had arrived and with it all the attendant miseries.

The Party's views of this period of socialist construction have differed widely. During the Khrushchev era the forced collectivization and industrialization of the late twenties and early thirties became known as the "dark years" of Stalin's rule. Brezhnev, however, sees this period as a "pioneering stage of Soviet history which merits unquestioning enthusiasm" from today's generation of Soviet youth. On occasion, he has even portrayed these years as an almost virtuous period of Soviet history. In his speech at the fiftieth anniversary celebration of the Great October Revolution in 1967 he said:

> Remember, comrades how people lived in those years: bread rations, shortages of clothing and footwear, an acute housing

shortage and many other difficulties and privations. Yet the country literally seethed with the labor enthusiasm of the masses; volunteers streamed to the ... places where the advance posts of socialist industry were being created.[18]

But what about the hardships and extreme cruelties of the period? He chooses to dismiss them:

> Unlike the bourgeoisie who already had tested appliances, our Communist Party had to pioneer the road to socialism, to build and test the "appliances" of the new society in practice.... It must always be remembered that for us every step was a quest and every advance was achieved in stubborn struggle against the enemies within the country and in the world arena.[19]

Speaking at a collective farm congress in 1969, Brezhnev said that the same extenuating circumstances also applied to the Stalinist period of forced collectivization: "Certain mistakes were made in the process of collective farm construction. But these mistakes were made during the process of search; mistakes made because of the lack of experience! The Party itself boldly brought the mistakes to light, told the people about them frankly, and corrected them."[20]

In short, Brezhnev holds that the hardships, the miscalculations, the errors and perhaps even Stalin's Great Purge could hardly have been avoided given the circumstances the Party faced at the time.

While Stalin was busy industrializing Russia and cleansing the Party of "alien" elements, in Germany Adolf Hilter was on the move. Germany was rearming. Japan's military might was also growing. Russia's Chinese Eastern Railway in Manchuria was sold to avoid an armed conflict with Japan, as the problem of preserving peace became one of primary importance to Stalin. In the mid-thirties the Red Army underwent modernization and expansion and in 1935 thousands of men were called up. In November 1935 Brezhnev too was drafted.

His late entry into the military was unusual. Under the national recruitment laws of 1925, 1928 and 1930, all male workers between the ages of 21 and 26 were required to serve on active duty in the regular army, in territorial armies, in centers of instruction, or in the defense industry. Brezhnev's military service, however, had been postponed for nine years.

There were several reasons for the deferral. The shortage of trained personnel for collectivization in the late twenties was one. Active military service for technical personnel in Brezhnev's field was frequently deferred to a later date. Futhermore, until 1930 Brezhnev was involved in important state work, after which he resumed student status at the Institute and further deferment. In addition, there was no clearly visible external threat to the country and consequently no major concern for the creation of a large standing army. However, the rise of Hitler and the recognition of both Germany and Japan as possible future military adversaries changed that.

Military life was not altogether new to Brezhnev. The same national service laws required young men to undergo training prior to active service. This was spread out over a two-year period and included about 420 hours of political and basic military instruction, incorporating 60 days of exercises. Brezhnev fulfilled these requirements while in school at Kursk.

In 1935, the length of active service required in the regular army was two to four years and in the territorial army eight to twelve months. Brezhev served in the latter.

He made good use of the 11 months he spent in the barren Transbaykal region of Siberia. He attended a tank tactics school there which put him a cut above other Party *apparatchiks* who entered the war with Germany six years later. Upon graduation he became a platoon sergeant, but his political experiences was soon put to practical use in the platoon as its political officer. The latter in part paved the way for his selection as Dnepropetrovsk *oblast* ideological and indoctrination secretary in 1938 and as a political worker in the Red Army during World War II.

Far reaching changes occurred in Kamenskoye during Brezhnev's absence. The town acquired a new name. On February 1, 1936, it was renamed Dneprodzerzhinsk, immortalizing Dzerzhinskiy forever.

Upon returning home in the autumn of 1936, Brezhnev fully expected to resume work at the factory. Instead his attention was turned to teaching. The Workers' Faculty had been converted into a Technical College. Its curriculm and its facilities had been expanded. Its director though had become a victim of the purge, leaving the vacancy open. Brezhnev got the job. A photograph in a 1976 Soviet pictorial book shows a young Brezhnev on the cover of the school's first class album.[21]

Brezhnev held this post until May of the following year when he was "elected" to the Executive Committee of the Dneprodzerzhinsk *soviet* as one of its two vice-chairmen, that is, deputy town mayor. This time too he stepped into the shoes of a Stalin victim. Brezhnev was 30 and fully recovered from his earlier setback.

IV

Khrushchev's Loyal Propagandist

*No matter what the pursuit or field, he must choose a
protector, a patron among those already in power,
and he must put himself in the relationship of a client
and rely upon his favor.* — Franz Borkenau on the
Soviet political system.

IN MAY 1937 WHEN DZERZHINETS, the combined organ of
the Dneprodzerzhinsk Party Committee and city *soviet*, announced
that "comrade and fellow worker" L.I. Brezhnev had been elected a
vice-chairman of the *Gorsovet* (city *soviet*) it received scant attention in the face of headlines warning of activities by "bourgeois
nationalists," "alien elements," "capitalist agents" and "saboteurs" in
Dnepropetrovsk. According to Stalin and Postyshev the *oblast*, and
for that matter the entire Ukraine, was crawling with anti-Soviet
vermin. Earlier, Postyshev had testified that Trotskyist "double
dealers" had wormed their way into the Dnepropetrovsk district Party organization. And during his trial, Pyatakov, the chief defendent
at the second Moscow trial in January 1937, described how these
groups had been organized in Dnepropetrovsk.[1] These allegations
and the absence of a Moscow representative to the May 1937
Thirteenth Ukrainian Party Congress were omens of another purge.

Postyshev, though renowned as a liquidator of Trotskyites
and Bukharinites, had been removed in March without explanation.
Only later at the Thirteenth Ukrainian Party Congress was he formally charged with promoting hero worship (his own) and relaxing
Party vigilance. Stanislav Kosior, who succeeded Postyshev in Kiev,
accused him of letting Trotskyites and nationalists infiltrate the
Ukrainian Party apparatus and "seize control of important posts." In
reality, Postyshev was removed because he had incurred Stalin's
displeasure by developing a pro-Ukrainian outlook and by coming to
Bukharin's aid at the February 1937 Party plenum.

Stalin's dissatisfaction, however, did not stop with Postyshev;
it encompassed the whole of the Ukrainian Party which everyone
thought Postyshev had purged to Stalin's satisfaction. By the Thirteenth Ukrainian Party Congress Stalin had already decided that all
members of the Ukrainian Party and government must go. New men

without any Ukrainian loyalties would have to be found and put in charge at all levels so Stalin could effectively rule the Ukraine.

Stalin diligently prepared by setting up a Special Security Commission of the Party's Central Committee, consisting of himself, Nikolay Yezhov, Russia's chief policeman (who was later crowned the "flaming sword of the revolution" for his role in the Great Purge only to be executed by Stalin when the purge was finished), and Vyacheslav Molotov, to investigate the Ukrainians. The Ukraine was subsequently inundated with agents sent to gather evidence. In August, with such evidence firmly in hand, Stalin dispatched a special purge troika composed of Molotov, Yezhov and Khrushchev to present an ultimatum to the Ukrainian Central Committee.

Guarded by "special" NKVD troops sent from Moscow, the three arrived in Kiev, immediately called a special plenum of the Ukrainian Party Central Committee, and proceeded to lay down the charges. Molotov demanded a vote of no-confidence in Kosior, in Khatayevich who had succeeded Postyshev as Second Secretary, and in the other Ukrainian Party and state leaders. In a totally unexpected move, Molotov demanded that all be expelled from the Central Committee and Khrushchev be "elected" Ukraine Party Secretary.

But the old guard Bolsheviks of the Ukraine would not relinquish their positions. The next day a second plenum was held, but again they refused to quit. Molotov then called Stalin who offered a "compromise" discussion of the matter with the Party Central Committee in Moscow. Except for one, Panas Lyubchenko, the premier, who took his own life, the Ukrainian leaders reluctantly agreed to go. Most were never heard from again.

In the sweeping purges which followed, Khrushchev orchestrated the removal of the remaining high ranking officials of the Ukrainian Party and government. However, the "smashing of enemies of the people" did not begin in earnest until Khrushchev's actual arrival as head of the Ukrainian Party in January 1938. The 1943 edition of the Soviet *History of the Ukraine* tells us: "With the arrival in the Ukraine of the close comrade in arms of Stalin, N.S. Khrushchev, the eradication of the remnants of the enemy and the liquidation of the wrecking activities proceeded particularly successfully."

On January 29, 1938, *Pravda* carried the news of Khrushchev's assumption to the Party secretaryship of the Ukraine. A large portrait of the new viceroy of the Ukraine, wearing a wide smile and a traditional embroidered Ukrainian shirt, accompanied the article.

Edward Crankshaw described Khrushchev as a "man who had no justification except as Stalin's instrument and he had to go to very great lengths to demonstrate that he was nothing but Stalin's instrument."[2]

Born in 1894 to peasant parents in Brezhnev's ancestral home province of Kursk (whether this endeared him to Brezhnev in some small way is hard to tell), Khrushchev joined the Party in 1918, rose from a private in Trotsky's Red Army to head the Stalino Party organization in the Ukraine, becoming a delegate to the All-Union Communist Party Congress in Moscow in 1925. As a functionary of the Ukrainian Central Comittee, he was already making important speeches to Ukrainian Party congresses by the time Brezhnev graduated from the Land Teknikum. However, it was not until Khrushchev entered the Industrial Academy in Moscow in 1929, at a time when Stalin was looking for faithful followers, that he caught Stalin's eye.

After joining the Academy's Party Committee, he became its Secretary and at Stalin's bidding purged the Committee of its rightest elements. Stalin rewarded Khrushchev in 1931 by making him Secretary of Moscow's prestigious Bauman district Party Committee. Between 1932 and 1938, Khrushchev became a Stalin protégé, was promoted to Second and then to First Secretary of the Moscow city and regional Party Committee, and oversaw the building of the spectacular Moscow subway. Just before his departure for the Ukraine, Stalin rewarded him with candidate membership in the Party's Politburo, making him one of the top dozen Party leaders in the country.

As the new ruler of the Ukraine, Khrushchev's job was to expeditiously conclude the purge, build a new Party organization in the Ukraine and Russify the republic. At last here was the man who would engineer Stalin's master plan for the Ukraine, "the rich jewel of Moscow's crown," and Brezhnev was to help.

The first phase of the job was accomplished by late summer, though officials continued to be removed on a smaller scale until the Germans marched in in 1941. "I pledge myself," Khrushchev told Stalin in May, "to spare no efforts in seizing and annihilating Trotskyites, Bukharinites, and all agents of fascism and despicable bourgeois nationalism on our free Ukrainian soil."[3] Indeed, Khrushchev and his NKVD chief, Fyodor Uspenskiy, left no stone unturned as they cleansed every Party committee, Soviet state enterprise, schools and other institutions of "recidivist elements" and "cold followers of the Ukrainian Party."

The results were staggering. The Ukrainian Party leaders Kosior and Postyshev were found guilty of mass murder and executed. Of the Politburo, the Orgburo, the Control Commission and the Ukrainian Party Secretariat, not a single member was left. Only two remained free of the 62 full members and 42 candidate members of the Central Committee elected at the May 1937 Ukrainian Party Congress. All 17 members of the government were arrested and most were executed. All *oblast* secretaries were liquidated, as were many lower level functionaries. Nothing was left of the former Ukrainian Party organization.

The rebuilding process began in early May 1938. Men of the Stalin era, careerists and functionaries, were imported from Moscow. And Stalin empire builders and colonizers, loyalists like Demyan Korotchenko and Semyon Zadionchenko who had been associated with Khrushchev in Moscow, fanned out across the Ukraine to search out promising apparatchiks to build up a new efficient Party apparatus at the *oblast* level and organize a new regiment of Khrushchev followers. In the spring, Khrushchev promoted 1600 Party members to district and city Party jobs. Podushka, who became a secretary in the Dnepropetrovsk Party organization, reported to the Eighteenth All-Union Party Congress in March 1939 that about 300 of the best Party members were picked to head various posts in the *oblast* vacated in 1938.[4] She was one, Brezhnev was another.

It was in May of 1938 then that Brezhnev moved from vice-chairman of his hometown city Soviet into a direct Party function: He became head of the Dnepropetrovsk regional Party Committee's Department of Ideology and Indoctrination. An entirely new element in his career had begun, that of a full-time Party organizer and Khrushchev protégé.

He thus became a participant in *shefstvo*, a Russian term which means the placement and promotion of persons loyal to oneself or to one's ideas and goals in important jobs to build one's own base of support and personal following. By the same token, in order to rise in the Soviet political system, the aspirant is compelled to choose a protector, a patron among those who are powerful. The client backs his patron and he rises, or falls, as his patron moves up or down the hierarchical ladder. No other factor would play as important a role in Brezhnev's rise to national political prominence. Just as Khrushchev was Stalin's instrument, so Brezhnev became Khrushchev's advocate, his troubleshooter, expeditor and co-conspirator.

What exactly did Khrushchev see in the young deputy mayor of Dneprodzerzhinsk that persuaded him to make him part of the new regiment? At a minimum, the loyalty and competence of Brezhnev were known through NKVD sources. There is, of course, also the possibility that they had met earlier in Moscow. The fact that Brezhnev was a Great Russian in nationality as well as outlook and already in the Ukraine was a definite asset. He was also a proven Stalinist and a qualified engineer. Stalin regarded technical training, especially engineering training, as the most desirable general preparation, other than specific training in a Party school, for a young man hoping to reach a high position in the Soviet hierarchy. Brezhnev had a clear police record, none of his friends or relatives had even been arrested, and he knew his *oblast* from back to front. Moreover, he was tough. As *Partorg* at the Institute and later as a city official he had demonstrated a certain capacity for intrigue which could be useful.

Above all, Brezhnev came highly recommended by none other than Demyan Korotchenko, third in Khrushchev's entourage. Though a Ukrainian by birth, in the course of Korotchenko's work in Moscow and later as Party secretary of the Western Province Committee and then Smolensk City Committee of the All-Union Communist Party in the mid-thirties, he had been completely russified. In Smolensk he even used the Russian name of Korotchenkov. His credentials as a Khrushchev follower and confidant were established in the Moscow District Party Committee where he had worked as one of the secretaries. He was sent to Dnepropetrovsk in late 1937 as its new Party secretary to clear the way for Khrushchev's takeover. Brezhnev caught his eye during the course of this transition. One month after Khrushchev arrived in the Ukraine, Korotchenko went to Kiev and became the chairman of the Ukrainian Council of People's Commissars.

A great deal of reshuffling took place in the Dneprodzerzhinsk City Party Committee on the eve of Korotchenko's departure. Several of Brezhnev's classmates from the Institute moved into responsible Party positions at the city level. Two of them, Pavel Alferov and Konstantin Grushevoy, whom we will have occasion to meet again, graduated from the Institute one year ahead of Brezhnev. They became department heads at the factory. As a result of a mini-purge in Dneprodzerzhinsk, Alferov was appointed city Party head in 1937. Grushevoy succeeded him in 1938. But only Brezhnev was elevated to the *oblast* level. He impressed Korotchenko as the most

promising young Party member of the Dneprodzerzhinsk
organization and Korotchenko, prior to departing for Kiev, recommended Brezhnev for the vacated (by purge) post of ideology and indoctrination chief.

The inside link with Khrushchev was maintained and
strengthened through Semyon Zadionchenko, Korotchenko's successor in Dnepropetrovsk. Like Korotchenko, Zadionchenko was a
Khrushchev protégé, but from the Bauman district of Moscow. He
was also associated with Khrushchev's takeover of the Ukraine.
As head of the Dnepropetrovsk Party organization, Zadionchenko
often spoke highly of his propaganda chief Brezhnev.

In his capacity as head of the *oblast* Department of Ideology
and Indoctrination, and later *oblast* Secretary for Propaganda when
that office was created in February 1939, Brezhnev functioned as
Khrushchev's (and thus Stalin's) propaganda transmitter to the
worker and Party member in Dnepropetrovsk. He was given complete responsibility for both public propaganda and Party indoctrination. He assumed command and supervision of all oral and
printed propaganda, relying heavily on the press and radio to
reach the masses. He became the chief editor and censor for nearly
200 newspapers and magazines published in Dnepropetrovsk between 1938 and 1940; he controlled hundreds of propaganda
"agitation points" in schools, clubs, reading rooms, "houses of
culture," libraries, museums, study circles, hostels, indeed virtually
everywhere political literature could be kept or disseminated; he
broadcast important speeches by Stalin and Khrushchev, and
organized political rallies, talks and lectures in support of their
policies. As the oblast's top ideologist, he also had the tough task of
providing Party members with a Stalinist political education. Long
and tedious indoctrination courses for factory and *kolkhoz* Party
secretaries had to be prepared as well as preliminary papers and
reports of all kinds for Party plenums.

The job would not only test Brezhnev's imagination,
organizational abilities and stamina, but it would, for better or for
worse, open him up to particularly close scrutiny by Stalin, Khrushchev and the NKVD. Yet he displayed not the least bit of apprehension
about stepping into the shoes of his dead predecessor. The risks
were great, but the danger and violence of the Civil War, famine,
collectivization and the Great Purge had been great too.

Brezhnev revealed himself at once to be a propaganda wizard.
On July 11, 1938, *Izvestiya* printed a full-blown article on Brezhnev's

8000 agitators and propagandists who had worked on the recent "election campaign." They were described as nothing less than a "Great Army... strengthened by more and more cadres every day." Coming from the government's central newspaper, that was significant praise of a junior Party apparatchik. "Some in the army," the newspaper concluded, "have years of Party experience.... Others are new cadres of agitators demonstrating their organizational talents for the first time." The report accurately summed up Brezhnev and his colleagues.

With the Soviet election over in late July, Brezhnev enthusiastically turned the attention of his "army" to other, more pressing tasks. Russification now received his undivided attention and he geared up his propaganda machine accordingly. He was about to undo Stalin's own policy of "Ukrainianization" so fervently implemented in the twenties and thirties and crush the Ukrainian social consciousness that had dared to rear its head in his *oblast*.

In no other policy area did Stalin so completely reverse himself. In an attempt to appease those segments of the population rebelling against his collectivization and industrial policies, and to avoid a clash with Ukrainian patriots by early insistence that Russian be made the official language of the Ukraine, he had permitted Ukrainian to remain the official language of the Ukrainian Soviet Socialist Republic even to the extent of castigating those Russian-speaking officials who failed to study the language. Though beaten, forced to collectivize and industrialize, and later pressured to adopt Russian ways, the Ukrainians of the Dnepropetrovsk *oblast* clung to their mother tongue and customs. Brezhnev was to destroy these last elements of national identification.

Brezhnev presented his anti-Ukrainian propaganda with the skill and flare of a born agitator. The propaganda was calculated to stir up an atmosphere of revulsion for everything Ukrainian.

Ukrainian bourgeois nationalism was now the main enemy. At the Fourteenth Ukrainian Party Congress called in June 1938 to approve and consolidate the results of the recent purge, Khrushchev alleged that Ukrainian "bourgeois nationalists — Polish and German spies" who feared the "power and influence" of the Russian language — had subverted Russian language and culture in the Ukraine.

Brezhnev alleged that these mad nationalists had driven the Russian language and culture from the schools in the Dnepropetrovsk *oblast*. This provided the backdrop for Brezhnev's purge of the

Ukrainian language from the schools. Under his watchful eye Russian was established in all non-Russian schools in the *oblast* in accordance with Khrushchev's April 1938 decree which made it a compulsory school subject.

All the newspapers, periodicals and pamphlets were now printed in Russian. The switch was explained by Brezhnev thus:

> Bolsheviks study the German language in order to read the theories of Marx in the original. The theories of Marx and Engels were developed further by the theories of Lenin and Stalin in the Russian language. Hence comrades, the people in all areas are studying and will study the Russian language in order to study Leninism and Stalinism and be taught to destroy their enemies.[5]

In addition, the Ukrainian language itself was tampered with to make it more like Russian. Brezhnev rewrote the history books to depict bourgeois and Communist national leaders of the past as traitors to the Ukrainian people and their republic. The history of the Ukrainian Communist Party was russified. The unique Ukrainian culture was lost in many areas. There were endless tributes to Stalin, to the Russian culture, to the eternal friendship of the Russian and the Ukrainian peoples written by Ukrainian editors who recognized their new "Russian" heritage.

In March 1939, Brezhnev took time out to propagandize "The great historical step toward greater socialist democracy and strengthening of the All-Union Communist Party" taken by "comrade Stalin" at the Eighteenth Communist Party Congress.

The recent purges had so drastically reduced Communist Party membership that Stalin was compelled to lay down new Party rules designed to broaden the base of support for the Party by enrolling new members into its ranks, particularly in the Ukraine where the population was the furthest removed in sympathy from the Party. Many of the Party's earlier restrictions on admission were now dropped. Common rules were adopted, a set period of probation established and a bill of rights, of sorts, for Party members was added. Theoretically any Party member could now participate in "free and business-like discussions" of Party policy, criticize "*any* Party worker," elect representatives and stand for election to Party committees, and be present when his activity or conduct was being questioned.

In her speech to the 1939 Eighteenth Party Congress Podushka provided a capsule of Brezhnev's promotion of the new rules. The

Congress met from March 10th through the 21st. She addressed the gathered delegation on the 21st and noted that within that ten-day period "over 60 percent of the members and candidate members of the primary Party organizations in the *oblast* have participated in discussions of the new rules." The campaign is a success in the *oblast*, she told the Congress. "Hundreds, no, thousands of Party and non-Party Bolsheviks in the factories, brigades, institutions and educational establishments have been told about the rules.... Everyone is discussing them."[6]

A rare insight into Brezhnev's view of the Party purges is provided by his commentary on the provision in the new rules prohibiting "mass cleansings" of the type carried out during the Great Purge and during Khrushchev's Ukrainian purges. Such cleansings, Brezhnev admitted: "were a means of *improving* the composition of the Party during the transition period," but he added, "they are no longer necessary in conditions of *victorious socialism* when capitalist elements have all been eliminated" (italics added).

Yet Brezhnev continued to accuse the "bourgeois nationalists" of being "German and Polish [*i.e.*, capitalist and fascist] spies" and thereby perpetuated the sense of danger at home. It is doubtful that leaders like Lyubchenko, who was accused of having led a renegade gang known as the "Ukrainian National Fascist Organization," and others had secretly connived with Hitler, or his representatives, to overthrow the Bolsheviks in the Ukraine. However, the accusation served as a useful political tool against domestic opposition, so it continued to be used. In part it also reflected Stalin's concern about Germany's growing challenge to the Soviet Union.

The Ukraine was a particularly vulnerable part of the Soviet empire and German leaders, including Hitler, had shown special interest in it. Hitler even cultivated anti-Soviet Ukrainian émigrés, possibly for future use in the republic.[7] Patriotism was therefore emphasized much more in the Ukraine than other Soviet republics.

What Brezhnev sought to do was, on the one hand, continue his slander and character assassinations and, on the other, stir up hatred for Germany and support for the Soviet government as protector of the republic. These themes were intricately laced with anti-Polish propaganda which stressed the ambitious nature of the "vicious and depraved Polish government" and the torturous and brutal nature of Polish rule in the "Western Ukraine" (*i.e.*, eastern Poland).

There did not appear to be a central policy for building mass support. Rather, each *oblast* propaganda secretary developed his own devices and pursued his own campaign toward that end. A month after the Eighteenth Party Congress met in Moscow, Brezhnev devised his implement: a series of *oblast* "workers' conferences." The conferences, designed to demonstrate the patriotism of "Dnepropetrovsk metallurgists," were an enormous success and received national recognition.

The first conference was held on April 20, 1939. Thousands participated, raising a hue and cry over the "Hitlerite menace" and the brutality of the Polish government. The highlight of the rally was, without a doubt, its concluding statement—a 1500-word pledge of support to Stalin and to the Soviet government which Stalin considered significant enough to print in the April 23 edition of *Izvestiya*. The pledge received special half-page coverage and contained Brezhnev's unique treatment of the themes of unity, patriotism and Soviet might (military power), which remain his central themes today. Extracts from the pledge are as follows:

> Our dear Comrade Iosif Vissaronovich [Stalin], once more we pledge that ... with all our might we will fight for the further blossoming of our socialist nation. We firmly heed your warning of capitalist encirclement and will ... strengthen the defense of our country and promote revolutionary vigilance.... Nobody will ever succeed in halting our victorious movement toward the final triumph of communism.
>
> Our country possesses sufficient metal to make strait-jackets for those lunatics who have lost their heads, who imagine that they can attempt to violate our inviolable borders.... The volleys of Voroshilov will flatly smash each and every enemy of our country.
>
> If the fascist aggressors attempt to violate our inviolable borders they and their filthy hides will experience all the mighty wrath of our many millions of Soviet people, welded Stalinist people, of their united hatred of the enemy, of their unswerving attachment to the Bolshevik Party, of their united indivisible love for you, dear Iosif Vissaronovich. The 1st of May is near.... On this joyous day the fortunate people of the Soviet Union will join the First of May columns in the city square to once more demonstrate before all the world, our love, and our dedication to our Bolshevik Party, to you, Comrade Stalin. Together with all the Soviet peoples, the metallurgists of Dnepropetrovsk *oblast* proclaim from the bottom of their souls:
>
> Greetings to our socialist nation.

Greetings to our Party of Lenin and Stalin.
Greetings to the leaders of Party and people,
  our dear and great Stalin.

Brezhnev's propaganda themes naturally shifted after the Nonaggression Pact was signed with Germany on August 23, 1939. Coming as it did in the wake of Stalin's particularly rabid anti-fascist attacks in the spring and continued security negotiations with the Western powers, the treaty signed by Russia's new Foreign Commissar Vyacheslav Molotov and Germany's Joachim von Ribbentrop stunned the Russian people, as it did the rest of the world. But the treaty offered the best chance of security for the Soviet Union, at least in the short run, since the collective security arrangements with the West had failed to check Hitler. Perhaps Stalin hoped that Germany and the Allies would become involved in a drawn-out struggle that would leave Russia the arbiter.

With the advent of the Pact, Brezhnev halted all attacks on Germany's interest in the Ukraine. As it now appeared that Stalin had jettisoned his anti-fascist ideological framework, the *oblast* adopted a policy of scrupulous neutrality toward Germany. Though blind as to Stalin's reasoning, on the day the treaty was officially announced Brezhnev loyally summoned yet another Workers' Conference. Its purpose: to demonstrate the *oblast's* solidarity with comrade Stalin on the matter of the Soviet-German pact.[8]

This neutrality prevailed despite some incidents of air space violation and even attacks by German planes. When Hitler's planes bombed the Komintern factory in Dnepropetrovsk in October 1939, Brezhnev all but disregarded it. When the bombing was mentioned in the press it received no more than a few lines and then Brezhnev would only say that the bombing had been done by (unidentified) "enemy planes."

In return for Soviet neutrality in the future war in Europe Hitler had agreed to give Stalin control of Finland, the Baltic States, the eastern part of Poland and the Romanian province of Bessarabia. On September 1, 1939, Hitler's Panzer divisions invaded Poland, thereby triggering World War II. At the same time, Russia mobilized. On September 17, the Soviet Union began to occupy the eastern areas of Poland.

When Molotov announced over Moscow radio the Soviet government's decision to send in Red Army units to secure the eastern Polish districts, Brezhnev organized yet a third rally. This

time he drummed up mass support for the Soviet invasion. The rally
also gained national recognition and press coverage. On September
17, 1939, the Ukrainian Party Central Committee's newspaper *Industriya* announced:

> The people of Dnepropetrovsk *oblast* warmly welcome the
> decision of the Soviet government to defend ... the lives of
> peoples living in western Ukraine and western Belorussia. We,
> the Soviet people, are forever devoted to the great Party, and to
> the leader of all working people of the world, comrade Stalin.

Three days later the newspaper again reported: "Workers in
Dnepropetrovsk ... are working harder than ever to build the defense
of their country and show a patriotic spirit."

The invasion went swiftly. Semyon Timoshenko, commander
of the Kiev Military District, led the Red Army forces which occupied the entire area in three days. Khrushchev then set about
preparing it for annexation to the Soviet Ukraine.

From his lookout in Dnepropetrovsk Brezhnev took it all in:
the deportation of nearly 1.5 million Poles to prison camps in Siberia
and northern Russia, the establishment of an effective secret police
and Party apparatus, and the arrest and execution of 10,000 Polish
officers — six years later he would do the same thing in
Czechoslovakia.

Brezhnev treated Stalin's decision to wage war on Finland in
late November 1939 the same way. In a resolution published in *Industriya* on the 30th of the month, he proclaimed:

> We metallurgists fully support the decision by our government
> to cut diplomatic and economic relations with Finland. For a
> long time Finland has been an impudent provocateur of war.
> We believe that our valiant armed forces will be able to teach
> the Finnish political landgrabbers a lesson.

Similarly on December 3, the Komintern factory in
Dnepropetrovsk resolved:

> The oppressed people of Finland together with our heroic
> armed forces are engaged in a battle with reactionary elements
> who dragged themselves into a war with the Soviet Union....
> We submit that the workers will, in only a short time, be able to
> defeat the Finnish bourgeoisie.[9]

Pledges to produce more steel for the Soviet armed forces, all
of them signed by workers from this or that factory, always accompanied Brezhnev's resolutions of support for Stalin's conduct of
foreign policy.[10] Not all pledges, however, were kept.

At a plenum of the Dnepropetrovsk Party organization in

November 1939, Zadionchenko reported that four factories in the *oblast* did not fulfill their production quotas for the ten-month period. He told the Fifteenth Party Congress of the Ukrainian Communist Party held that year that neglect of ideological work on the part of some factory Party secretaries had been to blame.[11]

Had Brezhnev overlooked propaganda work in some factories because of his devotion to foreign policy propaganda and work on the Electoral Commission of the Ukrainian Supreme Soviet to which he had been elected in October 1939?[12] It is doubtful. This hint of trouble only became recognizable a short while later when propaganda in the Ukraine as a whole was subjected to a complete review.

Nevertheless, Brezhnev immediately got to work on the problem. He again organized a series of political campaigns while his "army" conducted crash courses in Marxist-Leninist ideology for secretaries of factory Party organizations.[13] These received favorable mention in *Pravda* on February 16, 1940.

In 1940, all propaganda organizations in the Ukraine underwent critical review and a report of the findings was published in *Pravda* on September 29, 1940. The Central Committee's investigation revealed that the quality of propaganda was below par in many Party organizations. While foreign policy propaganda had "become popular," the report concluded, the teaching of Marxism-Leninism was being neglected, independent study of the newly published *Short Course of the History of the VKP (b)*[14] was not being pursued, and many Party organizations had failed to adequately investigate the advantages of the lecture system for oral propaganda.

How did Brezhnev fare in the investigation? All the Central Committee report said was that the level of theoretical ideological propaganda in the Golonyanskiy *rayon* was poor. "It isn't surprising that of 941 people in the district who are studying the *Short Course*, 627 are still on Chapter 1," the report concluded. But that was it. On the whole, the feeling was that his organization was in pretty good shape.

By 1950, Stalin was the absolute master of the Ukraine. Khrushchev had successfully dispelled its separatist ambitions, liquidated its Trotskyites, Bukharinites and bourgeois nationalists. He had also added new territory (the "western Ukraine"), restored Party vigilance and built up an efficient, Stalinist Party organization. Stalin was highly pleased.

By helping to create mythical enemies, saboteurs and spies and thus contributing to the paranoia by which Stalin and Khrushchev could justify their purges, Brezhnev had done his part too. He publicly defended the purges as completely legal. He helped destroy the Ukrainian language and culture and he organized the russification of the *oblast*. His foreign policy propaganda won national recognition. All this of course profited Khrushchev. He was promoted to full membership in the Party's ruling body, the Politburo, in March 1939.

V

The Battle for Dnepropetrovsk

Arise, arise, great land,
For mortal strife arise.
'gainst fascist forces stand,
'gainst the darkness we despise.
Let noble anger seize you
And surge up like a wave,
The war you wage is holy
All peoples shall it save. — Fighting
Song of the Red Army, 1941.

IN EARLY 1941 CLOUDS OF WAR once again settled over the Soviet Union. The uneasy alliance that had existed between Hitler and Stalin for some time had deteriorated markedly in the winter of 1940. Russia's territorial demands in November 1940 as the price for joining the Berlin, Rome, Tokyo Axis outraged Hitler. The Führer would not abandon Finland, place Bulgaria in the Soviet sphere of influence, or persuade Turkey to allow Soviet bases on the Straits of Bosporus. Instead, Hitler decided to conquer the vastness of Russia itself.

By the middle of 1941, with Germany secure in the Balkans and the eastern Mediterranean and free from any immediate threat of invasion from the west, Hitler was ready to embark on that venture. He chose June 22, 1941, to strike.

That Sunday at sunrise four million German soldiers crossed the western Soviet border along a front extending from Finland to the Black Sea. Outnumbering the Red Army units guarding the border areas, Panzer and mechanized units of the German Army drove deep into the Soviet defense lines, quickly overrunning the territory Khrushchev had annexed to the Ukraine and the Baltic states. So effective was the German blitz that by the time the terrible winter of 1941 had set in the German forces had seized much of the Ukraine and central Russia.

Russia was caught unprepared for the war she was now forced to fight. There had been ample warning. Rumors about German preparations for an attack circulated in Europe in early 1941. Churchill had personally warned Stalin, as did Stalin's own military attaché in Berlin. But, as Khrushchev later told the conclave of gathered

59

delegates at the Twentieth Party Congress in 1956, "Stalin ordered that no credence be given to information of this sort. In order not to provoke an initiation of military operations, the necessary steps were not taken to prepare the country properly for defense."[1]

Still, Stalin was not completely idle. In the months preceding the war he hesitantly ordered some limited economic mobilization, mainly in munitions. Though not on the scale required, some new production capacities were also added for tanks and aircraft. The mobilization, however, was limited mainly to a few large industrial enterprises in the south. Industries in the Dnepropetrovsk *oblast*, particularly those in the city of Dnepropetrovsk, which produced about one-fifth of the country's iron, steel and rolled metal, naturally figured in the limited mobilization.

In February 1941 Stalin ordered Zadionchenko to begin conversion of two of the *oblast's* factories to military production. One enterprise in the city of Dnepropetrovsk already producing gun barrels was to increase its output and begin limited production of automatic small arms. In addition, part of the Dzerzhinskiy factory in Brezhnev's hometown was to be converted to production of ammunition and artillery shells.[2]

Brezhnev was chosen to direct the economic mobilization; he became the *oblast's* secretary for defense industry, a position, to be established in each *oblast*, that was created at the Eighteenth Conference of the Communist Party held in February 1941.

Yevgeniy Malyarevskiy, a member of the Dnepropetrovsk Party Committee, explains why Brezhnev was picked for the job in Dnepropetrovsk. *Oblast* Party Secretary Zadionchenko nominated Brezhnev at a special Party plenum because the job required "a man who is energetic, has a technical education and rich experience in production, and most importantly, is respected by the workers, foremen, and engineers.... The present Secretary for Propaganda, comrade Brezhnev, is just the man for the job."[3]

Thus, donning his new title of Dnepropetrovsk Secretary for Defense Industry, Brezhnev, in the months before the outbreak of the war with Germany, put the *oblast's* "mobilization plan" in action. Everything was coordinated through Khrushchev. Soviet propaganda provides two illustrations of Leonid at work in these months. Both are furnished by Iona Andronov, a Soviet journalist who has written extensively about Brezhnev's war exploits.

One is based on a telegram sent to Aleksey Shakhurin, the People's Commissar of Aircraft Industry, on May 7, 1941. The message contains an appeal to Shakhurin for assistance and reprimands the Commissar's subordinates for holding up technical specifications and machine tools needed by a Dnepropetrovsk factory.

In a second writing Andronov praises Brezhnev's energies and dedication as the *oblast's* Secretary for Defense Industry:

> The Regional Committee Secretary for Defense Industry worked indefatigably from the early hours of that sinister June 22, 1941, to save the factories in the Dnepropetrovsk area and to harness them fully to serve the needs of the fighting forces.
>
> He had been busy in his office long after midnight to complete an urgent report to Moscow on the output of ammunition at local enterprises and the construction of a new military airfield and was planning to go at dawn to see how things were progressing at the airfield, though this did not seem too urgent considering that June 22 was a Sunday.[4]

Brezhnev was a stickler for detail. "We knew that the *obkom* report on construction and production would reach I. V. Stalin," Konstantin Grushevoy recalls, "therefore, we checked every word and figure."[5] Grushevoy, who was second secretary of the *oblast*, and other *obkom* secretaries had stayed back with Brezhnev to work on the important report.

Andronov's picture of Brezhnev is gilded. In reality the reorganization implemented to increase defense production was performed without fanfare, national recognition for Brezhnev, or haste for that matter, since Stalin, and presumably Khrushchev, still saw little immediate danger of attack by Germany.

Gun barrel production was increased and conversion of two factories to small arms and munitions production was achieved under Brezhnev's supervision. In May one factory was partially retooled to produce aircraft parts. Refurbishment of the local civilian airfield also began that month. Contingency plans were drawn up to facilitate the transition of industry to a war footing if necessary.

All in all defense output in the *oblast* increased about 60 percent.[6] This was hardly adequate, even for the *oblast's* own defense, as events were soon to prove. The relatively puny nature of these preparations is suggested by Grushevoy's recollection that "the restructuring of industry along military lines in the *oblast* required *immense efforts* on the part of the Party, soviet and economic organizations, and of all the workers"[7] when war finally did come.

In the early morning hours of June 22, General Dobroserdov, commander of the 7th Regiment in Dnepropetrovsk, telephoned Grushevoy with an urgent message.

I was ordered to report immediately to headquarters. There I
was shown a telegram stating that German troops had attacked
the Soviet Union and ordering complete mobilization.

I telephoned Leonid Ilyich Brezhnev and relayed the contents
of the telegram and the news that Kiev was being bombed. We
arranged an immediate meeting of all the secretaries and members of the *obkom* bureau.

Everyone was stunned. For the next several days havoc
reigned. Instructions from Moscow or the Central Committee of the
Ukrainian Communist Party, desperately awaited, did not come.

Meanwhile, Brezhnev and Georgiy Dementyev, who had
taken Brezhnev's place as *oblast* Propaganda Secretary, got in touch
with the local Party organizations. The next day, Kiev rang and said
that Stalin would make an announcement about the war and issue instructions at noon.

On the 23rd, Khrushchev and the Council of People's Commissars issued detailed instructions and set production quotas for
the mobilized industry.

Brezhnev's contingency plan had already been hastily implemented. Metal works, pipe rolling mills, rail and sheet metal mills,
steel construction works, clothing, leather, lumber yards and food
industries were all now harnessed to war production. *Vse na fronty,
vse na fronty* ("Everything for the front, Everything for the front")
became the slogan for all. Day and night the work pressed forward.
Brezhnev found himself driven by the most challenging task he had
yet faced. He was completely taken up with the fight. Interludes for rest
and diversion were few.

It was an uphill battle all the way, an impossible race against
time. Physically, mentally and technically, the population was unprepared for the colossal task. Brezhnev flung masses of engineers
and workers into converting the industry. "But it did not all come off
without a hitch,"[8] Grushevoy recalled.

Innumerable problems arose. German planes bombed the
railroads, cutting supply lines and leaving Brezhnev dependent solely
on local supplies. Manpower shortages also became acute. As
before, the drafting of workers into the Red Army left the factory
work force severely depleted. Yet in order to meet the required
production quotas factories were placed on 24-hour shifts. In many
factories, Brezhnev was forced to rely on children, too young to fight
in the Red Army, and women to run the complicated machinery.
Natalya, Vera, and Viktoriya all went to work. Women and children
harvested the fields as well.

As a result of the collective labor, hardships and sacrifice, the munitions production quotas for June were all filled. The Dzerzhinskiy, Komintern, Lenin and other factories in the *oblast* turned out anti-tank devices, metal spikes and jeep, tank and airplane parts. By mid July mortar and small arms production in Dnepropetrovsk was well under way.

The demands on all Dnepropetrovsk Party secretaries were great in those terrible days. There was much to do; not the least of which was the recruitment of Communists for political work in the Red Army. During the first six months of the war more than a million Party and two million Komsomol members from all parts of the country were mobilized for political work. Dnepropetrovsk alone sent 14,000 Party and 80,000 Komsomol members.

They were the most dedicated politically, a feared and hated lot. It was their task to supervise the "green" military officers, cajoling and threatening to obtain maximum performance since Stalin's liquidation of many of the more competent commanders in the Great Purge had demoralized the Red Army. They also had the even more difficult task of trying to instill the "spirit of patriotism," supreme devotion to the socialist homeland, and hatred of the enemy in the soldier through raising his "revolutionary consciousness and discipline;" eliminating "sluggishness and other negative phenomena" and strengthening the authority of the commander.[9] If difficulties arose in accomplishing these goals they called on Lavrentiy Beria's special NKVD units which had orders to shoot any soldier who illegally retreated. So powerful a force were the political workers that Hitler gave orders to shoot them on sight.

Recruitment of these Communists began on the 23rd. It was up to each secretary to recruit Communists for political work. Brezhnev found them in universities, technical schools, factory workshops and collective farms. Later, he became a "Military Commissar" responsible for supervision of hundreds of such political workers.

Two of those recruited were Vladimir Shcherbitskiy and Nikolay Mironov.[10] Born in Dnepropetrovsk, Shcherbitskiy had just graduated from the Dnepropetrovsk Chemical Engineering Institute. After the war he became a dedicated Brezhnev follower and chief of the Bureau of Preventive Maintenance at the coke chemical plant in Brezhnev's hometown. In 1948, Brezhnev brought his young protégé into the Dneprodzerzhinsk Party Committee as Second Secretary. Three years later he became head of the Committee. He has continued to rise under Brezhnev's sponsorship and is a Politburo member and the Party Secretary for the Ukraine today.

Mironov, who in his position as chief of the Party's Administrative Organs Department, in 1964 connived with Brezhnev to overthrow Khrushchev, was a university student in Dnepropetrovsk in 1941. He was seriously wounded during the war, but recovered and also became a Brezhnev protégé rising high in the KGB hierarchy.

Later on we will come back to Shcherbitskiy and Mironov and meet many more men like them who had early career ties, even "schoolboy" ties, to Brezhnev and hold high positions in the Soviet Union today because of his patronage.

But to return to the events of the summer of 1941: On June 25 Stalin sent General-Major Ivan Prostyakov and an impressive staff to Dnepropetrovsk to recruit 20,000 men to fill the ranks of new Soviet divisions. This involved extensive recruitment in the countryside and for Brezhnev a trip to Novomoskovsk. The Novomoksovsk Party organization was the hardest hit by the draft. Uneven recruitment practices had so depleted its Party organization that between factory visits Brezhnev had to personally recruit several hundred Communists from surrounding areas to keep the Novomoskovsk Party organization going.

Brezhnev hardly saw his family now. Viktoriya, herself busy in the factory, seldom knew when to expect him home. Brezhnev, like all Party secretaries, literally lived at the factories, plants, *sovkhozy* and *kolkhozy*, coordinating war production efforts and solving problems.

During all this nobody thought Dnepropetrovsk itself would ever become involved in the actual fighting. The front was still far away and everybody expected the hasty expulsion of the fascists. But the Germans pushed deeper eastward and closer to home. Concern grew for defending Dnepropetrovsk. Volunteer battalions were organized to penetrate the surrounding forest and search out parachutists, saboteurs and spies.

In early July, Stalin was forced to order the evacuation of industry and population from forward areas in the Ukraine, but for some areas it was already too late. Whole towns were destroyed or captured by the Germans. What industrial equipment could be quickly dismantled and evacuated to the east was. What could not be taken was demolished.

On July 5, the State Defense Council, the inner council established under Stalin's chairmanship to supervise the conduct of the war, ordered the evacuation of the Dnepropetrovsk Motor Plant. Brezhnev directed the evacuation, which was carried out smoothy, and the equipment, literally down to the last nut and bolt, was also packed off.

By July the war was going badly and Stalin needed top-notch military commissars to stop the massive retreats and desertions at the front lines. Many prominent Party leaders, members of the Party's Central Committee, and *oblast* Party secretaries were sent into action. The 1960 edition of the *History of the Communist Party of the Soviet Union*,[11] for example, lists Brezhnev alongside Mikhail Suslov, Nikolay Bulganin, Nikolay Ignatov, Yan Kalnberzin, Aleksey Kirichenko, Aleksey Kuznetsov, Vasiliy Mzhavanadze, and other "experienced Party leaders" who were pressed into important political work.*

Zadionchenko was the first to go from Dnepropetrovsk. He was ordered to report to the Military Council of the newly organized "Southern Front" to become its chief political officer, leaving Grushevoy to run the *oblast*. Brezhnev now became second in command.

"In accordance with the decision made by the Central Committee of the vκp(b) and his own wishes,"[12] Brezhnev was next to go. Realizing that his fortunes could best be advanced by active military service as opposed to Party work in the rear, Brezhnev "persistently requested his superiors to release him" for active duty. When permission was granted, "I left for the front with hardly a minute to rush home and say goodbye to the family." According to *obkom* archives he departed for active duty on July 14, 1941,[13] two days after Khrushchev began his gallant defense of Kiev.

In October, Brezhnev became first deputy chief of the Political Administration of the Southern Front. This group constituted one of two "front" armies defending the Ukraine and was under the

Ignatov had been involved in full-time Party work since 1934 and had been a secretary of a Party committee, and from 1937 to 1940 second, then first secretary of the Kuybyshev oblast. Kalnberzin, a Latvian Communist, had been a member of the Party since 1917 and was first secretary of the Latvian Party in 1941. Kuznetsov had been a Party member since 1925 and had been secretary of the Dneprodzerzhinsk Rayon Party committee and from 1937 to 1938 second secretary of the Leningrad oblast. Mzhavanadze had joined the Party in 1927 and had commanded political and infantry posts in the Red Army since 1927. Suslov was a Party member as early as 1921 and had been first secretary of Stavropol Territorial and City Party committees, a member of the Party's Central Revision Commission in 1939, and in 1941 a full member of the Party Central Committee. Since Brezhnev only became a full-time Party organizer in 1938, he was by far the junior of those Party member listed.

command of the South West "Direction," whose political officer was
Nikita Khrushchev. Between July and October Brezhnev worked
directly for Khrushchev.

The city of Dnepropetrovsk was already being bombed by the
time Brezhnev left. The front was drawing near, the lines now extending some 350 to 600 kilometers inside the borders of the Soviet
Union with fighting along a line drawn through Pyranu, Tartu,
Pskov, Vitebsk and south along the Dneper to Rechitsa, then on
through Novograd-Volyanskiy, Zhitomir, Berdichev and Dunay to
the Black Sea. Leningrad, Smolensk and Kiev were in grave danger.

Brezhnev kept Grushevoy informed by telephone of the day-
to-day situation at the front. Toward the end of July he ordered
Grushevoy, his former boss, to get construction of anti-tank
barricades underway: "The deputy head of the engineering section of
the Front, Engineer Lt. Colonel Shifrin will get the plan to you. He
will give you the details." On July 24, General-Major Andrey
Khrenov, head of the Engineering Section of the Southern Front, flew
in to direct the work.

In early August, Khrushchev sent Brezhnev to check on the
work and to establish Front Headquarters in Dnepropetrovsk. He
arrived home on August 7.

Grushevoy describes him at this time as "much the same. We
valued his erudition, industriousness and integrity, except that now
he was in military uniform with the rank of Regiment Commissar. He
was suntanned, slightly thinner, with dark circles under his eyes that
displayed concern and alarm, and he was somewhat more stern."[14]

Brezhnev now became the supreme military authority in
Dnepropetrovsk. "Brezhnev told us that he had been sent to
Dnepropetrovsk by the Military Council to assist the obkom with the
current situation," Grushevoy said. Brezhnev examined everything
and found the defense construction satisfactory; he told the local
people they had "done a good job." However, the reserve military
units were in critical need of arms and ammunition, which Brezhnev
had some success in procuring.

Judging by General Zamertsev's testimony (below), Brezhnev
did an incredible amount of work not only in converting the factories
in Dnepropetrovsk to war production, but also in assisting him:

> Our division was made ready in time thanks to the help given
> by the regional Party Committee, and in particular by Secretary
> Leonid Brezhnev. He and other leading functionaries of the
> Committee saw to it that our newly formed division and other
> units which were to defend the city were supplied with arms.[15]

A major evacuation of industries and population from the *oblast* was ordered on August 6. For the next two weeks the dismantling went on around the clock, often under heavy night bombing. In Brezhnev's own words,

> Most of the factories and enterprises in the region were evacuated, together with the industrial and office workers, engineers, technicians and their families. The state farms were evacuated with the tractors and other property of the machine-tractor stations. Many collective farms were evacuated, with all their property sent into the interior of the country.[16]

It was a colossal effort. A total of 99,000 boxcars of equipment and other freight and all rolling stock and locomotives were evacuated to the Urals.

Andronov gives Brezhnev exclusive credit for the evacuation: "The people of Dneprodzerzhinsk still remember how in the summer of 1941, just before the city was overrun by Nazis, Brezhnev came there and organized the evacuation to rear areas of industrial equipment so that not a single production unit would fall into enemy hands."[17]

Actually, the evacuation had already begun by the time Brezhnev arrived home. A. Sidorin, Party Secretary for Dneprodzerzhinsk, directed the evacuation of the Dzerzhinskiy factory. Its evacuation was in full swing and in fact Brezhnev's brother, who worked there as a workshop engineer, was helping in the move when Brezhnev visited the plant with Grushevoy on the 8th of August.[18]

On the trip back to Dnepropetrovsk that evening, Brezhnev's jeep became disabled with a flat tire. As he and Grushevoy changed the tire two German planes appeared in the sky. The pilots failed to see the jeep and continued on toward Dnepropetrovsk.

"That's strange; for some reason they didn't shoot. Usually the bastards chase any vehicle in sight, especially a jeep," Brezhnev commented.

"This is the first time we've seen planes like that over Dnepropetrovsk. They must be German planes," Grushevoy remembers saying.

"Yes, they're fighters—Messerschmitts. If fighters have come this far, that means that the front has moved closer."

It had. On August 13, Dnepropetrovsk came under heavy German artillery fire. The evacuation was completed that day, the last train load of people and the remaining equipment departing in the early morning hours of the 13th. Viktoriya, the children, Natalya, and Vera left on that train to spend the duration of the war

safe in the Kazakh Republic. Yakov Brezhnev went into the Red
Army. Later in the day, Brezhnev helped plant dynamite charges
which left the factory buildings and anything the Germans could put
to use, flattened. The unharvested corn in the fields was burned.

The next day Brezhnev left to help transfer the front
headquarters to the village of Pokrovskoye located in the center of
the *oblast*. That night the Southern Front tried to contain an assault
by the enemy directed at Aleksandr, Nikolayev, and Odessa.
Brezhnev returned to Dnepropetrovsk with Zadionchenko and
General Ivan Tyulenev, commander of the Southern Front, a week
later.

General Tyulenev took command of the Reserve Army (a
week later it became the 6th Army commanded by Rodion Malinovskiy) defending the city of Dnepropetrovsk. The Reserve Army
fought valiantly since Stalin had ordered Dnepropetrovsk held at all
cost. Enemy planes and artillery bombarded the city continuously.
On August 18 the Germans began their final assault.

Franz Halder, chief of the German General Staff, wrote in his
diary:

> August 18, 1941. Von Kleist's group is rapidly advancing on
> Nikopol near Dnepropetrovsk. Enemy aircraft are intensively
> attacking our advancing forward units.
>
> August 21. Heavy fighting west of Dnepropetrovsk where the
> enemy has sent into action newly formed, but not yet combat-
> ready divisions.
>
> August 23. Stubborn fighting on the west bank of the Dneper
> at Dnepropetrovsk. The situation there calls for sending Kleist's
> main forces into action.
>
> August 24. Our units are engaged in heavy fighting at
> Dnepropetrovsk. The enemy is sending in all available and
> newly-formed units and our tank forces operating in this area
> are making slow progress.[19]

On the 25th, Dnepropetrovsk became engulfed in flames as
von Kleist's panzer divisions rolled into the streets of a city defended
by men armed with little more than rifles, machine guns, improvised
petrol bombs, and mortars that pounded away at point blank range.

According to both Grushevoy and Zamertsev, Brezhnev fought
in the city's heroic defense right up to the last minute — until 6 a.m.
on the morning of August 25, when Stalin ordered the 6th Army to
retreat to the left bank of the Dneper. The valiant fight for
Dnepropetrovsk had been lost.

VI

Colonel Brezhnev

*During the Great Patriotic War (i.e., World War II),
Marshal Zhukov invented a foolproof
plan for routing the Germans at Stalingrad.
When he presented the plan for Stalin's
approval, Stalin looked at the map outlining
the proposed battle, curled his mustache,
and remarked: "I will check with Colonel
Brezhnev and if he approves then you
may proceed."*—Popular Soviet anecdote.

QUITE A LEGEND has been built up around Brezhnev's war
time military service giving rise to amusing anecdotes like the one
above—a favorite among Moscovites. Like Khrushchev, and Stalin
before him, as Party chief Brezhnev has made an immense effort to
promote and glorify his own war service for personal political gain,
which makes the true story of his war years a difficult one to tell.

Soviet authors who write about Brezhnev emphasize his
ability as a military commissar to motivate and lead men in war. The
position of "military commissar," introduced in 1937, had been
abolished in August 1940, giving unit commanders full responsibility
for all aspects of troop control. The position was reintroduced in
1941, because there "were not enough officers," the "reserve officers
lacked a military education," the "war complicated the commander's
job" and "he needed assistance in both the military and the political
sphere."[1] Inspiring the troops on to glory was a monumental task in
the fall of 1941, when Soviet troops deserted by the thousands or were
taken prisoner. Chaos reigned at the Southern Front. The Front had
successfully forestalled the German advance at the Dneper Bend
through September, but on October 5 von Kleist's 1st Panzer Group,
fresh from its victory in Kiev, moved southward and from its staging
area in Dnepropetrovsk maneuvered in behind the Southern Front in
the Bredyansk area; 106,000 Russians were taken prisoner or deserted.[2] Brezhnev personally described the seige as "extremely difficult"
and the retreat eastward as "pushing us to our limits."[3]

Brezhnev was unable to stop the desertions at Bredyansk.
Only he knows the punishment dealt out to those who disobeyed orders in the helter-skelter retreat to the east. Usually disloyals were

Top: *Colonel Brezhnev and officers of the Red Army Southern Front at Rostov, October 1942.* Bottom: *Good news from the Front is shared with Ivan Kravchuk, a personal aide.*

shot on the spot by Beria's Special Units. Brezhnev handled the troops and the green officers as well as he could. In 1941, bitter feuds often broke out between the commissar and the military commander because the commissar could and often did countermand the commander's orders. But soldiers and officers alike respected Brezhnev and admired his ability to "fire the fighting spirit of the man," [4] or so the official propaganda says.

In the winter of 1941, the military situation improved in favor of the Southern Front. By November the Front was able to gather its strength and launch a counteroffensive against the Germans at Rostov.

Mikhail Kotov and Vladimir Lyaskovskiy who were correspondents with the Southern Front published an article about Brezhnev's political work at Rostov in a 1972 edition of *Ogonek* magazine. They give him credit for "spiritually" perparing the men for the successful offensive. "The realization that the work of the Front's political organs would soon undergo its most serious test" was very much on Brezhnev's mind as he traveled to Dyakogo to meet General Kharitonov whose 9th Army was engaged in fighting. [5]

Brezhnev coaxed, cajoled and threatened in order to instill in the troops at Dyakogo supreme devotion to the Soviet homeland, and with postive results:

> In these terrible days [he wrote in the Front's newspaper], in the smoke of great battles for our homeland, the leadership by the party organization of the Army Komsomol has been strengthened. It has become more flexible and military. In glorifying themselves on the battlefields the communists of the Southern Front have inculcated the qualities of courage, bravery and fearlessness in their faithful assistants, the Komsomolites, and like the great Russian General Suvorov they say to the young fighters going to war for the happiness of their homeland "Take as your example a hero of olden times, observe him, follow him, equal him and surpass him.... Glory be with you." [6]

Brezhnev wrote articles for the Soviet press and he edited books about the war. Kotov and Lyaskovskiy wrote a small pamphlet on the Battle of Rostov which Brezhnev edited and published as a supplement to the Front newspaper *Vo Slavu Rodiny* in 1941. An edition of this book appeared with Brezhnev as editor in 1972. [7]

In January through April 1942, the Southern Front commanded by General Malinovskiy made gains east of Stalino. Together with the Southwest Front they were able to penetrate the enemy's defense at Lozovskiy and Barvenkogo where Brezhnev won the Order of the Red Banner for gallantry with an artillery regiment. The victors, however, were soon forced to beat a hasty retreat back to Rostov. By July, the Southern Front was again in a state of great confusion. Despite Malinovskiy's valiant attempt to hold his position, Rostov was lost. The Germans initiated an offensive along three bridgeheads on the Don and successfully crossed the river.

On July 28, the Southern Front, decimated by the losses at Rostov, was amalgamated with Marshal Semyon Budennyy's North Caucasus Front. Brezhnev now lost his job as Front deputy political officer. Since the position in the North Caucasus Front was occupied by a senior officer, Brezhnev was reassigned to a lower echelon command as deputy political officer of General Yakov Cherevichenko's Black Sea Group of Forces of the Transcaucasus Front. The official accounts say both this move and his transfer to the 18th Army the following April were designed to move Brezhnev closer to the troops. Actually, they gave him greater opportunity to distinguish himself in the field.

In 1971, the Soviet journal *New Times* published two wartime photographs of Brezhnev. One shows Brezhnev and other Soviet officers at the edge of a forest. The inscription on the back reads: "In memory of the days of the Patriotic War, Georgiyevskoye village, L. Brezhnev." According to the Tuapse city museum the photo was taken in August 1942 when Soviet forces were retreating into the mountain passes northeast of the city.

That month heavy fighting broke out in the Caucasus foothills after Hitler sent in Wehrmacht divisions against the Black Sea Coast defended by General Cherevichenko's Coast Group. Stalin ordered the 18th Army as a contingent of this group to prevent a German breakthrough to Tuapse.

It was for that reason that Brezhnev was commissioned in August to organize special detachments of 500 Party and Komsomol members to assume positions on the front line. Four such detachments were formed.[8] Discussing them in his book *Bitva za Kavkaz*, the late Marshal Andrey Grechko, who served with Brezhnev in the Caucasus, asserted that the troops of the Black Sea Coast had faced a perilous situation in the summer of 1942. They were heavily outnumbered. Moreover, Soviet defenses had been considerably weakened by the "psychology of retreat" and fatigue. The only way to overcome this and raise the "morale of the soldiers" was for Communists and Commissars to go into battle first.[9]

A second photo dated September 1942 shows Brezhnev smiling and shaking hands with Aleksandr Malov as he hands the soldier a Party Card. In the early days of the war few soldiers belonged to the Party, but Party membership was now conferred as an honor on those who had performed well in combat.[10]

Indeed, Brezhnev handed out hundreds of Party cards and conducted numerous political rallies to instill Bolshevik firmness in the troops. He issued instructions and directives to his political cadres working in divisions, companies and detachments at Tuapse. A meeting held at the village of Anastasiyevka in the autumn of 1942 is typical. Mikhail Lukyanov, then a political officer, recalls the meeting:

> It was held at night because of the daylight air-raids. Commissar Brezhnev presided. As usual he appealed to us to set examples of bravery and staunchness, saying that we were Party organizers and represented the core of the defense. We had need to demand strict military discipline, he said, but must not permit any bullying in dealing with the soldiers.[11]

Lukyanov portrays Brezhnev as an extremely benevolent commissar, but war commissars were anything but benevolent and Brezhnev was no exception. Many, in fact, carried things to the extreme. After Stalin ordered the military political departments to enforce "iron discipline" to prevent retreat following the loss of Rostov, overzealous disciplining of troops, including illegal executions, became a serious problem[12] — so serious that in October 1942 the Party retracted the commissar's right to discipline and punish troops.[13] Brezhnev, on the other hand was always concerned about the soldiers' safety, health and welfare. "When he visited units and subunits Leonid Ilyich was interested in the welfare of the soldiers and commanders and saw to it that they had everything they needed,"[14] one comrade recalls.

The Political Department of the 18th Army was not supposed to be in charge of supplies, but according to all accounts Brezhnev believed that it was up to his department to ensure that the necessary supplies got to the troops. The following dispatch to General Nikolay Vatutin, commander of the 1st Ukrainian Front, on the eve of the Kiev offensive in December 1942 is an example:

> The food situation is bad in the units.... Delivery of the ammunition and food issued to us is delayed for lack of motor transport.... The first train arrived only yesterday. We have been issued 195 tons of petrol, but that is enough to fill the tanks only once. We are badly in need of winter uniforms.... Please

render the necessary assistance on the questions that I have
enumerated. [Signed] L.I. Brezhnev, December 11, 1942.[15]

It seems that Brezhnev also concerned his department with
evacuating the wounded and giving medical assistance. A directive
issued three days before the Kiev offensive instructed subordinates to
"pay particular attention to the medical corps. The political departments of units are to detail special personnel to be responsible for
evacuating the wounded from the battlefield and rendering them
timely medical aid."[16]

Ivan Kravchuk, who worked with Brezhnev in the factory in
Dneprodzerzhinsk before the war and who became his personal aide
when Brezhnev visited the factory in August 1941, recollects another
side of Brezhnev. Kravchuk says that despite Brezhnev's relatively
"good nature," he was after all a "strict and demanding commissar."
He would not tolerate mistakes or half-hearted efforts and if he
caught someone neglecting his duties he would not hesitate to punish
the offender severely.[17] General Anton Gastilovich, who later commanded the 18th Army, adds that Brezhnev wielded a firm hand in
dealing with troublesome situations that would periodically develop.[18]
These views are more in line with the traditional role of the commissar as a strict disciplinarian.

The public image of Brezhnev is that of a commissar who was
dedicated to the cause of socialism and to Party work; a multital-
ented individual embued with burning enthusiasm, fighting spirit and
the desire and ability to motivate men; benevolent, yet demanding of
subordinates; disciplined, vigilant, self-sacrificing; a defender of the
country, respected by subordinate and superior alike. The same man
"spent most of his time in the trenches"; was on "the same line as the
Malaya Zemlyans with a machine gun in his hand"; "knew all the
Army from the commander down to the soldier" and "was their
favorite."[19]

Brezhnev "made the impossible possible," Sergey Borzenko,
another war correspondent, writes and through "his words and
deeds, his personal behavior, and firm composure, his profound
ideological conviction and great adherence to Party principles ... he
caused the troops to take hold of themselves, pull themselves
together" and "inspired the men on to new heroic heights."[20]

These are indeed lofty qualities and whether they really
belonged to Commissar Brezhnev is a matter of conjecture. They are
the same revered qualities sought in the ideal Soviet man, the model
Communist, Party and military leader. Propagandized, they demon-

Brezhnev greeting Khrushchev (left) on the North Caucasus Front, 1942.

strate to Soviet audiences that only Brezhnev is well suited to lead the Soviet Union today.

Planning combat operations was not within the purview of a commissar's duties, but Brezhnev allegedly helped plan many such operations. Marshal Konstantin Moskalenko, then commander of the 38th Army, and Grechko assert in their memoirs that Brezhnev was competent in both political and military matters. Other Soviet publications state directly that Brezhnev took an active part in planning and carrying out several large scale Soviet Army operations.[21]

Brezhnev never participated in any of the very big battles of World War II, though in October 1941 his reserve political cadres were quartered at Stalingrad and he visited the city once that month. The battle for which he is famous was fought at Malaya Zemlya, a small beachhead just south of the city of Novorossiysk on the Black Sea coast. Though insignificant compared to the battle for Stalingrad, the amphibious assault at Malaya Zemlya by the 18th Army in February 1943 and the liberation of Novorossiysk seven months later are today acclaimed as together forming one of the most important stragetic operations in the war. They have become symbols of courage, endurance and military prowess, and have inspired books, plays and songs. A national requiem is dedicated to those who died at Novorossiysk and in September 1973 Brezhnev awarded the city the title of "Hero City."

The real purpose of these accolades has been to focus on Brezhnev's association with the liberation of Novorossiysk which he claims, "laid the foundation for liberation of the Ukraine." The belated "Hero City" award, for example, was designed in large part to honor Brezhnev and provide an opening for the claim that he was responsible for the liberation of the city.

The claim first surfaced in the September 1973 issue of *Ogonek*. There Kravchuk boldly asserted that Brezhnev had suggested the diversionary landing operation at Malaya Zemlya leading to its liberation. Brezhnev believed that by using the element of surprise, a diversionary force could successfully storm the beachhead and divert the enemy's attention long enough for a landing force of three infantry brigades and a tank force to penetrate the main German defenses further south.[22] Though the latter failed, a beachhead at Malaya Zemlya was established.

Brezhnev personally claimed credit for the plan when he presented Novorossiysk with its award in 1974. He stated, "Together with Commander Leselidze [commanding officer of the 18th Army] I worked out a plan for landing a force." In this same light a play about Malaya Zemlya staged in Tashkent in 1975 portrayed Brezhnev as the principal character.[23] This was a major departure from his previous portrayal as simply an energetic and dynamic commissar.

One Soviet biography also credits Brezhnev with supervising the training of landing forces and recruitment of experienced soldiers and officers for the Novorossiysk operation in September 1943.[24] Vice Admiral Kholostyakov, who was in charge of the landing, recalls that Brezhnev did participate in planning both the amphibious landing and the plan for the overland offensive. Still another version observes that the plan was worked out by Konstantin Leselidze and his chief of staff, and General Pavlovskiy, with the aid of the commander of the Black Sea Fleet, Vice Admiral Lev Vladimirskiy, Rear Admiral Sergey Gorshkov (today commander-in-chief of the Soviet navy), and other top Soviet infantry, air force and artillery officers who discussed it in detail with leading political workers, among them Colonel Brezhnev.[25]

After Novorossiysk the 18th Army took the Taman Peninsula. "By this time," Brezhnev recalls, "we were moving so quickly through Taman that we got caught up in our own bombing."[26]

Kerch was next. Brezhnev reportedly helped plan this offensive too.[27] According to Misha Kraskin, Brezhnev's orderly, the commissar suggested evacuating the Kerch beachhead and postponing the Crimean campaign until the Soviet navy could convert several coastal tankers into tank landing craft. The plan required lining up a dozen tanks and self-propelled guns on the ship's upper deck and then sinking the ship close to the shore. The tanks and guns would then move over floating pontoon bridges stretched between ship and shore. The plan was never tried because General Leselidze opposed it. Brezhnev then bypassed channels and appealed to Marshal Timoshenko, Stalin's personal representative on the Black Sea battlefront. Timoshenko had Leselidze replaced.

In July 1944, Stalin reactivated the reserve 4th Ukrainian Front under the command of General-Colonel Ivan Petrov and transferred Brezhnev, the 18th Army, the 1st Guards Army and the 8th Air Army to the front. Their assignment was to capture the passes of the Carpathian range leading to the political centers of Uzhgorod and Mukachevo where Brezhnev was to establish a base of political operations for occupied Czechoslovakia.

Brezhnev is praised in Marshal Grechko's memoirs for his work in the political and *tactical* preparation of the 4th Ukrainian Front for the difficult mountain crossing. A book published in Uzhgorod in 1968 claims that Brezhnev was given chief responsibility for training the troops because he had extensive mountain experience.[28] Grechko, who commanded the 1st Guards Army and worked directly with Brezhnev, and other military authors remark on the excellent political preparation that Brezhnev gave everyone. But they view his organization of tactical training encompassing a broad program of detailed mountain instructions and *praktika* (exercises) as his greatest contribution to the operation.

Despite the heavy losses incurred in crossing the Carpathian mountains in August the offensive was a success, ensuring Soviet control of eastern Czechoslovakia.[29] Moving further westward, the Red Army occupied Slovakia in early January 1945. Seizure of the important Moravska-Ostrava industrial region began the following spring. The area was taken, but only with great difficulty and heavy Soviet losses. The 18th Army had some success in the initial attack, but an enemy counteroffensive in late March prevented any further advance.

Political commissar Brezhnev (front) with battle weary soldiers, ca. 1944.

General Yevgeniy Zhuravlev, commander of the 18th Army, pressed on with futile attacks which cut the 18th Army to pieces without making any substantial gains. Brezhnev again wired his friends in Moscow and a commission headed by Marshal Timoshenko investigated. As a result, Generals Zhuravlev, Petrov, and his chief of staff were all dismissed. Zhuravlev was replaced by General-Lieutenant Anton Gastilovich and Petrov by Marshal Andrey Yeremenko. Brezhnev reportedly then moved up to become political chief of the Front.

According to Moskalenko, however, General Petrov was removed in March for inadequate preparation of his armies for the offensive. Zhuravlev, on the other hand, had been relieved of his duties by January. Brezhnev became chief political officer of the 4th Ukrainian Front only at the end of the war. It is nevertheless possible that Brezhnev was instrumental in the dismissal of his superiors since the final attack on Moravska-Ostrava was successfully executed along the lines that Kraskin says Brezhnev counseled.

Accounts of Brezhnev in combat and leading troops into combat abound in Soviet literature. Brezhnev saw action in fighting at Rostov, Tuapse, Kerch, Novorossiysk, and in the Ukraine and Czechoslovakia. He fought in the defense of Dnepropetrovsk, came under heavy German fire and was almost killed enroute by jeep to 9th Army Headquarters. Grushevoy states that Brezhnev won the Order of the Red Banner at Barvenkogo and "revealed himself" in "military combat" in Kiev. General Gastilovich claims Brezhnev led troops into battle in Czechoslovakia. The seven months Brezhnev spent at Malaya Zemlya was the most difficult period of the war for him: "I was in the front ranks of the battle for Malaya Zemlya. I confess to you comrades, that in the four years I spent at the front, I never saw a more difficult or bloody battle."[30]

Kravchuk remembers that "wherever the Nazis pressed hardest in order to drive the landing force back that was where Brezhnev set off for."[31] Malaya Zemlya, for example, could only be reached by crossing the embattled Tsemenskaya bay from Gelendzhik and then the trip had to be made by slow launches or seiners through mine-filled waters dodging German torpedo boats and submarines while under heavy artillery fire and air attack. Brezhnev made the trip often.[32]

The first time a magnetic acoustic mine nearly killed Brezhnev but the charge went off astern of the boat and he was only shaken. He was less fortunate on the next trip when his boat hit a mine and he was thrown overboard. The incident was reported in the press in 1943, but no details were given.

More recently, Vanya Solovyov, then a 13-year-old cabin boy, recalled seeing Brezhnev pulled from the icy water of the bay. Solovyov's launch was sailing across the bay through extremely bad weather when he saw the outline of the boat he later learned was carrying Brezhnev. "The next minute a column of water shot from under its bow," he recalls. "It's hit a mine," someone yelled. Seven men from his seiner had been thrown overboard by the blast, but all were all right and were picked up by the launch in a matter of minutes.[33]

In another version of the incident told by Kraskin the survivors drifted for five hours under heavy enemy fire before being rescued by a Soviet torpedo boat. Brezhnev reportedly suffered from shock and was possibly wounded by the blast.[34]

That wasn't the last trip Brezhnev made to Malaya Zemlya. Sergey Borzenko writes in his book, *Life at the Front*, that Brezhnev made the trip 40 times for a total of 80 crossings of "death row" between March and September 1943.

A photo taken just before the Novorossiysk offensive in September shows Brezhnev wearing a second Order of the Red Banner. This medal is awarded for recognition of conspicuous bravery or self-sacrifice in time of war, special capacity for leadership, or the performance of some action contributing decisively to a Soviet military success. Brezhnev won the second medal at Malaya Zemlya.

It was in connection with the move to Kiev in November 1943 that K.S. Moskalenko first met Brezhnev:

> We handed over part of the zone for the next assault to the 18th Army which had just arrived from the northern Caucasus.... He [Brezhnev] and other officers of the 18th Army met us and we introduced them to the divisions of the 52nd Infantry who were being relieved. During the general discussion and afterwards in private talks, Leonid Ilyich expressed his satisfaction with the fact that the troops had joined the 1st Ukrainian Front.
>
> I liked his simplicity, courage, and decisiveness of thought and action. We understood that in Leonid Ilyich we had a person who was an excellent organizer and Party political and ideological worker; someone who also had a wide understanding of military matters.[35]

A few days later Brezhnev justified Moskalenko's faith in him. On the night of December 11, Brezhnev received word at Army headquarters in the village of Kolonshchina near Kiev, that two

German tank divisions had unexpectedly launched an attack on the Army's weakest sector at Stavishche. After dispatching his political officers to various sectors of the fighting, Brezhnev and Kravchuk set out for the fighting by jeep. About a kilometer and half from the front line they left their jeep and made their way to a trench where thirty soldiers were located. The soldiers had been forced to fall back from the first line trenches after most had been killed.

"The explosions came one after another and men were hit left and right.... The German machine guns opened up again and the infantry attack began. We had only one machine gun left and it too fell silent in a matter of seconds," Kravchuk recalls.[36]

"Brezhnev ran towards the machine gun and I after him, jumping over men lying motionless at the bottom of the trench. Brezhnev shouted to me over his shoulder: 'You've got your first-aid kit with you, see if you can help any of them.' I hurriedly bent over two or three of the men, but they were dead.... Just then the machine gun sprang to life again. When I reached it I found that Brezhnev had taken the place of the dead machine gunner.... I noticed that we were running low on ammunition and the Germans were still coming on: they were now only 30-40 meters away and were already beginning to throw hand grenades. Several times I tried to push Brezhnev down below the parapet when the enemy fire was particularly heavy, but each time he shoved me aside. As he reached his last machine gun belt, he ordered me to go down to the trench and tell the men to save their hand grenades until the very last and to prepare for hand to hand fighting.... I counted only about a dozen survivors in our trench..... It seemed that we had no more than ten or fifteen minutes to live—until Brezhnev's machine gun fell silent, until the hand grenades came, until the Nazi attackers poured into the trench.

"But as happens so many times in war, we made it. The Katyusha rocket launches opened fire and a sergeant soon appeared with an anti-tank gun, followed by a platoon and then a company of soliders."[37]

Four days later the 18th Army took Korostyshev and pressed on toward Zhitomir itself. Its capture took another four days of bloody battle which Brezhnev described in this dispatch to Front Headquarters:

> Our troops carrying out deep flanking maneuvers are pressing the enemy back, dealing him heavy losses in men and material. But the enemy is offering stubborn resistance, clinging to every line, to every inhabited point. The Nazis have brought

up more artillery and are using thermite shells. Exceptionally fierce resistence was encountered on the approaches to
Zhitomir. Having dug in along the railway line, the Nazis
levelled all their fire power at our assault lines, but could not
withstand our blows and, abandoning a great many mortars,
guns and other arms, fled in panic from the battlefield.[38]

On January 5, 1944, the 18th Army reached Berdichev where
fierce tank and infantry battles ensued. Once again Brezhnev reportedly demonstrated initiative and courage. Soviet troops became
pinned down by machine gun fire coming from the railway station
and barracks. Colonel Volkovich ordered a frontal attack on the em-
placements, but when he reached a position near the barracks he
discovered that Brezhnev, leading a handful of men, was already
there.

Two more times Brezhnev personally led troops into battle. In
one case, he assumed command of a rag-tag band of soldiers; another
time he took charge of troops under heavy enemy fire. "When difficult situations arose during the fighting, L.I. Brezhnev personally
led the soldiers."[39]

Brezhnev's propagandized war record has served him well.
The prestige of a Soviet leader is, after all, built around a record of
accomplishment and the most critical test of executive ability in the
recent history of the Soviet regime was the guidance of military
operations during World War II. The claims about helping plan
combat operations are clearly intended to establish his credentials as
a military strategist and tactician. Moreover, it is important for the
leader of the Party to be identified with an "outstanding event" in
history. "For the older generation of our Party," Brezhnev says, "the
Great October Socialist Revolution and the Civil War were such
events. For my generation it was the Great Patriotic War" (World
War II).[40]

VII

Conquering a Foreign Land

The Ukrainians were only able to achieve full freedom and the opportunity to express themselves freely for unification with the Soviet Ukraine and for the liquidation of land ownership thanks to the Red Army and the great Soviet people which extended to us the hand of brotherly help. — From the Transcarpathian *Oblast* Party Archives.

BREZHNEV HAD NO DESIRE to return to civilian work after the Red Army liberated the Ukraine. "I asked permission to stay at the front because the Red Army was triumphantly sweeping the country free of Fascist invaders."[1] His real motive was probably otherwise.

In October 1944, Brezhnev and his Political Department became secretly responsible for Communist political organization in occupied Czechoslovak Carpathian-Ruthenia, better known as Transcarpathia. This was the eastward thrusting tail of Czechoslovakia stretching across the Carpathians toward the Ukraine. It was a bridgehead assuring the U.S.S.R. of military domination of Central Europe, and Brezhnev was to impose Soviet Communist rule on this strategic region in a manner strikingly similar to Khrushchev's annexation of eastern Poland to the Ukraine five years earlier. He would engage in deceit, intrigue and ruthless force to acquire this territory for Stalin.

He took his orders from Lev Mekhlis, Stalin's personal emissary. General-Colonel Mekhlis had been assigned to the Military Council of the 4th Ukrainian Front to orchestrate domestic political operations inside Czechoslovakia.

In 1944, Transcarpathia was a social, political and economic hodgepodge. A mix of people, including a half-million Czechs, Hungarians, Romanians, Russians, Ukrainians and other nationalities lived there. Divisions in social status were vast. The region was politically volatile, its territory often contested. Czechoslovakia ruled the region from 1919 through 1938 when it became subject to Hungarian domination although there had always been a pronounced national Ukrainian sentiment among the people.

In 1919, Carpatho-Ukrainians sought union with the national Ukraine, forming during the Second World War a clandestine Ukrainian national movement called the Organization of Ukrainian Nationalists (OUN). The OUN was anti-German and anti-Soviet.

The capture and occupation of Mukachevo and Uzhgorod, the two principal political centers of Transcarpathia, was central to the Soviet design for the region. On October 18, 1944, troops of the 4th Ukrainian Front commanded by General Ivan Petrov crossed the Carpathian Ridge, captured the passes from Lupkovskiy to Tatarskiy, and moved 20-50 kilometers deep inside Czechoslovakia across a 275-kilometer front. General-Colonel Grechko's 1st Guards Army pressed on westward while the 18th Army engaged the Germans in fierce fighting and succeeded in liberating both cities. On the 28th, Brezhnev entered Uzhgorod; his future base of operations.[2]

That day was a time for joyful celebration. When the 18th Army rolled into town, weary and battle-worn, the people heartily welcomed their Red liberators. A blaze of color could be distinguished amidst the destruction and ruin as Red flags and welcoming banners were stretched between the buildings. The liberators were greeted with flowers, fruit, wine, kisses and tears of gratitude. Brezhnev wrote, "The population of the Czech villages are giving the army a hearty welcome. Upon entering villages our troops are met by the remaining inhabitants who come out into the street with offerings of all kinds of produce. They are greeting us with extraordinary hospitality."[3]

Thanks to the Red Army Transcarpathia was free, or so everyone thought. The Red Army should have now allowed a free government to be set up in accordance with a treaty signed with the exiled Czech government in London in 1943 which specified that once Transcarpathia was liberated it would become part of a new Czechoslovak Republic headed by exiled President Eduard Beneš.

Believing that the 18th Army would honor the treaty, Beneš ordered the organization of a regional democratic government. He had Brezhnev's word the Army would not interfere: "We have no intention of interfering in your affairs. That [organizing a government] is your own business, and it is up to your people to decide."[4]

But Brezhnev already had orders to establish a Communist government using the same Comintern guidelines issued to Marshal Josip Tito in May 1941 for seizure of power in Yugoslavia. According to the instructions: "(1) The Communist Party, until the seizure of power, should be careful to maintain in the countries where the revolution is being prepared good relations with patriotic and religious circles. No discrimination should be made against the churches.... National traditions should be respected. Wherever necessary ... representatives of the churches should be allowed to contribute in the preparation and carrying through of the revolution....

"(2) The press should be used....

"(3) Immediately after the seizure of power the Central Committee will set up a new government. This shall be representative of the broad masses of people and appear democratic....

"(4) Opponents of the new administration should be removed as soon as possible, but in a democratic fashion — that is to say, be brought to trial before a regular court or a people's court. The latter should be comprised of one known member of the Party and two secret members or sympathizers....

"(5) The country should not apply for inclusion into the Soviet Union until instructions to this effect have been received....

"(6) Traitors to the Party are to be liquidated without trial once their treachery has been submitted to the Party organization.... The death penalty is prescribed for treachery of any sort against the interest of the communist revolution.

"(7) The term 'class enemy' comprises the following groups: members of ideological movements of a nationalist or religious character, priests, members of the police force, officers, diplomats and civil servants when they refuse to side with the revolutionary forces; all members of dynasties, any individuals known to have opposed the preparation or the carrying out of the revolution.

"(8) After the Party has seized power, it shall dispose of funds, separate from state funds, taken from the following sources: property belonging to class enemies who have been liquidated, or whose possessions have been confiscated ... property confiscated from the churches, the ruling dynasty and war profiteers."[5]

Thus Brezhnev's solemn assurances had hardly been given when local Communists emerged from the underground and began organizing a Soviet Communist government. In the next few weeks Brezhnev prepared a remarkably efficient fifth column of indigenous Communists to take over Uzhgorod and Mukachevo. Many of them, indoctrinated in the Soviet Union or in the Red Army, were now returned to Transcarpathia to be assimilated into the population.

The official history of Transcarpathia tells us:

Colonel Brezhnev, chief of the 18th Army's Political Department, rendered *great political and ideological assistance* to the Party's organs and People's Committees of the liberated country. The Transcarpathians remember well his appearance at assemblies and meetings of workers, his sincere *advice on setting up the new way of life* with the organs of the people's government."[6]

A propaganda blitz launched the Communist campaign. The full weight of Brezhnev's know-how was thrown into an avalanche of propaganda designed to arouse local patriotic feeling and popularize the concept of unifying the territory with the Soviet Ukraine.

About 25 years earlier a Popular Congress of Carpatho-Ukrainians meeting in Khust had voted for the incorporation of this part of Czecholsovakia into the national Republic of the Ukraine. Therein lay the key to Brezhnev's propaganda strategy. He sought to exploit the region's past national aspirations and to persuade the population that their future still lay with the Ukraine and not Czechoslovakia.

But the 1919 Congress had voted to join the national Ukraine, not the Soviet Ukraine. Consequently, Brezhnev's campaign for annexation was met with fierce resistance by many Ukrainians. These Ukrainians, aware of Khrushchev's atrocities against Ukrainian national leaders in the prewar years and opposed to unification, countered with propaganda of their own. Posters carrying such anti-Soviet slogans as "Union with the Ukraine is a beautiful slogan, but with which Ukraine? The Soviet Ukraine is presently oppressed by Russian Bolshevism" appeared overnight, pasted on the war-gutted buildings. Many Carpatho-Ukrainians had decided to cast their lot with Czecholsovakia and with the prospect of free national and cultural development.

It was the Russophiles in the region, most of whom were previously anti-Communist and Hungarian collaborators, who took to the streets in support of unification with the Soviet Ukraine. They did so in part to redeem themselves. When it became apparent in 1944 that Germany was losing the war, these Russophiles took up the banner of Soviet patriotism. They fully cooperated with Red partisans fighting in the mountains and pretending to be Ukrainians they engaged from the beginning in the Soviet political campaign. Many became faithful Communists.

Meanwhile, a permanent domestic propaganda network was being developed. Collaborating with Ivan Turianitsia, a native of the region and a fellow commissar, Brezhnev's Political Department established three Communist newspapers. The *Molodj Zakarpata*, *Zakarpatska Pravda*, and *Zakarpatska Ukraina* deluged the country-side with convincing patriotic propaganda. Although they denounced with equal fervor past Hungarian and Czech regimes, their pro-Soviet orientation was not immediately apparent.

Brezhnev's propaganda was particularly effective among potential Czech army recruits who were promised service in their home region if they would join the Red Army. This factor, when coupled with Brezhnev's heavy censure of Czech recruitment material, hindered Czech efforts to recruit men to fight in Slovakia.[7]

In the early fall a popular uprising backed by a coalition of Social Democrats, Liberal groups and Slovak Communists broke out in Slovakia. It took several German divisions more than two months to crush the insurrection. Indirectly Brezhnev's propaganda hindered Czech military efforts to help their brethren in Slovakia. He stood by and watched this national tragedy. Almost 30,000 Slovaks of various political convictions were killed, preparing the ground for the later Soviet takeover.

Brezhnev ultimately halted the efforts by Beneš loyalists to form a government. He declared the legitimate City Council they established in Uzhgorod on October 28 illegal because "anti-people elements acting under the direction of Czech reactionary circles in London attempted to take control of the town. However, their subversive activities were discovered, and their self-appointed Committee [city council] dispersed."[8]

Meanwhile, Uzhgorod and Mukachevo "elected" Communist city councils:

> As early as October 28, a city council [in Uzhgorod] was formed consisting of representatives of the working class and the progressive intelligentsia. At its first meeting the chief of the 18th Army's Political Department, Colonel L.I. Brezhnev, told those present about the liberation mission of the Red Army. He stressed that the Army's mission was to annihilate the enemy and help enslaved people acquire freedom and independence.[9]

By mid November, with the Communists firmly in place, the drive for unification shifted into high gear. Posters and leaflets, portraying the joys of life in the Soviet Ukraine and the rewards awaiting the workers and peasants reunited with their brethren, saturated the towns and villages. A democratic constitutent assembly to vote for unification was the only ingredient missing. For this, Brezhnev applied the procedure that had worked so well for Khrushchev in Poland in 1939. Communists in Mukachevo and Uzhgorod set up an organization committee for a People's Congress to meet later in the month.[10]

A wave of meetings began in support of the Congress. Resolutions were adopted and petitions for union with the Ukraine were collected by Brezhnev's department and sent to Moscow and Kiev. Priests and members of the local clergy signed to show that even the Catholic Church supported unification.[11]

When the People's Congress met at the municipal cinema in Mukachevo on November 25, quite a display was made of it. The Congress' theme of "Long live the union of Transcarpathia to the Soviet Ukraine" was played up in all the local newspapers and in the Soviet media. All political constituencies were represented by over 633 delegates who came by army jeep, truck, any way Brezhnev could get them there. The Beneš government was not allowed a representative.

Everything had been prepared ahead of time, all was foreseen. The vote for unification was unanimous. Neither Brezhnev, Mekhlis nor any Soviet official attended the Congress. They directed the machine from behind the scenes. Vasyl Markus, a delegate to the Congress, recalls that while some non-Communist delegates were opposed to the union and other suggested a plebiscite on the matter all voted for unification after Soviet officials threatened them with imprisonment.[12]

On November 26, the People's Congress issued a manifesto "demanding" that the Soviet Ukraine make Transcarpathia an integral part of the Republic. This document became a kind of constitutional act, but not before Brezhnev collected some 250,000 signatures blessing it. According to Markus signatures were acquired by devious means, even blackmail. "People were promised clothing and food if they would sign. People signed more than once, and school children in elementary grades were even made to sign."[13]

For this fine work "distinquished for its variety and effectiveness" Brezhnev was promoted to general-major.[14] He had been so thorough in preparing for the Congress and Stalin so confident of its outcome that Brezhnev was allowed to pin on his general's star even before the Congress had finished its business.

The use of Brezhnev's immense political and organizational talent was not to end with the Congress, nor apparently was it to be limited to Transcarpathia. Formal unification with the Ukraine would come only after the Beneš government of Czechoslovakia could be pressured to cede the territory legally to the Soviet Union in an internationally recognized treaty. In the meantime the region was to be made Soviet in everything but name.

The first order of business was to establish a central government. The Congress proceeded to elect a governing body — the Popular Council — composed of 17 members, with Ivan Turianitsia as President. Communist bureaucrats were brought in from Kiev and strategically placed in all levels of the government. All decisions were made in Kiev. Located in what had been the proposed offices of the Czech regional administration in Uzhgorod, the Council governed by decrees published in the local newspaper.

The Soviet NKVD ran the security and police organs which were modeled after the Soviet apparatus. In conjunction with these a Soviet style civil and criminal court system with special tribunals was formed and a chief prosecutor's office established to try "class and state enemies," who seemed to be everywhere. Former officials of the Hungarian regime, deputies to the Parliament in Budapest, and former collaborators with the Hungarian regime who refused now to cooperate with the Communists became the first victims. Ukrainian nationals who remained committed to a free Transcarpathia were next. For the most part, these "fascist agents working in the pay of foreign espionage agencies"[15] were hanged.

The threat of resistance was very real. Angry Ukrainian nationalists opposed to Soviet rule in Transcarpathia organized the Insurrectional Ukrainian Army (IUA) and from the dense forests of the Carpathians conducted terrorist raids. Commissars, high ranking Army officers, and the NKVD were their favorite targets. Numerous officials were killed. In 1946, the IUA presented a real obstacle to sovietization and a personal danger to Brezhnev who ranked high on their hit list. They made several attempts on his life, but the armada of army and NKVD bodyguards surrounding the commissar warded off the potential assassins.

The police raids, the arrests, the trials, the executions, the mysterious disappearances of prominent leaders, the deportations, went on around the clock. The number of victims rivaled the 10,000 Polish officers and thousands of Poles deported from eastern Poland by Khrushchev in 1939.

Following the outbreak of World War II, the Czechoslovak Provisional Government in London signed an agreement with the Soviet Union for joint military action against Germany. At the end of 1943, Beneŝ, naively believing that Stalin would guarantee democratic Czechoslovakia a secure position in Europe and optimistic the country could act as a kind of bridge between the Soviet Union and the West, went to Moscow and signed a treaty of friendship, mutual assistance and postwar collaboration. In it Beneš and Klement Gottwald, the exiled head of the Czechoslovak Communist Party, worked out the principles for the future organization of the Czech state. These principles were implemented in Kosice, Czechoslovakia, in January 1945.

The 18th Army liberated that city on January 21, 1945. Brezhnev may have been instrumental in the formation of this government too. A partisan from Poprad recalls that "an impromptu meeting was held in the town square. A Soviet General [Brezhnev] stood in an open car and told us that now we must elect popular organs of power, set up National Committees." Anton Rasla, a member of the new government, recalls that he was sent by the Kosice government to the headquarters of the 4th Ukrainian Front to consult with Generals Petrov, Mekhlis and Brezhnev on various matters concerning the "Kosice Program."[16]

This famous "Program" became the blue print for sovietization of Czechoslovakia. Its two most significant features were the avowed Russian orientation and the instrumentality of the national committees like those established in Transcarpathia. A National Front composed of Communists, Socialists, and a smattering of Liberals and Catholics became the only legal political authority in Czechoslovakia. Communists were put in key government positions and in the 1946 elections they gained almost half the seats in the Prague Parliament. A Communist coup d'état two years later brought Czechoslovakia in line with the other Eastern European states as a satellite of the Soviet Union.

On May 6, 1945, United States Army General George Patton's advance forces moved to a point eight miles outside Prague. They were ordered to withdraw because of Soviet protests. The liberation of Prague, the capital of Czechoslovakia, was to be the privilege of the armies of the 4th Ukrainian Front. Brezhnev would help.

The war officially ended for the Soviet Union on May 9, 1945. But for Brezhnev it dragged on for another three days. Hitler was already dead but German divisions under the command of General Field Marshal Ferdinand Shörner, commander of the German Army Group Center, refused to lay down their arms and attempted to fight their way out of Czechoslovakia. "The enemy ... poured on ammunition on our forward positions and began a hasty retreat,"

*Generals P. I. Zubov (left), unidentified, Brezhnev, and V. I. Kofanov,
members of the special Combined Regiment of the 4th Ukrainian Front in
Stalin's victory parade, Red Square, June 1945.*

Brezhnev reported on the night of May 10. "All day on May 9 and 10 our troops pursued the withdrawing enemy and engaged him on one defense line after another. Now our troops are incessantly pursuing the Germans."[17]

On June 24 Brezhnev had the great honor of participating in Stalin's Red Square Parade celebrating the war victory. "In recognition of his great service to his country,"[18] Brezhnev was designated military commissar of the combined regiment which represented the 4th Ukrainian Front in the parade. It was a gala event. Donning full military regalia, Brezhnev marched proudly alongside Grechko, Moskalenko, Gastilovich and other officers down the sacred Red Square for Stalin's review. Banners of the vanquished enemy were thrown down at the foot of the Lenin Mausoleum and the whole event was captured on film which is shown widely throughout the Soviet Union each May.

On the night of the 24th, Stalin hosted a lavish party for the victors. But Brezhnev did not attend. He had been quietly whisked away to Transcarpathia to finish his work. By pressuring the new Czech government and promising Soviet support for Czech territorial claims elsewhere, Stalin persuaded Dr. Beneŝ on June 29, 1945, to sign the long awaited treaty ceding Transcarpathia to the Soviet Ukraine. Brezhnev would prepare Transcarpathia for the transition.

There was still a good deal to do to make the region politically acceptable. Many opponents of the regime still had to be eliminated. Property and industry had to be fully nationalized and since the area was mostly agricultural, the liquidation of kulak elements had to be carried out and collectivization begun.

Industry and commerce were nationalized within three weeks of Brezhnev's return. Turianitsia had earlier undertaken some nominal nationalization, but it was limited mainly to the banking industry and foreign assets. Now the entire economy was laid to seige.

For twenty years land had been a burning political issue in Transcarpathia. No preceding government had ever been able to resolve the land problem, particulary the plight of the landless peasant. But the Communists seized the precious properties of rich Hungarian and German landlords and the Catholic Church and divided them up among the poor peasants. The former landowners reacted violently. "The class enemy mounted opposition to the people's government. The richer peasants sabotaged the spring sowing campaign in 1945 and tried to bring disorder into the reconstruction of the agricultural economy."[19]

"Accidental" fires destroyed acres of grain creating a maddening dilemma for Brezhnev. But he gave the saboteurs no quarter. "Communists were obliged to expend considerable effort on breaking the counteraction of village hoarders and uniting the poor peasants in overcoming the difficulties."[20] Backed by Red Army units, he annihilated the kulaks in the classic manner.

Brezhnev knew better than to talk about collectivized agriculture in 1945, but it was only a matter of time before it came. "People's educators," who urged the peasants to form collectives, soon flooded the countryside. A year or so later all land given to the peasant was taken back for collective farms and peasants were made to join the farms. Those who resisted were uprooted from their cherished earth and sent by trainload into slave labor. In early 1946, Transcarpathia, with its population beaten and broken, became the Transcarpathian *Oblast*. Turianitsia became the Party Secretary.

To this day the illegal Soviet annexation of Transcarpathia remains a thorn in the side of most Czechs. The wound occasionally festers. Brezhnev could not have been too pleased when during the heat of the Czech crisis in 1968, the Czech press questioned the legality of the annexation and recalled the blood of innocent victims shed to achieve it.

VIII
Rebuilding the Dneper Valley

*When I have occasion to visit the places dearest to me
I do not merely admire the beauty of the Dneper
banks. I recall this road built before my eyes, that
Palace of Culture built during my tenure, and these
factories, power plants, mines, city streets and
kolkhozy — all of which contain a part of my labor,
my thoughts, my worries and my sleepless nights. —
L. I. Brezhnev, 1978.*

WITH TRANSCARPATHIA in Stalin's pocket, Brezhnev's work
in Czechoslovakia was over. He was tempted to stay in the Army but
the military's fall from grace and Stalin's deflation of its role both in
war and in postwar society persuaded him instead to board the train
bound for the Dneper valley and the family he had left behind in 1941.

Natalya, Viktoriya and the children were again at home.
Dnepropetrovsk, however, had changed drastically. The white two-
story apartment building was gone and they found themselves cram-
med into a one-room apartment in a partially burned building on
the outskirts of town. Natalya put treasured family pictures on the
bare walls, but the place was still empty without Leonid. Galina
would be 17 soon and was blossoming into an attractive young
woman. From Viktoriya's letters Brezhnev learned that Yuriy, proud
of his "papa the general," had joined the Young Pioneers. So much
had happened during those painful war years with the family apart
that Brezhnev could never recapture.

In Kiev, Khrushchev, who dutifully returned to reclaim his
political parish when the Germans retreated, was now busy reassem-
bling his "boys." Without them he could not reestablish his authority
in the Ukraine ravaged by the war and plagued by lawlessness. They
were his tools and he went to great lengths to locate them and
arrange their return. Brezhnev was easy to trace since he had
worked with Khrushchev in the final stages of Transcarpathia's annexation. Khrushchev pulled strings in Moscow, arranged Brezhnev's
discharge from the military, and sent him to the Zaporozhye *oblast*
as its Party Secretary. The *oblast* was close to home. In fact, it was
right next door.

The journey home was long and tedious. It took two weeks by

train. The trip gave Brezhnev a panoramic view of vast stretches of country devoid of life. He saw destitute people living in primitive dugouts; pits in the ground covered over with branches and earth. He saw charred fields where yellow corn had once grown and mounds of twisted steel beams and rubble where major industrial centers and cities had once stood. The Ukraine lay prostrate. It was utterly depressing. Perhaps only the anticipation of being reunited with his family kept his spirits up.

On August 30 when the Kiev Express pulled into Dnepropetrovsk a weary Brezhnev clad in a wrinkled general's uniform stepped off the train to a hero's welcome. He momentarily forgot about the war and the destruction around him as he embraced Viktoriya and their children. But the walk home sadly brought back reality. The damage to Dnepropetrovsk was worse than he had imagined.

What would Zaporozhye be like, where the fighting had been worse? He could not help but wonder what scene of devastation awaited him in the seat of the Zaporozhye *oblast*, just an hour's drive from Dnepropetrovsk:

> I recall[ed] the tree-shaded squares, fountains, attractive apartment buildings in which the residents took special pride, the vacation resorts on Khortitsa Island and the wide, green Lenin Avenue that extended through the entire city right down to the Dneper River. In the evenings when I normally returned home [from a visit] there was always a ruddy glow in the blue sky above the furnaces of Zaporozhstal [Iron and Steel Works] and hundreds of fires reflected in the water, framing the famous [Dneproges] dam in a kind of arch.[1]

Brezhnev set out for Zaporozhye early the next morning to assess the damage first hand.

> But I managed to reach only the by-product coke plant, or more precisely, the ruins that remained of its large facilities. There was no road beyond it, so I had to walk. I wandered around until late in the day. I saw raised pavement, broken bricks, piles of rubbish and tangled beams everywhere.[2]

More than 400 factories in the *oblast*, 21 of national significance, lay in ruins. The huge Zaporozhstal Iron and Steel Works, once the Soviet Union's sole producer of thin sheet steel for making automobiles, pipe and tin, lay before Brezhnev like a toppled giant. Piles of debris lay where its blast furnaces, aluminum and ferrous alloy plants, the buildings of Kommunar, the engine works and many other enterprises had stood before the war. Dneproges, the magificant dam once accorded the lofty title of "patriarch of Soviet energy," was a total loss.

"Disfigured by fire and metal, laying in ruins was my native land."[3] Brezhnev would rebuild Zaporozhye. It was a challenge even greater than defeating Hitler. From that moment on Brezhnev saw little of his family. The work required every waking moment, every bit of energy he could muster. As the demands of work and politics became all-consuming, he was forced to put the family forever second in his life.

German economists estimated that restoration of the region to prewar production alone would take 25 years. But Stalin decreed it was to be done in five. Announcing the first postwar Five Year Plan in February 1946, he told the Soviet people they could not rest until Zaporozhye, indeed the whole of Soviet industry, was not only restored but significantly expanded. Despite the heavy toll the war had taken on Russia's human resources Stalin set the nation to the task of surpassing the prewar level of production and overtaking the capitalist countries, thereby securing for Communism an economic victory over capitalism.

> We must achieve [Stalin said] a situation whereby our industry is able to produce each year up to 50 million tons of pig iron, up to 60 million tons of steel, up to 500 million tons of coal, and up to 60 millions tons of oil. Only under such conditions can we regard our country guaranteed against any accidents [*i.e.*, safe from attack]. This, I think will require perhaps three more Five Year Plans, if not more.[4]

This kind of growth was imperative because the world as Stalin saw it had become divided into two antagonist camps, with Communists on one side and aggressive imperialists (the West) on the other. There was to be a war of a different kind, one calling for boldness, dedication and sacrificial toil, and Brezhnev was ready to participate: "I realized full well that this was an important objective for the state, not only from the standpoint of the economy, but politically."[5]

Brezhnev worked round-the-clock supervising the various sectors of construction. He carried an army cot with him and slept at Zaporozhstal one night and at the dam site the next. One minute he would be knee deep in mud personally supervising the mixing and pouring of cement, the next he would be out giving pep talks to workers. He worked as though the very future of the Soviet Union depended upon his *oblast*; of course Brezhnev's personal political future really did.

The dam received highest priority. The Germans had blown up all the turbines, generators and valves, and only 14 of 47 spillways remained intact. Brezhnev's predecessor, Fyodor

Matyushin, had begun rebuilding the dam but the pace of work dissatisfied Stalin. Moscow accused Matyushin of failing sufficiently to rally the *oblast* Party organization. But Brezhnev would not err in this regard. He put Party work to the fore, and moving his *oblast* Party Committee headquarters to the dam site and putting the Party organization there directly under his control were just the initial indications of how far he was prepared to go in successfully completing his assignment.

Everything was analyzed politically. Brezhnev reprimanded those who neglected "Party political and indoctrination work" at the dam:

> As soon as you begin to talk about political work, your discussion leaves something to be desired. What is needed is political analysis, but you have not done this. Without an understanding of the [world] political situation, you cannot draw the correct conclusions. And without correct conclusions, we cannot advance even a single step.[6]

He scolded those who considered the "acquisition of cement" and other materials in short supply more important than political work:

> There is no doubt that cement is needed. Without cement, we cannot mix concrete. But it is much more important for the individual who loads the cement into the pier of the dam to understand why this cement must be loaded and packed in freezing 20-degree weather at a height of 40 meters.... This is why Party organizations must place the task of indoctrination at the top of their list. Then the cement and everything else will arrive much more quickly and things will go much better for us.[7]

He implored his peacetime Party subordinates to hussle like wartime commissars. "If a man cannot make a passionate speech to an audience and explain what the Party Central Committee wants and what our Party is fighting for, if he cannot set an audience on fire, then what kind of administrator, what kind of Bolshevik, is he?[8]

Brezhnev drove his "construction soldiers" to compensate for the desperate shortage of manpower. Millions of able-bodied men died in the war and as many as 10 million civilians had been executed by the Germans, died in labor camps or starved to death. If this wasn't enough Stalin's continued efforts to purge Ukrainian nationals, political untrustworthies and Nazi collaborators further aggravated the shortage. Nevertheless, Brezhnev managed to round up some 50,000 people to perform the backbreaking work of rebuilding the dam. Although slave labor from the prison camps helped, it still meant long arduous toil for the labor forces. Workers used wheel barrows, picks and shovels and mixed and poured cement by hand in freezing winter temperatures, always under the watchful eye of an army of NKVD troops.

The dam was slowly raised from the ashes. Within two months the republic press jubilantly reported that six holes in the dam's wall had been plugged, the spiral tube in the first generator plant had been assembled and the construction plan for the third quarter of the year had been fulfilled early.[9] Three months later, Brezhnev proudly announced completion of the first stage of construction. The main turbine was ready for testing.

A gala ceremony was organized for the occasion. When the day arrived Brezhnev inspected everything thoroughly, checked everything out, measured everything, then, after ordering the band to strike up the music, pulled the switch starting the turbine. The test was a success and so was Brezhnev in receiving wide publicity for the achievement. Stalin graciously thanked those whose "hands had assembled the turbine" and those through whose "strength and determination the dam had been brought back to life," among them "comrade Brezhnev."[10]

Reconstruction of the Zaporozhstal Iron and Steel Works was not so immediately successful. This gigantic plant had taken ten years to construct, but Brezhnev was expected to rebuild it in less than five, with resumption of limited production in one year.

Disregarding recommendations by the United Nations to completely scrap the plant, reconstruction commenced in early 1946 under the direction of the Zaporozhstroy [building] Trust headed by Veniamin Dymshits. But it was slow going; construction was plagued by continued shortages of material and labor, as well as rampant crime.

Criminal activity presented a grave problem. Not a week passed without armed gang attacks on one part of the city or another. Zaporozhye was without street lights and nighttime robberies, assaults and murders seriously hampered organizing work for the night staff. Efforts to track down the gangs were hampered by the NKVD's devotion to detecting and exposing Nazi collaborators. Brezhnev was left to deal with both problems; the traitors and the criminals. "I had to divert Communists and Komsomol members to this front."[11]

But too much time was spent chasing criminals. On February 5, 1947, *Pravda* assailed Brezhnev for neglecting the work at Zaporozhstal. "Neither the Party Committee at the site or the Zaporozhye *oblast* Party Committee seem very interested in the reconstruction of Zaporozhstal whose output the country so desperately needs," *Pravda* concluded.

The news struck like a bolt of lightning. Suddenly all eyes were on Brezhnev. Everything he had achieved, everything he considered a success had been turned around and turned into a near defeat. The criticism was hardly fair.

He knew something was wrong in Kiev. Khrushchev had apparently become too big for his boots. His rivals, namely Georgiy Malenkov who was chairman of the nation's committee for economic rehabilitation of liberated regions, and Andrey Andreyev, agricultural overlord of the Soviet Union, had Stalin's permission to take Khrushchev down a notch or two by pointing an accusing finger at his Party organizations.

"That night Stalin called me. The conversation was serious," Brezhnev remembers. "Stalin moved the completion date for the entire complex up and told me the production of steel was to begin in the coming autumn."[12] Brezhnev was caught up in a power play and was under fire from two sides. His patron was in trouble, his enemies were pointing accusatory fingers at his work, and now Stalin had made almost impossible demands on him.

Brezhnev went swiftly into action. According to Dymshits, "Zaporozhstal became his whole life. He moved his office there and also his bed."[13] He beefed up the labor force at the steel works—to 47,000 at one point—by diverting workers from the dam. He also stepped up Stakhanovite competition. One of his brigade pipeliners, Ivan Rumyantsev, became famous for introducing the time-saving idea of large block assembly of pipeline.

If Brezhnev had been tough on Communists and workers at the dam before, he was doubly tough on them at Zaporozhstal now. With Bolshevik persistence, he pulled up the slack in all directions. The key was organization.

There were 40 building administrations and subcontractor organizations working under the jurisdiction of various national ministries at the site. "I immediately had to deal with the absence of contracts between these offices, their endless disputes and mutal accusations. They started jobs everywhere, but never finished them. Discipline was poor, there was no interaction or collaboration. In other words, there was nothing to transform a crowd into an organized team."[14]

Flying in the face of such opposition, he set up a single work schedule for everything from sorting pipe to pounding nails. This was to be his method, to "check, make demands, provide incentives

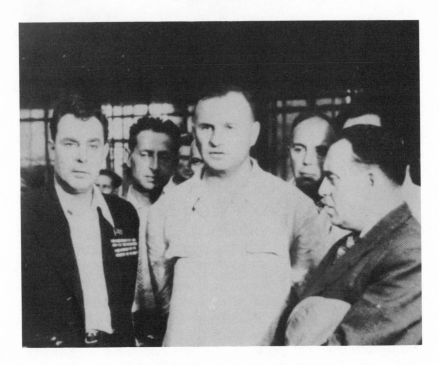

Brezhnev (left) with workers of the Zaporozhye Trust, 1947.

and, if necessary, punish the workers."[15] Brezhnev inspected everything hourly to make sure the schedule was followed. He resolved disputes on the spot. Work went on around the clock in three shifts.

By March, the plant showed dramatic improvement. On the 19th of the month *Pravda Ukrainy* proclaimed Zaporozhstal the nation's "Pioneer Builder." It was a good thing too because the political tide had turned.

In early March it looked like the end for Khrushchev. Stalin forced him to relinquish his post as Party Secretary of the Ukraine to Lazar Kaganovich, Khrushchev's old boss in Moscow during the building of the Moscow subway. Two weeks later, Khrushchev "asked" to be relieved as Party Secretary of the Kiev Regional Party Committee. Finally, on March 24, he gave up his position as head of the Kiev City Party Committee. Then he dropped out of sight.

It looked as though Brezhnev's end was also near. But Kaganovich kept him on; the achievements at Dneproges and Zaporozhstal had bought him time. However, on April 8 the Party

Central Committee in Moscow issued a decree harshly criticizing him and the Zaporozhstal Party Committee. Malenkov was pushing for his removal.

Brezhnev had to pull something off, and soon. He called a special meeting of Zaporozhstroy. It was a heated meeting and Brezhnev was unmerciful. He made it clear that everyone's head was on the line. He demanded "the pace be doubled," "more workers be found," "lags be tightened up," and "new plans and schedules be drawn up," he schemed and plotted and came up with a plan.

On April 20, 1947, Brezhnev published a grandiose pledge in *Pravda Ukrainy* outlining a detailed work schedule to have a blast furnace and the combined electrical power and heat generating plant operating by June, a slabbing mill by July, a sheet metal shop by August, and a cold rolled sheet metal shop by September. Stalin would get his precious metal.

To enforce the rigid schedule Brezhnev organized a "fist" of shock Communists to squeeze every last drop of energy out of the workers. He explained: "We have thus far operated with an open hand [a slap in the face] so to speak, rather than with a fist. But a hand cannot deliver a sharp blow. We all learned that year to do exactly that, to gather our strength in our fist, and then to use it as our tool."[16] Brezhnev drove everyone with a disregard for the limits of human flesh and blood. After all, he concluded,

> Many of us are not even aware of our own capabilities. People differ. Some throw up their arms before you even finish giving them an assignment and proclaim: "What are you saying, what are you talking about! I can't do that!" But you convince them to try. You see that same person later and he has done more than he was supposed to. "I didn't know I could do that," he explains. Well, after all, when people go into battle do they know they will become heroes?[17]

The days sped by, the work grew intense, corners were cut, and Brezhnev produced. For five consecutive months Zaporozhstroy won the nation's all-union building competition. Furnace No. 3 produced its first cast iron on June 30.

> I recall that day in every detail. The furnace roared evenly, one had to shout to be heard, but metallurgists were accustomed to it. The noise was music to my ears because deep in my heart I still considered myself a metallurgist. The oxygen torch burned through the taphole and a thin trickle of white-hot metal appeared. We followed each ripple in the stream and watched the bucket being filled for the first time. I remember ... we kissed all the blast furnace operators.[18]

A month later the slabbing mill went into production. Brezhnev sent the first consignment of rolled steel to automobile factories in Moscow and Gorky on October 1, 1947. On October 3 the Soviet Trade Union newspaper *Trud* reported that Zaporozhstroy had "honorably kept its word to comrade Stalin." Brezhnev had not only completed the work ahead of schedule, but he had exceeded the plan by 150 percent. "Well done," *Trud* concluded.

Stalin and Kaganovich sent congratulatory letters and telegrams to Brezhnev for his "great victory." Stalin personally wrote: "The Soviet people place a high value on the selfless labor of these men who successfully rebuilt Zaporozhstal and whose work exemplifies the application of the advanced methods of Socialist labor."[19]

A total of 20,000 workers received medals. The Zaporozhstroy Trust, the plant, many workers, engineers, production managers and Party members won the highest honor; the Order of Lenin. Stalin personally awarded Brezhnev's Order of Lenin in December 1947.

Brezhnev was not so successful in agriculture. In fact, his management of agriculture in Zaporozhye was appalling. Here was an area Khrushchev's opponents could readily exploit with legitimate criticism.

Matyushin had reestablished many *kolkhozy* and generally got agriculture back on its feet. But threshing was slow in the *oblast* in 1946 and the annual grain deliveries to the state were late. On March 4 *Pravda Ukrainy* warned Brezhnev not to make the same mistakes for 1947. The article offered a critical analysis of the Rozovskiy *rayon* which had failed to fulfill its plan for fallow land and was last to deliver its grain in 1946. Harvest failures in the *oblast* were attributed to neglecting fully to utilize resources at hand and organize political and ideological work. It was strange, *Pravda Ukrainy* concluded, that "the *oblast* leadership had failed to notice the reprehensible functioning of the Rozovskiy *rayon* and probe deeply into its state of affairs at the time."

Brezhnev did get the harvest for the new year off to a good start; The collective farms made the most of the high moisture in the soil to begin early ploughing and the sowing of crops was finished ahead of schedule. However problems occurred elsewhere. Harvestor machinery production at the Pervomaiskiy plant fell behind, much of the harvesting had to be done by hand.

On June 7 the editor of *Pravda Ukriany* implored Brezhnev to take decisive action to correct this lag in production. Little was, or could be, done, however. The *oblast* began harvesting first, but with limited use of mechanized harvesting only half the crop was in by the beginning of July.

Brezhnev's adversaries attacked again on July 6 in a terse press article which accused Brezhnev of failing to deal satisfactorily with the matter either on a political or a practical basis.[20]

Several times during July and August Brezhnev called meetings of the *oblast* Party Committee, but each time only desultory measures were adopted. Rural Party activities were stepped up and in some cases disciplinary action was taken, but nothing seemed to speed up the harvest. *Pravda Ukrainy* again accused Brezhnev of flatly neglecting political work. "It is not a matter of passing one more resolution," the newspaper proclaimed, "what is needed is concrete political work."[21]

Brezhnev was told to conduct an "educational campaign" among *kolkhoz* workers and young Communists. *Pravda Ukrainy* asserted that the distribution of agricultural newspapers in the field would help. Suggestions were made that rural officials should work through the primary Party organizations and conduct political work in the countryside personally; that Communists be more evenly distributed among the Party committees and appointed to vital positions in the harvest campaign—in some cases Communists had not even been attached to the brigades in control of work in the fields—and that the *rayon* organizations should teach the art of Party work to new and inexperienced Party secretaries.

In a special editorial entitled "Party organization of the country-side—the leading forces in the campaign for economic welfare of the *kolkhoz*," published in the *oblast* agricultural newspaper *Chervonye Zaporizhzhya* on September 20, Brezhnev indicated that he was trying and that he had put a number of Kiev's recommendations into effect. But grain deliveries during September and October improved almost imperceptively. In subsequent issues *Chervonye Zaporizhzhya* praised progress made in other areas of agricultural activity rather than continue the attack. This brought criticism in a *Pravda Ukrainy* article on October 6 which assused Brezhnev of "political shortsightedness."

Such negligence is seldom tolerated by the Party. But Brezhnev's success in rebuilding industry in Zaporozhye was his saving grace. Had it not been for that he would have been swiftly removed from office and banished forever. But Stalin had already decided that Brezhnev should go to Dnepropetrovsk and reorganize the industry there. For the moment judgment on Brezhnev's agricultural failure was postponed.

On November 22, 1947, Pavel Naydenov, a former Brezhnev schoolmate and colleague, was sacked as Party head in Dneproptrovsk for "neglecting to follow Zaporozhye's example of management." Brezhnev was named to replace him because "it would be a crime not to put this [Brezhnev's] experience to work in Dnepropetrovsk." Moreover, "Bolshevik initiative and firmness are sorely required in the *oblast*."[22] The former Propaganda Secretary had become Party Secretary of his home *oblast*.

The assignment was challenging. Many shops were still inoperative and the mines flooded. Industry was making a comeback, but production had to be boosted and the city of Dnepropetrovsk needed substantial renovation. Karl Marx Avenue was still in ruins and workers were without housing. There were no telephones, no street cars, no automobiles. In the countryside, agricultural production was below prewar levels, which worried Brezhnev. On top of all this Malenkov men had been planted in the Dnepropetrovsk Party organization by Nikolay Patolichev. In early 1947, this Malenkov protégé had been assigned as second in charge of the Ukraine under Kaganovich.

In December 1947 Khrushchev got his old job back, that of Party Secretary of the Ukraine. Kaganovich almost certainly helped him. Since Kaganovich could not stay in Kiev forever, Patolichev was his logical successor. However, making Patolichev Party chief of the Ukraine would give Malenkov control over the republic—something neither Kaganovich nor Khrushchev wanted. Khrushchev's first action upon resuming control as Ukrainian Party head was to throw Patolichev out, which heightened the conflict with Malenkov, effects of which reached Dnepropetrovsk.

Brezhnev proceeded to overhaul the weak Party organization he found in Dnepropetrovsk, aiming to raise its effectiveness in directing industrial and agricultural output in the *oblast*.[23] In early 1948 he introduced two measures aimed at Party reorganization. One called for more and stronger primary Party organizations in industry and agriculture; the other ordered closer coordination between the *oblast* and lower level Party organizations.

It was the second that got him into trouble at Party meetings in March 1948 and again in June 1949. Several delegates to the March conference called for condemnation and expulsion of the "elementary *administrirovaniya*"—or rule by fiat—method characteristic of

Naydenov's regime. They wanted decision-making based on "suggestions and recommendations from workers and Communists" instead. These delegates, all Malenkov agents, complained that Brezhnev ignored them.

"Many decisions of the Party Committee still smack of orders from landlords," they said.[24] One delegate cited Brezhnev's insistence that Party Secretary Turov of the Likhovskiy *rayon* be reelected Party head despite the fact that he was an obnoxious little dictator who was hated by his colleagues. Brezhnev defended him on grounds that he got the job done. The squabble that ensued between Brezhnev and the *rayon* resulted in the dismissal of several *rayon* officials.

More complaints about Brezhnev's "style of leadership" accompanied Khrushchev's promotion to Moscow as Party Secretary for agriculture in January 1949. At the *oblast* Party meeting that month Secretary Shepilkin, Turov's successor, claimed Brezhnev was "still treating the *rayon* Party Committee in an inconsistent manner." He said:

> Save the token visit by Brezhnev, not one member of the *oblast* Party Committee or anyone from the *ispolkom* of the Soviet of Worker's Deputies visited our *rayon* in 1948. Yet throughout the year we were flooded with decisions and directives from the Party Committee and the *oblispolkom*. At harvest time we would receive from seven to ten directives daily and we didn't even get time to read them.[25]

During 1948 and 1949 Brezhnev took a good deal of flak from Shepilkin and Party members who ultimately paid dearly for their criticism. Three men who fell into this catagory were A.R. Blinov, head of the Dnepropetrovsk city Party Committee, S.P. Shevchenko, formerly head of the Dnepropetrovsk city *soviet* when Brezhnev was *oblast* Propaganda Secretary, but city Propaganda Secretary in 1948, and a city secretary named Khrapunov, about whom little is known.

It was Shevchenko and Khrapunov who had likened Brezhnev to a landlord. Party policy welcomed criticism and self-criticism but this pair had stepped way out of line. For a long time Brezhnev simply chose to ignore the city Party Committee in decision making. Protests did little good. Shevchenko, for example, suggested that since Brezhnev did not consult with him on propaganda matters, the least he could do was advise him on decisions that had been made, which "shouldn't be too difficult since my office is located in the same building."

The quarrel went on for over a year. Finally Brezhnev "uncovered" a scandal involving misappropriation of building materials against Blinov. Brezhnev's investigation led to criminal charges against Blinov and he, Shevchenko, Khrapunov and other subordinates were swept from office.

The *oblast's* agricultural problem boiled down to tightening discipline over the collective farms so that production could be improved. Party organization in the collective farms was seen as the key to success.

The overall percentage of primary Party organizations to collective farms was much lower in Dnepropetrovsk than in other *oblasts* in 1949 and those in existence were generally politically weak. To correct the deficiency Brezhnev dispatched as many Party activists to rural areas as he could and recruited local collective farm managers to build Party organizations. The greater number of organizations appear to have been forced by the redistribution of existing rural Party members.[26]

Similar emphasis was given to primary Party organizations in industrial enterprises. Brezhnev told the Ukrainian Party Congress in 1949 that the number of these organizations in local industry had increased from 236 when he took office to 387 by January 1949.[27]

What is most striking about Brezhnev's Party work as a whole for the two years 1948-1949 was the effect it had in the countryside. The *oblast's kolkhozy* attained prewar levels of cultivated land and produced an excellent harvest. Field teams and brigades utilizing advanced methods of agrotechnology grew harvests of grain and other crops that considerably exceeded the *oblast's* average indicators and allowed the *oblast* not only to fulfill the state's agricultural plan but for two years running, deliver early.

In industry, Dnepropetrovsk completed its annual production plan by December 10, exceeding state plans for steel, iron, coke production and mining. Some 1950 plans were even surpassed.

The city of Dnepropetrovsk was rebuilt in a grand style. Vast apartment complexes were constructed, cast iron fences graced the squares, street lights and street car lines were erected. Trees, shurbs and flowers were planted. Two of the most beautiful parks in the Ukraine today, the Chkalov and Shevchenko parks, were established. Brezhnev even restored a "Palace of Culture" dating back to the era of Catherine the Great. It was all quite a sight to behold.

These wonderful achievements were made possible, Brezhnev told the Ukrainian Party Congress in 1949, by the "increased effectiveness of the Party organization in the *oblast*, the advanced ideological training of personnel ... and the *style of leadership."*[28]

Part II

Developing the Leadership Formula

IX

True Son of the Bolshevik Party

A Bolshevik must soberly assess the results of his work without using success as a pretext to flatter himself or take life easy. Rather, he must endeavor to work all the more energetically and solve the problems facing him even more efficiently. A good Bolshevik is one who unmasks shortcomings and bravely smashes all that is old and outdated to pave the way for progress. — L.I. Brezhnev, 1951.

KHRUSHCHEV NOW DECIDED he should have Brezhnev closer to him. So in 1950, Brezhnev moved to Moscow, the center of all power. Up to now the Party veteran's 21-year career had been limited to *oblast* field posts. Henceforth, all assignments would come from Khrushchev personally and an entirely new pattern would emerge as Brezhnev prepared for future national leadership.

The key event generating this upward move in Brezhnev's career was Khrushchev's own assignment to Moscow in December 1949, made possible by the untimely death a year earlier of one of Stalin's most able lieutenants.

Andrey Zhdanov, who was two years Khrushchev's junior, had had a spectacular political rise, becoming at age 38 both a member of the Party Secretariat and a candidate member of the Politburo. He was smart, obedient and had he lived he might have become Stalin's successor. But his death in July 1948 and the vicious purge of his followers left Malenkov with a concentration of power too vast for Stalin's liking.

This situation prompted Stalin to recall Khrushchev to Moscow to head the city and regional Party Committee and as a Party Secretary counterbalance Malenkov's growing power. Khrushchev was also given the unenviable task of whipping the country's agriculture into shape, a tough job which had resulted in the demise and fall of nearly all of his predecessors. Now more than ever Khrushchev needed his best men around him.

Brezhnev's arrival in Moscow was timed to coincide with the national elections to the U.S.S.R. Supreme Soviet, the Soviet parliament, in early March 1950. Brezhnev had been nominated in January to stand for election to the Supreme Soviet, and, running alone on the Party ticket for Dnepropetrovsk, he was elected two months later to the chamber of the "Soviet of the Union." Thus he came to Moscow a legitimate representative of his constituency. That Khrushchev had summoned Brezhnev there for other reasons was apparent by the fact that he arrived a good three months before the Supreme Soviet was due to meet and he resigned from his post in Dnepropetrovsk before leaving the Ukraine.[1]

Khrushchev put Brezhnev to work on his agricultural staff in the Party's Central Committee apparatus. It was a job that would groom him and introduce him to the highest levels of the Party. Brezhnev had no real power relative to the Party leaders in Moscow though, so he had to rely solely on Khrushchev for protection. He needed it. Moscow was a hive of activity and the political climate was hostile to a young (Brezhnev was then 43) hot shot from the provinces. Colleague and foe alike watched him with suspicion.

Here he met his adversaries face to face. The power Malenkov wielded was astounding. Brezhnev realized for the first time that his association with Khrushchev could cost him dearly, maybe even his life. Malenkov was responsible for the executions of Zhdanov's colleagues and this undoubtedly loomed in Brezhnev's mind over the next several years when his adversary sometimes gained the upper hand.

For four months Brezhnev shuffled papers, prepared background reports and position briefs, and did Khrushchev's leg work as his boss subjected the nation's agricultural policies to a complete review. Drawing on the collective expertise of the apparatus he helped Khrushchev formulate agricultural policies designed to do away with the "link" system of agriculture. It consisted of small groups of farmers, headed by a leader and assisted wherever possible by the machine tractor stations, who worked plots of land in common. It was replaced by the "brigade" system which employed large "brigades" of peasants. Brezhnev also became intimately involved in the policy of *kolkhoz* consolidation whereby small contiguous collective farms were joined together to form large farms. And in June he addressed the nation's agricultural ills in a speech before the Soviet parliament.

Brezhnev looked, listened, kept his mouth shut and learned a great deal. He discovered at first hand the ins and outs of Party affairs at the top. It was an invaluable education and it would continue. But in the summer of 1950, Khrushchev's needs took Brezhnev to rural Moldavia.

Unlike Brezhnev, Nikolay Koval, the Party Secretary in Moldavia, was a man who had no patron in Moscow and whose fortunes had turned sour. As a long time Communist he had been Moldavian Party head since 1946, and was responsible for the immediate postwar reconstruction of the republic. His inability, however, to liquidate the last vestiges of capitalism in the republic and bring about the socialist victories called for in the five year plan for the Moldavian S.S.R. adopted in July 1946, angered Stalin. On June 5, 1950, Stalin called a special Central Committee and fired Koval.

If Khrushchev did not initiate the process which led to Koval's dismissal then the brilliant tactician at least saw an opportunity he could exploit. Here was a chance to extend his influence beyond Moscow and the Ukraine. Having Moldavia in his pocket too would enhance his power vis-à-vis Malenkov, and he could use the loyal Brezhnev, providing he could arrange the latter's appointment as Party Secretary of the republic, to achieve that goal.

It wasn't easy. Malenkov vehemently objected, but he could do nothing to stop Khrushchev. Stalin agreed to appoint Brezhnev because he too wished to further offset Malenkov's power. In short, Brezhnev's appointment to Moldavia was made to promote Khrushchev and to benefit the great leader himself by balancing the political power of his two top subordinates. All Malenkov could do was to make trouble for Brezhnev whenever the opportunity presented itself and hope that Brezhnev would repeat his earlier agricultural blunders.

There was reason to believe that Brezhnev would botch the job on his own for in Moldavia he inherited an almost impossible situation. Moldavia was one of the last outposts of socialism reclaimed from German rule in 1945, and with the small republic Brezhnev inherited a recalcitrant agricultural economy and a highly concentrated multinational-multilingual population including a peasantry long independent and hostile to Soviet attempts to collectivize them. His chore was to regain control over the republic's nominal collective farm system and reintegrate socialist agriculture.

But Brezhnev did not botch the job; quite the contrary. His two-and-a-half year rule in Moldavia rivaled for regimentation, brutality and human suffering the earlier period of collectivization in the Soviet Union. "Strength," Brezhnev remarked in 1952, "characterizes and makes effective the Party's leadership in Moldavia. "A good bolshevik is one who unmasks shortcomings and bravely smashes all that is old and outdated to pave the path for progress."[2] That is exactly how Brezhnev gained Party control in Moldavia.

Even after five years of Soviet rule the old way of farming persisted in the republic in 1950. The principle difficulty lay in the fact that Koval had not adequately reinforced the collective farm structure set up immediately after the war. Almost all of the land had been collectivized but a Central Committee investigation in the spring of 1950 revealed widespread violation of kolkhoz statutes, particularly those pertaining to the collective farmer's responsibility to the state: the size of his garden plot far exceeded the legal limits; much of his livestock and machinery remained outside the collective farms; and there was no enforcement of the mandatory labor hours that each farmer was obliged to devote to collective production for the state. Overall, little collective farming was being done. Brezhnev released figures in July 1950 which showed that of 5000 collective farmers registered in Moldavia, half had never participated in any kind of collective farm production.[3]

Brezhnev interpreted this unacceptable state of affairs as a resurgence of capitalist elements in Moldavia. In part, this view stemmed from the republic's long domination by Romania and the attitudes and policies of Stalin associated with the ideological threat seen in Soviet border areas at this time because of the Cold War. Moldavia was an important buffer to the West and had to be protected.

In Brezhnev's eyes the republic was particulary susceptible to counterrevolutionary activity and imperialist encroachment: "All of the history of Moldavia has been a history of constant struggle for national independence against landgrabbing aggressors, Germans and capitalists who coveted the rich Moldavian land, and this continues today," he wrote in September 1950.[4] He had to deal with the threat daily. Nighttime raids on collective farms and machine tractor stations by anti-Soviet partisan groups often reinforced by more organized and dangerous bands from the western Ukraine caused no end of trouble. The "imperialist threat" was real and personal.

Brezhnev dealt with the renegades first. Military units stationed in Kishinev, the capital of the republic, were ordered to hunt them down. By day, however, many renegades were regular farmers, so he instructed the Minister of State Security and Party organs to launch a full-scale war to "dekulakize" the countryside. He went about the whole operation as though he were conducting a military campaign.

Two dekulakization drives had been conducted in the republic before — one in 1940 and another in 1946 — but Brezhnev's "battle plan" was altogether different. It was directed primarily at farms that had already been collectivized. Brezhnev explained:

> Some collectivization had transpired in the right-bank regions of the republic after its creation in 1940, but during the war the republic was seized by the Germans. In the four years that the imperialists occupied Moldavia they established a network of bourgeois nationalists which penetrated every sector of the economy. After Soviet liberation in 1945, these bourgeois nationalists infiltrated the collective farm movement. They penetrated the collective farm leadership, established themselves in positions of authority, and are working to undermine the economy and deliver a lethal blow to the Moldavian Socialist Republic.[5]

Brezhnev's "thesis" was a unique modification of the Twenties' collectivization theme and signaled a purge of the existing collective farm leaders who Brezhnev accused of being "imperialist" agents. In this way he shifted the blame for conditions in the farms onto the *kolkhoz* leadership instead of the republic Party organization. When he took charge of the republic he retained all of the top Party and government leaders and made only minor changes at the lower levels. By doing this he was able to maintain continuity of leadership and realign the existing Party organization under his direction without further weakening the structure.

Collective farm leaders became the first casualty of Brezhnev's blitz in 1950. Violence now came naturally to him, and by the end of the year over half of the *kolkhoz* chairmen had been purged and disgraced or tried and sentenced on grounds they had violated *kolkhoz* laws and conspired with imperialists to overthrow the republic. New tough *kolkhoz* leaders were imported from other parts of the Soviet Union and particularly from the neighboring Ukraine to replace them, though some posts were purposely left vacant in anticipation of *kolkhoz* consolidation.

Of course dekulakization enveloped not only collective farmers but those in still uncollectivized regions of the republic, where the policy was used to facilitate collectivization. In areas already collectivized, it was used to force compliance with *kolkhoz* laws. Peasants everywhere resisted and as Brezhnev forced the issue, those who had earlier sat idly in protest turned to violence. One member of the

Moldavian Party Committee described the trouble this way: "We had a very difficult and bitter struggle with many obstacles: The tenor of life, people's old habits, but most of all the hostile activities of the national kulak element rendered *desperate opposition to everything new the Party tried to do.* Economic construction, it goes without saying, was not achieved without high cost."[6]

The cost in both property and lives escalated daily, becoming especially alarming after October 1950. Two factors were responsible: the imposition of tougher penalties for violation of *kolkhoz* laws and *kolkhoz* consolidation.

In 1951, Brezhnev combined stiffer penalties with reorganization of the collective farm structure aimed at dragging the peasant by the nape of the neck away from his precious garden plot, long the thorn in the side of socialist agriculture. On October 14, he announced that anyone "caught idle" — failing to work the mandatory labor hours — would be "swiftly and severely punished." At the same time he declared that continued dekulakization "is absolutely necessary to establish the fundamental conditions needed for future development of socialist agriculture in the republic." The latter would take the form of "consolidation of the collective farms in accordance with Party policy."[7]

The idea of merging smaller contiguous collective farms into large production units was Khrushchev's; it became official policy in March 1950. The whole concept was linked with his grander scheme to regroup collective farm peasants into large "agro-towns" to consist of newly built homes or apartments with all the social, medical, Party and administrative facilities centrally located. Brezhnev liked the idea. He constantly referred to the political, social and economic benefits to be derived from "large collective farms" and he wholeheartedly supported Khrushchev's program for *kolkhoz* consolidation as an obvious step toward the larger scheme.

At the Party's plenum on October 4, 1950, Brezhnev lauded *kolkhoz* consolidation as a panacea for the republic's agricultural ills. Parroting Khrushchev on the subject, he argued a long list of advantages ranging from reduction of administrative costs, improvement in the selection of qualified cadres and promotion of reliable collective farm leadership, to substantial increases in labor discipline, farm production and deliveries to the state.

While Brezhnev worked to strengthen the Moldavian Party organizations, their weakness and complete absence in many villages was an important motivating factor for consolidation. With consolidation most farms would have at least one resident Communist. The larger farms would also provide for more efficient use of the desperately scarce resources of skilled management and machinery.

Why did Brezhnev wait so long to begin consolidation? The answer lay in the fact that collectivization in the western regions had to be completed before a uniform consolidation plan could be put into effect. That work was finished in August. Certain "fundamental conditions" relating to dekulakization also had to be at least partially realized. However, if he felt that adequate progress had been made by the end of 1950 to proceed with consolidation unencumbered he was mistaken.

This kind of upheaval aroused the wrath of the peasantry because it decreased the size of their garden plots, and threatened their traditional means of livlihood. They soon found themselves hardpressed to produce enough on their private plots to sustain themselves, much less enough to sell on the open market. Sabotage and plundering became rampant. At the January Party plenum Brezhnev blamed "resurgent kulak and other enemy alien elements who were purposely attempting to sabotage economic help to the *kolkhozy*."[8]

He responded by expanding the categories of "crimes against the state" and he organized a final drive to liquidate all opposition to his regime. A new wave of arrests, trials and speedy convictions swept across the republic. "Prosecutors, judges, ministers of justice and legal consultants" who were "sent into the villages to give lectures on socialist law"[9] worked around the clock trying cases of sabotage. The death penalty, which had been reintroduced by Brezhnev in 1950 for cases of sabotage, now claimed a multitude of victims. But in just 15 months Brezhnev cut the number of farms in the republic in half.

Stalin fully backed the repressive measures and Brezhnev used the elections to the Moldavian Supreme Soviet to publicly demonstrate Stalin's support. On January 11, 1951, for the first time ever, Brezhnev's name appeared in print side by side with Stalin's. The occasion was the joint announcement in the republic's newspaper *Sovetskaya Moldavia* that both had been nominated by the Frunze Agricultural Institute in Kishinev to stand for election to the Moldavian Supreme Soviet. Brezhnev's name not only appeared with Stalin's, but it appeared in the same size print and equal space was devoted to listing the credentials of each: Stalin received the usual exalted praise, while Brezhnev was described as a "true son of the Bolshevik Party, noted for his long service in the leadership of *soviet* and Party work and one who devotes all his strength and energies to the task of communist construction." This enhanced Brezhnev's authority.

It also reflected the reorientation and bolstering of propaganda in Moldavia that had begun in the fall of 1950. The peasantry not only had to be disciplined and taught to obey, they had to be educated to believe in the great wisdom of Stalin and the good life under socialism. Propaganda dissemination in the republic was decentralized and haphazard. Brezhnev frequently expressed dissatisfaction with the state of propaganda and agitation and it soon became apparent that the propaganda apparatus needed overhauling.

Three brand new themes dominated propaganda in 1951: the benefits of *kolkhoz* consolidation, achievements and future tasks of socialist construction, and the crises of capitalism. Thirty-five new newspapers appeared to herald the coming of Communism; local and national radio stations began broadcasting around the clock; movies depicting the benefits of socialist agriculture were shown regularly; and agricultural exhibits and libraries were established in the *kolkhozy*.

Brezhnev made the same Stalinist demands of culture. His cultural policies were typical of the policies applied to all non-Russian nationalities at the time. He demanded that Moldavian literature and art be ideologically strengthened to instill a greater sense of Soviet patriotism and political consciousness among Communists, and that history be rewritten to show Russia's involvement in Moldavia's struggle for independence as far back as Peter I. He tampered with the Moldavian language "to give it a more Marxist-Leninist character" and to accommodate publication of the complete works of Lenin and Stalin.[10]

Anything that could serve as a national rallying point was quickly suppressed — or should have been. A case in point was *Pravda's* complaint that "Moldavian composers have written few musical compositions, they continue to limit themselves to the so-called arrangements of folk music which have little use."[11] Intellectual resistance to such change was strong. Brezhnev continually complained and so did Moscow about the "Moldavian intelligentsia's serious ideological faults and errors stemming from a bourgeois nationalist approach to every aspect of life."[12]

Like propaganda, overhaul of the republic's machine tractor stations (MTS) was long overdue. The MTS were a basic feature of the Stalinist farm system and the fact that in Moldavia they fulfilled only one-half of the state plan for 1950 was unsatisfactory by anybody's standard. Brezhnev had ambitious plans for these mechanized sectors of socialist agriculture. With more stations and newer machinery they could mechanize the whole of socialist agriculture and, at the same time, stand guard as political watchdogs over the collective farms. His views on their purpose and function were orthodox Stalinist.

Brezhnev told the Third Moldavian Party Congress in 1951:

> Our machine tractor stations are absolutely indispensible for socialist agricultural production and for strengthening the economic and political organizations of the kolkhoz. They are essential for strengthening Party-organizational and mass-political work in the villages and directing the development of Communist consciousness and labor discipline among the collective farmers."[13]

The MTS had to be rebuilt. The problem was the damage done to the machinery during the recent peasant rebellions. To ensure that proper repairs were made Brezhnev created a special supervisory commission and gave it punitive powers and a mandate to oversee repairs and maintenance. He also saw to it that maintenance norms were set up and promised that "those responsible for wasting materials would be held accountable to the Party and the state." An inventory was taken to protect against theft and plundering.

Tractor and combine drivers and mechanics were badly needed. Brezhnev recommended that women be trained for these jobs. Continued shortages of qualified personnel and the need for political reliability motivated him to assign workers from industry and the trade unions to the MTS. This move previewed a larger policy recommending "urbanization" of the MTS which Khrushchev introduced in August 1953.

Reinforcement of MTS political departments was one of Brezhnev's major goals. In 1950, he sent 500 Communists out to work in these departments. They played a major role in enforcing labor discipline: "The political departments together with Party committees initiated major political, organizational and mass political work among *kolkhoz* and MTS workers, giving particular attention to observance of *kolkhoz* regulations, to the consolidation of labor discipline and to the increased activity of field workers."[14]

Besides disciplinary measures, reorganization of propaganda and the MTS, Brezhnev increased the number of primary Party organizations, brought new members into the Party and into Komsomol, trained cadres in courses on agronomy, zoology and ideology, and initiated socialist competition to bring the peasants and agriculture into line. He also mobilized the trade unions: "L.I. Brezhnev highly valued the activity of the trade unions ... which played a significant supplementary role in preparing and building collectivized agriculture in the right bank of Moldavia, strengthening and developing the *kolkhozy, sovkhozy* and MTS."[15]

The urgency with which Brezhnev carried through the transformation of Moldavia was motivated by existing ideological and economic conditions, but most of all by personal considerations. When he assumed command of the republic he had 10 months in which to bring about substantial change and to prepare a favorable report for the upcoming Moldavian Party Congress scheduled to meet in March 1951. In addition, he had until July 1951 to complete Moldavia's five year plan for reconstruction and development. The plan had been decreed by Moscow and its slow pace had cost Koval his job. Lastly, Brezhnev was very much aware of the rumors that Stalin would soon hold the first postwar all-union Party congress and he wanted to be in the best possible shape for that.

Things did look better by March of 1951. Labor discipline was up and collective farmers were working more hours than ever. Some farmers, however, were still not fulfilling their minimum work requirements. Brezhnev never solved this problem completely. Nevertheless, the achievements accomplished represented substantial mobilization on Brezhnev's part and improvement over 1950. At the Third Moldavian Party Congress in March Brezhnev reported:

> A deep revolutionary transformation has taken place in the villages. This has delivered our peasants from kulak exploitation and poverty and created infinite possibilities for development of all branches of the agricultural economy. The last of the exploiting class – the kulak – has been liquidated. The collectivization of agriculture is entirely complete.
>
> The Party organization in Moldavia with the significant help of the Central Committee of the All Union Communist Party (bolshevik), the Soviet government and Stalin personally, has made significant advances ... in socialist reconstruction of the villages, organizations of agricultural economy, strengthening of *kolkhozy*, and improved the work of the MTS. The Moldavian countryside is now undergoing a great political and labor advance.

In fulfilling the resolution of the Central Committee of the VKP(b) of June 5 the Central Committee of the Moldavian Communist Party undertook measures to raise the level of organizational Party work in villages and to strengthen mass political work among the *kolkhozy*, workers of the MTS and the *sovkhozy* and thereby mobilized all collective farmers for the fight for further development of the agricultural economy.

All of this [Brezhnev proudly concluded] goes to prove that the Party organization of the republic had fulfilled the resolution of June 5 and has successfully strengthened the leadership of agriculture.[16]

Although Brezhnev claimed a sizeable victory for himself, he was careful to point out that a great deal still had to be done. Indeed, in his speech to the Congress, he failed to report successes in actual economic production. A report published in *Sovetskaya Moldaviya* on January 31, 1951, explained why. Of 28 areas of agricultural production cited in the newspaper, over half never fulfilled state plans for 1950. Brezhnev's punitive campaigns were responsible.

It was therefore not surprising that all Party meetings held in early 1951, and a special agricultural conference called just before the Congress, concentrated on implementing organizational and technical measures and further mobilizing the peasantry to bring about an upturn in production, Brezhnev's immediate concern being a successful annual harvest.

The real surprise was his success in turning agriculture around. A July article in *Sovetskaya Moldaviya* announced "completion of all aspects of the postwar five year economic plan for Moldavia."[17] In a letter to Stalin in August Brezhnev boasted that Moldavia had reaped a good harvest. An update in November announced overfulfillment of production quotas in several agricultural areas, including wine production. The latter had been the primary objective of a longterm agricultural development plan presented to the Moldavian Party Congress: a grandiose scheme to develop 13,000 new hectares of vineyards and to develop related industries.

Pledges like this were indicative of Brezhnev's tremendous confidence as the Nineteenth Party Congress approached. He repeatedly made promises which seemed next to impossible to achieve. But his position continued to be reinforced right up to the Fourth Moldavian Party Congress (held September 1952), which Brezhnev used to spotlight his achievements on the eve of the all-union congress. "Every third collective farm in the republic is now a millionaire," he told the Moldavian Congress.[18]

At the Moldavian Congress Brezhnev also focused attention on his other achievements, especially social, where his major contribution had been an improvement in education:

> Conspicuous successes have been achieved in the development of Soviet culture. Illiteracy has been eliminated. The bourgeois landowning Bessarabia never had higher education institutions. Today, the most gifted Moldavian youth are working on masters' and doctoral dissertations in the institutes of the U.S.S.R. Academy of Sciences in Kishinev and in other towns, in the university, and in seven higher educational institutions. In the last five years more books have been published in the Moldavian language than in the last 100 years.[19]

He also took this opportunity to point out that Moldavia's constitution had been amended to reflect the recent changes.[20] One of those changes involved reorganization of the republic's administrative structure. Since collective farm consolidation had come to include several villages, the village *soviet* lost its importance and was abolished. Its powers were transferred to city *soviets.*

Brezhnev was in almost perfect form for the Nineteenth All-Union Party Congress; the accumulated effect of his tyrannical rule and economic measures had produced outstanding results. However, an uncomfortable situation arose just three weeks before the all-union Congress was scheduled to meet.

Errors in the selection and deployment of political instructors were brought to light at the Moldavian Party Congress in September. Brezhnev himself had raised the matter, but only to demonstrate that he had already taken action to remedy the problem. However, this didn't satisfy Andrey Kozyrev, head of the republic's collegium for economic matters. Kozyrev blatantly challenged Brezhnev to tell the Party why he hadn't punished those responsible for the errors. Kozyrev particularly wanted to know why no action had been taken against A.M. Lazarev, the Party Secretary in charge of cadre selection.

Pravda took Kozyrev's side: "It is necessary to say that such assertions made in comrade Brezhnev's speech as 'We members of the Bureau attempted to carry out the plenary sessions strictly and without sparing the self-regard of our leaders and to remain on a high level of principle' were met with bewilderment. These assertions made by the speaker did not genuinely reflect the situation."[21]

In fact, *Pravda* hinted that Brezhnev was even trying to gloss over his subordinates' mistakes to save face himself: "Comrade Kozyrev had pointed out that ... comrade Brezhnev, in speaking of the errors in selecting and training cadres of instructors, did not say anything about the actual perpetrators of those errors, in particular comrade Lazarev." *Pravda* also alleged that favoritism had been at the bottom of promoting some unqualified individuals to leading positions. This action and others were to blame for the high turnover of cadres in the republic and in turn raised questions about the quality of Brezhnev's ideological work.

Pravda's attack took Brezhnev by complete surprise. It wasn't difficult to figure out that neither Kozyrev nor *Pravda* had acted alone. Their attack had been well planned and timed, and obviously launched by Malenkov to discredit Brezhnev and thus Khrushchev. Khrushchev at the time was making allegations of corruption and nepotism against Malenkov's subordinates. How embarassing for Khrushchev should his own protégé turn out to be corrupt.

The allegations infuriated Brezhnev. He retorted and Khrushchev, equally provoked, used his influence with the editor of the Party's influential journal *Bolshevik* to publish Brezhnev's retort, an article entitled "Criticism and Self-Criticism — the Tested Method of Cadre Training."[22] It was a superb piece of prose.

He began by lauding the new Party rules which were released by Stalin in August 1952 and which emphasized the need for fearless criticism and self-criticism by Party leaders. The rules were up for formal ratification. Therefore Brezhnev's article served a dual function: it argued in support of the rules which were in turn used as his defense.

> The general instructions of comrade Stalin in this historical document say that members of the Party should solicit criticism from below, expose shortcomings in work and remove them, fight against complacency and intoxication from success. That is absolutely correct. Members of the Party have the right to criticize their beloved workers of the Party at Party meetings.

But, Brezhnev warned:

> The changes encompassed in the new rules state that each Communist should observe Party and state discipline. The same obligation applies to Party members.

He berated the Kozyrevs in the Party for failing to abide by this principle and prevailed on them to remember that:

> When armed with Party and state descipline, such things as frauds and lies before the Party are a great evil and are incompatible with continued tenure in the ranks of the Party. Courageous criticism and self-criticism should not be used to downgrade the Party or for hairsplitting [as Kozyrev and *Pravda* had done]. Hairsplitting is not an exercise in criticism at all.

Rather, it defrauds the Party on the actual state of things.
Workers should not step down from a principled position and
forfeit the feeling of responsibility for confidentiality of Party
business and become hairsplitters.

In Brezhnev's opinion such people were not worthy of continued Party membership and neither were "those who stifled
[genuine] criticism or substituted it for windowdressing or eulogy."
Both were criminals. This had been a factor in Koval's removal. After
all, Brezhnev pointed out,

Criticism and self-criticism has historically been a great source
of strength and invincibility of our Party and a source of new
life and activity of the Party. Only through it can the correct
development of all sections of the Party, cultural and scientific
work take place. It is the source of our strength.... No one
should be afraid to expose mistakes and shortcomings, but
criticism and self-criticism must be used correctly.

Brezhnev admitted to some truth in personal favoritism in
cadre selection but he claimed no personal responsibility. Moreover,
he had fired the nepotists. One republic Party secretary was
removed in 1951. D. Tkach, Brezhnev's immediate deputy, left office
in 1952, and the Komsomol Secretary was dismissed in May of the
same year. They were replaced by Moldavian Party members, and
while some cadres from the Ukraine were assigned to vacated posts
this was standard practice.

In the case of comrade Demin, the Minister of Light Industry,
Brezhnev condemned nepotism on grounds that it stifled efficiency:
"By forgetting Bolshevik rules for cadre selection and surrounding
himself with friends, relatives and people from his own region,
comrade Demin created within the ministry a situation of servility
and toadyism, incompatible with an efficient approach and fundamental criticism of shortcomings."

The Central Committee, Brezhnev carefully pointed out, did
not tolerate this practice: "Comrade Demin was severely criticized
for this abuse of power, but he was not dismissed from his post. He
heeded the criticism against him and corrected his errors."

The subtlety of Brezhnev's remarks was not lost on those who
had sought Lazarev's removal. By dismissing Lazarev, Brezhnev
would have admitted poor judgment. Besides, Lazarev had mended
his ways. He had only recently replaced Tkach who had also been
found guilty of "selecting cadres on the basis of personal relationships" and had been dismissed by Brezhnev because "he had attempted to discredit the communists who were criticizing him." Under

other cricumstances, Brezhnev would not have hesitated to sacrifice anyone who stood in the way of his own success.

Pravda's criticism of the high turnover of cadres was valid but Brezhnev claimed the turnover was understandable: "Of the more than 8000 people sent into the field in 1951 through 1952 ... not all could be expected to have the necessary knowledge or experience to cope with the conditions. In the factories and *kolkhozy* and even among the people, the cadres ran into serious difficulties because of the strength of the old order and bourgeois tradition."

Brezhnev not only countered each accusation or inference against him, but concluded with a final positive appraisal of his record, driving the point home that through his leadership Moldavia had become a model republic and a symbol of Leninist-Stalinist ideals:

> Two years ago the Central Committee of the vKP(b) uncovered serious shortcomings in the Moldavian Party leadership and in economic and cultural construction.... But in just a short time concrete changes have been made. Socialist construction has taken place ... which ... has built a mountain of socialist agriculture, with shining culture, nationalist in form, but socialist in content.
>
> In Party work the Central Committee ... paid a great deal of attention to the fact that the principle of intra-Party democracy be strictly adhered to in every Party organization, that the collective be the fundamental condition in all Party work, that Party meetings, plenums and conferences maintain a high standard. The fact that the plenums of the Central Committee have been called more frequently than in the past demonstrates this.

The attempt to discredit Brezhnev rebounded on his and Khrushchev's mutal adversaries. It had also afforded Brezhnev an excellent opportunity to reaffirm his record, enhance his image as a dedicated and able Stalinist and, at the same time, strengthen Khrushchev's position.

X

The Succession Struggle

The road to the top is open to all, just as every one of Napoleon's soldiers carried a marshal's baton in his knapsack.

In history, it is not important who implements a process, it is only important that the process be implemented. — Milovan Djilas, *The New Class.*

IN THE NEXT 11 MONTHS the converging threads of two careers were drawn together to form a common bond which linked Brezhnev to Khrushchev and each to the web of intrigue that wove its way through the Party hierarchy immediately preceding and following the death of Stalin in March 1953. This period was characterized by the constant interaction of rivalries, jealousies, hatred and power politics within the Party. It was a climate in which Brezhnev thrived, and it nurtured his development as a Party leader during the last days of Stalin's life.

The Great Leader himself was the ultimate compelling force behind Brezhnev's elevation to the top of the Party in the early part of this period. But it was Khrushchev who initiated the sequence of events leading to Brezhnev's rise to the top. Edward Crankshaw wrote about Brezhnev's benefactor:

> Khrushchev — almost certainly in alliance with Mikoyan who was interested only in efficiency, and the comparative newcomer to the Party Secretariat, Mikhail Suslov ... and with Bulganin as well, who knew all about the hatred and contempt of the military high command for the Party ... — managed to persuade Stalin that something had to be done. The Party, Malenkov's special preserve, had to be sorted out, purified, rejuvenated, reorganized, and he, Khrushchev, with his healthy Ukrainian background, uncontaminated by the Moscow rat race was the man to do it. From now on it was war to the knife with Malenkov....[1]

Khrushchev's first line of attack had been to strike deep into Malenkov's territory with charges of crime, corruption and graft against his subordinates, demanding that the corrupt and inefficient in various sectors of the Party and bureaucracy be tossed out. No wonder Malenkov struck back by bringing the same charges against the precious protégé, Brezhnev.

A major purge was in the offing in 1952. Indeed, there was evidence that Stalin, his paranoic personality now more active than ever, even planned to liquidate some of the Party's top leaders. Khrushchev accused Stalin in his secret speech to the Twentieth Party Congress in 1956, of plotting to rid the Party of Beria, Kaganovich, Molotov, Kliment Voroshilov and Anastas Mikoyan.

Moves to check the personal power of Beria had, in fact, already begun. Viktor Abakhumov, Beria's Minister of State Security, was purged in 1951 and replaced by Sergey Ignatyev, a Khrushchev man, thus making Khrushchev's hand obvious. Beria's followers were purged from the bureaucracy, the Georgian republic (his real stronghold), and other areas controlled by the police chief.

Then, at the Nineteenth Party Congress in October 1952, Stalin promoted a large number of second-level officials to the Party's top organs, thereby providing an immediate reserve hierarchy to carry out his will, to swallow up and ultimately replace those he planned to get rid of. The Party's Central Committee was expanded to 125 full members and the Orgburo, which along with the Party Control Committee was traditionally responsible for the business of organization and discipline, was amalgamated with the Secretariat. It in turn was expanded from five to ten members, and the Party's ruling body, the Politburo, was reorganized into a weighty Party Presidium of 36. The Politburo had originally consisted of only 11 members. The break with tradition was symbolized by a change in the name of the Party itself to the Communist Party of the Soviet Union (cpsu).

The significant expansion of the Party leadership gave Khrushchev — and even Malenkov since Stalin now determined that both had to be strengthened vis-à-vis Beria — an opportunity to bring some of their protégés and closest followers into the Moscow fold. What a break for Brezhnev! This was the opportunity he had waited and worked so hard for, a chance to go right to the top.

As an ably qualified and proven Stalinist, as Khrushchev's top protégé, and as the Party Secretary from Moldavia, he was strategically placed on the eve of the Nineteenth Party Congress to move into at least some of the Party organs, or even all three if luck were with him and if Khrushchev and Stalin wanted it that way. Further, the prospects for a purge of Party leaders such as Beria, whose days were in fact numbered though he was not to fall until after

Stalin died, Kaganovich, who had fallen from Stalin's favor, and Voroshilov, one of the old guard Bolsheviks who had commanded the Red Army but who Stalin now suspected of being a foreign agent, would, once Brezhnev got his foot in the door, provide an opportunity for him to become one of the half-dozen top leaders in the Soviet Union. But the first step was to get elected to the new Party organs.

For ten days Brezhnev sat at the October Congress. He spoke briefly, listened attentively, applauded the speeches and simply waited for his inevitable election to one or more of the Party's organs. There was nothing particularly eventful or even interesting about his own participation in the Congress, except that he was elected to the commission charged with verifying the credentials of the delegates. His speech to the Congress was a carbon copy of his earlier report to the Moldavian Congress.

Finally, on October 15, *Pravda* published the list of the 125 full members of the newly elected Central Committee. In alphabetical order Brezhnev came fourteenth. Two days later *Pravda* revealed the composition of the new Party Presidium and Secretariat. Brezhnev was first on the list of candidate members of the new Presidium and third on the Secretariat list.

For all appearances Brezhnev ranked with and in some cases even above, the most important leaders of the Party thanks to Stalin's replacement of the old system of ranking important officials first with the Cyrillic alphabetical listing. The published list, however, belied Brezhnev's importance.

All republic Party secretaries, 15 of them, were elected to the Central Committee at the Congress. Brezhnev would probably have been elected to the Central Committee too without any special help from Khrushchev. But only four of the 15 became members of the Party Presidium. They were Nikolay Ignatov, Patolichev, who had become Party Secretary of Belorussia, Leonid Melnikov, Party Secretary of the Ukraine and a Khrushchev man, and Brezhnev.

Brezhnev, Ignatyev, Korotchenko, who was now chairman of the Ukrainian Council of Ministers, and Melnikov constituted the core of the Khrushchev group in the Presidium. Only Brezhnev made it into the Party Secretariat, the body responsible for executing Party policy and managing the Party apparatus.

Brezhnev held only candidate or non-voting status in the Presidium. This reduced his political status but made little practical difference as far as policy formulation was concerned since the body had been watered down by its size, and Stalin dominated the policy-making process in the Party Presidium as he had done in the Politburo anyway. Nevertheless, Stalin intended Brezhnev's candidate status to be only temporary. Khrushchev told the Twentieth Party Congress later:

> Stalin evidently had plans to finish off the old members of the Politburo. He often stated that Politburo members should be replaced by new ones. His proposal after the Nineteenth Party Congress concerning the selection of 25 persons to the Central Committee Presidium was aimed at the removal of the old Politburo members and bringing in of less experienced persons.[2]

On November 7, 1952, instead of being down in the crowds that filled Red Square straining to catch a glimpse of the Great Leader, Brezhnev stood within a few feet of Stalin himself atop the Lenin Mausoleum and reviewed the anniversary parade celebrating Lenin's capture of power in Russia. This was Brezhnev's first public appearance as a national leader.

It was a significant appearance. The lineup of Party leaders on Lenin's Mausoleum during national celebrations is a measure of a leader's political importance. Not all members of the Party's ruling organs are privileged to attend. Those who do are the cream of the crop, the top line of Soviet leadership, the ones to watch. Brezhnev's presence objectified his status as a member of the elite.

But his presence was further significant. Though he came 17th in the lineup, of the relatively new leaders standing on the mausoleum only Brezhnev and Averkiy Aristov, who were on Khrushchev's side, and Nikolay Pegov and Panteleymon Ponomarenko, both dedicated Malenkov men, were members of both Presidium and Secretariat. They would be the ones most likely to succeed those Stalin planned to purge, constituting, along with Khrushchev and Malenkov, and possibly Bulganin who now commanded the armed forces, an inner core of leaders, a smaller "ruling" committee of the Presidium called the Presidburo.[3]

In the winter of 1952, Stalin cranked up the vast Soviet propaganda machine in preparation for the purge. There were new calls for "vigilance" against saboteurs and subversives, foreign spies and Zionists. Vigilance became the watchword and Stalin's cold war "Hate America" campaign reached a fever pitch. The Soviet anti-semitic campaign, which claimed the lives of 400 leading Jewish writers, artists and musicians in August 1952, was now intensified. In Czechoslovakia 14 ranking Party and government leaders were put

Stalin and the Soviet leadership reviewing the October Revolution parade from atop the Lenin Mausoleum, November 1952. Left to right: J. V. Stalin, K. E. Voroshilov, G. M. Malenkov, L. P. Beria, N. S. Khrushchev, L. M. Kaganovich, V. M. Molotov, N. M. Svernik, M. G. Pervukhin, M. Z. Saburov, A. I. Mikoyan, P. K. Ponomarenko, M. A. Suslov, M.F. Shiryatov, A. B. Aristov, N. M. Pegov, and **L. I. Brezhnev.**

on trial in one of the biggest judicial shows ever in a satellite country. In the meantime, Stalin stretched his imagination to devise a scheme comparable to the 1934 Kirov murder to use as a pretext to remove Beria and the others. An atmosphere of paranoia and tension seeped into the Party organs.

Brezhnev now found himself in extremely hostile company. Khrushchev's men encountered bitter opposition from the Malenkov faction. Patolichev, Mikhail Pervukhin and Maksim Saburov, both technocrats who were made deputy chairmen of the U.S.S.R. Council of Ministers in 1949 and 1950 respectively, Pegov and Ponomarenko made up this group. The new Presidium and Secretariat were divided between these two factions, forcing other members to choose sides. The "old Politburo" members tried to remain aloof, but were sometimes forced to technically ally themselves with one side or the other. Generally they were hostile to the younger generation of men whom they rightfully viewed as a personal threat.

By January 1953, Stalin had devised the scheme he wanted. On the 13th of that month he announced to an already terror-struck Russia that the police had uncovered a plot contrived by mainly Jewish physicians to kill important Party and government leaders on behalf of American and British intelligence agencies. This was the so-called "doctors' plot." The accused were charged with having already murdered Andrey Zhdanov by inadequate medical treatment during his illness and were arrested and beaten to confess to other murderous schemes.

This was to be the beginning of the end for Beria, Kaganovich, and almost certainly Molotov and Mikoyan too; for Brezhnev and a select few others it meant the beginning of a move upwards. Men now went to extremes to jockey for position and Stalin's favor.

But in retrospect it was all rather futile. Stalin's health was not good. He had not been up to giving a long and detailed report to the Party Congress in October 1952; the strain was simply too great. His health deteriorated rapidly in the remaining months of 1952 and early in the new year. Finally, on the night of March 1, in his bed in the Kremlin Stalin was overcome by a massive brain hemorrhage. The "Greatest Leader of All Humanity," as Malenkov described Stalin at the funeral, was dead.

The regime without its leader was cast into an abyss. Stalin's colleagues waited days to announce his death, fearing public panic and disorder. Stalin had ruled Russia by fear and terror. The question of ruling the vast empire that he had built now became an immediate reality and a real concern. He had made no arrangements for succession because he distrusted everyone. "No one had dared bid him prepare for death, none dared to try on the crown in his presence."[4] Who was to assume Stalin's key role? Malenkov? Khrushchev? Or was it to be the dreaded Beria? One thing was for certain. There would be no purge of the top leaders now. There would be no promotion for Brezhnev either.

Those Stalin had intended to purge now exercised collective control over the Party, and it was determined in the first hours after Stalin's death that dramatic changes were needed if public "disorder and panic" were to be avoided. Fear dominated the decision making, deals were made, bargains were struck, and compromises were hastily fashioned. The cumbersome Party Presidium was reduced to half its size (to 14 men), while the Secretariat was reduced by one with some new men being elected.[5] When the new composition of these bodies was announced on March 7, Brezhnev was conspicuously absent from each. He had been struck from the Party leadership just as swiftly as Stalin had catapulted him to the top.

The dismissal of some lesser figures from the Presidium and Secretariat was to be expected with the reduction in the size of these bodies, but why in particular had Brezhnev's head been put on the chopping block? That his Party activities were incompatible with those of the people who formed the new Presidium of the Central Committee was only part of the matter. It seems that in the panic of the succession crisis the following situation developed.

Although Malenkov came out way ahead of Khrushchev in the race for Party control in those first hours and days of feverish maneuvering among Party leaders—being designated Party and government head—Khrushchev was still a powerful force to be reckoned with. Nevertheless, he was unable to retain his important men in the Party leadership because of another, more pressing need. Brezhnev's removal as well as the firing of other key figures from both the Khrushchev and Malenkov factions was the result of an early compromise between the leaders of these groups and the "old leaders" to temporarily call off the infighting and neutralize the warring factions for the sake of Party unity.

Of Khrushchev's supporters, Brezhnev, Ignatyev and Korotchenko left the Party Presidium. Their dismissals were roughly balanced by the removal of Pegov and Patolichev. Saburov remained in the Presidium, and Ponomarenko and Melnikov were reduced to candidate status and left to counterbalance each other. Brezhnev, Ponomarenko and Pervukhin were relieved of their duties in the Secretariat. Ignatyev was briefly left to counterbalance Nikolay Shatalin, a lone-time Malenkov associate now brought into the Secretariat.

All of Malenkov's associates were transferred to government posts. Pegov was made Secretary of the Council of Ministers Presidium. Ponomarenko and Ignatov were relieved from the Secretariat and transferred to the Council of Ministers, suggesting that Ignatov was also a Malenkov associate.

Khrushchev's supporters, Korotchenko, Melnikov and ultimately Ignatyev were returned to provinces. It was disclosed on April 4 that Ignatyev had been responsible for "political blindness and gullibility" relating to false charges in the doctors' plot conspiracy. He was exiled to the remote Bashkir Soviet Republic in the Urals. Melnikov resumed his post as Party Secretary of the Ukraine and Korotchenko returned as head of the Ukrainian Council of Ministers, though that summer he was accused of "distortions of the Lenin-Stalin nationality policy" and dismissed from his post.

On March 7, the official newspaper of the armed forces, *Krasnaya Zvezda*, announced Brezhnev's fate: "L.I. Brezhnev had been released from the Presidium and Secretariat in connection with the transfer of his duties to head of the Political Administration of the Navy."

So, in March 1953, Brezhnev dusted off his general's uniform, his reserve military status now activated for an indefinite time. Although his political power had been neutralized, there was one consoling factor: he was allowed to stay in Moscow and work at the Central Committee level. Thus he was saved from the obscurity of the provinces. He owed Khrushchev for that.

The Navy's Political Administration and its successor, the Main Political Administration of the Army and Navy, functioned as the "department of the Central Committee" responsible to the senior Party secretary,[6] Malenkov. On March 14, however, Malenkov resigned from that position and from the Secretariat, and on the following day the Ministry of Defense was organized and Brezhnev made a deputy chief of the Main Political Administration,[7] giving him wider political responsibilities and facilitating his larger access to the military establishment. Now Khrushchev, who was left the senior

secretary when Malenkov departed (though Khrushchev was not officially designated Party First Secretary until later in the year)
became Brezhnev's boss. This unique arrangement would soon bear
the fruit of political conspiracy.

For now Brezhnev's job was simply to project the image of
continuity and unity of the collective political succession among the
military. Increased ideological vigilance, discipline of personnel and
rapid growth of Party organizations and political academies in the
armed forces in the interregnum reflected the intention of the leadership to reassert the principle of Party control. According to the official Soviet military encyclopedia, "Brezhnev directed the work of
increasing the ideological consciousness of military personnel and
strengthening these Party organizations."[8] Attention to his official
duties, however, was soon turned elsewhere — namely, Beria.

With Stalin dead, Lavrentiy Beria, the man guilty of brutal
violence against Soviet soldiers and citizens and a reign of terror
against Ukrainian and Russian peasants, succeeded in making a
remarkable comeback from his weakened position in the last months
of Stalin's rule. According to Khrushchev, Malenkov "fell under the
complete influence of Beria and acted as his shadow and tool."[9]
Now certainly in close alliance with Malenkov, Beria moved into the
number two position in the reorganized Party Presidium and became
Malenkov's deputy in the government. Beria arrested the comman-
dants of the Moscow city garrison and Kremlin guards and made the
Political leadership dependent upon his secret police (MVD) troops for
protection. He declared the doctors' plot a hoax designed to discredit
the police (for failing to discover the "conspiracy" in time). He began
to also place his men back in positions of power in the republics, to
make his secret police independent of the Party, and to put
colleagues in the Party leadership under around-the-clock surveillance. Beria was so successful in reinforcing his power that by the
summer of 1953, it appeared that he was angling to seize the reigns of
power by force if necessary.

The famous coup against the MVD chief on June 26, consum-
mating weeks of careful planning and coordination between Party
and military leaders, however, put a stop to that scheme. The coup
was the first major event of the post-Stalin regime to have a far-
reaching impact on the political scene, especially on the matter of
Party leadership succession. While Beria's removal benefited the entire Party leadership except for Malenkov, who lost an ally, it served
Khrushchev's ends most.

Khrushchev's role as the chief engineer of the coup and even executioner of Beria has been well documented.[10]   Khrushchev later testified that the Party Presidium had been left with no choice but to liquidate Beria, but first they had to trap him, to catch him when he was vulnerable and without his bodyguards. Toward the end of June 1953, a phoney meeting of the Presidium was staged for that purpose.

Khrushchev gave several conflicting versions of how Beria died. He claimed to have personally shot him ("Beria came into the conference room one day without his bodyguard and I shot him"[11]), though it was also rumored that Beria had been strangled by his colleagues with the help of the Red Army generals. Colonel Oleg Penkovsky related that "Beria was shot in the basement of the Moscow Military District Headquarters building. Beria's corpse was soaked with gasoline and burned there in the cellar."[12]

However Beria died, the phenomenal plot against him had required careful coordination with top military leaders to prevent an armed counter coup by loyal elements of Beria's secret police. That delicate job was Brezhnev's. He was under surveillance too, anyone who entered the Kremlin was. But since Brezhnev's official duties allowed him free access to both the Ministry of Defense and Party headquarters his comings and goings were not suspect. He was able to orchestrate things on the military side of the house without arousing suspicion.

Although Khrushchev never publicly disclosed Brezhnev's role, Brezhnev's public activities following Beria's fall indicate his involvement in the conspiracy against the police chief. Brezhnev had remained totally removed from public view since March 7. His name appeared nowhere in the Party or military press. Then immediately after Beria was killed he became strangely visible again: on August 10 he opened the annual Air Force Day celebrations[13]; on August 21 and 22 he attended diplomatic receptions for East German representatives visiting Moscow[14]; on August 23 he attended the diplomatic gathering of M. Dalya, Romania's ambassador to the Soviet Union[15]; on September 8 he signed the obituary of V. Vershinin, a prominent general lieutenant of the tank corps[16] and on September 13 he opened Tank Day.[17] Nearly all of these activities were in one way or another related to events surrounding the coup.

Because they possessed the only force that could successfully counter Beria's police force should it come to a showdown, the armed forces were given a key role in Beria's removal. They were grateful.

The fact that Brezhnev opened Air Force Day and Tank Day celebrations would even under normal circumstances have been unusual since this task is reserved for high ranking professional — not political — officers associated with the services concerned. But in 1953, Brezhnev had the honor of opening both festivities.

The celebrations were especially fitting that year because both air and tank forces could claim some credit for the removal of Beria. Besides Brezhnev the principal speaker at Air Force Day celebrations was General-Colonel Pavel Zhigarev, commander-in-chief of the Soviet Air Force, who had assured the support of the Air Force in the coup. Earlier in the year Beria had arrested the young General Vasiliy Stalin, Air Force commander-in-chief of the Moscow Military District, on charges of drunkeness for which he was sentenced to eight years' imprisonment. The Air Force may have had some interest in revenge.

The "visit" to Moscow by German Democratic Republic Party and state representatives on July 21 to "conclude new political and economic agreements" was also timely. Six weeks earlier East Berlin had been rocked by strikes and riots in all major industrial centers. To the international embarrassment of the Soviet Union, Soviet troops and tanks had to be brought in to restore order. These events are generally believed to have precipitated the arrest of Beria ten days later.

It seems that Beria had long controlled the East German Socialist Unity Party and in a bid for power in Moscow began a modest process of "liberalization" in East Germany which got out of hand and resulted in the Party's loss of control over the population. A later explanation claimed that the trouble had been caused by "the adventure of foreign hirelings and Western agents in Berlin," with Beria acting as their principal.[18] Consequently, he was charged with being a British agent, and East German Communists were credited with having exposed the "capitalist plot."

It was therefore appropriate that those who had effected Beria's downfall should attend the reception on August 21 to show Soviet appreciation for East Germany's role in exposing Beria. At the reception given by the German ambassador the following evening Brezhnev and the others were no doubt warmly thanked for delivering East Germany from the hands of the "filthy bourgeois agent and traitor Beria."

Brezhnev's "diplomatic" schedule was extremely heavy that week. He attended the Romanian reception celebrating the ninth year of Romania's independence won by the Red Soviet Army. His attendance there can only be explained by the purge of Beria's large security apparatus in Romania being carried out under the direction of the Main Political Administration.

Brezhnev's signature on the obituary of General Vershinin is also unusual, except perhaps in the context of Brezhnev's wartime association with the ground forces and in particular their shared role in the Beria coup. It is customary for a Soviet official to sign the obituary of a deceased comrade only if they have had a close working relationship. While Brezhnev's association with General Vershinin can only be traced to the coup, Brezhnev's affiliation with other military figures instrumental in Beria's removal such as Malinovskiy and Moskalenko dated back to the Second World War.

Beria's execution did not end Brezhnev's involvement in the affair. He took an active role in the subsequent purge of the police apparatus. The Main Political Administration staged mass meetings designed to whip up even greater hostility toward Beria in the military districts. In many instances the military took direct control of Party organizations controlled by Beria's protégés. In Georgia, for example, Khrushchev arranged to have Vasiliy Mzhavanadze, a Khrushchev supporter and an old army buddy, made the Party Secretary.

With Beria gone, the challenge to Malenkov could now be effectively mounted. The role of the armed forces in the Beria affair elevated the military in the Soviet hierarchy and compelled the Party leaders to recognize its increased importance as a pillar of support for the regime.[19] Brezhnev was early to recognize this factor and in the second half of 1953, he anxiously exploited this and the ill-feeling in the military caused by Malenkov's introduction that August of new economic policies.

Malenkov sought to court the Soviet people by promising more food, lower prices and higher wages, and a better standard of living. His "new course" presented to the Supreme Soviet in early August 1953 called for a change in priorities to accommodate development of food and light industries at the expense of heavy industry and ultimately armaments. This naturally aroused the anger of the military and in that Khrushchev and Brezhnev saw an opportunity to rally forces against Malenkov. Brezhnev quickly let his colleagues in the military know that Khrushchev was the champion of their needs and during 1953 he campaigned to rally the military's support for Khrushchev.

Brezhnev earned a reputation as a spokesman for military interests and as a strong advocate of arms development. The latter was particularly timely in 1953 because the Soviet Union had just acquired the hydrogen bomb. Those in the Party like **Malenkov** advocating reduced military spending to allow for development of consumer goods argued that the United States would not launch a nuclear strike against the Soviet Union because the risk of destruction for both countries was simply too great. The military, on the contrary, argued that the development of new strategic systems was especially important. Barely three years later, when production of Soviet nuclear armed ballistic missiles got underway, Brezhnev became Party manager of the project which resulted in the successful flight of Sputnik in 1957 and the development of the Soviet Strategic Rocket Forces.

As Brezhnev purged the MVD and rallied military support for Khrushchev, his benefactor packed regional Party organizations with followers and finalized the plans for a strategic offensive against Malenkov. A major part of that offensive was to be played out by Brezhnev over the next three years in the hitherto virgin lands of Kazakhstan.

XI

The Struggle Continued from the Provinces

There is no moral code ... to restrain the aspirants to the succession from framing each other and killing each other. In so far as they follow the precedents bequeathed to them, and in so far as they follow the real inner laws of the total state, that is precisely what they will have to do. —Bertram Wolfe, *Ideology in Power.*

KHRUSHCHEV WAS A GAMBLER. In February 1954, he emerged from the shadows and introduced a scheme to plow and cultivate an area in the semiarid steppes of Kazakhstan and Siberia equivalent to the total crop-producing regions of Great Britian, France and Spain. It was a bold and risky undertaking designed to provide a quick solution to the country's grain shortage and to cut the ground out from under Malenkov.

The so-called "Virgin Lands Program" was to be the instrument through which Khrushchev secretly planned to defeat Malenkov and put himself fully at the helm of the Soviet Union as Stalin's heir. His protégé Brezhnev would help by directing a major part of the cultivation and by collaborating in the systematic attacks on Malenkov and his Party and government subordinates for administrative incompetence and even sabotage during the course of the cultivation.

A tornado of controversy surrounded the project which was approved at the Party's February plenum. Malenkov, officially cut off from the Party apparatus at this juncture and using the government as his power base, would have nothing to do with it for it contrasted with his more cautious suggestion of making farming of existing agricultural land more intensive through the judicious use of peasant incentives. He rallied Molotov, Kaganovich and others whom Khrushchev later dubbed the "anti-Party" group to oppose the scheme. They became a major obstacle to its proper implementation and to hear Khrushchev and Brezhnev tell it, they purposely attempted to wreck the project. They certainly succeeded in blocking

Khrushchev's attempt in February 1954 to install Brezhnev in the key administrative position as Party Secretary of the Kazakh Republic.

Khrushchev naturally wanted a free hand in running the virgin lands program, particularly in Kazakhstan. Over half of the land to be cultivated was in the Kazakh Republic and the existing Party leadership there would not do. They were anything but enthusiastic about plowing up the Republic and when they recommended a slow rate of cultivation for Kazakhstan, Khrushchev drew the conclusion that they were either lazy or on Malenkov's side. Only by appointing Brezhnev Party Secretary of the Republic would Khrushchev have the kind of leadership and management needed to make the scheme he was betting his life on pay off.

Yet he was unable to directly appoint his protégé while Malenkov continued to exercise control over the levers regulating key agricultural appointments. Khrushchev tried, but it was no use working through regular channels. In the end he took the matter to the Party Presidium.

The fight there was bound to be tough. Earlier he had appealed to the larger Central Committee over the opposition of the Party Presidium to get the virgin lands program approved. Now, however, he had no recourse to the larger body. After all, the proposed appointment was a cadre and not a policy matter.

Khrushchev pursued the matter doggedly in the face of determined opposition. Party leaders resented the tricky way he had gone about getting the virgin lands scheme passed and now saw a way to get even. In addition, in view of the circumstances under which Brezhnev was removed from the Party leadership eighteen months earlier and his role in Beria's murder, personal animosity toward Brezhnev may have also been a factor in the opposition.

Malenkov led the opposition in the nine-member Presidium. He dragged out Brezhnev's past agricultural failures in Zaporozhye to damage him. Khrushchev countered by presenting his client's excellent record in Dnepropetrovsk and, more importantly, in Moldavia, but it did little good. The Presidium would simply not listen.

Then Malenkov played his hand. He insisted that his own protégé, Ponomarenko, be appointed Party Secretary of the Kazakh Republic. If by choosing Ponomarenko Malenkov had it in mind to sabotage the program then his choice was a good one. Ponomarenko not only lacked the necessary savvy and managerial expertise, he was totally uninspired by the project. He called the work in the republic "so much humbug."[1] The pro-Malenkov Presidium nevertheless saw fit to pick him over Brezhnev.

Still, Khrushchev could not be completely ignored — he was after all Party head. So the Presidium sued for a "negotiated settlement," with the result that Brezhnev was made Ponomarenko's deputy. On February 8 the Kazakh Republic Party newspaper, *Kazakhstanskaya Pravda*, hinted at the appointments of this most unlikely pair by announcing that a collective of Alma-Ata workers had nominated them to stand for election to the Soviet of Nationalities chamber in the U.S.S.R. Supreme Soviet. Three days later their appointments were made official.

This was the second time in recent months that Brezhnev lost out in maneuvering and there would be scores to settle. Moreover the Presidium had put him in an invidious position: as the agricultural expert of the team, he bore the brunt of the responsibility for ensuring the success of the new lands cultivation in the republic. His, not Ponomarenko's, head would roll should it fail. How could he hope to get the job done while Ponomarenko controlled all the requisite levers of power in the republic, would probably fail to back him on important decisions, and probably even work against him on principle? Ponomarenko was an obstacle that would have to be removed.

Thus, when these two enemies took their respective posts in early 1954, the issues were already defined and the arena of conflict drawn. And they were enemies, despite Brezhnev's clouded recollection of Ponomarenko 25 years later as an "able and dependable" comrade.[2] Public confrontation occurred within weeks of their arrival in the republic. The occasion was the celebration in Alma-Ata marking their nominations to the Supreme Soviet. Ponomarenko spoke first, Brezhnev second.

Ponomarenko downplayed the importance of the virgin lands project for the country's agricultural production, saying that it held only limited importance. No amount of prodding could get him to fire inspiration for the program. He chose instead to emphasize the familiar Malenkov theme of improving the country's living standard through the development of light industry and increased production of consumer goods.

This cut Brezhnev to the quick. When his turn came he stepped up on the podium and blasted Ponomarenko for his economic priorities. He stressed the necessity of a strong grain-based agricultural economy as the *real* first step in raising people's living

standards. He pointedly reminded Ponomarenko that despite
Malenkov's claim that the country had a sufficient supply of grain,
the Party and the people had determined otherwise.

Brezhnev lavishly praised the Party's decision to cultivate new
land in Kazakhstan, calling it a "lofty and noble" task. In fact, he
elevated it to the level of a "grand national venture" that "is inspiring
and rallying the patriots of our motherland."[3] The latter remark was
meant above all to cast aspersions on those who displayed any less
enthusiasm for virgin lands cultivation than Brezhnev.

Conflict between Brezhnev and Ponomarenko over the next
15 months was publicly visible. One had only to read the
newspapers. In three public appearances of the Kazakh Party leadership in May, September during the Third Writers' Conference, and in
October at the anniversary celebration of the October Revolution,
the two leaders stood physically apart symbolizing their differences.

There were also the systematic attacks on Ponomarenko in
the national press. Brezhnev's revelations of incompetence on the
part of the republic's *oblast* and *rayon* Party committees in directing
the MTS and collective farms were particularly damaging to
Ponomarenko since the Party in September 1953 had transferred
responsibility for the daily managment of these two institutions to
local Party secretaries. Brezhnev earnestly undermined his "boss" in
Kazakhstan, ensuring that Ponomarenko was unmistakenly identified as belonging to that force working to sabotage virgin lands
cultivation by purposely neglecting the means of socialist
agriculture.[4] Ponomarenko fought back, but Brezhnev, having
assumed the offensive, kept at it.

Brezhnev simultaneously plotted to destroy Malenkov's
governmental machinery in Kazakhstan. He confronted the various
ministries in the republic with accusations of incompetence and ob-
structionism to the virgin lands program in a three-pronged strategy
designed to strip the ministries of their economic prerogatives, particularly in agriculture, give him total control over the republic, and,
ultimately, bring down the Malenkov government.

Malenkov regarded the big corporation-like state farms, as
opposed to the collective farms, as "grossly inefficient." Consequently he tried "in every way to hinder the formation of new *sovkhozy*."[5]
Khrushchev and Brezhnev, however, saw in them a major means to
extend virgin lands cultivation since they could be staffed by young
single workers who could be prevailed upon to endure extremely
primitive living conditions in the remote areas of the country.

Brezhnev's starry-eyed vision of adventurous young people forging a whole new frontier, farming the land and building new settlements surrounded by golden fields of grain was a foolish notion to Malenkov. He knew better.

Studies had shown the *sovkhozy* to be extremely costly to run, but Brezhnev claimed that "their economies are obvious as they produce cheaper goods and agricultural produce" than the collective farms. At the Nineteenth Party Congress Malenkov had labeled the state farms the "chief cause of the country's agricultural ills," but Brezhnev hailed them as the answer to those ills and to the future demands that would be placed on agriculture by the country's rapidly growing population.

When Malenkov continued to harp on the inefficiency of the state farms, Brezhnev reminded him to turn to Lenin for guidance: "The Party has always been vitally interested in the *sovkhoz* system. On the second day after the October socialist revolution, the Second All-Russian Congress of Soviets treated the question of the creation of Soviet farms in the Decree of the land. The *sovkhozy* were created from the original idea of the great Lenin as exemplary state enterprises in agriculture."

Malenkov was not impressed. Brezhnev again evoked the authority of Lenin in campaigning for equipment for his *sovkhozy* as well as to demonstrate the ideological error of Saburov and others in the State Planning Commission who, upon Malenkov's secret instructions, refused to allocate funds and resources for much needed tractors and other equipment. Citing Lenin's collected works, Brezhnev insisted that: "Vladimir Ilyich considered the furnishing of the *sovkhozy* with the most advanced technology as an important step in order to, in large scale farms, produce better, cheaper and more than before."

Malenkov could not be swayed, but the Central Committee was. They approved a plan in which by 1960 state farm land would constitute nearly half of the land under cultivation and account for nearly half of the grain crop. This was a good start, but looking way beyond that Brezhnev predicted greater things for these "seeds of the future" whose production in his view "represents the only rational approach to socialist agriculture."

In was this kind of thinking that did serious damage to the collective farms throughout the country in the mid 1950s, since many of them were converted into large-scale state farm enterprises. Brezhnev was an early advocate of this policy, which Khrushchev sponsored, though expediently joined the opposition against the policy when it became an issue in the ouster of Khrushchev in 1964. When Brezhnev became Party head he repealed the conversions policy on grounds that both farm systems "have an important and complementary place in socialist agriculture."[6]

But all this was in the future. In 1954 through 1956 Brezhnev established 134 new state farms and rejuvenated or enlarged another 233 existing farms in Kazakhstan. In March 1955, he declared "our *sovkhozy* are indeed advanced socialist enterprises (just as Lenin had envisaged) and play the principal role in increasing production." Moreover, he proffered his farms as proof that Malenkov had been wrong all along and that the state farm was superior to the collective farm for the development of socialist agriculture.

Brezhnev's state farms did produce. Figures he presented to the Twentieth Party Congress showed that Kazakhstan would provide two-thirds of the nation's grain supply for 1956. But the cost of production would be extremely high, as Malekov predicted. In fact, a report published a few months before the Congress met showed that while excellent production gains were made in Kazakhstan in 1954, only one-third of the *sovkhozy* produced above cost, and in the second year of the program the overall percentage of "profitable" farms actually declined.

How did Brezhnev account for the huge expenditures? He blamed them on mismanagement of the farms by the Ministry of Sovkhozy and other ministries responsible for state farm operations: "Unprofitability is unmistakably the result of unsatisfactory management of the *sovkhozy*, especially on the part of the ministries which should look into the present conditions and set about solving them."

This kind of railing became a familiar Brezhnev theme in the months preceding Malenkov's ouster from the government. Even after Malenkov was stripped of his premiership in February 1955, Brezhnev continued to make political capital out of it. In a speech in early March, for example, he expressed dismay at the government's failure to make an attempt to improve the management situation in the state farms. "Why hasn't the ministry bothered to look into the present conditions and solve the principal problems?" Brezhnev asked. This line of argument was carefully calculated to imply that Malenkov continued to manipulate the government through his loyal administrators. Otherwise, Brezhnev suggested, "the problem may be beyond the competence of the ministry to handle." In any case, he proposed that "the ministry turn to the local Party and Soviet organizations for help."

Its head was fired instead. A.I. Kozlov, long associated with Malenkov as chief of the Central Committee's agricultural section, had been named Minister of Agriculture and Procurement in 1953 and subsequently shifted to the Ministry of Sovkhozy. Brezhnev got tremendous satisfaction out of seeing this Malenkov administrator reduced to the menial status of director of the Khristovskiy State Farm in northern Kazakhstan and made subordinate to him in 1955.

Brezhnev's attacks on the Ministry of Sovkhozy and his upbraiding of local Party officials for failing to take a more aggressive role in the daily management of local economic affairs also bolstered the policy of decentralized agriculture that Khrushchev was promoting. Khrushchev, having long seen the technically-trained managerial Party member as having great practical value (a factor in Brezhnev's catching his eye in the early years), began to promote these Party members over the ideological element of the Party as a means to realize his vision of transforming every local Party organization into a technically functional unit capable of handling its own agricultural affairs as distinct from simply disseminating abstract doctrine.

In this regard, Brezhnev consistently lashed out at Ponomarenko for laxity in implementing the September 1953 Party plenum order decentralizing agricultural management. Brezhnev described the management situation in the Republic's collective farms as "appalling": Ponomarenko had too long tolerated poor placement and supervision of collective farm management by his district Party secretaries. "Now that the threads of political and economic leadership are in our hands, the demands on us are simply too great to let such a situation continue," Brezhnev concluded.

Brezhnev attempted to establish absolute control over the Republic's state farms. The September 1953 plenum provided for the strengthening of Party organizations in the state farms in order to intensify their role in developing agriculture," but did not give the Party direct responsibility for management. Nevertheless, using the precedent set for management of the collective farms and the MTS, Brezhnev, with Khrushchev's blessing, implored district Party secretaries to "deal with the *sovkhozy* in a concrete manner on a daily basis."

The Party had the right to intervene in the management of state-run enterprises in emergencies. Brezhnev argued that ministerial mismanagement of some state farms was so bad that it justified the immediate exercise of the Party's prerogative. He told district Party secretaries that "responsibility for the state of affairs in the *sovkhozy* is borne by the Central Committee of the Kazakh Communist Party and its personnel and *we must act accordingly*." But government administrators resisted such encroachment and local Party secretaries were reluctant to act because they were unsure just how far they could go as long as Malenkov was still head of the government. That was soon fixed.

Back in Moscow the battle raged on. That summer, Malenkov lost all control over Khrushchev, who won Party approval for an extension of the virgin lands cultivation. In December, Abakumov, Malenkov's collaborator in the murder of Zhdanov's colleagues in 1948, was brought to trial and executed. Malenkov's power in the government steadily weakened until on February 8, 1955, Malenkov resigned as Premier.

In the spring of 1955, Khrushchev cautiously tried for Ponomarenko's removal, treading lightly to avoid unnecessary criticism. The ouster was achieved in early May, cloaked in the festivities of the country's May Day celebrations. It was all very hush hush and made without so much as a public announcement. However, the fact that a smiling Brezhnev stood next to Ponomarenko during the 1955 May Day parade review in Alma-Ata should have tipped off the politically astute. Ponomarenko simply disappeared after that. People speculated that he had fallen into the clutches of the secret police, but on May 11 the newspaper reported his presence in Poland. Stripped of political power he became the Soviet ambassador to Warsaw.

Brezhnev fully assumed the helm in Kazakhstan, while in Moscow, Khrushchev, free almost to do what he pleased, took one more step in decentralizing agriculture. A new agricultural Planning Order was passed by a Central Committee plenum in March 1955. The Order, proposed by Khrushchev as early as January 1954, but stymied while Malenkov was head of the government, decentralized agricultural planning to the extent that the *kolkhozy* and *sovkhozy* were given a large degree of independence in determining local production.[7]

In one case Kazakhstan was specifically cited in the Order issued on March 9 for failing to exploit local possibilities for breeding fine and medium wool sheep. Brezhnev blamed the government. He gave a convincing display of disdain for bureaucratic red tape, standardized methods, and the government bureaucrat who lacked initiative, obstructed progress and actually symbolized the opposite political camp.

Later on when he became Party chief, he reversed the policy of decentralized agriculture though he retained some measure of decentralized planning. In fact, for a while Brezhnev even appeared willing to go further than Khrushchev to make the farms "free in fact, not just in words" but he never kept his promise. The primary advantage of decentralized planning for him in 1955 was that it betokened the urgency for competent authority—i.e., greater Party authority—in the state farms, and it enabled him to implement a number of pet projects that had hitherto been bogged down in bureaucratic red tape.

One such project was the establishment of vineyards. Brezhnev had actually proposed the venture in June 1954, based on his experience with wine production in Moldavia. The idea, however, floundered in the Ministry of Agriculture until the Planning Order was passed. Consequently, 1955 brought a marked expansion of vineyards in southern Kazakhstan and the establishment of related industries, which was a start on Brezhnev's boast to turn Kazakhstan into the "Soviet Union's greatest eastern industrial area." He established the basis for such industrialization, but he was unsuccessful in making any substantial gains in industrializing the republic before 1956.

Throughout 1954 and after Malenkov's departure from the government Brezhnev successfully moved in unison with Khrushchev to increase the authority of the Party apparatus and strip the government of its administrative and economic prerogatives.

Judging by the charges later brought against Malenkov and other members of the anti-Party group, they put up determined opposition to these encroachments and to the virgin lands program in particular. Malenkov was charged with obstructing state farm organization by delaying the establishment of farms Brezhnev wanted. Kaganovich was accused of pressuring Gosplan, the central government planning office, to claim that it had neither the money nor resources for the virgin lands program, and Saburov's state planning committee allegedly hindered the flow of machinery and supplies to Kazakhstan.

"The anti-party group zealously opposed the gigantic task of developing the virgin lands," Brezhnev proclaimed in his keynote speech on Lenin's birthday in 1959. Referring to Molotov and

Kaganovich specifically, Brezhnev asserted that these "so-called agricultural experts strongly resisted by various means the development of the virgin lands. But their opposition," Brezhnev concluded, "was successfully resolved and the project became an outstanding feat on the part of the entire Soviet people and our Party."

Just how successful was Brezhnev in producing? Agricultural production in Kazakhstan at the beginning of 1954 was below prewar levels, but by the end of the year, and despite Ponomarenko, Kazakhstan had nearly doubled the original first-year cultivation estimate for the republic and thanks to good weather, an excellent harvest was gathered. Brezhnev told the February 1955 session of the Supreme Soviet that almost half of the grain scheduled for delivery to the state over a three-year period was supplied in 1954 alone.

This remarkable progress was a tribute to Brezhnev. It also validated, along with results reached elsewhere, the economy of the virgin lands program. Brezhnev belabored this very point at the February Supreme Soviet. He attributed a measured rise in the country's standard of living and reduction in the cost of grain production in 1954 to the large scale cultivation of new lands. Data which he presented to the Supreme Soviet showed that Kazakhstan had succeeded in cutting its grain production costs by half and even more in some *sovkhozy* of superior efficiency. Brezhnev argued that even greater savings could be achieved through expansion of the virgin lands projects and corresponding extension of the *sovkhoz* system. This good news disproved Malenkov's earlier judgment that the program was adventurous and financially unsound, and it actually contributed to his downfall from the government.

At the February Supreme Soviet session Brezhnev also promised to triple the area sown in 1954 and produce a record-breaking grain harvest for 1955. He doubled the pace of construction and cultivation when he returned to Kazakhstan. But that summer what Malenkov and Molotov had predicted and Khrushchev and Brezhnev feared the most happened: drought enveloped all of the virgin lands.

The drought shook the confidence of Khrushchev's supporters. In August Brezhnev alluded to the fact that "there are those who are now casting aspersions on the whole vigin lands project by pointing to the unfavorable weather conditions." But he continued to defend the program and appealed to the critics to "look to the future and forget momentary disappointments." Khrushchev defended the program on the basis of Brezhnev's cost data, arguing that "even if these regions rendered two good crops in a five year period the effort would still be worth while because of the relatively low cost of large scale grain production."[8]

In Kazakhstan itself morale was shattered by the lack of rain, and "negative trends" developed among the rank and file of farm workers and the Party. "There are those," Brezhnev grumbled, "who would rather moan than mobilize themselves and others to gather what crop there is." In state farms, managers, frightened by the poor harvest, asked to be allowed to "retire." Shortages of basic necessities — especially food and water supplies for the coming winter months — caused panic. Brezhnev underscored the urgency of the situation at the August plenum: "Comrades, we have got to do everything in our power to calm the people and keep the situation under control."

Now the darker side of Brezhnev reemerged. As in Moldavia he threatened, cajoled and punished the faint hearted: "If we have to we will punish severely those *sovkhoz* managers who wish to resign. When it is a question of providing the state with 200 million *poods* of grain we have the right to expect exceptional activity and enthusiasm and *we will get it.*"

Everything hinged on saving as much of the crop as possible. Brezhnev's career was still on the line and the survival of thousands of people in Kazakhstan depended on at least a moderate harvest. He resorted to tried and tested Stalinist tactics, but he also gave the requisite measure of encouragement and promised to "honor the Party's contract with the *kolkhozy* to provide them with at least one kilogram of grain per day, and to continue to pay the state farm workers a good wage." He also postponed *kolkhoz* loan repayments for one year to allow for winter food and supply purchases.

In the end, Brezhnev gathered a harvest amounting to about 65 percent of the 1954 harvest. The following year was particularly difficult for him. Though Brezhnev failed to triple the amount of land cultivated as he had promised, he did double it, which still surpassed the revised state plans. On that rested his sole claim to success in 1955. At the Twentieth Party Congress he reported: "The republic Party organization has honorably fulfilled the task of developing the virgin lands program: 15.3 million hectares of virgin land were to be cultivated in the republic over a period of two years. In fact, 18 million hectares have been plowed."[9]

But what about the bad harvest in 1955? Brezhnev attempted to mollify the skeptics by predicting plenty of rain and promising a bumper crop in Kazakhstan for 1956. He told the Congress: "The considerable increase in the area of land sown will enable the production of grain to be increased to 1.4 million *poods* this year in the Republic. The wishes of the Party are being fulfilled.... Kazakhstan is becoming one of the most important grain producing regions of the country."[10]

This was exactly what Khrushchev wanted to hear. His fate rested on the 1956 crop. But Kazakhstan received good rains that year and produced a crop fivefold that of 1955. In fact, the crop was the best for the five years of the period 1956 through 1960.

For this great achievement, which compared in magnitude and importance to the rebuilding of the Zaporozhstal Steel Works a decade earlier, Brezhnev received a second Order of Lenin. But more importantly Khrushchev rewarded him with reelection to the CPSU Central Committee, to the Party Presidium (as a candidate member) and to the Secretariat at the Twentieth Party Congress. Brezhnev had personally done more than any other member of Khrushchev's team between 1954 and 1956 to defeat Malenkov in the government, enhance the Party's prestige, consolidate Khrushchev's power and secure his sizeable victory over his opponents.

XII
The Battle Won

*Life, with its great and undefeatable Leninist feeling
for what is new, sweeps from its path everything old,
routine, and ossified and, like a fresh spring wind,
blows it out the wide open window.*

*The Party unanimously and resolutely, ideolog-
ically and politically, routed the contemptible anti-
Party group of plotters and splitters.... Our Party
removed these renegades from the road with the
same ease that a train runs over a splinter.* — L.I.
Brezhnev, 1959, 1961.

THE TWENTIETH PARTY CONGRESS in February 1956 was a very
real victory for Khrushchev and his disciples. Stalin was repudiated,
beginning the process which we in the West came to call "de-
Stalinization:" all of the high Party posts that Brezhnev had held under Stalin were restored to him vindicating his earlier losses; more
Khrushchev men were brought into the Party Presidium; the Party
Secretariat was enlarged with Khrushchev supporters as was the Central Committee; a new bureau of the All-Union Central Committee
for the Russian Soviet Federated Socialist Republic (R.S.F.S.R.) was set
up with Khrushchev as chairman; and a new foreign policy of
peaceful coexistence, revolution without violence, and the aban-
donment of the inevitability of war doctrine, was inaugurated.
But the battle with Malenkov, Molotov and Kaganovich was far
from over. In fact, the toughest round had yet to be fought.

Though Khrushchev emerged in 1956 as Lenin's real heir,
something happened after the Congress to dangerously return his
opponents to the political stage. Two factors were involved: the up-
surge of national democratic and liberalizing forces in Poland and
Hungary in the fall, and Khrushchev's drastic reorganization of the
Soviet economic administration early in the new year.

People, particularly those enslaved in Eastern Europe, misunderstood Khrushchev's denunciation of Stalin. His secret speech on
Stalin at the Party Congress was instantly leaked to the satellites
where the masses concluded that Khrushchev authorized them to
openly denounce their bosses. All the satellite countries were ruled

by little Stalinists who had hanged most of their antagonists, except in Poland and Hungary where important Communists, survivors of Stalin's purge, were now prepared to begin liberalization.

Inspired by the wake of cynicism de-Stalinization created, on June 28, 1956, factory workers in Poznan, Poland rioted in protest of the existing police regime and atrocious working and living conditions. Wladyslaw Gomulka, a moderate Communist and the former General Secretary of the Polish Workers' Party who had been arrested and imprisoned by Stalin's henchmen, saw in the "popular movement" an opportunity to do away with his captors, size power, and establish a degree of independence from Moscow hitherto unknown to Poland. Exploiting the country's anti-Stalinist sentiment, he made a successful bid to take control of the Polish United Workers' Party.*

By fall the situation had got completely out of hand. Elements in Warsaw were now claiming that only "democratization" of the country could quell the internal disorder. This was something Khrushchev had not counted on. Moreover, he was blamed for the trouble not only in Poland, but in Hungary too where similiar events were already taking place. Molotov, who opposed the "liberal line," particularly Khrushchev's attack on Stalin and rapproachement with Marshal Tito's Yugoslavia, now pointed an accusing finger at Khrushchev for the political repercussions that his policies were causing. By September, Khrushchev was in immediate danger from the Stalinist faction in the Presidium.

Khrushchev's disciples now assumed the defensive. Brezhnev defended him tooth and nail. Only political expediency could explain labeling Stalin a criminal and a mentally deranged tyrant responsible for the murder of a large number of people. Brezhnev may have personally thought Khrushchev's denunciation unwise, even harmful to the cause of Communism in the long run. But being a practical politician, he was willing to go along with it if Khrushchev deemed it necessary. He did not like what he saw in Poland and elsewhere anymore than Khrushchev's accusers, or Khrushchev for that matter, but he jumped to defend Khrushchev against the storm created by striking down Stalin.

Still, he knew that his boss would have to act fast to eliminate the explosive situation in the satellites. Brezhnev watched anxiously as Khrushchev, Malenkov, Molotov and Kaganovich rushed to War-

*In 1948 the Polish Workers' Party and Polish Socialist Party were united to form the Polish United Workers' Party, sometimes simply referred to as the Polish Communist Party.

saw in early October to stop the re-election of Gomulka as Communist Party head of Poland. Breathing fire, Khrushchev threatened Gomulka with the use of Soviet warships and tanks. But Gomulka, backed by the people of Poland who openly declared their determination to fight the Russians, stood firm. Khrushchev was forced to back down.

When news of Gomulka's bloodless victory reached Hungary where volatile conditions indicated a more violent and costly upheaval because of long-standing grievances against the Soviet regime, students demonstrated in support of Gomulka's regime. Mátyás Rákosi, infamously known as Hungary's "bald-headed murderer," had become discredited as head of the Hungarian Communist Party, forcing Moscow to appoint Ernő Gerő, his faithful henchman, in his place. Nevertheless, public anti-Stalin sentiment continued to build and was given an outlet in student demonstrations in late October. When the demonstrations turned into riots and the police fired into the crowds all hell broke loose.

Khrushchev tried to patch up the situation as best he could. Negotiations proved fruitless. In October 1956, in a final effort to diffuse the explosive situation in Hungary, Brezhnev, along with Bulganin, Madame Yekaterina Furtseva, Aleksey Kirichenko, Voroshilov, and others accompanied Khrushchev to the Adriatic and Black Sea coasts to engage Tito's help. On November 16 the Yugoslav newspaper *Borba* reported their meeting with Ernő Gerő. A few days later, Soviet troops were ordered into Hungary.

We know from the *Borba* report that Brezhnev played a role in the negotiations. But in November 1956, did he vote to send Soviet troops to savagely put down the popular revolt in Hungary?

Provided that the decision to send troops was reached by a majority of voting Party Presidium members in formal balloting, then Brezhnev could not have participated. He lacked voting status as a candidate member of the Presidium.

It was Brezhnev's job as the secretary responsible for military affairs that made him eligible to vote on the matter. The decision to use Soviet troops in Hungary was probably reached in the Higher Military Council first. The Council was made up of the top Soviet political and military leaders and functioned as the highest security policy-making body in the U.S.S.R., responsible for deciding not only matters of military construction but also security matters involving the use of the Soviet Armed Forces. If the Council then was run anything like its successor, the Defense Council, is today, decisions reached in that body were final and only pro-forma presented to the Presidium for ratification.

Brezhnev later hinted that he had voted to restore socialist order by military means: "Thanks to the [military] aid of the Soviet Union ... the forces of counterrevolution were routed." Hungary, he alleged, had been part of a larger "imperialist conspiracy" aimed at "launching an open offensive against all socialist countries" in a desperate attempt to "stop further disintegration of the imperialist colonial system," namely in the Middle East.

Citing the conflict in Egypt in 1956 as a specific example of "Anglo-French reactionism" and a manifestation of an imperialist plot to "break up the process of largescale international cooperation between states," Brezhnev rationalized that Hungary had been chosen as the launching pad for the conspiracy because that country was "politically vulnerable." The "imperialists' aim," he declared, "was to provoke a counterrevolutionary rebellion in Hungary, overthrow the people's regime, destroy the socialist gains of the Hungarian working people, and establish a fascist regime in Hungary, thereby creating a hotbed for a new war in Europe."[1]

But there was never a conspiracy. Brezhnev collaborated in sending 2,500 tanks and 100,000 Soviet soldiers to Hungary to smash what another would call a "rising of the workers against exploitation, of the intellectuals against thought control, and of the whole nation against Soviet imperialism."[2]

Another man in the Gomulka mold was the moderate Communist Imre Nagy, once Hungary's Prime Minister, who had assumed the reigns of the freedom struggle in Hungary, declared an end to the system of one-Party rule in the country, announced that Hungary would be withdrawing from the Warsaw Pact, proclaimed the neutrality of Hungary and asked the United Nations for protection. But no one came to Hungary's aid. "We in Moscow felt as if we were sitting on a powderkeg," Colonel Oleg Penkovsky later wrote. "But what did the West do? Nothing. This gave Khrushchev confidence and he began to scream: 'I was right.'"[3]

Twelve years later Brezhnev would send Soviet troops into Czechoslovakia to crush a second so-called "imperialist-inspired counterrevolution." Just as Khrushchev's annexation of Poland had served as Brezhnev's example in Transcarpathia in 1944, so Hungary in 1957 would serve as Brezhnev's model in 1968.

The brawl over the direction of the national economy was the final catalyst sparking a bold move by Malenkov, Molotov and

Kaganovich in June 1957 to oust Khrushchev and his disciples from the Party leadership.

Having returned to the stage, in December 1956 the powerful coalition of the old Stalinists Molotov and Kaganovich along with Malenkov and his economists and technocrats put on their own performance. In fact, theirs was the feature act. At the December Party plenum they discussed at length the issue of economic reorganization with the result that the State Economic Commission was reorganized.

In that reorganization Malenkov's protégé Pervukhin became chairman of the Commission which had been created in May 1955 to deal with short-term economic planning. Almost all of the first deputy chairmen and deputy chairmen of the Council of Ministers were transferred to the Commission, giving it considerable strength. This downgraded Gosplan, which had previously been responsible for long-term economic planning, though in 1955 Khrushchev had given republic governments increased authority to make detailed plans and fix production targets for their own areas. The lastest reorganization was in the interest of the state and Malenkov's economic groups and strengthened the centralized planning mechanism that Khrushchev and Brezhnev had been fighting.

The Khrushchevites reacted swiftly. They called a Party plenum for February. Brezhnev campaigned hard in the provinces in early January, enlisting the help of rank and file Central Committee members to overturn the opposition's December victory. Aristov, Nikolay Belyayev and Madame Furtseva campaigned too, while Khrushchev himself made a nationwide trip paying personal visits to Central Committee members and calling in debts from many local leaders who, like Brezhnev, owed their political fortunes to Khrushchev.

Rallying support to overturn the recentralized economic structure was the real purpose of Brezhnev's visit to Omsk in late January—though the official occasion was to award the *oblast* the Order of Lenin for success in virgin lands reclamation. Brezhnev made an impassioned speech which was broadcast over national radio on January 20, and focused on the benefits of localized planning and Party management of agriculture. It was very clear what he was up to when he neared the end of his speech and began expanding the concept of localization to the larger economic picture, priming the regional Party leadership and his national listeners for the February plenum.

He appealed to the vested interest of the Party apparatus and to provincial ministerial officials and industrial leaders whose enterprises were bogged down by Moscow's government bureaucracy and red tape. This coordinated effort swung the Central Committee vote. When the committee met in February it proclaimed the need to rearrange the work of the State Economic Commission. The positions of Gosplan and the Commission were again switched, but Gosplan's duties were limited to coordinating the work of the administrative organs in the economic regions.

In early March Khrushchev abolished the central all-union industrial and economic ministries and set up regional Councils of the National Economy called *Sovnarkhozy*. Malenkov, Molotov and others bitterly resisted the change because it entailed a significant readjustment in the balance of political power between the Party and state and economic groups and because they genuinely believed that it would lead to economic anarchy.

Against such attacks Brezhnev defended Khrushchev's point of view as Leninist and decentralization as pursuant to the Leninist line of the Party.[4] Later alluding to the specific intrigues of the anti-Party group against the scheme, Brezhnev said: "Against the background of the successes of the Party's economic policy was the complete political bankruptcy of the anti-party group of Malenkov, Kaganovich, Molotov, and Shepilov who joined them, who tried to divert the Party from the Leninist road."[5]

By June 1957, almost all of the statewide economic organizations had been wiped out. Malenkov's back was to the wall and while Khrushchev was away visiting Finland (returning on June 14) Malenkov and Molotov called an ad-hoc meeting of the Party Presidium, chaired by Malenkov. Khrushchev and, by implication, Brezhnev were charged with "rightest peasant deviation."

According to Michael Lucki, Moscow correspondent in 1957 for the Polish newspaper *Trybuna Ludu*, at least Malenkov and Molotov asserted that the risky virgin lands program had upset the economic balance and detracted from the country's industrial development, thereby affecting the U.S.S.R.'s international position.[6] Matters relating to the "question of opening up the virgin lands" occupied the top of the list of the various charges brought by the anti-Party group.[7] The group demanded not only that Khrushchev resign as Party head, but that Khrushchev's secretaries go with him.[8]

Kirichenko and Mikoyan were the only two voting members of the Presidium who defended Khrushchev at the inquisition.

Suslov, who was away when the proceedings began, evidently remained neutral, but later chaired the Central Committee meeting at which Khrushchev was exonerated and the anti-Party group accused.

Early in the Presidium proceedings Malenkov insisted that a formal vote be taken to decide Khrushchev's fate. A three-day quarrel on the question ensued. According to Guiseppi Boffa, an Italian Communist with high level contacts in the Kremlin, it was during the debate that Khrushchev appealed to the Central Committee.

Brezhnev and other Central Committe members who lived in Moscow responded immediately with a letter to the Presidium stating: "It has become known to us that the Presidium is in constant session. We also know that you are discussing the question of the control over the Central Committee and the leadership of its Secretariat. Questions of such importance to our Party cannot be concealed from members of the plenum of the Central Committe."[9]

Eighteen Central Committee members then rushed to the building where the meeting was being held and demanded that they be admitted into the room and informed of the proceedings. According to the 1959 edition of the official Party history, Brezhnev was one of the 18 who "acted decisively against the anti-Party group and dealt a crushing blow at the latter's violent deviations from the Leninist line of the Party and its Central Committee."[10]

He was not immediately admitted into the Presidium room, nor were any of the Presidium candidate members (six out of seven of whom supported Khrushchev) or other Central Committee members. But Brezhnev, Madame Furtseva, Belyayev and Frol Kozlov nevertheless intervened in the inquisition. According to Boffa, they harangued outside the door until they were allowed a brief audience. Once inside, they invoked Party rules to demonstrate that the Presidium was responsible to the Central Committee and that only the Central Committee plenum could legally decide the fate of Khrushchev and the Party Secretariat.[11]

While the Party Presidium was in session a mad scramble was made to get the right Central Committee members to Moscow. In three days Soviet military aircraft under the command of Marshal Georgiy Zhukov flew in specially selected members (all Khrushchev devotees) from the provinces. Altogether, 309 Central Committee members attended the emergency Party plenum and sat in judgment not of Khrushchev but of the anti-Party group.

Two hundred and fifteen members asked to speak. Brezhnev

laid down a barrage of hard evidence to show that the group had sabotaged Party work in the virgin lands and had undermined the Party's economic reform. The presentations went on. Other speakers accused the group of imposing their policies without democratic debate, and still others showed that Malenkov, Molotov and Kaganovich were personally responsible for the mass slaughter of Party cadres and gross violations of Soviet legality during Stalin's reign. Shepilov was labelled a "political prostitute." The meeting lasted seven days, with time for only 60 speakers — the rest submitted written declarations.

Overwhelmed by the barrage of accusers, the anti-Party group withdrew its demands, admitted its errors, and, adding a farsical note to the whole affair, all except Molotov voted for their own explusion from the Presidium. Brezhnev, Aristov, Belyayev, Madame Furtseva and Marshal Zhukov immediately stepped into fill the vacancies.

The rout of the anti-Party group was complete, or almost complete. Malenkov was subsequently excluded from all government and political life and given a post as head of a hydroelectric power station in Ust-Kamenogorsk in east Kazakhstan — no doubt Brezhnev's idea. Molotov became the Soviet ambassador to Mongolia, and Kaganovich went to the Urals to become the director of a cement factory. Pervukhin and Saburov were silently demoted, but not publicly disgraced until the Twenty-first Party Congress. Bulganin's fall was not final until the autumn of 1958. Shepilov was sent to teach in Tashkent. Saburov eventually became director of a plant in Sisrani.

The June 1957 Party plenum was an overwhelming victory for the Khrushchev Party machine, but the machine was still not satisfied. It now organized a propaganda campaign aimed at public condemnation of the anti-Party group. Brezhnev was very much in on it and so was Madame Furtseva. All of Khrushchev's henchmen traveled around the country addressing Party elements. Madame Furtseva talked to the Moscow Party *aktiv* on July 2; Frol Kozlov spoke in Leningrad on July 4; and Brezhnev addressed numerous military organizations and commands.

On July 5, 1957, *Krasnaya Zvezda* printed a lengthy Brezhnev speech on the "G.M. Malenkov, L.M. Kaganovich and V.M. Molotov anti-party group" given at the headquarters of the Moscow Antiaircraft Defense District. Brezhnev told his audience that the goal of the group had been to split the ranks of the Party, change the

Party line, and restore the Stalinist methods of Party leadership that had been condemned at the Twentieth Party Congress.

Brezhnev made several more speeches condemning the anti-Party group before the extraordinary Twenty-first Party Congress met. He stressed that the policies of the "contemptible" group had been divorced from life and that the group had tried to divide and divert the Party from the Leninist path. But nowhere did he accuse Malenkov or the others of sharing responsibility for Stalin's crimes.

Why Brezhnev did not pursue this line of condemnation too cannot be explained with any degree of certainty. Speculation can be offered. Once he attained full membership in the Presidium he may have thought it unnecessary since the anti-Party group had already been politically discarded. Or he may have had mixed feelings about the Stalinist heritage. He never did condemn Stalin personally and in fact came to portray the "mistakes and errors of the past" as "understandable" in light of the "unbroken ground that had to be trodden."[12]

Later, at the Twenty-first Party Congress held in May 1959, Khrushchev pressed for a public trial of the anti-Party group. An extremist bloc of Leningrad Party members wanted to try Malenkov for murdering Zhdanov's colleagues. A more moderate bloc considered the matter of the anti-Party group closed, and a third group, headed by Mikoyan, remained neutral.

Brezhnev put himself between the first and second group. He brought specific charges against the group for sabotage of the virgin lands program, but he was satisfied that the group had been beaten and discharged from the political leadership. Furtseva, Kirichenko, and most other high ranking leaders who had intervened in the June Presidium proceedings agreed with him. As a result, no further action was taken.[13]

Brezhnev's stand on the group at the Party Congress in 1961 is easier to understand because concrete political issues were involved. These are discussed in detail later. It is enough to say here that Brezhnev adopted a position that mainly benefited himself and exerted a considerable impact on the outcome of the attempt to expel the group from the C.P.S.U. and try them for crimes. But after the rout of the anti-Party group in June 1957, Brezhnev seemed only interested in promoting Khrushchev's rise.

XIII
Khrushchev's Missile Czar

The Party and the people will spare no effort to provide the glorious defenders ... of our motherland with the most technically advanced weapons. We shall implement Lenin's appeals still more stubbornly and resolutely, be always on guard, guard the defense potential of our motherland like the apple of our eye, and multiply the strength of our glorious heroic Soviet armed forces. —L.I. Brezhnev, April 22, 1959.

BETWEEN DEALING WITH HUNGARY and rescuing Khrushchev from the clutches of the anti-Party group, somehow Brezhnev found time for his work in the Party Secretariat. It was important work of a top secret nature. His attendance at the Party *aktiv* meeting of the Moscow Antiaircraft Defense District in July 1957, his address to the Army *aktiv* in the German Democratic Republic in November of that same year, and his participation as the Party representative at the fourth DOSAAF (the Voluntary Society for Assistance to the Army, Air Force and Navy) Congress in 1958, only hinted that his work might be military in nature.

In June 1961, Brezhnev was awarded the title of "Hero of Socialist Labor." According to the official announcement published in *Pravda* on June 21, the award was for "outstanding service in the development of rocket [missile] technology and work in assuring the successful flight of Soviet man into space on the spaceship Vostok."[1]

The true nature of his work wasn't revealed until 1973. Just before Brezhnev's trip to India in November 1973, Moscow Radio announced:

> As [a] secretary of the Central Committee of the Communist Party of the Soviet Union in that period [1957-1960], Leonid Brezhnev was immediately occupied with the organization of diverse jobs in the country which were linked with space exploration. Leonid I. Brezhnev, holding a top Party post in Moscow, gave a great deal of his time and attention to matters devoted to the advancement of Soviet heavy industry and construction and reinforcement of the defense capacity of the country."[2]

Brezhnev's secret role as Party expeditor for the development and deployment of the U.S.S.R.'s first intercontinental ballistic missiles (ICBMS) was revealed not long after that.

Following his consolidation of power in 1956 — and while publicly pursuing disarmament negotiations with the United States — Khrushchev set out to revolutionize Soviet strategic thinking by developing a military force of "intercontinental ballistic rockets armed with nuclear warheads." The military advantages of such a force were obvious: unlike bombers, with the missiles' hypersonic speed they could penetrate any defense; they could be camouflaged and located in hidden sites thus reducing vulnerability to counterattack; and, deployed against an evolving nuclear threat based largely on the periphery of the U.S.S.R., they would be the ultimate deterrent. The political potential of these new weapons was even more promising and Khrushchev knew it. After the dramatic launching of Sputnik I, the world's first artificial satellite, in October 1957, the Soviet tone in international relations altered noticably and threats of atomic retaliation against the European NATO powers became the recurrent theme of Soviet diplomacy.

The Soviet Union had reached atomic warfare capability by 1956. But the really important part of the strategic equation still missing for the U.S.S.R. was "a missile powerful enough to cover intercontinental distances and deliver a nuclear payload with tremendous destructive force." All subsequent work of Soviet missile designers and bureaus was directed at creating such a missile. By 1956-1957 the Soviets had deployed the T1 intermediate range ballistic missile (IRBM). Development of the ICBM in one year was then given top priority.

Leonid Brezhnev was selected to secretly direct the project. That's why his work in the Party Secretariat was kept secret. This was a brand new field for Brezhnev, though he had some very early exposure to Soviet missile technology.

Mikhail Yangel, at one time second only to the father of the Soviet ballistic missile, Sergey Korolyev, in Soviet missile research, was one of the top German specialists brought back to the Soviet Union from Germany with plans, machines, and a large part of the staff responsible for building the German V2 rocket from which the first Soviet missiles were developed. Malenkov's "Special Branch" of the Soviet government had seized the plans and everything related to production of these rockets when Germany was defeated. An obituary of the late Yangel, signed by Brezhnev and published in the

Soviet press in October 1971,[3] praised the scientist for his distinguished contribution to the field of *raketno-kosmicheskoy tekhniki* (missile-space technology). The obituary indicates that Yangel had been a leading figure in this field in the late forties and fifties. He was also long-time head of the "secret" automobile factory in Dnepropetrovsk which bore his name and which, since its construction, has been a major producer of missile components.

Brezhnev, as a trained engineer and Party Secretary of Dnepropetrovsk *oblast*, supervised the early constuction of that important plant. In 1949, orders went out from the Ministry of Heavy Machine Building, the nominal name for the government ministry still responsible for missile development and production, to convert the automobile factory and one or two other factories to the production of required missile components for the Soviet follow-on versions of the V2 rocket.[4] In fact, Brezhnev was probably reporting on the progress of construction when he told the Sixteenth Congress of the Ukrainian Communist Party in 1949, "The *oblast* Party organization is taking all measures to ensure the fulfillment of the plans for building and installation at the motor car plant."[5]

Likewise, Brezhnev was Party Secretary of Kazakhstan when the important "Baykonur" ballistic-missile and satellite-launching complex was built near the rail stop of Tyuratam, in Kazakhstan. This site is the Soviet "Cape Canaveral." The first Soviet ICBM was launched from there as well as Sputnik I and all early manned space flights and communications and military intelligence satellites.

Sometime in 1956, Brezhnev, in conjunction with Dimitry Ustinov and the scientist Mstislav Keldysh, became the nucleus of a top level management board for nuclear ballistic missile development and production. They, along with Brezhnev's old war comrades Rodion Malinovskiy, and marshals of artillery Nikolay Voronov, Mitrofan Nedelin, Nikolay Yakovlev and Aleksandr Vasilevskiy, "led the difficult work of creating and developing Soviet nuclear armed missiles and forming the early missile units (of the Strategic Rocket Forces)."[6]

While Brezhnev sat at the top of the pyramid for the Party, Dimitry Ustinov became the linchpin of the effort on the government side. No one was better suited for the job. Given his extensive background as Minister of Armaments and then Minister of Defense Industry until 1957, he was responsible for setting up the nuclear ballistic missile industry and supervising its operation. Shortly after World War II, a supraministerial organization charged with missile development was attached to the U.S.S.R. Council of Ministers and a number of Brezhnev's war colleagues belonged to it. Ustinov became its head in 1957 and held this position in conjunction with his job as a deputy chairman of the Council of Ministers until 1963. He and Brezhnev worked feverishly in the remaining months of 1956 and early 1957 to build a ballistic missile which could "strike at the heart of any capitalist country." A 1975 Soviet film on the Armed Forces described Brezhnev's role in the months before the launching of the first Soviet ICBM in the summer of 1957. In one segment of the film the camera pans to a missile site while the narrator notes that Brezhnev "had been responsible for the development of these weapons systems." In another segment a Strategic Rocket Force colonel recalls his "lengthy discussions with now head of the Communist Party, Comrade Brezhnev, who was responsible for the development of this weapons system."

Progress was swift. Several secret tests of nuclear weapons were conducted in late 1956. That same year the Soviet Union rejected no less than 14 American proposals on disarmament and control of nuclear weapons.

Then in May 1957, the Brezhnev team test-fired a missile carrying a payload of 4,840 pounds, which soared to an altitude of 132 miles. Three months later, on August 27, 1957, a second missile was fired from Baykonur. "A multistaged intercontinental ballistic missile has been built and tested in the U.S.S.R.," Tass, the Soviet News Agency, proudly reported. Moreover, "the most important stage of Soviet missile building has been successfully concluded," Tass added. When the August tests were completed the world learned that the U.S.S.R. had conducted a series of ICBM tests that sent military payloads higher than 800 miles to targets more than 5,000 miles away.

This was alarming news for the United States which had yet to test at full range its ICBMs. But the event which really shocked the world, and particularly shook Western confidence in its technological superiority over the Russians, was the launching of the Soviet satellite Sputnik I two months later. On October 4, 1957, Moscow Radio announced: "As a result of very intensive work by scientific research institutes and design bureaus, the first artificial satellite in the world has been created. On October 4, 1957, the first satellite was successfully launched in the U.S.S.R."

The familiar "beep, beep" of the tiny Sputnik satellite became familiar to all of us. Its launching was an unprecedented scientific and technological achievement which did much to reorient American thinking. Yet as dramatic as the space launch proved to be, the Soviets had been methodically working on the space probe. As early as November 1953, Academician Aleksandr Nesmeyanov (head of the U.S.S.R. Academy of Sciences) had said that "science has reached a state where it is feasible to send a stratoplane to the moon, to create an artificial satellite of the earth."[7]

According to Korolyev, however, the decision to build and launch Sputnik I was not actually made by the Party until August, prompted by the prospect of the launching by the United States of its *Vanguard* satellite by the end of the year. Korolyev depended on Khrushchev to spare nothing for the project in the interests of the colossal scientific and propaganda effect that the launching of the first space satellite would have. Indeed, Khrushchev spared nothing. He put a special research institute at Korolyev's disposal as well as a factory in Kaliningrad which was to build the satellite and make the necessary modifications to the missile.

"Moreover, the office of the Secretary [i.e., Brezhnev] ... became a kind of headquarters where decisions were made on the most important problems of space exploration. Meetings were held here with prominent scientists, designers, and technical specialists. Brezhnev was [also] often seen at the plants producing rocket equipment."[8]

An article in *Krasnaya Zvezda* on Brezhnev's seventieth birthday in 1976 elaborated on his role in the Sputnik program and in the actual launch of the satellite. The author, a launch site engineer, says that Brezhnev worked in the design bureau with Korolyev and went frequently to the factories and to Baykonur to check on the progress of the work and launch preparations.

The article's author recalls the launch of Sputnik I in detail. Brezhnev, Korolyev and Ustinov were on hand for it, but there was no mention of Khrushchev. Brezhnev is portrayed as being the supreme Party authority on the site supervising the launch. As the final preparations were made, Korolyev explained the launch procedures and briefed Brezhnev on the expected flight path of the satellite. When the engineers indicated that everything was ready, it was Brezhnev who gave the word to launch.

By the time Yuriy Gagarin made his famous space flight on April 12, 1961, Brezhnev had left the space program. His 1961 award was for the earlier work he had done in the program culminating in the Gagarin flight.

Few presidents or prime ministers have expertise in the field of strategic weapons that they control. Brezhnev does. For five years he was in charge of nuclear warhead factories, guided missile plants, and rocket test sites. Between 1956 and 1960, he had 17 missile plants, 11 missile engineering development centers, and 300,000 administrators, scientists, engineers, technicians and production workers at his disposal. Missile plants in Dnepropetrovsk, Irkutsk, Kalinin, Kazan, Kharkov, Kiev, Riga, Omsk, Novosibirsk, Leningrad, Moscow and other cities scattered across the U.S.S.R. turned out ICBMS in increasing numbers in those years. Khrushchev once boasted that the U.S.S.R could produce 250 ICBMS a year.

These missiles went to arm bases at Alma Ata, Aralsk, Irkutsk, Komsomolsk, and Magnitogorsk, all of which became part of the Strategic Rocket Forces (SRF) when this branch of the Soviet Armed Forces came into being. Its formation as the "principal arm" of the Soviet Armed Forces was officially announced on January 14, 1960. Marshal Mikhail Nedelin commanded the SRF until his death on October 20, 1960, in an airplane crash, at which time Marshal Moskalenko took over.

During Lenin's birthday celebrations in 1959, Brezhnev told a crowd gathered in Red Square that the Party would "perfect still further" and "multiply the strength of the glorious and heroic Soviet Armed Forces." To do otherwise, "to weaken the socialist state," he said, "would mean to embark on a course of betrayal of all working classes everywhere."

Indeed, today's generation of powerful Soviet supermissiles armed with multiple nuclear warheads which threaten the United States, were developed from the first ICBMS of the 1957-1960 era which Brezhnev helped to develop and deploy. From those first missiles the Soviet Union has succeeded in building the largest missile force in the world.

XIV

President Brezhnev
and the Roots of Soviet
Policy in Africa

Comrades! In our time, when the socialist system has become the decisive factor in world development, the Leninist peace-loving foreign policy of the Soviet Union and the other countries of the socialist camp assumes special importance. And in this sphere, too, new paths have been laid in recent years. Hardened methods and ossified dogmas have been discarded. The Party has restored in all its fullness, and has developed in accordance with the new conditions in the world, the Leninist policy of peaceful coexistence, a policy that is deeply principled and at the same time flexible and closely linked with life. —L.I. Brezhnev, Address to the 22nd C.P.S.U. Congress, 1961.

IN THE CLOSING SESSION of the U.S.S.R. Supreme Soviet on Saturday, May 7, 1960, Marshal Kliment Voroshilov, the 79-year-old fellow founder of the Party with Lenin and head of state, asked to retire from his position as Chairman of the Presidium of the U.S.S.R Supreme Soviet (President of the Soviet Union). Khrushchev stood up, accepted Voroshilov's resignation, graciously thanked him for his contributions to the Party, walked over to the Marshal and kissed him on both cheeks. The Party chief then moved for Brezhnev's appointment as President, hailing him as an "outstanding public figure."[1] The appointment was unanimously approved and the ceremony was capped with a final round of embracing amidst roars of approval and applause from the deputies.

This unorthodox display in the usually somber Supreme Soviet was interesting and, in retrospect, symbolic of the extraordinary role that would be played by its new head. However, the outside world missed the significance of the change in leadership. Western observers concluded that it was a sign of Khrushchev's weakness. In fact, it reflected several important changes in the Soviet system.

Voroshilov's departure should not have come as a surprise. He had erred politically when he failed to join Khrushchev with sufficient alacrity during the Presidium crisis in June 1957. On several occasions he had taken stands against Khrushchev who began to associate him with the anti-Party group. Voroshilov's exit from the Supreme Soviet Presidium thus marked the removal of the last anti-Party group member from the government.

It marked as well the end of an epoch begun with Lenin and a generational change in the leadership of the Supreme Soviet. Stalin had left the steel-cable maker Mikhail Kalinin in a purely ceremonial position from 1919 to 1946 until, almost blind, he requested retirement. Nikolay Shvernik, Kalinin's successor, found himself in the middle of a shakeup of the Party and the government following Stalin's death in 1953. He was replaced by the doddering old "Marshal Klim." Brezhnev, on the other hand, at 53, belonged to the younger, post-1917 generation and was a dynamic and ranking member of the Party leadership.

Brezhnev's appointment aided the political ambitions of Brezhnev's chief competitor for the position of Khrushchev's heir. In fact, it may have marked a personal victory for Frol Kozlov. (The Brezhnev-Kozlov relationship will be discussed later.)

This was also a period in which Khrushchev undertook several new directions in Soviet foreign policy. In that regard, it is possible to view Brezhnev as cast once again in his traditional role as chief administrator of yet another Khrushchev program, this one in the diplomatic arena. Two West German newspapers, the *Suddeutsche Zeitung* and the *Münchner Merkur* predicted that "the formal chief of state of the U.S.S.R. will no longer be the 'state grandpa,' but a hard, ambitious, and well versed functionary and an exponent of the new ruling class of leaders." Brezhnev they elaborated, "is reportedly such a dynamic individual that more can be expected from him than his merely becoming a figurehead."[2] They were right. He was to transform the nominal post of head of state into an instrument of foreign policy through which Moscow would espouse its interests in the Third World.

Except for trips to North Korea and East Germany in 1957, Brezhnev had never traveled abroad. In April 1960, he made his first visit to a capitalist country when he headed a three-man delegation to the Twelfth Congress of the Finnish Communist Party in Helsinki. Here he made an important declaration that was to guide his work for the immediate future. The declaration, cited below, was made exactly one month before he became President.

Communist Chinese criticism of the Soviet policy of peaceful coexistence with the West had mounted in the months preceding the Finnish Congress. At the Congress Brezhnev praised the policy, as did the other delegates. But he qualified his praise with the declaration that "war [with the capitalists] is not a fatal inevitability ... [but] of course as long as capitalism remains on this earth there will be reactionary forces which are capable of trying to unleash a war."[3]

This was not a new Soviet line; Khrushchev had stated it often enough at home. What was new was that for the first time it was affirmed publicly by a highly placed Soviet official outside the Communist bloc. The fact that it was purveyed in a capitalist country indicated that the statement was designed to demonstrate to Communists everywhere the erroneousness of Chinese allegations that the Soviet Union had abandoned the anticapitalist ideological struggle. On the contrary, Brezhnev would soon strike at the very heart of the capitalist system — the colonial empire.

Soviet global strategy is subject to change, readjustment and reinterpretation. So it was that following Khrushchev's introduction of the concept of "peaceful coexistence," it had to be transformed into a workable world strategy. During an era of nuclear stalemate it was felt that meaningful political gains could only be scored with relative impunity in the fertile zones of Africa and Asia. The Soviet leadership saw manipulation of the Third World as the key to "peaceful" struggle against the West and with China too as differences between the two Communist superpowers became greater. Some exploration of what came to be called the Third World had been undertaken earlier, but except for agreements signed with Syria and Egypt in the Middle East and Guinea in Africa actual Soviet diplomatic activities remained small. Thus, Soviet Afro-Asian relations had to be reassessed and a policy developed and implemented in a dynamic and effective fashion.

Brezhnev's remarks in Finland prefaced the introduction of just such a policy. The strategy he helped work out consisted of expanding positive ties with national movements and nonaligned countries by supporting their anticolonial sentiment and economic needs and by appealing to their vanity with arms and showpieces of greatness. These seductive techniques were aimed at eliminating anti-Soviet influence in Africa and Asia and ultimately establishing socialist governments there.

The basic theoretical framework was drafted by the "eighty-one Communist parties' conference" chaired by Brezhnev in November 1960, which gave birth to the concept of the "national democratic state." Defined as "a state that consistently defends political and economic independence and struggles against imperialism and imperialism's military blocs; opposes military bases on its territory; struggles against new forms of colonialism and the penetration of imperialist capital; and rejects dictatorial and despotic methods of government; a state in which the people are assured of broad democratic freedom....,"[4] the concept described many former colonial states in Africa and Asia. Instead of the customary "dictatorship of the proletariat," the "national democratic state" was to be the vehicle for social change in these states.

In the months that followed, Brezhnev articulated the concept in considerable detail.[5] He implied that the traditional concepts about the class nature, composition and methods of the liberation struggle in the colonial world had become outdated. Former colonial nations could no longer be automatically considered the preserve of the imperialist camp because many of them held strong anti-Western views. Therefore, while traditional ideology held that only indigenous Communists could be genuinely interested in carrying out the struggle against colonialism, alliances with other reformist elements were now allowed. National bourgeois leaders were to be viewed as progressive, some even revolutionary, certainly anti-imperialist, and consequently worthy of Soviet support.

Africa was chosen as the testing ground for the regime's new Third World policy because, in Brezhnev's words, "all eyes are turned toward Africa." Indeed, a bloody civil war in which the Soviet Union had been humiliated was raging in the Congo and Moscow needed a greater African support in the United Nations for its positions on the Congo and Khrushchev's effort to oust Secretary General Dag Hammarskjöld and create a three-man commission to run the United Nations.

So in February 1961 Brezhnev set out for Africa promising noninterference in the internal affairs of African states and offering these states aid, trade agreements and arms. On his departure for the dark continent, Moscow Radio predicted that "a period of tempestuous development in Soviet-African relations is just around the corner."

The trip went well from the beginning. Brezhnev even scored an unexpected bonus of world publicity en route when his plane was strafed by an Algerian-based jet fighter. According to the Soviet version of the incident, Brezhnev's Aeroflot Il-38 was flying at an altitude of 8250 meters and 130 kilometers north of the city of Algiers over international waters when a French jet fighter made several passes and then fired on the airplane.

Khrushchev quickly capitalized on the incident to heighten anti-Western feeling among Africans. Moscow's domestic and foreign radio service delivered no less than 10 lengthy commentaries by Soviet and African leaders accusing France of deliberately trying to sabotage Brezhnev's trip. President Sékou Touré of Guinea in particular charged the French with "abiding hostility to any form of international detente and cooperation" between the Soviet Union and Africa.

Brezhnev personally used the incident to draw attention to the war in Algeria, probably hoping to harden the attitude of rebel forces in anticipation of upcoming negotiations with France. The Moroccan ambassador to the Soviet Union, who had been aboard the plane, likewise accused France of trying to "spread the war." Yugoslav newspapers reported "the attack" as "a deliberate act of violence against a highly placed statesman."

Morocco's outspoken criticism of France over the incident symbolized its shift eastward. In fact, in view of Morocco's previous neutrality, its swing to the East — which was further demonstrated by King Mohammed's acceptance of an undisclosed amount of Soviet aid and arms — represented a major achievement for Brezhnev.

The Soviet President had been scheduled for only a brief refueling stop in Rabat, but the reception he received there was such a warm one that he decided to stay over. Khrushchev had made limited arms overtures before but the Moroccans were infinitely more receptive to Soviet aid this time, particularly in light of the delivery of 12 MIG fighter-interceptors and two trainers accompanied by a crew of Soviet technicians which had arrived aboard Soviet freighters ahead of Brezhnev.

Brezhnev's successful diplomacy in Morocco alarmed the West. The King agreed to demand the removal of United States Air Force Strategic Air Command bases from the country three years earlier than their scheduled withdrawal, and Brezhnev received approval to use Morocco as an intermediary shipper for Soviet arms destined for the Algerian revolutionaries.

Guinea was the next stop on Brezhnev's agenda. That country was of tremendous political value because through Guinea Moscow had been able to secure a toehold in sub-Saharan Africa. Guinea had gained independence from France in 1959 and had sought and received Soviet economic assistance.

President Touré received Brezhnev with open arms. Crowds sang and danced along the road from the airport to the capital, children ran out of their classrooms to greet Brezhnev and in Conakry, the capital, large portraits of Brezhnev with inscriptions reading "Long live the President of the Presidium of the Supreme Soviet of the U.S.S.R." hung everywhere. Touré even awarded Brezhnev Guinea's highest medal, the Order of the Fighter for Independence.

It was quite a show, a "profound experience," Brezhnev recalls. Touré spared nothing, leaving Brezhnev to conclude that Guinea had made a profound commitment to socialism.

Touré's intention was to secure substantial aid and new trade agreements from the Soviet leader. The fact that an official of Brezhnev's standing accompanied by the Deputy Minister for Foreign Affairs, Culture and Foriegn Trade, the Deputy Chairman of the State Committee for Foreign Economic Relations, and the heads of the first and second African Departments of the Ministry of Foreign Affairs had come to Guinea indicated that Moscow was ready to subject Soviet-Guinean relations to a complete review. In light of American offers of aid which Touré used as a trump card, the Soviet Union appeared most accommodating.

Indeed, Brezhnev tried hard to prove that Moscow could outdo Washington. He promised "Guinea will get whatever aid it needs." Moreover, Brezhnev undertook a new and more favorable five-year trade agreement with Guinea. Exactly how many million rubles he spent there has never been made public, but it was substantial. Touré would only say that Guinea had been promised "stupendous economic, financial, technical and cultural assistance."[6]

All sectors of the international community credited Brezhnev with raising Soviet-Guinean relations to an all-time high. Touré told reporters: "President Brezhnev's visit ... is of great importance to us.... It shows that our relations are as close and friendly as our people desire them to be." Soviet commentary aired in English reported that "cooperation between our countries is the direct outcome of President Brezhnev's visit." William Attwood, the American ambassador to Guinea, described Brezhnev's visit as a "triumph," leaving American prospects for influence hardly bright.[7]

This assessment proved accurate in early February when President Touré sent an angry letter to President John Kennedy accusing the United States of having a direct hand in the assassination of Patrice Lumumba. The timing of the letter — it was written almost a month after Lumumba's death, but during Brezhnev's visit to Guinea — makes it certain that Brezhnev inspired it. Similarly,

Brezhnev was probably responsible for pressure in high levels of the Guinean government to expropriate foreign firms operating in Guinea, notably the American firm of Olin Mathieson which had $75 million invested in mining Guinean bauxite.

Brezhnev visited Ghana next. The year 1961 was a watershed in Ghanaian politics, the division between the old and the new Ghana, between the pro-Western Ghana and the Ghana that promised and tried, albeit unsuccessfully, to follow "scientific socialism." Brezhnev's visit marked the turning point.

For over a year President Kwame Nkrumah had been moving toward an anti-Western position due in part to his failure to gain a dominant position in Leopoldville after having made a heavy investment in troops there during the Congo crisis. His new foreign policy called for the elimination of Western influence from Africa and unification of the continent under Ghanaian leadership. This coincided with his decision to build Ghana's economy via socialist methods. Nkrumah only had to convince his guest that Ghana too was marching down the road to socialism to get the aid needed.

Nkrumah's political acumen and his programs for the socialization of agriculture and ideological education impressed Brezhnev. Letting the Soviet President break ground for construction of the new Marxism-Leninism Ideological Institute at Winnebu symbolized Nkrumah's assurance that Ghana would be properly socialized. Consequently, Brezhnev agreed to double the loan of $40 million approved six months earlier and to provide technical and military assistance to Ghana—this in part by training Ghanaian military officers in the Soviet Union to replace British and Canadian officers in command positions in the armed forces. Discussions on building an atomic reactor were also begun; they were concluded during Nkrumah's visit to the Soviet Union the following June.

The question of why Brezhnev failed to include Mali on his agenda is an important one. Mali had only broken from the French colonial yoke six months earlier and its leaders professed a socialist outlook. They were seeking aid and were being actively courted by both the United States and China. What probably happened is that Brezhnev overspent in Morocco, Guinea and Ghana—one Soviet commentator labeled the aid packages "colossal"[8]—and was unprepared to extend similar commitments to Mali.

Brezhnev decided to wait. Further expenditures required Presidium approval. No doubt some in that body were skeptical of the need to include Mali. After all, the country was not strategically important — though it had some military importance to the national liberation struggle in Algeria — and Mali was a dismally impoverished land with limited resources.

However, Brezhnev did send a cordial greeting to President Modibo Keita prior to departing Africa, and within weeks of Brezhnev's return home an offer of a loan and modest military assistance was made to President Keita. Brezhnev argued convincingly for Mali. One concern was the French bases in Mali from which desert patrols operated to prevent Algerian rebels from crossing the border into Algeria. After the aid agreement was concluded Keita demanded immediate French withdrawal from Mali.

In retrospect, no regime in Africa turned out to better exemplify the potential of Soviet expectations in Africa than that of Modibo Keita's. Until his overthrow in November 1968, Keita worked to build a socialist society by means of a highly centralized and well-developed Marxist-Leninist trained political party committed to socialization of the economy.

Of those African colonies not yet liberated, Angola attracted Brezhnev's attention the most. The staging of a bloody "popular uprising" in the capital city of Luanda while he was visiting neighboring Guinea and the emergence of the Popular Movement for the Liberation of Angola (MPLA) convinced Brezhnev of the need to provide direct military assistance to the MPLA. Guinea agreed to handle the Soviet shipments of small arms.

Thus, direct Soviet military sponsorship of the rebels in Angola was tied to Brezhnev's trip to Africa in February 1961. The following June he reported on the progress of the national liberation struggle.

"Now Angola is one of the most active sectors of the struggle. Now tangible blows are being dealt to the colonists. Now there are few people who doubt that the day is near when the victorious voice of independence and national freedom will also rise over the land of Angola."[9]

From all accounts — Soviet, Western, African and Brezhnev's own — his 18-day shuttle around Africa had a significant impact on the balance of political influence there, giving the Soviet Union an edge over its Western and Chinese competitors. Brezhnev demonstrated a remarkable ability to use diplomacy as an effective ideological weapon and he was particularly successful in bringing about tough anti-Western policies among several African governments.

He recognized "progressive national democrats" like Presidents Touré and Nkrumah as the principal driving force in the anti-imperialist sturggle in Africa. Nowhere did he discuss the revolutionary mission of the proletariat, nor did he ascribe an important role to the Communist parties in the African states. Rather, he stressed the revolutionary importance of the coalition of classes rallied around the exisiting nationalist parties and "the development of an independent national (democratic) state."

What impact did Brezhnev expect this development to have on Marx's inevitable historical process? "It will have significant historical importance." Citing Guinea as an example, he explained that Guinea was at the forefront of the revolutionary process which would determine the future of Africa. Merely by choosing the non-captialist path of development Guinea had chosen between oppression and socialism.

However, it was one thing to formulate doctrine about the role of the national democratic state, but quite another to come to grips with theoretical formulations about how these states should develop internally. Brezhnev's failure to remark on many aspects of the problem relating to internal development, social structure and corresponding class relationships represented an intentional sidestepping of points that were in disagreement with African views.

Marxism teaches that revolutions must pass through two phases: a bourgeois-democratic one first and a socialist one second. Brezhnev indicated that Africa was the exception; there the two phases could be telescoped. Acquiring national independence constituted the prerequisite "revolutionary" act analogous to the October 1917 Revolution.

Brezhnev's postulation of a similarity between Guinea's gaining independence and Russia's October Revolution in his March 3 speech in Conakry is an example:

> We know that currently the people of Guinea will have to do a lot to overcome all the remnants of the colonial regime. All this is very close to our hearts and understandable to us since our people too had to overcome a great number of difficulties after the victory of the 1917 revolution. Even though our country was not a colony, the czarist government had kept it in a state of economic, political and cultural backwardness.

Brezhnev's praise and pledge to support the pan-African movement — though the Soviet Union had previously objected to such movements because of their ethnic base and tendency to gloss over the class struggle — was a clear attempt to curry favor with the

Africans. Twice in Guinea Brezhnev publicly recognized the movement as an acceptance of unity among Africans in the common struggle against imperialism. Pan-Africanism, he said, is "a decisive factor in the liberation of African peoples from the colonial yoke and the growing unity of the African states. The Soviet Union welcomes the efforts of the Guinean Republic and other African states aimed at achieving such unity."

Brezhnev's own assessment of the trip reflected a firm conviction that prospects for the entire liberation of Africa and the eventual establishment of communist governments there were excellent. He was thoroughly convinced by Touré's display and by Nkrumah's probably more serious commitment to socialism. Everywhere Brezhnev looked, in Morocco, in Ghana, Algeria and in Angola he saw the liberation struggle unfolding. He believed Africans had a genuine desire to embrace socialism, and Guinea and Ghana, in his eyes, were striding quickly ahead: "We are profoundly convinced that the time is not far away when African nations will shake off the last fetters of colonial slavery and the sun of national freedom and independence will shine over the whole of the African continent."[10]

XV
Prosecuting the Global Ideological Struggle

Lenin foresaw that the enslaved peoples would rise against imperialism and break the chains. Lenin's prophetic words are coming true. The colonial and dependent peoples will achieve such development as cannot fail to lead to a crisis of the entire world of capitalism. — L.I. Brezhnev, 1961.

HEARTENED BY HIS AFRICAN VENTURE, Brezhnev turned anxiously toward Asia, hoping, especially there, to counter Chairman Mao Tse-tung's growing influence on the continent. The Chinese were effective competitors in Asia and projecting Soviet influence in this part of the world would be difficult. But probes were made and by the summer of 1961 Brezhnev had closed an arms deal with Indonesia's President Achmed Sukarno, which turned out to be next to the largest Soviet military assistance package ever granted to a foreign country. The exception, of course, was Stalin's very early assistance to the Chinese.

Khrushchev and a host of Soviet officials participated in the discussions with the Indonesians held in Moscow in June 1961, but Brezhnev was in charge of the negotiations. His role as the chief Soviet negotiator was vividly revealed when he received personal recognition from President Sukarno and the Indonesian Silver Star medal for his "personal struggle for peace and happiness of people everywhere."[1]

The arms deal concluded nearly twelve months of wooing by the Soviet Union, preliminary aid and arms agreements with Indonesia having been signed in Moscow and Jakarta in early 1961, but with Andrey Gromyko, the Soviet Minister of Foreign Affairs, presiding because of Brezhnev's presence in Africa. The June agreement stipulated that Indonesia would be supplied with 30 of Russia's finest MIG fighter aircraft equipped with air to air missiles, 25 TU-16 bombers, IL-28 bombers, AN-2, AN-12 and IL-14 cargo planes, MI-4 and MI-6 helicopters, and a host of SA-2 antiaircraft missiles. Her navy was to receive a Sverdlovsk cruiser, 12 attack submarines, seven Skoryy class destroyers, seven frigates, 24 motor torpedo boats, seven minesweepers, 12 Komar class motor patrol boats, two submarine support ships, and the list went on.

At a friendship rally for the Indonesians² Brezhnev told them he hoped Indonesia would now assume the leading role in the national liberation struggle in Southeast Asia. The idea coincided with Sukarno's desire to establish his country as the leading nation in the region and to eliminate Western military presence there beginning with the Dutch withdrawal from West Irian, New Guinea, which Indonesia claimed for itself and which was being hotly contested with the Dutch government.

Brezhnev naturally interpreted Sukarno's territorial aspirations in Marxist-Leninist terms. The Soviet President went to great pains to demonstrate masterfully the "similarity of the historic destinies of our peoples" by comparing the "imperialist predators who are converging on the Indonesian archipelago to pick the newly established country clean" to Russia's early period under socialism. "In the dawn of our own socialist existence," Brezhnev told the Indonesians, "we too had to crush the intervention of fourteen imperialist states, and during the Great Patriotic War we had to repel the attack of Hitlerite hordes backed by the military potential of the whole of Europe."

The latter remark is particularly interesting for here Brezhnev tarred all European nations with the same brush, implying that they had been collectively responsible for the German invasion of Russia in June 1941. The full significance of the remark can only be understood if it is viewed in the context of the 1961 Berlin crisis when the Soviet Union and the United States locked diplomatic horns over that city. Indonesia's claim to the Dutch colony of West Irian provided Brezhnev with a perfect opportunity to foment intense anti-Western sentiment in another part of the world and hopefully take some of the heat off Berlin.

One principal concession sought from Afro-Asian leaders at this time was their endorsement of Soviet policies toward Berlin. Brezhnev succeeded in obtaining both Nkrumah's and President Sukarno's endorsements in the summer of 1961, and, with his promise of Soviet support for the Indian liberation of the Portuguese occupied territories of Goa, Daman and Diu later in the year, he evidently got India's endorsement too.

At the Moscow Indonesian rally Brezhnev drew very explicit

parallels between West Irian and West Berlin. As one of the chief spokesmen in support of Indonesia's claims, he addressed the threat posed by Dutch military presence in the colony, underscoring the need to reunify the colony with its "mother country." "Indonesia does not want a local or a world war," Brezhnev concluded, but "should the imperialists persist, military force will be needed to secure Indonesia's total independence." Only a simple transition of thought was required to similarly picture unwanted Western presence in Berlin and the threat of Soviet military action there.

The threat posed to India's position on the Asian subcontinent by the buildup of American arms in neighboring Pakistan, and Indian claims to the Portuguese colonies of Goa, Daman and Diu, promoted India to take Brezhnev up on his offers of military aid. One agreement was signed in November 1960 for $31.5 million in military equipment and supplies and another in September 1961 for the purchase of Soviet jet fighter engines for supersonic aircraft under development in India.[3]

But it was the liberation of the Portuguese colonies in December that commanded Brezhnev's undivided attention for most of that month. Here actual "capitalist colonies" were liberated by Soviet (and European) weapons and Brezhnev was an eyewitness.

Despite tremendous domestic pressure to take military action against the Portuguese, for a long time Prime Minister Jawaharlal Nehru resisted using force to settle the decade-old dispute with Portugal over the colonies. He hoped the Portuguese would follow the French example in Pondicherry and withdraw peacefully. However, on December 7, 1961, Nehru went before the Indian Parliament and told the legislative body that the situation had become exacerbated and force would have to be used.

Troop mobilization got underway immediately, but India needed Soviet endorsement of military action before it could act since a military offensive against Portugal would surely prompt a sharp reaction from the West and maybe even countermeasures. India, in fact, had been promised Soviet moral and political backing. During Nehru's visit to the Soviet Union in September 1961, Brezhnev reassured him: "Chairman Khrushchev agrees that colonialism in all its forms and manifestations should be resolutely condemned. He also declared that he deeply appreciates and sympathizes with the desire of the Indian people to immediately liberate Goa, Daman and Diu from Portuguese colonialism."[4]

But as of December 7, the Soviet Union had not specifically endorsed the Indian invasion. Brezhnev arrived in Bombay a week later to do just that. He went to India to personally approve and then observe at first hand the military liberation of the colonies. The timing of the trip, the rousing welcome he received — which even overshadowed President Dwight D. Eisenhower's earlier visit — the delay between the massing of Indian troops on the Goan border and the final order to invade, which came only after he announced Soviet support, confirmed this.

Brezhnev spent three days in secret meetings with Indian government and military officials to review the invasion plans and to squeeze out of Nehru last minute political concessions, among them support for a separate peace treaty with East Germany. The preliminary announcement on December 15 that "India and the Soviet Union are cooperating in solving the most important international problems" was an indication that the question of a German treaty had been one of the topics under discussion.

On the evening of the 17th, Brezhnev made his long awaited speech approving the invasion. He said:

> The Soviet people and our Party regard it as their international duty to help people who are achieving and strengthening national independence.... Regarding as inalienable the right of all peoples to a free and independent life, the Soviet Union is for the immediate abolition of colonialism in all its shapes and forms. As for the problem closest to the Indian people, that of liquidating the vestiges of colonialism here on Indian soil, the Soviet Union has full understanding and sympathy for the Indian peoples' desire to achieve the liberation of Goa, Daman and Diu from Portuguese colonialism."[5]

Military operations began at midnight.

Three times over the next few days Brezhnev defended India in the face of moves by the United States, Great Britain and France to censor India in the United Nations. Each time he pointed to the anticolonialist struggle in the Third World and to the "international obligation" of the Soviet Union to help nations wishing to strengthen their national independence:

> The position of the Soviet Union on the question of abolishing colonialism has been set forth with utmost clarity by the Chairman of the Council of Ministers, N.S. Khrushchev. We regard as inalienable the right of people to put an end to foreign oppression and we shall support their just cause. Here in Bombay we feel most acutely the satisfaction and enthusiasm

Viktoriya (left) and Leonid Brezhnev warmly welcomed by Indian officials upon their arrival at Dum Dum airport, December 1961.

with which the Indian people have reacted to the news about the commencement of the liberation of Goa and other territories captured by Portuguese colonialists on Indian soil. The Soviet people understand well the feelings of the Indian people who have long awaited the hour when the whole territory of India will finally be free from colonial oppression."[6]

At the end of the military campaign Indian officials held public ceremonies to thank Brezhnev for Soviet support of "India's liberational struggle." Mr. Mazumdar, the mayor of Calcutta, summed up the government's feelings best in a special thank-you to Brezhnev, when he said: "As friends who lead the way you have been giving us all kinds of aid with no stint. Our salutations go out to you on this battleground redolent of the memories of numberless patriots." Brezhnev was so taken by the tribute that he publicly thanked the Indian people for letting him "share personally in the joy of the people in listening to the exciting news of Goa's liberation."[7]

The People's Republic of China was the loudest critic of Brezhnev's diplomatic activities in India and elsewhere in the Third World, particularly in Asia. Mao alleged that countries receiving Soviet economic and military aid were being forced to pay dearly by foregoing real social progress. The years 1962 and 1963 saw a sharp upturn in these attacks as China intensified the already heated polemics with the Soviet Union and made an all-out effort to undermine Soviet influence in Asia. The earlier implied rivalry between the two communist giants now broke out into a bitter ideological battle. China sought the support of the uncommitted Asian nations and the Soviet Union labored to prevent them from succeeding.

Two nations wooed were Cambodia and Laos. Brezhnev made a secret offer of $18 million in aid and arms to Cambodia in early 1960 during Prince Norodom Sihanouk's visit to Moscow that year, but Sihanouk, hoping to maintain Cambodia's neutrality, had turned the offer down. In mid 1963, however, he accepted a Chinese grant of $50 million for Cambodia's economic development, which led to a second Soviet offer. This time Brezhnev agreed to provide Cambodia with a small national air defense system consisting of MIG 17s, antiaircraft guns, a radar station, jet trainer, trucks and mobile field units.

In this way, Brezhnev was able to bring about a respite in Cambodia's pro-China leanings and effect a major shift in that country's military purchasing policy; until then Cambodia had bought its

Brezhnev receives a silver casket containing a mayoral address from Rajendra Nath Mazumdar, mayor of Calcutta, during celebrations marking the liberation of Goa in December 1961.

major weapons from France and the United States. Cambodia severed all military and economic ties with the U.S. in 1963.

A visit to Moscow by the Laotian King and Prime Minister, Prince Souvanna Phouma, in 1963, gave Brezhnev the opportunity to use some devious diplomatic techniques in order to secure the maximum propaganda value for giving aid to the neutralist Laotian government, while also underhandedly supplying arms to the Communist Pathet Lao forces.

This complicated turn of events was preceded by years of conflict between the three main Laotian political groups. The neutralist Souvanna Phouma approached Brezhnev in November 1960 to counter American-backed rightest forces operating in Laos. When Phouma was later forced to flee into exile, an alliance was formed with the Communist Pathet Lao and military aid was redirected to the combined forces. Soviet deliveries during the latter part of 1960 and early 1961 included petroleum, light artillery pieces, antiaircraft guns, armored cars, ammunition, combat rations, and other war materiel.

Then, in June 1962, a three-way coalition government headed by Phouma was formed and in July a "Geneva Agreement" was signed which called for the recognition of Laotian neutrality. Seven months later the Pathet Lao faction left the coalition to continue the socialist struggle in hope of ultimately achieving a Communist victory in Laos.

While Khrushchev and Brezhnev hoped that a pro-Soviet Communist government would come to power in Laos, Brezhnev attempted to exploit Soviet policy appeal to other Asian countries by emphasizing Moscow's readiness to support the non-aligned coalition government and the concept of neutality established at the International Geneva Conference in July 1962.

"We share the satisfaction of our Laotian friends on the agreement of Laos' neutrality achieved at the Geneva Conferences," Brezhnev told the Laotian delegation at a dinner reception in Moscow on February 13, 1963. "We believe that this agreement, together with the political program proclaimed by the coalition government of Laos with his highness Prince Souvanna Phouma as its head, forms a good basis for the development of Laos as a united, independent and peaceful neutral state."[8]

Throughout most of 1963 Brezhnev prodded the King to emphasize Soviet political disinterest in extending aid and assistance to Laos, and on several occasions the King gave Brezhnev the propaganda ammunition he sought. Moreover, the King personally praised Brezhnev for his understanding of the Laotian political situation and the position of the country in Asia: "Mr. Chairman of the Presidium of the Supreme Soviet, we are satisfied with all those sincere and heartfelt conversations which we had with you," the King told his host in Moscow in 1963. "We are also overjoyed by the understanding which you showed with regard to our country and our problems."[9]

The amount of Soviet aid promised to Laos in 1963 is uncertain, but in summing up his Moscow visit the King indicated that he was "highly satisfied with the readiness of the Soviet Union to help the Laotian people in their efforts to reorganize, renovate, and develop our country. Our visit was ... a fruitful one."[10]

Nowhere was it more obvious that Moscow intended to use its state-to-state relations as integral elements in the ideological struggle with China than in its handling of Brezhnev's visit to Afghanistan and in the October 1963 series of visits to Moscow by First Vice Chairman to the Algerian Council of Ministers and Minister of National Defense Colonel H. Boumedienne, Nepalese Prime Minister Tulsi Giri, and Ceylonese Prime Minister Sirimavo Bandaranaike. An October 19 *Pravda* article, "The Policy of Peaceful Coexistence in Operation," and subsequent media reports made this quite clear.

The *Pravda* article criticized short term opportunistic policies toward the developing countries and sought to reassure the Afro-Asian states of Soviet good intentions by arguing that Soviet policy was not dictated by "temporary tactical calculations," as Mao alleged, but "governed by the international duty of the U.S.S.R. to assist new nations, liquidate monopolist exploitation in them and develop their national economies."

Similarly, broadcasts heard throughout Southeast Asia and Australia in the early part of October emphasized the importance of strengthening the already friendly relations with Afghanistan in order to combat Chinese influence.[11] Broadcasts in Bengali to India and Pakistan cited Brezhnev hailing Soviet-Afghan relations as a good example of peaceful coexistence between a powerful industrial nation and a small country striving hard to overcome age old backwardness.[12]

Thus, the final communiqué concluding Brezhnev's six-day visit to Afghanistan served Moscow's purposes nicely. It provided Asian endorsement of a wide range of Soviet foreign policy propositions challenged by the Chinese, in particular the value of the policy of nonalignment and the nuclear test ban agreement signed between the United States and the Soviet Union. Like much of the daily press coverage of the visit, the communiqué stressed Afghan satisfaction with Soviet economic assistance.[13]

The greatest propaganda value, however, came from Brezhnev's talks with the Algerians that October. Mao had capitalized on Moscow's failure to extend credits to Algeria after the country gained its independence in July 1962, charging the Soviet Union with abandoning the Algerian national liberation struggle. However, Algerian press reports, citing the "high satisfaction of the Algerian people and the government" with previous Soviet aid, refuted those allegations. Moscow's $100 million loan to Algeria in October of 1963 immediately provoked a loan of $50 million by China, which forced Brezhnev to up the ante by yet another loan of $128 million in May 1964.

The obvious exceptions to Brezhnev's successful diplomatic

sweep occurred in his talks with Tito in 1962, aimed at officially restoring relations with Yugoslavia after a hiatus of nearly eight years, and in his visit to Iran in November of the following year.

The trip to Yugoslavia in September 1962, was the most important diplomatic mission Brezhnev had to perform that year. The talks were carefully watched, particularly by the nonaligned countries. Tito had become very influential among many Third World leaders and in the context of Brezhnev's prosecution of the struggle against the West and China, that factor alone provided great incentive to reconcile Soviet-Yugoslav differences. Moscow hoped to capitalize on the reconciliation.

However, ideological differences between host and guest came to the fore early in Brezhnev's visit. Tito turned out to be an anomaly. Despite so much talk about independent roads to socialism and about nonalignment, Brezhnev could not come to grips with this veteran Communist's neutrality. Tito was amenable to supporting many Soviet policies, but he refused to join Brezhnev in rabid ideological attacks on the West and on the United States in particular. Brezhnev's increasingly militant tone in Yugoslavia reflected his utter frustration with Tito.

The pressure for strong foreign policy coordination and a common front against the West as the price of friendship was unmistakable in Brezhnev's speeches. He conjured up images of future imperialist aggression which he claimed could be effectively fought only "through a mighty alliance of socialist states."[14] Tito, though accommodating on some points, remained firm in his commitment to neutrality and was careful to avoid alienating the United States. About as far as he would go was to say that there were "certain reactionary forces" at work in the world.

Brezhnev's chief intent was to draw Tito into declaring Yugoslavia's support for the proposed separate peace treaty with East Germany. This was not unrelated to Brezhnev's goals in the Third World. As one observer put it, Moscow hoped to get Yugoslavia's support for a treaty, then use Tito to put pressure on the nonaligned for open partisanship of the Soviet Berlin policy.[15]

The diplomatic community in Belgrade expected Brezhnev to raise the Berlin question, but they believed he would be discreet about it. His public utterances in Kragujevac on the second day of the visit, however, indicated that would not be the case. Evidently he assumed that Tito would go along with the Soviet Union on Berlin, probably because Tito had vaguely suggested several months earlier that Yugoslavia's position on Germany differed little from the Soviet stand.[16]

In light of Brezhnev's speech in Split, Croatia, two days later in which he specifically referred to a peace treaty, it became clear that his remarks in Kragujevac had been intended to prime Tito. In Split, Brezhnev said: "The consistent struggle of our country for the conclusion of a German peace treaty which should put an end to the remnants of the Second World War, provides a basis for solution to the problems of West Berlin."[17]

The fact that the first sit-down talks with Tito at Brioni were only two days away and news of the United States decision to end the most favored nation trade status theretofore accorded Yugoslavia reached Belgrade on September 27, had probably prompted Brezhnev. The shaky Yugoslav economy would suffer from the American decision. Brezhnev anticipated a strong anti-American reaction from Tito and believed that Yugoslavia would now surely side with the Soviet Union on Berlin to get back at the U.S.

Neither occurred. A Yugoslav commitment to a separate peace treaty was simply not forthcoming. Tito felt that a solution must be found in an agreement with the West. Yugoslav negotiators plainly reminded Brezhnev that possibilities for reaching an agreement with the Untied States over Berlin had not yet been exhausted.[18]

Brezhnev was more than a little annoyed. In a speech commemorating the Soviet dead of World War II at a cemetery opening in Gornji Milanovac on October 2, he gave vent to his feeling:

> In our hearts the memory is still alive of the millions of Russian and Yugoslav boys who were killed in the last war. Today imperialists and aggressive forces headed by imperialists of the United States are trying to start a new war, this time over Berlin and Cuba. With U.S. support, German militarists are again raising their ugly heads, reaching for atomic weapons and entertaining territorial aspirations towards Poland and Czechoslovakia while the posionous spiders of NATO strategists are drawing their slack nets of conspiracy against peace.... One can hear the sound of drums from the shores of the Rhine and the shouting of their masters across the seas encouraging the revanchists to another invasion of the East.[19]

If this wasn't enough, Brezhnev went on to criticize the European Common Market — on which Yugoslavia depended for approximately 30 percent of its foreign trade — as an economic base for predatory imperialism. To round off the stinging attack on the West, he concluded by saying that American policy towards Cuba was a cause for war.[20]

From Brezhnev's tone one would have thought that the Yugoslavs were 100 percent Peking hardliners. His loud outbursts only served to embarrass the Yugoslavs, personally irritate Tito, cause an immediate Western reassessment of Brezhnev's believed moderate foreign policy outlook and a boycott (by the Western diplomatic community in Belgrade) of the activities surrounding Brezhnev's visit.

Brezhnev quickly backpedalled after his cemetery talk. It was Brezhnev, not Tito, who eventually compromised, making some rather painful concessions in order to retain Yugoslav friendship and save face. He acknowledged the 1955 Belgrade declaration recognizing the right of Communist parties to pursue separate roads to socialism, stating that future Yugoslav-Soviet relations could be based on this declaration. He also agreed to a higher trade package. From where Tito stood, there were important economic gains to be made and he seized upon the opportunity. Goods were to be traded for Yugoslav-built ships for the Soviet merchant fleet and the exchange of goods was to be increased to $180 million, which represented a considerable increase over 1962.

The Soviet Union got little out of the deal. The joint communiqué that was issued contained nothing new and received little press attention.

What caught the eye of Western reporters instead was Galina Brezhnev's debut on the diplomatic circuit. While Papa was out touring industrial plants and making just about everyone in Belgrade mad at him, Galina, a tall and shapely blond, was busy charming her hosts. Dressed in her fashionable French dress, Italian spiked heels and huge dangling earrings, she was the darling of the social circuit. She completely overshadowed Khrushchev's daughter Rada, wife of the *Izvestiya* correspondent Aleksey Adzhubey, who was also along on the trip. Galina dazzled everyone. "She may well turn out to be the Kremlin's answer to Jackie Kennedy," one reporter concluded.

Brezhnev's trip to Iran in September of the following year was mainly made in the context of the ideological struggle with China. This was evident both in the timing of the trip—it came as the last in the series of state visits in late 1963—and in Brezhnev's speeches in Teheran which rehearsed familiar themes.

Brezhnev also hoped to counter Western influence in the Middle East. Iran had been the target of an intense Soviet propaganda campaign because of its Western sponsored defense alliances. But in 1962, Moscow attempted to undermine Iran's links with the West by taking a conciliatory approach towards its government. To facilitate this in July the Soviet Union signed an economic and technical agreement which provided for construction of a dam on the Asar River, construction of grain silos, and the development of the Caspian Sea fish hatcheries. Brezhnev's trip therefore culminated a 16-month effort to improve relations with Iran.

There was an atmosphere of expectancy in the country prior to his visit. Many Iranians hoped that trade and economic cooperation would be expanded. Yet, Iranian officialdom was not eager to overplay the importance of the visit. The Iranian attitude was given greatest clarity when the Shah made a public appearance with the American ambassador to dedicate new American built housing in earthquake damaged villages. This was given careful publicity, as was the news of new American aid to Iran. Thus, a large share of the publicity that should have gone to Brezhnev was preempted by other news, including that of President Kennedy's assassination. Moreover, the itinerary arranged for Brezhnev isolated him from crowded cities and thus from Iran's public.

Brezhnev was taken aback by this kind of treatment and showed his displeasure by his failure to endorse the Shah's economic and social reform programs that the latter had been working so hard for. On the one occasion at which Brezhnev might have exploited an important opportunity to support the program he chose not to. His address to the joint session of the Iranian Parliament was perfunctory.

No aid agreement came out of the visit, though the Shah desperately wanted a new steel mill which the United States had refused to finance. That he approached Brezhnev about financing the mill is apparent by the two-day delay in announcing that an Iranian survey plane had strayed across the Soviet border and been shot down by Soviet fighters.[21]

The downing of the Iranian plane occurred during Brezhnev's address to the Iranian legislative bodies. Two Iranian officials aboard the plane had been killed. Only the bare minimum of cordiality was maintained after news of the incident reached Teheran. The incident could not have come at a worse time and some Westerners speculated that well placed Soviet elements were trying to sabotage Brezhnev's trip and, more importantly, Khrushchev's foreign policy.

The net assessment of Brezhnev's trip to Iran was mainly

negative. At most, the visit served to symbolize the normalization of relations between the U.S.S.R and Iran.

There is no question that Brezhnev entered the foreign policy arena in 1960 with great skill and over the next three years transformed the nominal post of head of state into an important instrument of foreign policy. As Khrushchev's roving ambassador he became something of a Henry Kissinger and the personalized style of diplomacy that he practiced became the hallmark of his Presidency and of Soviet foreign policy in general between 1961 and 1963. Moreover, Brezhnev's travels revealed a personality and character to Third World leaders quite distinguishable from Khrushchev's.

Unlike Khrushchev, Brezhnev was generally always calm and composed. He engaged in some demogoguery, but on the whole he avoided clumsy political agitation in dealing with foreign dignitaries. The exception of course was Yugoslavia. He was a charming guest and an equally charming host, which made Third World diplomats comfortable with him and, at times, even casual.

Brezhnev owed much of his success to his genuine enthusiasm and charm. He was a meticulous dresser and was constantly anxious about public reaction to him. Like Khrushchev, he used every opportunity to meet people and was particularly good at dealing with crowds. He was always out in front shaking hands with onlookers and kissing babies, not unlike Western politicians when they are on the campaign trail.

Khrushchev would always approach social topics in a way that gave him an opportunity to emphasize the special achievements of socialism and score propaganda points. But Brezhnev refused to deal with things in purely propagandistic terms. In the carpet factories in Iran, for example, he examined the weaving methods and asked women employees about technical data, not labor conditions.

There were differences in the conduct of diplomacy too. Khrushchev was a horse-trader. No matter how serious and sincere he tried to be, there was always the air of the comedian, the gambler, the trickster about him. Brezhnev's bearing and meticulous manner, on the other hand, made his presentations more convincing, his logic more compelling, his arguments more credible, and won the Soviet Union friends.

Nevertheless, there were numerous disappointments and some painful lessons to be learned about dealing with the Third World. In some areas, a discernible pattern of broken promises followed Brezhnev's visits. President Touré of Guinea depended heavily on the meaningful aid that Brezhnev had promised in February 1961, but Soviet bureaucrats could not resist unloading cheap goods on the "natives," and in many instances Moscow chose to make only cosmetic improvements to the economies of Guinea and other countries. Whether this occurred as a result of Brezhnev's overconfidence in the socialist process in Africa and elsewhere or for other reasons, the result was often harmful to Soviet interests. Touré's expulsion of the Soviet ambassador to Guinea in 1961 was clearly a reprisal for Soviet second-dealing, which embarrassed the Soviet Union and made other African leaders suspicious of Soviet intentions.

Brezhnev's confidence about the prospects for establishment of socialist regimes in Africa and elsewhere was unquestionably misguided. Soviet aid to Africa and Asia helped strengthen and widen the base of nonalignment in 1961-1963, but nowhere did it go beyond that and bring about the formation of a Communist government as Brezhnev had expected, nor did the development of ties in all cases even lead to a relaxation of repression against local Communists. Brezhnev had to learn that even those who appeared to be staunch supporters of the Soviet Union were politically unreliable. With disappointing political returns in Guinea and elsewhere, Brezhnev's enthusiasm seemed to mellow into a more realistic and mature outlook reflected by ideological deemphasis in his post 1961 speeches.

In terms of the aid granted to the Third World, in 1961 alone Brezhnev signed agreements amounting to an estimated $547 million. He armed Indonesia's Navy and Air Force, and provided additional millions in aid and arms to the liberation movements in Angola, Algeria and elsewhere in Africa. By 1964, Soviet relations with the Third World had become extremely broad and the scope so wide that the Party could neither abandon nor radically transform this "fraternal alliance" without a full-scale revision of Soviet foreign policy and the doctrine associated with it. Nor did Brezhnev in 1964 wish to abandon the Third World, for regardless of the disappointments, he felt the political benefits in the long run would justify the expenditure. Indeed, they have.

XVI

The Road Not Taken

Two roads diverged in a woods, and I
Took the one less traveled by
And that has made all the difference.
      — Robert Frost.

FROM 1960 UNTIL OCTOBER 1964 the course of Brezhnev's career was dominated by foreign policy, and it was disagreement in this policy realm that sowed the seeds of dissension and caused a parting of the ways with Khrushchev. Brezhnev was to split with his mentor on several key issues in the last years of Khrushchev's reign, but the 1961 Berlin crisis marked the beginning of the trouble. Up to then, even through the U-2 incident in 1960 which many observers treat as pivotal to the Kremlin powershifts of the early 1960s, Brezhnev remained a loyal and obedient servant.

Once Khrushchev initiated the policy of peaceful coexistence, his peace campaigns were paralleled by threats and demands for Western withdrawal from many parts of the world. He seriously believed that West Berlin would be one of the first Western outposts to fall and, by proposing that it made a demilitarized free city, Khrushchev began his campaign for a Soviet takeover of Berlin. This escalated into a Soviet challenge to the international status of the city in early 1961, which became known as the 1961 Berlin crisis.

Brezhnev was actively involved in the crisis both as a Party leader and as President. Two Brezhnev speeches figure prominently in this respect. One was made in June 1961, just four days after Khrushchev's historic meeting with President Kennedy in Vienna to discuss Soviet-American relations, nuclear tests, disarmament and Berlin, and the other in September, during Brezhnev's second trip to Finland. In the four-month interval forces and alignments in the Kremlin shifted radically because of disagreement over Khrushchev's methods of handling this and other foreign policy matters.

At the start, Brezhnev supported negotiation with the United States over West Berlin and was optimistic that a solution to the status of the city and to a divided Germany could be reached. His optimism was most clearly expressed at the Soviet/Indonesian friendship rally on June 10, 1961.

In the speech broadcast over Moscow domestic radio,[1] Brezhnev asserted that the Soviet Union was doing everything it possibly could to avert war with the United States over Berlin and that the "meeting between the untiring champion of peace, Nikita Khrushchev, and President Kennedy a few days ago" was a positive step in reaching a peaceful solution to the problems facing both countries. The principal thrust and importance of the speech rested in the positive evaluation he gave the Vienna meeting:

> That meeting proved to be a great event in the development of international relations in recent times, an event inspiring hope. It is a hope held by all nations of the globe whose thirst awaits a stable peace. They expect this first useful contact of the leaders of the two powers to be followed by further measures aimed at the relaxation of tension and a search for agreed solutions to international problems. As for the Soviet Union, it will do everything in order to justify those hopes.

The report served multiple purposes. From the standpoint of the Soviet campaign being conducted in the Third World, the timing could not have been better. Sukarno was a leading light among neutrals in Asia. Indonesia's support of Soviet demands in Berlin would thus serve to further strengthen the Soviet case among the uncommitted nations. The military aid agreement with Indonesia and Brezhnev's promise to support Indonesia's claims to Dutch New Guinea were accompanied by demands for reciprocal recognition of Soviet claims to Berlin.[2]

Further, Brezhnev intended to show that the Soviet Union was genuinely interested in reducing world tension through an extension of its good will and reasonableness, hoping to gain world sympathy for specific Soviet demands in Berlin.

He also meant to reassure the Soviet people that the policy being pursued in the test of strength over the city was a reasonable one, based on sincere desire for peace and reduction of international tension. "If the state of affairs [in West Berlin and Germany] is allowed to remain as it is," Khrushchev had earlier told the Russian people, "then this would mean always having a spark in the powder keg that might cause an explosion" in Europe.[3]

But the chief significance of Brezhnev's speech lay in the fact that it was the first official statement about the Khrushchev-Kennedy meeting to be made by any Soviet leader since Khrushchev's return home. It was a unilateral view, however, one made without Presidium concurrence.

A joint Presidium statement had not been forthcoming because of internal disagreement over how much significance to attach to the meeting and differences over the conduct of future relations with the United States. Specifically, the themes of good will, mutual understanding, and cooperation among states had been extensively propagandized by the Soviet media before the meeting, but there was next to no support for what was called the "spirit of Vienna" afterward. Osgood Carruthers, a journalist for the *New York Times*, reported: "There was no talk of the spirit of Vienna or victories for Mr. Khrushchev's policies following the meeting."[4] Similarly, Robert Slusser in his penetrating study, *The Berlin Crisis of 1961*, wrote that the so-called spirit of Vienna "had come to an early halt because of lack of any concrete foundation for it," there being no substantive agreement at Vienna, "and because it encountered no subsequent support within the Soviet leadership."[5]

But Brezhnev supported the spirit of Vienna. He made an effort in his speech to promote it, and he praised "the untiring champion of peace" for giving the "spirit" substance in Vienna. Even Khrushchev, when he personally reported on the talks a week later, was not so enthusiastic, indicating that the Party chief had partly succumbed to Presidium pressure. "I must note that all in all I came away pleased with these talks," Khrushchev concluded. "If I were to be asked, was it worth making arrangements for the meeting, was it worthwhile holding it? I would answer without a moment's hesitation that it was."[6]

Brezhnev's support of negotiations with the United States did not mean that he or Khrushchev advocated a "soft" position on Berlin or on any other foreign policy matter. Khrushchev did not go to Vienna to make concessions. On the contrary, he made demands for a German peace treaty to be signed by the end of the year. He believed that changes in the world balance of forces left the West with no choice but to accept Soviet demands for a peace treaty with both Germanys, which would specifically designate West Berlin a "demilitarized city" minus Western presence.

In Brezhnev's mind it was best to continue negotiations to make any agreement by the West appear the fruit of Soviet efforts. Whether he had nagging doubts about the validity of this approach in the long run or not, he supported Khrushchev on it. By September, however, there was a noticeable shift in his attitude.

Brezhnev's rejection of continued negotiations over Berlin wasn't because his position had fundamentally changed over the

summer, but because Khrushchev had become unnecessarily conciliatory. Brezhnev's speech on Berlin during his state address to the
Finnish Parliament in Helsinki in September 1961[7] vividly demonstrated this point.

The speech addressed all the essential aspects of the problem
in a straightforward manner and bore all the earmarks of a carefully
prepared and calculated move. Quite simply, Brezhnev told the
Parliament that the Soviet Union's goal was to achieve a lasting peace
in Europe. He reaffirmed in ringing tones the determination of the
Soivet Union and its allies to go ahead and conclude a separate peace
treaty with East Germany and thus seal once and for all the status
quo of the boundaries drawn by World War II.

Khrushchev had earlier asserted—perhaps to appease ex-
tremists in the Party Presidium—that if the United States did not
show an understanding of the necessity for concluding a German
peace treaty, the Soviet Union would then have to sign a separate
peace treaty with East Germany. It had been hoped, Brezhnev said,
that a solution could be reached to the problem of Berlin through
negotiation. "Unfortunately, our former allies have not demonstrated as much interest in a peaceful German arrangement as in
solidarity with those forces in today's West Germany which are
openly seeking to change existing national boundaries in Europe and
are making war preparations," Brezhnev pointed out.

"The Soviet government has supported and supports the
general resolution on the question of a peaceful arrangement for
Germany by negotiation," Brezhnev concluded, but "If the Western
powers do not want this," and he implied they did not, "then there is
nothing left but to do everything that is presently possible for signing
of a peace treaty, but only with the German Democratic Republic.
This is the only legitimate solution to the problem of West Berlin"
(italics supplied).

Khrushchev had chosen not to inflict a major diplomatic
defeat on the West by forcing it to accept a *fait accompli* of a Soviet-
East German peace treaty, bringing with the treaty the end of
Western occupation rights in West Berlin; he chose instead to build a
wall separating East from West Berlin. But Brezhnev continued to
harp on a separate peace treaty as being the only legitimate solution
to the problem. Such a treaty would give East Germany control
over all access to West Berlin. President Kennedy, however, warned
that any forcible limitation of allied access would be considered a
belligerent act. Brezhnev replied in his Finland speech by promising

that any American attempt to gain forcible entry into Berlin would be met by force: "If the West believes that its military threats will stop us from signing a separate peace treaty, one can only say: neither the Soviet Union nor its allies fear these threats, and it would be well for those who seek to warm up the atmosphere to note that it is a dangerous road to follow."

Doing a little missile rattling himself, Brezhnev concluded: "Under conditions of modern warfare, it [nuclear war] could mean the destruction of millions of people, the obliteration of whole countries."

Brezhnev's missile threats contrasted sharply with the policy of prudence and restraint being pursued by Khrushchev in early September. In answer to a joint Nehru-Nkrumah message sent to the Kremlin as a plea for direct Soviet-American negotiation, Khrushchev expressed full assent: "In the name of ensuring peace we are ready for negotiations at any time, in any place, and at any level."[8]

That month Khrushchev personally initiated conciliatory moves toward the United States by abandoning earlier insistence that a German peace treaty be signed by the end of the year and by resuming the bilateral disarmament talks that had broken down in July. Resumption of the talks made world news headlines. Significantly, Brezhnev neglected to mention them in his Finland speech.

Moreover, Khurshchev stressed the prospects for peace and the feasibility of negotiation. Eight days before Brezhnev spoke in Finland, the Party chief had emphasized that "the Soviet Union does not wish to follow the rut of military rivalry with the Western powers,"[9] and at one point he flatly stated that "there will be no war," regardless of the outcome over Berlin. In contrast, Brezhnev stressed the implausibility of negotiation and the threat of war. Khrushchev gave foreign reporters the impression that there was no impasse over Berlin. Brezhnev at Helsinki implied that there was. Western diplomats reported that some Soviet officials in private conversations expressed optimism about the possibility of a settlement that would avert a war.[10] There are no recorded private conversations of this nature with Brezhnev.

The significance of Brezhnev's Finland speech becomes clearer if we recognize that Soviet foreign policy at this time was shaped not unilaterally by Khrushchev, but by agreement and disagreement among the collective leadership. His speech was an integral part of a broad campaign by hardliners for control of foreign policy. Some observers argue that while Khrushchev was pursuing a soft line, his subordinates were charged with making noises of war to weaken the Western position. This may have been true at one point, but clear divisions had been drawn among the Soviet leadership by this tme and from September to October 1961, Khrushchev was embroiled in a sharp conflict.

Those in the Party leadership—Brezhnev, Frol Kozlov, Andrey Gromyko, Mikoyan and Mikhail Suslov—who advocated an extremely tough position had gained the upper hand in late August and September 1961, particularly during Khrushchev's absence from Moscow from September 22 through October 4, when he was at his Black Sea resort. Evidence of this included resumption of the Soviet military buildup and nuclear testing; a direct challenge to unrestricted Western access to West Berlin; and a tough military propaganda campaign designed to stiffen opposition toward conciliation with the West.[11] The latter was launched by Brezhnev's old wartime comrade, Marshal Moskalenko, two weeks before Brezhnev's trip to Finland.

Three days before Brezhnev was due to speak in Helsinki, Gromyko stood up in the United Nations and resurrected the end-of-the-year deadline for a German peace treaty. The emphasis Brezhnev gave the treaty, formulated in almost identical language at Helsinki, and the threats to use Soviet military force, supported Gromyko's position. Other than Gromyko, Brezhnev was the only Soviet official to advance the hardline position in a capitalist country.

Thus, Brezhnev's actions in late September identify him as a hardline proponent on Berlin and a pressure factor on Khrushchev which created difficulties for the Party chief's negotiations with President Kennedy. Internal disagreement was set in motion by external issues in which Khrushchev's policies and methods failed to satisfy a large part of the collective leadership and Brezhnev personally. Khrushchev was censured because, in the words of one American journalist: "He had been weak in dealing with the issues of Berlin, Germany, and disarmament."[12]

The hardliners believed that compromise or conciliation meant betrayal of the ideological essence of Communism and represented a shortsighted approach to the problem. Brezhnev either thought the Soviet military could stand down the United States or believed that the U.S. would not really mount an armed clash over Berlin, or if it did, that President Kennedy would never escalate the local conflict into a nuclear war.

Up to this point, unquestioned loyalty and support for Khrushchev had characterized and explained Brezhnev's behavior in all phases of the Kremlin political struggle since Stalin's death. Now the pattern began to change, the erstwhile protégé's politics characterized by a continuing shift from support of Khrushchev to a moderate and finally opposing stand.

On just about every substantive issue dividing the Party leadership over the next three years, Brezhnev would assume a middle-of-the-road position, appearing at all times to see validity in both sides of the argument. He would support Khrushchev when it appeared feasible to do so or out of strong personal conviction for an issue, while taking refuge in praise of Khrushchev that gave the latter pleasure and caused little or no offense to potential allies. He would frequently appear the mediator of conflict, offer compromise, or cause a stalemate by the position he took. This was a calculated strategy which, while not always so orderly and at times even appearing contradictory, enabled Brezhnev, when the opportune moment presented itself, to seize the Party crown from Khrushchev.

But the pattern was immediately confusing, its existence blurred by continuing praise of Khrushchev's Party leadership which fitted completely into the Party chief's attempt to link his policies to Lenin's. Brezhnev's personal praise of Khrushchev at the Twenty-second Party Congress in late October 1961,[13] for example, was so effusive that if not for other factors, it would have disguised the importance of Brezhnev's Finland speech. It was, namely, Brezhnev's reluctance to support Khrushchev's bid at the Congress, to restore momentum to his Party leadership by further condemning the anti-Party group, that pointed to the seriousness of the differences.

A new anti-Party group drive was central to Khrushchev's political strategy at the 1961 Party Congress. His earlier attack on Stalin had been a potent weapon against the opposition. In 1961, he intended to use it to the same end. The renewed attack on the group, aimed at severe punitive measures against its leaders, would eliminate a potential rallying point for opposition and act as an instrument against current points of resistance. The key was Khrushchev's charge that its leaders bore "personal responsibility for many largescale repressions against Party cadres, the *soviets*, government, Armed Forces and the Komsomol during the era of the personality cult."

Brezhnev displayed no desire to press for further action against the group. He devoted fewer words (183 words; one paragraph) to the subject of the anti-Party group in his report to the Congress than any other Party leader,* and he took a moderate stand

*In contrast, Ignatov devoted 1,760 words; Madame Furtseva, 1,100 words; Nikolay

on the whole matter, which mainly benefited himself and had a considerable impact on the outcome of Khrushchev's attempt to expel the leaders of the group from the Party.

Unlike Khrushchev and his erstwhile supporters, Brezhnev made no mention of "mass repressions" or "gross violations of revolutionary legality" (Podgorny), "death of totally innocent people" (Ivan Spiridonov), "mass slaugther of Party cadres" (Kirill Mazurov), "a hand in the tragic death of Tukhachevskiy and Yakir" (Furtseva). Nor did he directly take the side of those who discounted the past by failing to mention crimes or repressions.

He did say however that the leaders of the anti-Party group were "burdened with the weight of the past and the mistakes and crimes that had been committed," and he added "they should bear responsibility to the people for these mistakes and crimes." This deliberate obfuscation, increased by Brezhnev's failure to give details on how they should bear responsibility, placed him in an ambiguous position on the matter of punishment.

He assumed a similar position on the "more recent activities of the group." While those who headed up the attack accused group leaders of organizing a conspiracy and engaging in activities "to put the Party back in those days when people weren't safe," others saw "no present danger to our Party." Brezhnev provided a third view, which held that "not everyone proved capable of understanding the enormous importance that the restoration of Leninist norms of the Party and state life and the all-around development of democracy had for our Party." But while the "factionalists, dogmatists and skeptics" broke their ties with the people and entered into "an anti-Party collusion," their only offense in Brezhnev's opinion was that "in both domestic and foreign policy they were and remained revisionists, sectarians and hopeless dogmatists, clinging to the old, outdated forms and methods, refuting everything new that had been born."

The matter of guilt for past repressions remained the pivotal question. Here, Brezhnev played the deciding role.

Michel Tatu's analysis[14] of the Presidium vote on this question concluded that on the eve of the Congress nine members (Khrushchev, Furtseva, Ignatov, Kozlov, Nuritdin Mukhitdinov, Polyanskiy, Podgorny, Suslov and Shvernik) approved the thesis of guilt for at least three of the accused. Three (Mikoyan, Aleksey Kosygin

Podgorny, 990 words; Dimitriy Polyanskiy, 870 words; and Ivan Spiridonov, 550 words, to revelations about the criminal activities of the group's leaders.

and Otto Kuusinen) did not approve it, and one (Brezhnev) was ambiguous (Aristov was in Poland on leave of absence and did not speak at the Congress).

By the end of the Congress, however, the composition of the Presidium had changed. Madame Furtseva, Ignatov, Mukhitdinov, and Aristov had been eliminated, while Gennadiy Voronov (an opponent of prosecution) joined the Presidium. This shift left Khrushchev, Kozlov, Polyanskiy, Podgorny, Shvernik and Suslov for recognition of guilt, while Mikoyan, Kosygin, Kuusinen, Voronov and probably Brezhnev were opposed.

Suslov and Brezhnev, who had been the most reluctant to commit themselves one way or the other, played the arbitrators. Thus, the vote of the new Presidium was 6-5 for, or 6-5 against, depending on Suslov's final vote. A review of Suslov's position indicates that he voted with those who opposed the guilty verdict in both the early as well as the later vote. This means that there was a tie in the Presidium, with Brezhnev holding the deciding vote. The fact that no mention of expulsion was made in the resolution passed by the Congress on October 31 indicates that he voted no.

If Brezhnev was soft on the anti-Party group, he displayed plenty of steel against the Albanian "dogmatists and sectarians." His answer to the question (raised at the Congress) of whether or not the Soviet Union should break publicly with the Albanian Party of Labor was a resounding affirmative. Unlike the anti-Party group issue, there was no serious disagreement at the Congress over the position that should be taken on Albania's independent stand, only degrees of condemnation, and in this matter Brezhnev was not among the counselors of restraint.

Khrushchev's attack on the Albanians focused on their resistance to de-Stalinization. Summing up his arguments against the Albanian Party leaders, Khrushchev told the Congress, Enver Hoxha and Mehment Shehu "want to return to the days of the Stalinist personality cult." Brezhnev added that Stalinization was in full swing in Albania: "We already know that they do not like the course of the Twentieth Party Congress of our Party," but they are also "whipping up an atmosphere of the cult of the individual in their own country." The idea caught on. Mikoyan, for example, quoted Albanian Party leaders as promising that anyone who disagreed with them "would be spat at in the face, punched in the mouth, and if need be a bullet would be put in his head."[15]

Unlike Mikoyan and others, Brezhnev did not go into the

gory details about the Stalinist methods used to liquidate pro-Soviet elements in Albania. He should have. Liri Belishova, the wife of the prominent intellectual Nako Spiru, a longtime friend of the U.S.S.R and a ranking member of the Albanian Party, spoke highly of "our respected Comrade L. Brezhnev" during a visit to China. On her return to Albania she was arrested and executed by Hoxha.

Brezhnev did add fuel to the fire, however, by calling for a "popular uprising" in Albania: "We have done everything necessary to ensure that Soviet-Albanian relations would develop and grow stronger, but as our efforts have been fruitless, we are convinced that the only way for the Albanians to prevent a *fatal development of events* is for the Albanian leaders to return to the position of friendship and cooperation with all socialist countries and the interests of our great common cause" (italics added). The same language had been used to justify military action in Hungary in 1956.

Brezhnev was the only speaker to support a "popular uprising." Even Mikoyan, for all his vehemence toward the Albanians, stopped short of endorsing it. Did Brezhnev really intend military action? If his statement about the "fatal developments of events" is taken literally, it would seem so. In reality, however, it is doubtful that he ever seriously considered it.

From a purely military standpoint it would have diverted focus from the Berlin issue and tied up forces when the possibility of military confrontation with the United States was still very much alive. Moreover, military action against Albania might have led to a military conflict with the People's Republic of China, which supported Albania. Brezhnev must have known that the majority of the Party Presidium would never agree under existing circumstances to such a move, so it did him no harm to back it. There was nothing to lose by threatening the Albanians, and agreement with Khrushchev would help compensate for dissension on the anti-Party group issue.

Brezhnev also took a dissenting position by a vote of silence on Khrushchev's proposed economic investment priorities. The Berlin crisis had fueled higher defense expenditures and investment in heavy industry at the expense of agriculture and light industry; two areas in which Khrushchev now wanted to rechannel substantial investment. Brezhnev's failure to comment on the proposed changes in economic investments indicated dissent. Similarly, other hardliners and heavy industry exponents failed to mention the proposal in their Congress speeches.

Part III
POWER IN THE KREMLIN

XVII

Titans Locked in Combat

*Accomplished leaders don't fall from the skies,
they are raised up only in the course of the
struggle.* — Joseph Stalin, 1924.

IN 1959, KHRUSHCHEV, EXPRESSING HIS OPINION of Stalin's
failure to select a successor, told Averell Harriman that the mistake
must not be repeated and that he, in consultation with Mikoyan, had
picked Frol Kozlov as heir to the Party throne. Kozlov, the second
most powerful man in the government, was not a Khrushchev protégé
in the real sense of the word. He had developed his career in the Party apparatus independently of Khrushchev, but later rose to high
places because he threw the full weight of the Leningrad Party
organization behind the Party chief at the most crucial stage in
Khrushchev's rise to power. Kozlov helped save him in 1957 and subsequently wormed his way into Khrushchev's total confidence. When
Khrushchev became head of the government, replacing Nikolay
Bulganin as Chairman of the Council of Ministers in 1958, Khrushchev made Kozlov, the Leningrad Party chief, his deputy.

But it wasn't all Kozlov's cleverness that gained him the spot.
For sundry reasons Khrushchev had turned against Aleksey
Kirichenko, the senior member of the Ukrainian clique in Moscow
and Party second in command, whom many Western observers considered Khrushchev's heir apparant. Rumors about Khrushchev's
dissatisfaction with him had begun to circulate, and the Party chief's
remarks to Harriman clearly indicated that Kirichenko was having
political trouble. His "style of work" was reportedly defective; he
allegedly clashed with "influential" Presidium members over his
arrogant manner; he opposed some of the decisions taken regarding
the military and the police; and he failed as Cadres' Party Secretary
to oppose with sufficient vigor nationalist tendencies in the non-
Russian republics. He was dismissed from the Secretariat in January
1960.

Khrushchev's coldness seemed to extend to the Ukrainian
group in general. He turned more and more to the Ukraine's
traditional rival, Leningrad, for political and administrative talent.

It wasn't going to be easy for Kozlov to become the successor designate in reality as well as name. Khrushchev would have to bring the Leningrad apparatchik into the Party Secretariat and then maneuver him into the second position in that body. Kirichenko's removal from the Secretariat eliminated a major stumbling block, but the Ukrainian group in the Kremlin now led by Brezhnev constituted a major obstacle. For the next five months, until his election to the Secretariat in May, they worked feverishly to counter Kozlov's growing influence.

So began the contest for power between these two senior representatives and their respective Party organizations; a contest which over the next three years typified the traditional rivalry between Leningrad and the Ukraine for power and influence in Moscow. The manner in which the fortunes of these two men, their protégés and associates rose and fell in the ensuing power struggle strongly recalled the battles earlier fought between Zhdanov and Malenkov, and then Malenkov and Khrushchev. It also suggested a purposeful balancing of power by Khrushchev.

Curiously, Kirichenko's downfall conferred on Brezhnev, as the remaining senior secretary, a number of important powers which he put to good use. In January 1960, Brezhnev went to Alma Ata and supervised the purge of Nikolay Belyayev from the Party leadership, leaving Dinmukhamed Kunayev, with whom Brezhnev had worked in 1954-56, in charge. He made personnel changes in the Ukraine and in the central Party and government administration too that widened his own influence.

But the record for the Central Committee plenum of May 1960 suggests that Kozlov did some clever behind-the-scenes maneuvering of his own in the five-month interval. The Secretariat was cleaned out in a manner which implied that the sole aim of the reorganizing done at the plenum was to give Kozlov a clear field. Aristov, Furtseva, Ignatov and Pavel Pospelov were all sacked. Of the remaining members in the reconstructed Secretariat, only Brezhnev could pose a real threat to Kozlov in a bid for power should a succession crisis occur: Mikhail Suslov showed no desire to become Party head; Otto Kuusinen was too old; and Nuritdin Mukhitdinov was too young. As Kozlov studied the competition and potential challengers to his crown, Brezhnev loomed very large on the horizon.

It was Kozlov's considered opinion that Brezhnev had to be removed from the Secretariat if his own status as heir designate was to be guaranteed. But if in fact Kozlov did try to convince Khrushchev to unseat Brezhnev during the May plenum, he failed. Important factors, however, militated against Brezhnev's continuation in that body for very long. The endless succession of functions he was required to perform in his new job as President, particularly his trips away from home, increasingly deprived him of valuable time to perform his Secretariat duties.

It is not likely that Brezhnev gave up his seat in the Secretariat voluntarily. Nevertheless, his departure was announced on July 17, 1960.[1] There is a strong possibility that in the end, Khrushchev personally prevailed upon him to vacate the position since a policy designed to prevent most Presidium and Secretariat office holders from occupying seats in both bodies simultaneously seemed to be in operation. Up to this point, Khrushchev, Brezhnev, Kozlov, Kuusinen and Suslov were the only exceptions.

Kozlov now enjoyed a near monopoly of power. He quickly began to place his clients throughout the country. In little over a year eight cohorts were appointed to high posts in the central administration, in the economy, in regional Party posts, and one, Ivan Spiridonov, Kozlov's successor in Leningrad, to the Secretariat. Spiridonov's appointment was made at the 1961 Party Congress when Kozlov's power and career peaked.

Kozlov's gains also meant the temporary loss for Brezhnev of one very important protégé and close friend, Andrey Kirilenko. Kirilenko and Brezhnev had been neighboring *oblast* secretaries when World War II broke out and later served together in the war as political officers until Kirilenko became the military liaison for the aircraft industry. Postwar contact was maintained. Kirilenko took over in Dnepropetrovsk when Brezhnev went to Moscow in 1950, and Brezhnev was instrumental in securing Kirilenko's selection as a candidate member to the Party Presidium at the Twentieth Party Congress. Forcing Kirilenko out of the Presidium at the Twenty-Second Party Congress was a successful move by Kozlov to further reduce Brezhnev's status.

But the political current following the Party Congress was extremely fluid, and within six months the situation was completely reversed. There were no personnel changes in Kozlov's favor after the Congress. In fact, the top level shifts that were made actually worked against him.

On April 28, 1962, the Central Committee convened and

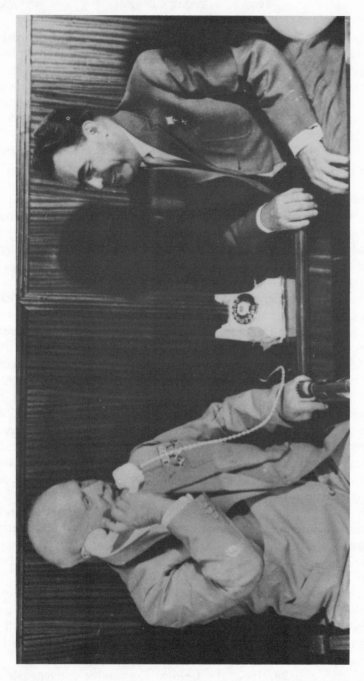

Khrushchev (left) and Brezhnev congratulate Cosmonauts Andriyan Nikolayev and Pavel Popovich on their historic flight, August 15, 1962. (World Wide Photos.)

removed Spiridonov from the Secretariat. At the same time they reinstated Kirilenko, giving him a handsome promotion to full Presidium membership to boot. Not only was Kirilenko's reinstatement a blow to Kozlov, but Kirilenko's additional assignment as First Deputy Chairman of the Bureau of the R.S.F.S.R. helped Brezhnev check Kozlov's power since the establishment of that body whittled down the traditional powers of the federal bureaucracy controlled by Kozlov.

The Spiridonov case provides a classic example of how Brezhnev used political circumstances and secret police connections to destroy an opponent. When Brezhnev left the Secretariat his job was filled on a makeshift basis, at least until Spiridonov came along. But the newcomer had made the mistake of placing himself at the head of the destalinizers at the Twenty-Second Party Congress when he recommended that Stalin's body, entombed in the Lenin Mausoleum since 1953, be removed. This liberal gesture sounded the alarm in the military and industrial sectors and prompted intrigue against him, since his assignment as military affairs secretary was interpreted as a Khrushchev move to stiffle that community by putting a "liberal" in charge. Brezhnev thereupon called on his friend Nikolay Mironov, who had been chief of the KGB in Leningrad where he had assembled a dossier on Spiridonov, and who was now head of the weighty Administrative Organs Department in the Party Central Committee. In no time at all Mironov unearthed information of a highly personal nature about Spiridonov, which Brezhnev used to slander and embarrass Kozlov's protégé, forcing his resignation from the Secretariat.

Brezhnev managed to recoup other losses, chiefly because of a serious dispute which erupted between Khrushchev and Kozlov in 1962 over at least two crucial issues. One was rapproachement with Yugoslavia. The second sprang from Kozlov's objection to special funding that Khrushchev wanted for agriculture. When Kozlov blocked the funding at the March 1962 Central Committee plenum, Khrushchev became angry. Subsequent personnel changes made in Brezhnev's favor at the central Party and government levels reflected this displeasure.

There were numerous signs in 1962 that Brezhnev was gaining momentum over Kozlov in the power struggle. During the May Day celebration parade Brezhnev stood next to Khrushchev on the reviewing stand, with Kozlov next in line.[2] At the height of the

Cuban missile crisis when the head of the Czechoslovak Communist Party, Antonin Novotny, met with Presdium leaders in Moscow, Brezhnev again stood next to Khrushchev in the protocol order.[3] Kozlov was number three in line in this instance also. Two weeks later, Brezhnev left for Czechoslovakia ostensibly to speak at the Twelfth Czechoslovak Communist Party Congress.

Novotny's visit, coming just 15 days prior to the Czech Congress, and Brezhnev's mission to Czechoslovakia were interrelated. They also pointed to Brezhnev's improved position vis-à-vis Kozlov. A number of high level meetings were held during Novotny's stay to discuss ways to handle the domestic opposition in Czechoslovakia which threatened a leadership crisis at the Congress. It was felt that the presence of a high-ranking Soviet official would prevent dissension at the Congress.

Kozlov more and more turned against Khrushchev. In the spring of 1963, as part of a direct challenge to Khrushchev, he began a new campaign against Brezhnev only to fall seriously ill before it could gather full steam.

The first signs of the offensive appeared on February 27, when the Party leaders campaigned in their constituencies for reelection to the R.S.F.S.R. Supreme Soviet. Tass characterized Brezhnev as "one of the most eminent figures of the Party and state, an energetic, talented, demanding and considerate leader who unswervingly puts Leninist principles into practice.[4] But such credits were not to be found in *Pravda* or in any other leading newspaper. *Pravda* actually took great pains to describe Kozlov as "a leader of outstanding qualities, lofty ideals and principles, one who has the gift of organization, practical sense, perseverance and firmness in the execution of Party and government decisions."[5] There was no mistake. This was a purposeful attempt to minimize Brezhnev's public image.

Similar treatment was meted out to Brezhnev's closest protégé. One March 12 *Pravda* dropped Kirilenko two places down, out of alphabetical order, in its listing of Presidium members attending an R.S.F.S.R. agricultural conference. Moreover, unmistakable criticism of Kirilenko was forthcoming on April 1 when a feature article by the Sverdlovsk Party chief, Konstantin Nikolayev, appeared in *Pravda*, criticizing the performance of his previous boss.

The inimical contest of strength went on. Then in April it

came to an abrupt halt. Kozlov suffered a sudden stroke, incapacitating him; recovery was not expected. Initially it appeared that Brezhnev had won the power struggle by default. But it was soon apparent that such speculation was premature.

If the Chinese stole the show at the June 18-21, 1963, ideological plenum (the plenum that ratified the near complete break with China), then the return of Brezhnev and the entry of Nikolay Podgorny, the Ukrainian Party chief, into the Secretariat at the plenum captured the remaining interest of the participants. Both appointments broke for the first time in over three years the pattern of organizational separation of the Party Presidium and the Secretariat, and immediately confused the issue of who was the new heir apparent. Knrushchev muddied the water still further by remarking to the visiting French statesman Guy Mollet that there were three possible successors—Brezhnev, Podgorny and Vasiliy Polyakov.[6]

Polyakov was Khrushchev's ghost writer on agriculture who immediately after Kozlov's disappearance from the political scene wrote an article in *Kommunist* (no. 6, 1963) in which he was most complimentary of Khrushchev. The article received widespread coverage in the provincial press. But it is difficult to tell what constituted the basis for Khrushchev's remark concerning Polyakov as a contender. Was Khrushchev spoofing or just trying to confuse the West? There appeared to be a little on which to base Polyakov's credentials as a real contender.

Several theories sprang up though to explain the appointments of Brezhnev and Podgorny. One school of thought contended that Khrushchev was now acutely aware of the potential danger of a single heir apparent. This school presupposed that both Brezhnev and Podgorny were Khrushchev men whose appointments would facilitate restoration of the Secretariat as the prime lever over the Presidium, thereby returning to the situation that Khrushchev had enjoyed in 1957.[7]

A modification of the theory recognized Brezhnev as second in command and heir apparent, while Podgorny was seen as counterbalancing Brezhnev in the Secretariat. Other observers fleetingly reversed the roles of Brezhnev and Podgorny. The *Daily Telegraph* for example, reported: "If as seems likely, Mr. Kozlov is now permanently out of the running, Mr. Podgorny must be regarded as Mr. Khrushchev's principal deputy and in theory at least, his potential successor."[8]

It seems clear, though, that if Podgorny was the chosen one, Brezhnev was actually the pick of those who had earlier rallied in opposition to Khrushchev and had provided support for Kozlov. The basis for this deduction can be found in the relative strengths of the contending forces within the Party leadership in March 1963. Only weeks before Kozlov was stricken, Boffa alluded to a "difficult struggle underway in Moscow."[9] Once Kozlov's illness was confirmed a scramble for power took place. Kozlov's challenges to Khrushchev had led to a strong reassertion of collective leadership in the spring of 1963, and the conservative forces behind Kozlov were far from resigned, despite the loss of their spokesman, to surrender the gains that had been made. They maneuvered to retain their political advantage.

The balance of power in the Kremlin shifted indeterminantly between April and June 1963, but the opposition clearly retained sufficient power to exert a major force on any decision about who was to replace Kozlov in the Secretariat. Most Party leaders expected that selection to take place at the scheduled May 28, 1963 Party plenum, but rescheduling of the plenum to June indicated failure to agree on a compromise candidate. Not one but two candidates emerged at the June plenum as a consequence.

Brezhnev can be ruled out as Khrushchev's choice. Unquestioned loyalty was a prime consideration and Brezhnev's as we saw earlier, had become suspect. Since the June plenum constituted Khrushchev's *last chance* to restore his once unchallenged position, he was careful to pick a candidate he could fully trust. He required someone more politically dependent on him and less ambitious than Brezhnev.

His choice would be a member of the Presidium whose career, like his own, had begun in the Ukraine. Kirilenko was ruled out because he was too close to Brezhnev. But Podgorny filled the bill. He had headed the Party in the Ukraine since 1957 and had a good record as a Khrushchev supporter. As a newcomer to Moscow he would be politically dependent on Khrushchev.

Brezhnev's selection as the choice of the opposition was a last minute decision. The opposition had lacked a ready-made candidate to promote in Kozlov's place. They had placed great hope in his speedy recovery and made every attempt to reassure his supporters and assert that although seriously ill, he was still a Presidium member and a Secretary of the Central Committee. But as Kozlov's condition worsened, selection of an alternative candidate became imperative since Podgorny was unacceptable.

Those very factors that had worked against Brezhnev before now worked for him. The choice for the opposition was nevertheless difficult. Brezhnev was a member of the Ukrainian clique and despite his policy declarations there was still the question of his strong links with the Ukraine. With regard to his philosophical outlooks, Brezhnev demonstrated a desire for a more orthodox approach to foreign policy, but his position on Khrushchev's domestic policies left lingering doubts in the minds of some of those who had supported Kozlov. Yet Brezhnev's hard line on the most crucial issues could not be overlooked. Moreover, he had good reason now to actively work against Khrushchev.

Twice Khrushchev had bypassed him in the selection of an heir. Moreover, Brezhnev had effectively competed with Kozlov and had obtained wide exposure and an extensive base of support with connections in the Party and state appartus (which Podgorny generally lacked). Too, his was a powerful voice in the Presidium. Force of circumstances then demanded that Suslov, the key figure in the opposition, place confidence in Brezhnev.

Selection of a qualified candidate was even more imperative if it was true that Suslov had contemplated a coup against Khrushchev in early 1963. Suslov reportedly went to see Kozlov in the hospital where the latter argued that the only way to alleviate the USSR's problems was to get rid of Khrushchev since no good would come of him.

It would have been foolish, however, for Suslov to expect Brezhnev to pick up where Kozlov had left off and further chip away at Khrushchev's armor. Brezhnev would play it cautiously. He was too old a hand at political maneuvering to make a rash move. He preferred to pursue a moderate line with Suslov's backing until assessment of the situation revealed it was time to move against Khrushchev. In the meantime, Brezhnev assumed a wide range of responsibilities in the Secretariat.

On the surface, the competition between Brezhnev and Podgorny appeared fluid. It was difficult to tell just who had the upper hand in the remaining months of 1963. Brezhnev's frequent appearances, though mainly related to his continued duties as head of state, tricked many observers into thinking that he was the front runner. For example, at the welcoming rally for cosmonauts

Brezhnev (left) basking in the sun with khaki-clad Fidel Castro and host Khrushchev (second from right) at the host's estate near Moscow in 1963. (World Wide Photos.)

Tereshkova and Nikolayev at Red Square on June 22 it was Brezhnev who stood next to Khrushchev. (Podgorny was in the background). Brezhnev was really there because of his connections with the defense industry and missile and space development; professional protocol, as it were, rather than Party rank. In fact, the media's failure to publish the photograph of Brezhnev with Khrushchev helped to demonstrate his eclipse, although the Party newspaper in Brezhnev's old bailiwick of Kazakhstan, *Kazakhstanskaya Pravda*, tried to make something of his appearance by publishing the photo.[10]

Despite the publicity that Brezhnev continued to receive, beneath the surface there was evidence that Podgorny, working less openly, began his new role with an organizational advantage. It was no coincidence that Brezhnev was required to continue his duties in the Supreme Soviet. These demanded an inordinate amount of time and restricted his politicking against Podgorny. Thus, again Brezhnev's functions in the Secretariat were bound to suffer. The obvious beneficiary of such a state of affairs was Podgorny.

The newcomer to Moscow had the authority to practice an active cadres policy. Barely a month after his selection to the Secretariat, several Kharkov officials associated with Podgorny were brought into the central administration, while Brezhnev suffered the loss of one of his chief protégés in the Ukraine, Vladimir Shcherbitskiy.

Brezhnev had succeeded in having Shcherbitskiy appointed Premier of the Ukraine only in 1960. By rights, Shcherbitskiy should have been made the Ukrainian Party chief when Khrushchev called Podgorny to Moscow. But Khrushchev himself, or Podgorny acting with Khrushchev's blessings, not only promoted Pyotr Shelest, a Kharkovite, to the position but arranged for Shcherbitskiy's removal from his Party posts in Moscow—Shelest subsequently receiving Shcherbitskiy's candidate membership in the Presidium—and dismissal as Premier of the Ukraine. Brezhnev could do nothing to prevent this axing, but he did manage to have Shcherbitskiy put in a holding pattern as Party head of the Dnepropetrovsk *oblast* until he was able to restore him to his former posts after the October 1964 coup.

Podgorny's range of responsibilities steadily expanded and he began to assume an increasingly prominent role in the leadership, particularly at the beginning of 1964. He told M. Bernard Firon, a French diplomat, during a visit to France in January 1964 that his role covered many fields.[11] There was even some indication that he had moved into Suslov's field of foreign Communist party relations, filling in during the summer and fall of 1963 when Suslov was ill. In April 1964, Podgorny's political status was considerably enhanced by his appointment to head a special commission to work out measures for strengthening the flagging livestock sector. He presided over six other Presidium members in this effort; Brezhnev was one of them. Podgorny's influence was also clearly reflected in portrait displays on national holidays.

Brezhnev during this period maneuvered against Podgorny. In the Ukraine, Brezhnev made a bid for control of the Ukrainian Party organization and also sought to improve his status in the central Party and government apparatus where cohorts in high level positions possessed the power to check Podgorny's thrusts. These powerful friends are discussed in the next chapter.

While it was true that Brezhnev's time-consuming duties as head of state limited his activities in the Secretariat, in the fall of 1963 he began turning more and more of his duties over to his deputy, Vasiliy Kozlov (no relation to Frol). By the following spring Brezhnev showed signs of political recovery. Khrushchev's policies and programs were now under heavy attack and Suslov was at his most active. As the pendulum swung back in Brezhnev's favor, he was relieved of his onerous Supreme Soviet duties at the July 13 session of the Soviet parliament. The reason according to the Tass announcement was the "The Central Committee considers it expedient to have L.I. Brezhnev concentrate on his duties in the Party Secretariat."

Again Western observers attempted to explain the change. Some believed that the Presidium had only just decided to let Brezhnev effectively return to the political mainstream. Another explained it on constitutional grounds: perhaps the Party had not wanted to appear to change presidents before the "formal expiration of his term." Others felt that Khrushchev had wanted to equalize the relative strengths of the two heirs to give Brezhnev more of a fighting chance to compete effectively and limit Podgorny's buildup of power.

Whatever the reason, the move was more than overdue. The Podgorny/Brezhnev dual authority in the Secretariat was inefficient, confusing and, in view of the Party apparatus, unnecessary. This, of course, did not mean that Podgorny's chances for succession had been nullified. Nevertheless, the announcement of Brezhnev's return to full-time work in the Secretariat was an omen of things to come. The phrasing that heralded Brezhnev's return to work had been used in March 1953, just before Stalin's death, in reference to Khrushchev. Khrushchev emerged six months later as First Secretary. It is ironic that five months after the announcement of Brezhnev's return to the Secretariat, he too became Party head.

XVIII
The Men Behind Brezhnev

Power as conceived by totalitarianism lies exclusively in the force produced by organization — Hannah Arendt, *The Origins of Totalitarianism.*

NOWHERE ELSE IN THE WORLD is the system of patronage so vital a factor in determining political fortunes as in the Soviet Union. Without Khrushchev, Brezhnev would never have made it to the top. His dependence on the Soviet version of the old-boy network twice brought him into the highest levels of the Party leadership. And once there he worked methodically to build up his own patronage network. A collective of loyalists, many with boyhood links or early career ties to Brezhnev, were subsequently promoted to key bureaucratic positions in the provincial and central Party and government apparatus, enabling him to accumulate power and influence. These men owed debts to Brezhnev and they backed him in the Kremlin power struggle and in his bold bid for Khrushchev's crown in October 1964. Many are in powerful positions today.

Brezhnev was particularly active in expanding an already intricate and complicated patronage network in the years immediately preceding Khrushchev's ouster from the Soviet leadership, promoting numerous officials to very high positions throughout the U.S.S.R. Within weeks of assuming Kirichenko's responsibilities, Brezhnev went to the heart of Podgorny's Ukrainian apparatus by maneuvering three cohorts into strategic positions within that organization.

Nikolay Drozdenko, an able and steadfast loyalist, was one of them. Brezhnev took the young graduate of the Dnepropetrovsk Railroad Engineering Institute under his wing in 1948. Later, under Andrey Kirilenko, Drozdenko became Propaganda Secretary, then Kirilenko's immediate deputy, and still later Party Secretary of the Ukrainian Komsomol organization.[1]

In January 1960, Brezhnev jockeyed his client into position as Party Secretary of the Kiev City Party Committee, where Drozdenko demonstrated his worth in the particularly heated battles with Podgorny in 1963. Later that year, Brezhnev elbowed out a Podgorny cohort to position Drozdenko as head of the powerful Kiev Regional Party Committee.

Yuriy Torsuev was an equally able Brezhnev supporter who replaced Drozdenko as head of the Ukrainian Komsomol apparatus in 1960. He had worked under Brezhnev in 1948-1949 too, becoming Dnepropetrovsk *oblast* Komsomol Secretary shortly after Brezhnev returned to the central Party leadership in 1956.

By far the most important promotion was that of the younger Vladimir Shcherbitskiy whom Brezhnev regards as a son. When Kirilenko left for Moscow in 1955, he turned the reins of the Dnepropetrovsk *oblast* over to Shcherbitskiy. The latter's star continued to rise and two years later Shcherbitskiy also left Dnepropetrovsk, but for Kiev where he had been elected a republic Party Secretary and Party Presidium member. Sponsored by Brezhnev at the 1961 Party Congress, he was elected a full member of the C.P.S.U. Central Committee and a nonvoting member of the C.P.S.U. Presidum.

Scherbitskiy's elevation to Premier of the Ukraine (Chairman of the Ukrainian Council of Ministers) in January 1960 vividly demontrated Brezhnev's selfish interest in Podgorny's republic. The premiership is a key lever of power in the Ukraine and regarded as a stepping stone to the top Party post in the republic. There was some speculation that Khrushchev might bring Podgorny to Moscow. If he did, Brezhnev was prepared to slip Shcherbitskiy into Podgorny's spot as Party chief.

But the ploy failed miserably. For three years as Premier, Shcherbitskiy labored earnestly to weaken Podgorny's grip over the Ukrainian government administration. Podgorny's success in removing Shcherbitskiy not only from the premiership, but from the Party Central Committee and C.P.S.U. Presidium as well in 1963, was payment for that kind of pressure and a slap in the face for Brezhnev.

A.Gaevoy and Leonid Lukich were two *Dnepropetrovtsy* who infiltrated Podgorny's apparatus in 1961. Both had helped Brezhnev rebuild Dnepropetrovsk in 1948-1950, Lukich as his Third Party Secretary. A graduate of the Dnepropetrovsk Metallurgical Institute (class of 1939), Lukich was chairman of the Dnepropetrovsk Sovnarkhoz and was elected to full membership in the Ukrainian Party Central Committee in 1961.

Gaevoy ranked much higher in terms of what he could do for Brezhnev. Succeeding Shcherbitskiy as Dnepropetrovsk Party head in 1957, Gaevoy's promotion in 1961 to Party Cadres Secretary was a major accomplishment. Control of cadre assignments throughout the Ukraine was essential if Brezhnev was to secure a grip on the regional power centers in the republic.

Brezhnev might have succeeded in this effort had Gaevoy lived. But a stroke and Gaevoy's death a year later seriously jeopardized Brezhnev's bid for power. The elevation of Ivan Grushetskiy, another *Dnepropetrovtsy*, to full membership in the C.P.S.U. Central Committee and to Chairman of the Ukrainian Party-State Control Committee in 1962 helped but it in no way fully compensated for the loss of Shcherbitskiy and Gaevoy.

The promotions of these six men amounted to nothing less than a brazen attempt by Brezhnev to wrest control of the Ukrainian Party organization from Podgorny. Had Khrushchev permitted Shcherbitskiy to succeed Podgorny as Ukrainian Party chief when the latter was called to Moscow — as Shcherbitskiy should have since he was senior in Party rank to the other eligible candidate for the job, namely Pyotr Shelest who was Podgorny's Second Secretary — Brezhnev might have achieved his goal. But he was checked, first by Khrushchev, then by Podgorny, through the demotion of Shcherbitskiy.

The open hostilities that followed between one faction in the Ukraine led by Brezhnev and the other by Podgorny and then Shelest, raged on for many years. Ultimately, Brezhnev was forced to disgrace Shelest.

While the Ukraine remained in Podgorny's hands in 1963, Moldavia belonged wholly to Brezhnev. Even Kozlov met with little success when he had tried to penetrate Brezhnev's Moldavian stronghold through the demotion of Nikolay Shchelokov. Kozlov did succeed in removing Shchelokov as Deputy Chairman of the Moldavian Council of Ministers in 1962, but he was unable to touch Brezhnev's highest ranking Moldavian ally, Ivan Bodyul.

Bodyul had been one of Brezhnev's most enthusiastic district Party secretaries during the 1950 collectivization drive in Moldavia. He held a number of Party posts in the Republic before graduating from the Higher Party School in Moscow in 1958 when his career advanced, again with Brezhnev's help, from instructor within a department of the C.P.S.U. Central Committee to Second Secretary of the Moldavian Communist Party. In May 1961, he was made Party head of the Republic, gaining full voting membership in the C.P.S.U. Central Committee in October.

President Brezhnev with Stalingrad war veterans, 1963.

The important Russian Soviet Federated Socialist Republic (R.S.F.S.R.), the largest of the Soviet republics, was in hand too. Here, Brezhnev's influence extended well down through the Republic's ranks, largely as a result of his own membership in the Republic's ruling body, the R.S.F.S.R. Bureau, from 1958 to 1960, which gave him an opportunity to place many clients in key posts. Kirilenko became Brezhnev's man in the R.S.F.S.R. in April 1962, when he was made First Deputy Chairman of the R.S.F.S.R. Bureau, assuming power second only to Khrushchev, the Bureau's Chairman.

Further, the R.S.F.S.R. Party State Control Committee, empowered to fine, reprimand and try "violators of state economic discipline," was in the hands of yet another trusted graduate of the Dnepropetrovsk Metallurgical Institute and Brezhnev's successor in Zaporozhye in 1947, Georgiy Yenyutin. He became head of the Committee in 1960, and was elevated to full voting status in the C.P.S.U. Central Committee at the Twenty-Second Party Congress.

At the *oblast* level, Ivan Yunak, a Party Secretary under Brezhnev in the late forties and Chairman of the Dnepropetrovsk State Executive Committee between 1955 and 1961, was elevated to Party head of the Tula *oblast*, one of the most important regions in the R.S.F.S.R. Similarly, Georgiy Pavlov, who had studied and worked with Brezhnev in Dneprodzerzhinsk in the thirties, became Party chief of the R.S.F.S.R. Mari *oblast*.

In Kazakhstan, Brezhnev's elevation of Dinmukhamed

Kunayev to Party head was a reward for many years of loyalty. Kunayev owes his entire Party career to Brezhnev. Until Brezhnev promoted him in 1960, he had had an uninspiring 18 years as Deputy Chairman, then Chairman (under Brezhnev) of the Kazakh Council of Ministers. However, Khrushchev's displeasure with Kunayev's poor performance in the harvest of 1960 and in 1961 led to his sacking. Brezhnev reinstated him after Khrushchev's overthrow and he has since remained Party head of Kazakhstan today.

At the Moscow and all-union levels an identical pattern of moving able backers into strategic positions in the Party and government emerged. Shcherbitskiy, Kirilenko, and Yenyutin have already been discussed. Veniamin Dymshits, encountered earlier in Zaporozhye, was another member of this group who rose progressively higher, being promoted four times in three years.

He was brought to Moscow in 1959 from a construction site in India to head the Capital Construction Administration of Gosplan, a position that gave him ministerial status. In July 1961, he became First Deputy Chairman, then Chairman of the State Planning Commission and a Deputy Chairman of the U.S.S.R. Council of Ministers, the highest government authority in the Soviet Union. Four months later his status improved immeasurably when he was promoted to Chairman of the newly established U.S.S.R. Council of the National Economy (Sovnarkhoz), then the most powerful economic body in the Soviet Union. Dymshits was labeled the "economic czar" of the Soviet Union in the Western press and, though a later reorganization did rob him of some of his power, he was still a powerful ally for Brezhnev.

Like Dymshits, Ignatiy Novikov, Brezhnev's neighbor in Dneprodzerzhinsk and classmate, became a Deputy Chairman of the U.S.S.R. Council of Ministers. That same month he was also made head of one of Russia's most important government construction departments, Gostroy.

The promotion of Nikolay Tikhonov was equally impressive. He was called to Moscow in 1960 from his post as Chairman of the Dnepropetrovsk regional economic council to become Deputy Chairman of the State Scientific Economic Council under the Council of Ministers. Born in Kharkov, Podgorny's old bailiwick, his loyalty lay with Dnepropetrovsk where he had worked as a boy until graduation from the Dnepropetrovsk Mining Institute in 1930. Working under Brezhnev in 1948-1950, he became famous for his efforts as head of the Southern Pipe Plant in Dnepropetrovsk.

Tikhonov and another Dnepropetrovsk cohort, Leonid Smirnov, were promoted in March 1963 to high positions in the central government; Tikhonov to Deputy Chairman of Gosplan and Smirnov to the Council of Ministers as a deputy chairmen.

While Tikhonov only gained candidate membership in the Central Committee in 1961, Smirnov gained full voting status. Here was an extremely valuable friend. Smirnov has close ties with the defense industry and with Dimitry Ustinov in particular, then head of that industry and a man on whom Brezhnev could also rely. In addition, Smirnov has strong ties to the military. Until his appointment to the Council of Ministers, he had been a Deputy Chairman, then Chairman of the State Committee for Defense Technology and finally Chairman of the Military Industrial Commission (VPK) where he works today. This is a key lever of power, linking the Party and government to the Soviet military and industrial complex. Smirnov's ties with Brezhnev are extremely close. He was director of the Dnepropetrovsk (Yangel) missile plant in the fifties and like Ustinov worked with Brezhnev in building the Strategic Rocket Forces.

The list goes on. For example, Konstantin Chernenko, a man who sits at Brezhnev's side in the Kremlim today — and someone to watch closely as a potential successor to Brezhnev — was also brought in on the government side. He had orchestrated Brezhnev's propaganda network in Moldavia and, as chief of the U.S.S.R. Supreme Soviet administration apparatus, he accompanied Brezhnev to Africa in February 1961. Similarly Georgiy Tsukanov, another alumnus of the Dnepropetrovsk Metallurgical Institute, long-time employee at the factory in Brezhnev's hometown, and Brezhnev's personal aide since 1958, was brought into the Supreme Soviet to help out. And Brezhnev's chosen successor in Moldavia in 1952, Zinoviy Serdyuk, was appointed in 1961 to the key post of Deputy Chairman of the Party Control Committee, which is charged with verifying and enforcing discipline throughout the Party's ranks.

Almost all of Brezhnev's henchmen promoted between 1960 and 1961 also gained either full membership or candidate status in the C.P.S.U. Central Committee at the 1961 Party Congress. Four who had been elected full members at the Twentieth Party Congress were retained (Gaevoy, Kirilenko, Kunayev, and Serdyuk), and eight more cohorts (including Bodyul, Dymshits, Grushetskiy, Novikov, and Vladimir Skryabin, First Secretary of Dnepropetrovsk *oblast*) gained full membership at the 1961 Congress, all eight bypassing the "mandatory" candidate status. Pavlov, Tikhonov and Tsukanov were brought in as candidate members. Brezhnev's lobby in the Central Committee therefore increased markedly from four at the Twentieth Party Congress to 15 at the Twenty-second Party Congress.

Thus, through a deliberate use of his power and influence to promote and transfer "boys from back home" to key bureaucractic and politically strategic positions, Brezhnev had firmly established his ablest supporters. They formed a solid foundation of personal support at various levels of the Soviet Party and government hierarchy that neither Kozlov nor Podgorny could match.

These officials with a personal loyalty to Brezhnev constituted a dangerous concentration of power from Khrushchev's viewpoint. Yet he had been partly responsible for their development as a group. After Kozlov's betrayal in 1963, the Party chief listened to Brezhnev's counsel and elevated officials to offset Kozlov's strengths, thinking it would reinforce his own position when combined with his own protégés already in high positions. (For example, three out of five new Party secretaries elected in October 1961 were close to Khrushchev — Nikolay Demichev, Aleksandr Shelepin, and Leonid Ilyichev; numerous others associated with Khrushchev were elected to full membership of the Central Committee.)

Rather than strengthening Khrushchev, the opposite occurred. By early 1964, Brezhnev had become a major force, and he drew freely on his foundation of support when the Central Committee assembled in Moscow to "consider" Khrushchev's ouster from the Party leadership.

Brezhnev's three terms in the Party Secretariat were even more important in rallying direct personal support for the coup against Khrushchev. As military affairs secretary Brezhnev was also responsible for supervision of the KGB and on some if not all of these occasions, he supervised the work of two highly placed figures brought into the central Party apparatus from the Ukraine during Stalin's last years. They were Aleksandr Shelepin, chief of the KGB from 1958 to 1961, and Vladimir Semichastny, Shelepin's successor.

Despite everything written in the West about Khrushchev's ouster, not enough attention has been given to the role of the KGB. Someday it may be throughly investigated. The available evidence now suggests that Brezhnev mobilized KGB officials to facilitate the coup.

One of those officials was the mysterious Nikolay Mironov[2] whose personal influence within the KGB was strong. He too was a

Dnepropetrovtsy and indebted to Brezhnev. When Brezhnev helped reorganize the KGB after Beria's removal, Mironov was planted in this vital organ where he took root and rose to prominence. A Moscow radio broadcast on December 24, 1957, indicated that he had achieved the high rank of general-lieutenant in the organization. By 1959, Brezhnev had succeeded in getting him promoted to the crucial post of chief of the Central Committee's Administrative Organs Department. Thus Brezhnev not only exercised control over that department via his official capacity at the time of Khrushchev's ouster, but also as Mironov's patron.

The Department exercises control over the civil police and the judicial system and controls the daily functioning of the KGB, which reports back to the Politburo through the Department. The Department's control over the KGB is so extensive that the KGB may not even hire staff officers without its approval and all assignments must be sanctioned by the Department.

Semichastny's appointment as KGB head would have passed Mironov's scrutiny. More importantly though, Mironov was empowered to initiate clandestine KGB operations. Thus, it was on Mironov's orders that special KGB agents replaced Khrushchev's regular airplane crew and flew the Party chief back to Moscow where he was met at Vnukovo airport and escorted to Party headquarters to be informed of his dismissal.

Immediately subordinate to Semichastny in the KGB itself were at least two identifiable Brezhnev men who checked and reported on the loyalty of their superior, verified his commitment to the coup, and helped organize and mobilize their organization. They were Brezhnev's two current KGB deputy chairmen, Semyon Tsvigun and Georgiy Tsinev.

Brezhnev recruited Tsvigun, a bald Ukrainian born in Odessa who fits the stereotyped image of the Soviet secret police agent, into the Moldavian Party Bureau in 1952 because Tsvigun's atrocious methods as deputy head of that republic's KGB had proven particularly effective in dealing with the recalcitrant peasants and nationalist renegades. There have been rumors in Moscow that he is related to Brezhnev by marriage. The position that Tsvigun held at the time of Khrushchev's ouster is unclear. Some Soviet biographies list him as the KGB Chairman for the Tadzhik Republic, but he may have been in Moscow in October 1964.

Tsinev's position in 1964 is known. He headed one of the main directorates of the KGB in Moscow. Born in Dnepropetrovsk, he

scaled the heights of the KGB bureaucracy under Brezhnev's sponsorship in much the same way as Mironov and Tsvigun and has a
"brotherly" relationship with Brezhnev. By 1964, this graduate of the
Dnepropetrovsk Metallurgical Institute also held the KGB rank of
general-lieutenant and headed the main directorate that played a key
role in the coup.

   Brezhnev's direct link with the KGB in 1964 was a vital factor in
his success in capturing the Party crown. Mironov's power was
especially important. His death in the same airplane crash that
claimed the life of the greatly disliked Chief of the General Staff,
Marshal Sergey Biryuzov, four days after the coup was a definite
setback for Brezhnev. The loss of Mironov was partly responsible for
the delay in Brezhnev's consolidation of power after October 1964,
and may have opened the way to later challenges to Brezhnev's
power by Shelepin. Mironov's position in the Central Committee was
left vacant for three years while a behind-the-scenes tug-of-war was
waged to determine who would fill it.

   Finally, top Soviet military marshals and generals bolstered
Brezhnev's arsenal of powerful friends. Many of his wartime
comrades belonged to a group sometimes referred to as the
"Ukrainian Marshals." Marshals Malinovskiy and Grechko held the
two top positions in the Armed Forces, Malinovskiy as Minister of
Defense and Grechko as his First Deputy, while Moskalenko, until
1962, was Chief of the Strategic Rocket Forces and also a Deputy
Minister of Defense.

   The fact that both Malinovskiy and Grechko were ethnic
Ukrainians strengthened their Ukrainian ties. They and other men
constituted a kind of inner circle who owed their high positions to
Khrushchev and had once been loyal to him. But Khrushchev, with
strategic doctrines and military policies, alienated even his staunchest
military supporters, while Brezhnev's own close relationship with
these men remained unchanged. As a member of the circle himself
and an advocate of a strong "combined arms" military posture,
Brezhnev was a political figure they could identify with and readily
back. Neither Podgorny nor any other poltical leader presented an
alternative in this respect.

   Outspoken criticism of Khrushchev's military policies led to
the dismissal of some of the top military officials in the early sixties,
including Brezhnev's friend and ally Moskalenko. In April 1962 his
position as Chief of the Strategic Rocket Forces was assumed by
Khrushchev's cohort Marshal Biryuzov, which only increased the

resentment fermenting in military ranks. Moskalenko was moved further down the ladder when he lost his position as a Deputy Minister of Defense shortly before Khrushchev's ouster. As Khrushchev's meddling in military matters increased, military leaders engaged in anti-Khrushchev lobbying and, ultimately, conspiracy with trusted and sympathetic top level politicians, foremost among them Brezhnev.

The *Christian Science Monitor* on October 17, 1964, shrewdly noted that Brezhnev would rely heavily on the military high command to back his Party leadership. That support, the newspaper concluded, should be readily forthcoming because "his political career was made in the Political Administration of the Armed Forces." They were, of course, stretching the point, but the idea of a close association was nevertheless true.

One explanation of Khrushchev's downfall expressed by some observers in 1964 was that the KGB and the Armed Forces had combined and conspired to rout the Party chief.[3] The base of personal support for Brezhnev was sufficiently broad to indicate that some combination of these elements assumed a significant role in bringing about Khrushchev's downfall and Brezhnev's installation as Party First Secretary. In short, with the Armed Forces and the KGB also on his side the power scale was heavily weighted in Brezhnev's favor in 1964.

Having infiltrated the Republic Party organizations, possessing powerful military friends, and with the KGB leadership in his pocket, Brezhnev simply had to choose his moment.

XIX

Policies That Started
a Political Crisis

*In an ever-changing, incomprehensible world
the masses had reached the point where they
would, at the same time, believe everything and
nothing, thinking that everything was possible
and that nothing was true.* — Hannah Arendt.

THE OUSTER OF KHRUSHCHEV in October 1964 can be viewed
as the culmination of conflicts and dissensions within the Party
leadership over his controversial policies in three key policy
areas — Party reform, resource allocation, and foreign policy.

One area for which Khrushchev came under attack was over
the failure of his "economics over politics" philosophy. At the
November 1962 Party plenum the idea of treating the Party chiefly as
an economic administrative apparatus was translated into a radical
reorganization that divided the Party into a dual hierarchy of Party
management, with industrial and agricultural Party committees
replacing the structure of single committees. Contention arose within
the Party leadership over whether the Party should intervene directly
in the economic process or should stand aloof, guiding and directing,
but not particpating in the actual management of production.

Khrushchev had long advocated direct intervention, which
was opposed by the top and middle level Party apparatchik who
owed his livelihood to his role as ideologist and propagandist and
who proved capable of mustering a large body of support, including
top level Party leaders, against it. Suslov and Kozlov each opposed
reorganization of the Party along economic lines. Neither spoke
favorably of the reorganization in their respective addresses to the
Bulgarian and Italian Communist Party congresses in 1963.

Where did Brezhnev stand on the issue? He favored both Party management and bifurcation of the Party to achieve it; he had
always supported the concept of direct Party management of the
economy. In Kazakhstan he had attempted to impose direct Party
management over the state farms, and at the Twentieth Party

Congress he seconded Khrushchev's suggestion that problems of "practical economics" should take precedence over ideological work.

In his speech to the Czechoslovak Party Congress held only a few days after the November 1962 C.P.S.U. plenum, Brezhnev asserted that bifurcation of the Party was justified in terms of "ensuring more concrete development of all branches of the national economy" and "enabling the Party to devote its main attention to production." He said that the plenum's "weighty measures" would play a "veritable historic role" in building the material and technical foundations of Communism and, in turn a Communist society.[1]

Brezhnev invoked Lenin at the Czech Congress to demonstrate his support of the new structural setup. The "discovery" of a Lenin document emphasizing the primacy of economics over politics in Party work was released in the Soviet media in September 1962. It provided Khrushchev with powerful ammunition to support his views and at the Congress Brezhnev cited the relevant Lenin passage to back those views.

Brezhnev also quoted Lenin to support a second major move associated with Khrushchev at the November 1962 plenum, a proposal to create a unified Party-State Control Committee. Up to this point only Khrushchev and Mikoyan had publicly associated themselves with the concept of unifying existing control agencies in the Party and the government into a single organ. Kozlov was the only figure to deal with the issue in negative terms. At the Czech Congress, Brezhnev noted that such a concept symbolized "restoration of Leninist principles" in the organization of control in the socialist state and was "equally important in building communism."

As envisaged by its original sponsors, the Committee was to be independent of the top executive body and wield wide investigative and disciplinary powers. Aleksandr Shelepin was appointed its head. The plenum, however, failed to define the agency's explicit powers, which suggests that there were differences among the Party leaders over what powers it should have. Brezhnev's speech to the Czech Congress indicated that contentions over the Committee's responsibilities did indeed exist and he came out firmly on the side of a strong agency.

He drew a direct parallel between "resistance to perfecting Party and State control" and "dogmatism and conservatism in thinking." He reminded the opposition that "putting an end to the harmful consequences of Stalin's personality cult'" not only means liquidating and correcting violations of revolutionary legality, but also "overcoming stagnation and conservatism" in one's own thinking. "The organizational forms of control ... which we have applied hitherto have played their positive part, yet life is speeding forward and what was right yesterday no longer corresponds to today's new tasks," Brezhnev concluded.

Such a philosophy is fully indicative of Brezhnev's approach to Soviet politics and demonstrates his predisposition toward expediency. He echoed these same words at the Party plenum that abolished the Party-State Control Committee in December 1965.

A major factor in Khrushchev's downfall was the continuing failure of agriculture to meet the nation's food requirements. Earlier Khrushchev had managed to increase agricultural production, and for a while it seemed likely that he could fulfill his promise to solve the country's chronic food shortage. By 1959, however, stagnation had set in. The last years of the Khrushchev era were filled with grandiose plans and utopian promises that only resulted in emergency crash programs to provide a minimal food supply. This inability to deliver the promised opulence brought a horde of accusers.

Brezhnev had been a faithful supporter and executor of Khrushchev's earlier policies for decentralizing agriculture and expanding grain production. So when Khrushchev came under attack for these and other schemes, Brezhnev initially came to the rescue, defending him not once but twice in major forums in 1962 and 1963.

At the 1962 Czech Congress, Brezhnev concluded his comments on Soviet agriculture by observing that "our agriculture has done very well ... mainly because of measures the Party and government adopted in the last few years." And in his Supreme Soviet pre-election speech to the Baumanskiy electorate in March 1963,[2] Brezhnev again strongly defended the policies. Not coincidentally, this occurred in the midst of Kozlov's challenge to Khrushchev. In this context, Brezhnev statements constitute an ambiguous mixture of defense of Khrushchev and an attempt to dissociate himself from him.

For example, Brezhnev noted that 1963 marked the tenth anniversary of that "historic day remembered by all the people when Comrade Khrushchev spoke to the Party Central Committee plenum" (the February 1954 plenum implementing the virgin lands program). This however, was the only reference to Khrushchev in his speech. Brezhnev attributed the gains that had been made in agriculture since

1954 to the efforts of the Party. He pointed out that "the Party" had returned "many times" to the question of agricultural development, examined the newest measures for ensuring development of "this important branch of our economy" and, as a result, significantly increased the amount of land devoted to grain production. Brezhnev attributed the "vast work of developing our agricultural production" to the "attentive and constant leadership of the Party." "The Party" (not Khrushchev), he said, "is doing everything to ensure that those conditions which meet the food requirements of the population are met."

Brezhnev made no public statements after March 1963 regarding Khrushchev's agricultural policies. However, failure to speak out at a time when criticism of Khrushchev was loudest, implied tacit concurrence with the criticism being voiced. Privately Brezhnev must have condemned Khrushchev after August 1964, when things became critical and Khrushchev threatened more radical measures in agriculture. Condemnation of Khrushchev's methods at this point would have been one way for Brezhnev effectively to extricate himself from his previous link with Khrushchev's agricultural policies.

In August 1964, Khrushchev revealed the main points of a proposal to undertake yet another reorganization of agriculture at the upcoming November Party plenum. There were two parts to the latest plan and both met with strenuous opposition. The first called for the creation of union-republic administrations concerned with each major farm product. Each trust (pig, poultry, etc.) at the republic and local administrative levels would have its own Party committee, an adjunct to the Party committee for agriculture. In addition, Khrushchev intended to place more restrictions on the private plots of the collective farmer, adding to the Party's record of instituting punitive measures against private holdings.[3]

Brezhnev opposed both measures. He had a clear understanding of the agricultural problem and how to solve it, but Khrushchev refused to accept his views. In a major speech following the October 1964 coup Brezhnev expressed sharp criticism of the deposed leader along these and other lines. Brezhnev played down the fact that 1964 was a record year for grain deliveries and condemned Khrushchev's "101" farm management reorganizations.

Brezhnev was particulary critical of Khrushchev's plan to cut the private plots of farmers. In a November 6, 1964, speech he declared that Khrushchev had placed unwarranted restrictions on the private plots "though the economic conditions were not yet ripe for such a step." Private plots accounted for nearly half of the livestock products, and a high percentage of other agricultural production. Brezhnev realized that Khrushchev's proposed new restrictions on the plots would merely reduce the national food supply.

Of course Brezhnev's most outspoken denunciation of Khrushchev's methods of managing agriculture came at the March 1965 agricultural plenum where he declared:

> Numerous, and at times far fetched, reorganizations resulted in an atmosphere of tension and confusion which deprived the leaders of a sense of perspective and undermined their faith in their own abilities. Instead of precise and painstakingly calculated work and a profound analysis of the situation, the state and collective farms are merely administered and ordered about.[4]

Resource allocation was the pivotal issue on which debate focused in Khrushchev's last years. Debate derived from Khrushchev's preference for a consumer oriented economy. Through numerous economic and military policies, Khrushchev aimed to undermine the traditional structure of the Soviet economy and neutralize or eliminate those sectors of opposition which were against realignment of economic priorities.

In 1954, Brezhnev zealously defended the traditional orientation. One might suppose that if he remained committed to the "old ways" he would similarly rise to defend them in the face of new challenges by Khrushchev. However, Brezhnev's stand in 1964 was not as clear as it was in 1954, nor is it easily explained. Each statement made in the course of the debate between 1961 and 1964 must be looked at carefully and in the context of the larger political picture.

Development of the chemical industry and the production of synthetic materials was an important means by which Khrushchev intended to propagate his consumer line. There is no question that Brezhnev supported development of this industry; his support, in fact, dated from 1958, when the chemicals program was first introduced. The program in 1958, however, had little success, was refurbished in late 1962, and devised as a plan to be submitted to the June 1963 Party plenum.

In his pre-election speech in March 1963, Brezhnev gave the revised chemicals plan favorable advanced billing on several counts. He pointed to "insufficient development" of the chemcials industry and concluded that "greater attention must be paid to the industry. A basic agrument that Khrushchev used to undermine traditional steel proponents was that synthetic products produced from chemicals could readily substitute for costly metals in many areas, including vast sectors of the consumer economy. Though Brezhnev was to attack this as an "incorrect view" at the 1966 Party Congress, he unmistakably supported it in 1963.

Brezhnev did not make the classical distinction between heavy industry on the one hand and consumer industry on the other, but referred to the application of chemical products to "all branches of industry." This formulation was strikingly similar to that which Khrushchev used at the Twenty-second Party Congress and after to purposely blur the distinction traditionally drawn between heavy industry and the consumer-oriented sectors of the economy.

In arguing that chemicals could now provide metal substitutes, Khrushchev devalued the metal criterion thereby enabling him to bring consumer goods in through the back door. Brezhnev placed similar utility on the chemicals industry, reporting that "chemicals will come to occupy an important place not only in industry, but in the everyday life of our people." He cited examples where plastic might be used in housing construction "in place of wooden floors, metal radiators, cast iron baths and a large number of other products." Moreover, Brezhnev concluded, "We want the increasing demands of the economy and population to be completely satisfied; this is the goal set by the Party and the government, and it will be reached."

Some Western observers have interpreted the chemicals program as Khrushchev's strategic plan in his renewed attack on the traditional structure of the economy in 1963.[5] If that was the case, then Brezhnev's statements on chemicals would seem to indicate that he supported that offensive. However, it is significant that Brezhnev stated that the demands of "the economy" must be met first, and then those of the populace. Moreover, a crucial distinction is made between the production priorities Khrushchev gave to the chemical industry and those Brezhnev prescribed. In his Baumanskiy speech, Brezhnev listed production for "atomic and rocket fields" first. "Their development," he said, "will depend to a large extent on the future availabity of synthetic materials with special characteristics." Agriculture was listed second and consumer related production last.

Brezhnev consistently placed defense at the top of the list. Various military spokesmen and the Minister of Defense himself also emphasized the program's importance to defense.[6] Brezhnev's emphasis on chemicals for defense gave him an alibi when the program encountered opposition. He wisely said nothing more about the matter after December 1963 as sentiment for the program soured.

Brezhnev's position on the consumer line must be approached in a different manner. Khrushchev's argument to shift larger resources to consumer production was predicated on the assertion that the Soviet Union had reached a satisfactory and sustained level of industrial output and was adequately defended. Did Brezhnev support these views? Possibly with regard to the first, he did.

In 1962, Brezhnev, observing a 45 percent increase in production (as opposed to the 39 percent increase planned) for the Seven Year Plan, noted that industrial production in the nation had gone "over and above" the planned levels. He concluded that the U.S.S.R. had not only begun to catch up with "the most powerful country in the capitalist world" in the "speed of industrial production," but had begun to surpass the United States in "the volume of production for a number of very important products."[7] Such references, however, were inconclusive.

Unmistakable, however, was the Brezhnev statement on the matter made exactly one week before Khrushchev fell. In Dresden, East Germany, on October 9, 1964, Brezhnev made this remarkable public indentification with the consumer line:

> New relations are being built in production and in everyday life, the new man of the socialist society is growing. Whom does all this tremendous work serve? ... By building socialism and communism, we certainly build the basis for the prosperity and happiness of our descendants. We are confident that our children and grandchildren will live better than we, but it is our immediate goal to achieve even today a steady improvement in the living conditions of the people."[8]

The statement is remarkable because it expresses direct support for the shift to consumer priority announced by Khrushchev at a joint meeting of the Party Presidium and Council of Ministers at the end of September. Consumer priority was to become the basis for long-term Soviet economic policy and appropriate reorganization of the economy would be made. According to the September 22 *Pravda* report of the meeting, Khrushchev told Party and government leaders that "the main task of the new economic plan was to ensure the preferential development of consumer industries."

If Brezhnev had previously wavered on the consumer line, his Dresden statement that "consumer protection and the need to increase the living standard" was not to be left to the future seemed to place him in the Khrushchev camp. However, the picture is still incomplete. What of the principal premise underlying the shift in priorities? What about the "adequate" defense posture? When the focus of examination is widened to include Brezhnev's military and foreign policy orientation, quite a different picture emerges.

Soviet internal and foreign policies are seldom unrelated. Therefore it should be remembered that from the outset of the debate over resource allocation, there existed an organic connection between the consumer policies advocated by Khrushchev, his reorientation of Soviet military doctrine, which placed emphasis on a single system of defense—the Intercontinental Ballistic Missile (ICBM)—and his planned reorganization of the Soviet Armed Forces to include troop reduction and replacement of service components with nuclear missiles. These proposed measures raised the specter of military opposition to Khrushchev.

Aside from the economic question, there were several interrelated aspects of Khrushchev's military formulations that brought opposition from Party and military officials. While recognizing the importance of the ICBM in the "missile age," his opponents continued to subscribe to the doctrine that "combined arms" would be used to fight any future war, nuclear or otherwise. These issues, plus increased political interference in the Armed Forces stemming from resistance to Khrushchev's military policies, became the focal point of the military's opposition.

Brezhnev never uttered one word of personal support for Khrushchev's military measures. In fact, he chose to pose arguments countering them.

Brezhnev's increasingly hostile portrayal of the West in speeches contributed to his anti-Khrushchev stand on military policy. Unlike other lines which could be switched on or off with relative ease or with little or no embarrassment, this one gained an intractable consistency. All of Brezhnev's speeches in Africa, Finland, Yugoslavia and elsewhere abroad and at home demonstrate this. They emerged as political and ideological justification for a strong military posture and removed the underpinnings of Khrushchev's more confident and optimistic assessments of Soviet military strength and the prospects of sustained détente with the West.

The thesis that "today imperialists and aggressive forces headed by the imperialists of the United States are trying to start a new war," advanced in Brezhnev's Milanovac cemetery speech in

Yugoslavia in 1962, and his warning in December 1963 (one week before Khrushchev announced Soviet troop reduction in East Germany) that "West German militarism" should compel the socialist nations to arm, not disarm,[9] crystalized the position of the Ministry of Defense.

Brezhnev's proclamations substantially diverged from the Khrushchev line, but were in tune with Malinovskiy's doctrinal thesis that "the imperialists are preparing a surprise nuclear attack against the Soviet Union and other socialist countries."[10] In short, when the country's military needs were weighed against the proposition of increasing the U.S.S.R.'s living standard, the perceived strategic objectives and military needs won out in Brezhnev's mind. This was best expressed in Brezhnev's Baumanskiy pre-election speech in which he pursued the dual line.

> *[Pro consumer]* We want the increasing demands of the economy and population to be completely satisfied. This is the goal set by the Party and the government, and it will be reached.
>
> *[Pro defense]* Comrades, we must consider the tasks of ensuring a reliable defense of the country. As much as we might like to direct all the national income of our people for purposes of peaceful development, increasing the standard of living and satisfying more broadly the varied needs of the Soviet people, *we must continue to divert large resources for the defense of the country* (emphasis added).

Brezhnev's principal differences with Khrushchev and his gaining of support from the Khrushchev opposition evolved from disagreement over major defense and foreign policy issues.

It is hard to tell to what degree, if any, Brezhnev fell out with Khrushchev over the handling of the Cuban missile crisis in October 1962, specifically the decision to yield to the American demand for withdrawal of all Soviet missiles from Cuba. In October 1964, Khrushchev was charged with having caused a Soviet defeat in the venture. He had been unable to use the newly acquired nuclear missiles to persuade the West to peacefully yield strategic sites. If Brezhnev pointed an accusing finger at Khrushchev in 1964, he nevertheless publicly supported him on the decision to withdraw the missiles at the time of the crisis, calling it "a sensible compromise."[11]

The situation with regard to Berlin was entirely different. In every speech he made between 1961 and 1964, including the October Revolution speech made a week after Khrushchev was deposed, Brezhnev emphasized the necessity of concluding a separate peace treaty and establishment of East German dominion over West Berlin.

No one could be certain what Khrushchev's intentions were with regard to the two Germanys in 1964. But one could speculate that he hoped to achieve rapprochement with West Germany. Khrushchev's son-in-law's visit to that country in August and the proposed state visit by Khrushchev in late 1964, seemed tailored to that end. The political unorthodoxy of the visits worried certain Presidium members. This concern was manifest in Suslov's militant speech in praise of Walter Ulbricht's Communist regime published in *Pravda* on October 6, 1964, and similarly transmitted in Brezhnev's arrival speech in the German Democratic Republic on the same day.

Brezhnev's speech was much more significant. He had assumed a strong anti-West German stand as early as December 1963. During his visit to Prague and over Prague radio he told the Czechs that Khrushchev was wooing "warmongers," and he warned West Germany "not to be consoled with futile hopes." In an attempt to reassure East Germany, he stated that the Soviet Union would never sell out its fraternal ally at any cost. Finally, raising the specter of Munich in 1938, Brezhnev concluded, "Today is not 1938. ... The continuing predatory intentions of the West German militarists" should "compel the socialist nations to strengthen their defense."[12]

The latter statement is extremely important for two reasons. First, it took clear exception to Khrushchev's troop withdrawal from East Germany announced less than a week later. Second, Brezhnev came out publicly against Khrushchev on the matter with a direct call for more, not less, military strength in Eastern Europe.

Brezhnev's speeches in East Germany reiterated these thoughts. There were serious implications for East German state security if Soviet troop withdrawals began. Malinovskiy's visit to the G.D.R. in April 1964, Marshal Grechko's visit, and Brezhnev's trip to East Berlin on the occasion of the fifteenth anniversary of the birth of the G.D.R. were to provide high level reassurances to Ulbricht that his country's interests would be protected by the Soviet Union.

Regarding the solution to the German problem, Brezhnev told his audience:

> We have exactly the same views as you on how the German problem must be handled. Despite the fact that no one in the West likes to hear it, we repeat, and shall keep on repeating, that there does not exist any more urgent a task than liquidation of the vestiges of World War II and realization of a German peace settlement. I can assure you dear friends that the Soviet Union will not slacken its efforts to conclude a German peace treaty."[14]

Khrushchev had already stopped insisting on a peace treaty with West Germany.

Khrushchev's China policy, specifically his announced intention of holding a meeting of Communist parties in Moscow in December 1964 to make a formal break with China, was a crucial element in his downfall. Khrushchev's collision course with China was too radical for most of his colleagues and contrasted sharply with the conciliatory line toward the dogmatic Chinese advocated by Brezhnev and Suslov since the summer of 1964.

There were those in the Party who favored a cautionary approach to the ideologoical battle with China for fear of an irreversible split in the world Communist movement. Brezhnev had worked hard with his aid and arms programs to counter Chinese influence in the Third World, but all of his statements on the subject, particularly those following his visit to Yugoslavia,* subtly hinted at finding alternative solutions to a complete ideological break.

The first indication of resistance from within the Party to Khrushchev's pro-Yugoslav moves appeared in the aftermath of the Cuban crisis on November 18, 1962, when *Pravda* printed an article by Boris Ponomarev, chief of the Central Committee's International Department, which took a position diametrically opposed to Khrushchev. Ponomarev invoked the 1960 Moscow Parties' Conference Statement designating revisionists (the Yugoslavs) and revisionism as the "main dagger" to the Party. The article opposed Khrushchev, who in the November *Problems of Peace and Socialism,* had chosen to treat revisionism as a dead issue.

Brezhnev took exception to both formulations. Citing the 1960 Moscow documents himself at the Czech Congress, he said that dogmatists and revisionists present an equal danger to the cause of socialism. His handling of the issue contrasted to Kozlov's as the latter, in agreement with Ponomarev, portrayed "revisionist splitters and opportunists of every kind" as the main danger.

Brezhnev's remarks suggest an attempt to reach a compromise at a time when Khrushchev's anti-Chinese offensive was at its height. An effort was underway in December 1962 to push the Soviet Union into a clear-cut pronouncement that "dogmatism" had become the main danger to the Party. The effort was aborted, however, perhaps due to Brezhnev's efforts to reach a compromise solution.

Rapprochement with Yugoslavia in 1962 risked escalation of the conflict with China, but Brezhnev believed that if Tito could be persuaded to follow the Soviet line on Berlin, the risk was worth taking.

That some compromise was reached was apparent by a C.P.S.U. letter sent to the Chinese Communists in February 1964, which showed signs of Soviet willingness to make limited concessions for the sake of unity. The compromise soon broke down, however, and when it did Khrushchev went ahead and declared that Yugoslavia should be considered a "socialist state."

Khrushchev had gone too far. Brezhnev now moved radically to the left on the whole matter. His new position was adequately stated in his funeral speech for Togliatti in Rome in August 1964, where Brezhnev posited the "splitters, pseudorevolutionaries and opportunists" — the Yugoslavs — as the main danger to socialism.[15]

Khrushchev's last initiatives with regard to Germany and China, coming as they did in a period of steady disintegration of Moscow's control over its satellites and the Communist movement, carried serious implications for Soviet foreign policy. They threatened to greatly accelerate the already powerful polycentric tendencies in Eastern Europe and among world Communist parties, and menace the security of the U.S.S.R.'s European flank. Only two years earlier Brezhnev had observed that "the correlation of forces in Europe is shifting ... in favor of socialism." Those gains were now threatened, and to Brezhnev, Suslov, and others the Soviet Union seemed to be on the verge of an irreversible setback in Communist Party relations and the world Communist movement.

Leading newspapers in France, Germany and elsewhere in Europe discerned a heightened internal conflict over the anti-Peking line in the months preceding Khrushchev's ouster.[16] Brezhnev hinted as much on October 6 when he neglected to mention the preparatory meeting for the December Communist parties meeting. And in East Germany, Brezhnev gave Ulbricht a completely different line on the purpose of the planned meeting. He told G.D.R. leaders that the C.P.S.U. would "strive for unity" among socialist countries on "an equal footing" and "on the basis of the correct combination of the common interests with the interests of the peoples of each country"[17] There would be no break with China.

In sum, Brezhnev's public statements on the most critical issues facing the regime in Khrushchev's last years revealed a mixed picture of support for some of Khrushchev's most controversial domestic policies, wavering and ambiguity on others, and clear disagreement and active opposition on still others. The collision course with the Chinese in December and the seriousness of the trouble in Soviet-East German relations, though, were the crystalizing agents causing Brezhnev and Suslov to act to depose Khrushchev.

Generally speaking, Brezhnev's position on many of Khrushchev's internal policies classified him as a "cautious reformer." Some of those forces in the economy calling for change could therefore identify with him. In October 1964, when reformers retained a sufficiently strong position in many parts of the Party and government apparatus to make debate on numerous controversial issues far from settled, when stability and an image of continuity with the previous regime was desirable to save face in the international community, this was particulary important. It was yet another factor working in Brezhnev's favor. Indeed, his first statements as Party head, repeating enough of the staples of Khrushchevian policy to sustain an image of continuity and enough of traditionalist doctrine to indicate change, painted a picture of Brezhnev as a unifying force.

XX
Prometheus Bound

He who seeks the salvation of the soul, of his own and of others, should not seek it along the avenue of politics, for the quite different tasks of politics can only be solved by violence. —
Max Weber.

IN OCTOBER 1964, THERE WERE FEW Party leaders whose career could match Brezhnev's. He was senior in experience and position to most in the Party hierarchy who might qualify as a possible successor to Khrushchev. None could claim such career diversity.

A Party member since 1929, he had been active in Lenin's NEP and Stalin's collectivization drives and held a variety of important state and Party posts. He had degrees in both metallurgy and agriculture and extensive practical, managerial and executive experience in each of these fields, giving him the necessary technical expertise — a condition *sine qua non* for the top Party post — and lending balance to his overall experience. Added to this was Brezhnev's responsibility for the military and the secret police.

The various stations throughout his career testify to the capabilities and connections to which Brezhnev owed his political rise. By 1964, the requirements for supreme Party leadership were no longer exclusively political or bureaucratic; extensive and varied experience was needed. Brezhnev was the only member of the Party Presidium in his fifties who had amassed the broad basis of experience in Party and government affairs that Khrushchev had described as desired prerequisites for Party leadership.

Brezhnev's political style counted highly too. The journalist Martin Page wrote at one time of his disappointment at finding Brezhnev so unimposing as President.[1] Indeed, this was an important aspect of Brezhnev's style. If Brezhnev impressed few outside his Party, he alienated fewer inside the Party. He maintained a low profile, quietly gathering support and when a coalition of those discontented with Khrushchev's policies and leadership reached a head, Brezhnev transferred these frustrations into political action.

Brezhnev's personality may even itself have given him an advantage. Khrushchev, with his shoe-pounding, maxim-spouting ebullience at the United Nations in 1960, had increasingly embarrassed the political leadership. He had become abrupt and offensive with fellow Party leaders and subordinates. This mixture of pathos, ridicule, impatience, and choleric outbrusts of anger was too much for his fellow Party leaders. Khrushchev's personality contrasted sharply with Brezhnev's deliberation, seriousness, sincerity, patience, and recognition of "collectivity" in decision making, prompting a colleague to comment: "He is an up and coming man ... a man to watch, smart, capable, modest and very popular in Party circles."

In short, Brezhnev projected the image that suited the Party. He was the kind of leader, at least in manner, the Soviet Socialist state required. As one West German newspaper pointed out in January 1964: "It is a consolation that a possible successor for the office of the most powerful man in the Soviet Union is a personality who, in addition to conviction and belief, also has will power as well as sober understanding of things as they are—plus well balanced judgment, which is very important in the ... dangerous issues of our time."[2]

Organizationally, Brezhnev also held the advantage. Of those generally eligible for the top Party post in 1964, Mikoyan (born in 1895) and Shvernik (born in 1888) could be disqualified because of age. Presidium membership alone was unlikely to be sufficient qualification, so Kirilenko, Aleksey Kosygin, and Gennadiy Voronov could be eliminated. Only Brezhnev, Podgorny and Suslov satisfied the criteria of Presidium and Secretariat membership.

Suslov never appeared to be a competitor. He had spent almost his entire career in the field of agitation, ideology and theory, and though a powerful figure he preferred the role of sponsor—in this case of Brezhnev. Podgorny was at a disadvantage because he had accumulated relatively little time in Moscow—one and a half years compared to Brezhnev's nine—and had only a short period of time in which to broaden his base of support. A strict Khrushchevite, Podgorny provided little comfort as a possible successor to those who were dissatisfied with Khrushchev's foreign and domestic policy lines. That left Brezhnev surviving the process of elimination. Brezhnev was the obvious successor; but the crucial element was the coup itself.

What was Brezhnev's role in the coup? Did he play the part of a Party bureaucrat whose support was necessary and who cast his lot with the faction most likely to win after a plan had been prepared?

Was he simply the *beneficiary of power*, or did he play a decisive, perhaps the key role?

The answers require a long hard look at Brezhnev the man. The Party bureaucrat characterization runs altogether contrary to Brezhnev's personal and political character. He was never a passive player, but always an active participant in each important reshuffle in the hierarchy since Stalin's death. Logic also militates against the second characterization. A cardinal rule of palace revolts, Soviet or otherwise, is that those who lead and succeed in revolution take power because the revolution gives them "legitimate" claim to it. Power is never turned over to the observer or sympathizer, regardless of rank.

Moreover, there is a crucial factor pointing to a decisive role for Brezhnev in the coup. Hannah Arendt observed in her characterization of totalitarian regimes that "the leader's ... power and authority is most conspicuous in the relationship between him and the Chief of Police."[3] Brezhnev exercised considerable influence over two crucial instruments of the coup, the KGB and the military. It is because of their relevance to political power that Brezhnev developed and has retained a strong degree of personal control over the KGB and the military by appointments and institutional aggrandizement.

The coup itself can be divided into three steps: conception, preparation and execution. The first stage may date from early 1963, the second from June 1964, and the third from September 1964.

Did Brezhnev conceive the plot? The answer depends upon the timing. If the coup was conceived at about the time Kozlov fell ill,[4] Brezhnev probably did not originate it. He strongly supported Khrushchev on the domestic issues then, while foreign policy with regard to Germany and China had yet to reach a critical stage. The coup idea may have been hatched by Kozlov and Suslov in 1963.

There is an equally good possibility that the idea entered Brezhnev's head after Khrushchev designated Podgorny as heir to the highest Party post. This would be particularly true if Brezhnev had felt a sense of personal betrayal. Despite policy differences with Khrushchev, there was scarcely a man in the Party who had devoted more years of personal loyalty and service to Khrushchev than Brezhnev.

There was also the possibility that Khrushchev would, as he had so often hinted, gracefully retire. Such an event would narrow Brezhnev's chances in the succession battle, for Podgorny, even though he lacked Brezhnev's range of experience and broad base of support, was moving rapidly forward and might well gain the inside track in any peaceful transition of power. Further, there existed a growing and potentially exploitable body of opposition to Khrushchev that under the circumstances might have tempted Brezhnev. He would act when the time was ripe. For the moment he could proceed, as he did, with broadening his base of support, extending his influence still more firmly over the KGB and the military, working to set the stage and sharpen the instruments for the coup.

Most plausible is the possibility that Brezhnev and Suslov, having moved to identical positions on other matters, reached a decision about the fate of Khrushchev at the same time. Sometime then, in late 1963 or early 1964, the core of the conspiratorial group was formed. It was probably completed by August 1964. Khrushchev's announcement that summer that he intended to effect a permanent break with the Chinese was the last straw, the pressing motive uniting Brezhnev and Suslov.

It may not have been entirely coincidental that the timing of Khrushchev's foreign policy moves coincided with Brezhnev's removal as President in 1963. Perhaps as the influential head of state he had become a thorn in Khrushchev's side on these issues. At any rate, the dismissal benefited Brezhnev. Was he now to "concentrate on his Secretariat activities," already secretly contemplating the October coup in collaboration with Suslov? Probably.

Brezhnev's last kind words about Khrushchev were made at the latter's seventieth birthday celebrations in April 1964, the famous grand occasion which created an illusion of unity around the First Secretary. Brezhnev's reserve on this occasion was clearly noticeable though. On April 16 when he, acting in his ceremonial capacity as President, awarded the Hero of the Soviet Union medal to Khrushchev at special ceremonies his praise was restrained.

When Khrushchev attempted to play up his own military accomplishments on his birthday, a good deal of the limelight fell on Brezhnev instead. Military officials speaking at the birthday ceremony merely noted that Khrushchev had participated and played a heroic role in the Great Patriotic War. Malinovskiy proceeded to list "eminent personalities" who had fought in the war. Brezhnev's name headed the list. Brezhnev's own assessment of Khrushchev's war experience applauded the Party chief's "heroic life as a Communist fighter."[5] This was not up to par with the usual praise he lavished on Khrushchev.

On July 30, 1964, Khrushchev publicly announced that

Moscow was sponsoring a meeting of 26 Communist parties on December 15. The announcement brought vehement protest from the Chinese and expressions of "concern" from fraternal parties. Argument over China at this time and the ramifications it had for the C.P.S.U. generated what became known as the "Togliatti Memorandum." Written during the Italian Communist leader's visit to the Soviet Union in the early summer of 1964, this memorandum was extremely critical of Moscow and painted a gloomy picture of the Soviet political scene. Soviet credibility among the fraternal Communist parties was threatened if the document were to be published.

Palmiro Togliatti died shortly after he wrote the memorandum. The official purpose of Brezhnev's visit to Rome in August 1964 was to attend Togliatti's funeral, but his real mission was to suppress publication of the memorandum. He failed.

In July 1964, Khrushchev's son-in-law made his trip to West Germany. He informed the West Germans that Ulbricht did not have long to live because he was dying of cancer and that Soviet-West German relations would soon see a marked improvement.

The KGB moved to sabotage the rapprochement effort resulting in the infamous "Schwikerman incident," in which a West German diplomat was injected with a toxic gas, and the "Khaborovsk incident," in which KGB agents broke into the hotel rooms of American and British attachés and searched their belongings. Such serious actions involving international diplomats would not have been carried out without orders from the highest KGB authorities, Semichastny, Mironov, Tsinev or Brezhnev. Brezhnev in his official capacity as Party Secretary responsible for the KGB could have been directly responsible for issuing orders through Mironov to create an international incident that would impair, if not sabotage, rapprochement with West Germany and soil the international atmosphere.

Brezhnev has been directly linked to the arrest of Frederick Barghoorn, the prominent American professor of Soviet politics, in Moscow several months earlier. John Barron discusses the arrest in his book on the KGB. The KGB had devised a plan to arrest Barghoorn on trumped-up charges of espionage during his visit to Moscow in order to barter for the release of a Soviet agent arrested in the United States. Barron notes that the morning of October 31, 1963, Semichastny telephoned Brezhnev who agreed with the "principle of reciprocity" and approved the plan.[6] Khrushchev, who had been out of town, reportedly flew into a rage upon his return and demanded to know "what idiot ordered the mad venture."

In the weeks preceding the coup, Brezhnev, Suslov and others were preoccupied with the troubled state of East German-Soviet relations. The Schwikerman, Khaborovsk and Barghoorn incidents brought a respite in the movement toward rapprochement with West Germany, but this did little to calm the East Germans. Worsening relations were pointedly revealed when Willi Stope, the East German Prime Minister, spent three days (October 1-3) in the Soviet Union (to open an exhibition) without paying the customary visit on Khrushchev.

The extent of the strained relations was exposed by Brezhnev's departure for East Berlin on October 5 and Suslov's blast at rapprochement timed to coincide with Brezhnev's arrival in East Berlin. Suslov, in a speech made at a rally in honor of the German Democratic Republic, forcefully stated, "The treaty between the U.S.S.R. and the G.D.R. puts a stop to the foolish illusions of West German revanchist circles about the possiblity of a deal with the Soviet Union at the expense of the G.D.R."[7]

Brezhnev reiterated support of the G.D.R. on the following day. If his secret talks with Ulbricht were ever published they would undoubtedly show the relevance of Brezhnev's visit to the coup itself. The content of Brezhnev's talks with Ulbricht was probably such that the coup must have come as no surprise to the East German leader. Ulbricht's congratulatory message to Brezhnev after the coup carried this flavor.[8]

It is impossible to determine the precise moment that the coup was set in motion. Of course, Suslov could have initiated it while Brezhnev, fully aware of the plan, was in Berlin. However, the presence of Podgorny in Moscow up to October 9 casts doubt on it.[9] It is more reasonable to assume that the machinery was set in motion on the evening of October 11, when Brezhnev returned home.

Mironov orchestrated his end of the coup. The KGB cut off Khrushchev's access to Party supporters or the public, to whom he might have appealed for support. The telephone numbers of those Central Committee members who might rally to his side were changed the night before Khrushchev returned to Moscow, and his regular plane crew were replaced with KGB agents. These precautions prevented most forms of active intervention in Khrushchev's favor.

The military's role, though generally passive, was nonetheless apparent. Military officers who might support Khrushchev were conveniently sent to Poland for the annual Polish Army Day celebration. Brezhnev's special toast to the Soviet military and his invitation to Malinovskiy to join the circle of toasters at the Kremlin reception on the October Revolution anniversary celebrations held a few weeks after Khrushchev's fall was a gesture of gratitude for the military's personal support.

Who could Brezhnev and Suslov depend on in a Party Presidium vote against Khrushchev? They knew they could count on at least five of the ten votes, two being their own. They could depend on Polyanskiy, who had become disillusioned with Khrushchev's formulation of agricultural policy and jealous of the favor being given to agriculturalist Polyakov. Andrey Kirilenko was a sure ally. Podgorny, Shvernik and Voronov would probably support Khrushchev. Mikoyan might join Khrushchev too. A 5-5 split in the Presidium would be insufficient to oust Khrushchev, but Mikoyan changed his mind once he became enlightened on the measures that had been taken.

With only eight or possibly nine members present, the Presidium met on October 12, at which time Brezhnev pressed for the immediate and summary removal of Khrushchev. However, a split apparently developed among those wavering, with Mikoyan negotiating a compromise. It was decided that Khrushchev would be given the opportunity to resign with honor from his Party and government posts but permitted to retain membership in the Central Committee. If, on the other hand, he refused to go along the matter would be brought before the Central Committee and the Presidium would recommend that he be voted out of office.

On the following day, Khrushchev returned to Moscow from his Sochi retreat. The Presidium had been in session for most of the morning when he arrived. Brezhnev chaired this meeting as he had the earlier meetings.

When Khrushchev entered the room Brezhnev refused to give up the place at the head of the table normally occupied by the Party chief, but motioned for Khrushchev to take a seat beside him. According to an account by a C.P.S.U. member[10] with knowledge of the events, Brezhnev told Khrushchev that the Presidium had deliberated and decided to accept the resignation he had so often talked about. Brezhnev told Khrushchev to appear before a televised session of the Central Committee, give a farewell address to the Russian people, and publicly nominate Brezhnev as his successor in the Party.

Khrushchev replied: "I don't have to account to you. Call a plenary session!"[11] Brezhnev had anticipated this. He told Khrushchev that the Central Committe had already assembled and was waiting. Khrushchev was informed that if he wished to fight no one would stop him, but he was warned that the "Party, government, Secretariat, Politburo and Armed Forces" were aligned against him and if he pursued the matter, he would be forced to retire with ignominy. Nevertheless Khrushchev persisted.

Suslov delivered the five hour indictment against Khrushchev at the Central Committee plenum. Khrushchev lost, but not without a fight and backing from some loyal Central Committee members. Brezhnev later tried to refute this division by declaring that the session had been held in "an atmosphere of complete unanimity among all the participants."[12] On October 15, 1964, Moscow TASS made this announcement:

> Nikita Khrushchev has been relieved of his duties as the First Secretary of the C.P.S.U. Central Committee and Chairman of the U.S.S.R. Council of Ministers. *Leonid Brezhnev has been elected First Secretary of the C.P.S.U. Central Committee.*

Part IV

THE MAKING OF THE
GENERAL SECRETARY

XXI

The Party Chief
Consolidates His Power

The thirst of power is insatiable and irresistable among Communists. Victory in the struggle for power is equal to being raised to a divinity, failure means the deepest mortification and disgrace. — Milovan Djilas, *The New Class.*

ON OCTOBER 15, 1964, LEONID BREZHNEV embarked on a new kind of political struggle. Having acquired the top Party post, he began to work quietly within the resurrected collective leadership to extend his role and enhance his position and stature. On the surface, he appeared to be generally satisfied to work within the oligarchial arrangement the Party leaders had agreed to, which prohibited the Party chief from simultaneously holding the post of Chairman of the Council of Ministers and committing him to a policy of "cadre stability." However, Brezhnev's early political maneuvering and manipulation of the executive organs of power, policy issues, and personalities, had all the appearances of classical steps to the Party leader's consolidation of power.

Brezhnev immediately acquired numerous additional posts until he had assumed all of Khrushchev's former functions except, of course, chairmanship of the Council of Ministers which went to the former deputy head of the government, Aleksey Kosygin, Russia's foremost economic administrator. The chairmanship of the potentially powerful Constitutional Commission, which had been set up by Khrushchev in April 1962 to draft a replacement to the "Stalin" Constitution, was Brezhnev's first gain.

As President, Brezhnev had been a member of the Constitutional Commission[1] and was aware that it represented his best long-term prospect for making a mark on the Soviet political landscape if the Party leadership could reach agreement on a new constitution. But for now, acquisition of the Commission's chairmanship was a personal gain, since there was no "constitutional" or other

247

provision which automatically entitled Brezhnev to succeed Khrushchev in this position.

The Commission operated under the jurisdiction of the Supreme Soviet Presidium. Both jurisdictionally and from the perspective of strict compliance with the leadership's collective agreement on the division of powers, the Commission's chairmanship should have been passed on to Mikoyan (as Chairman of the Supreme Soviet Presidium) or Kosygin. But at the December 1964 Supreme Soviet session Brezhnev became its head.

The Constitutional Commission with its 97-member constituency[2] provided a lever for Brezhnev to use against those in the state apparatus with whom he shared power. That he used the Commission in this way is substantiated by his declared intentions (early in his incumbency) to assert Party primacy over the state apparatus and by reports in subsequent years that a new constitution would soon appear, always followed by rumblings in the Party leadership over Party and state prerogatives. Numerous reports that Brezhnev hoped to bring the constitution project to completion in time for the fiftieth anniversary celebrations of the October Revolution were leaked in 1966 and 1967. Right after the Twenty-fourth Party Congress in 1971, there were new rumors that a constitution might be ready by the next Party congress.

Brezhnev's accession to the Chairmanship of the R.S.F.S.R. Bureau provided him with more immediate benefits. His protégé Kirilenko was the only top leader who functioned full time on the Bureau as its First Deputy Chairman. As the Bureau was tangential to the power equation, acquisition of its chairmanship was a logical step toward strengthening Brezhnev's position in the Central Committee.

It is not clear when Brezhnev took office as the Bureau's chairman but he was publicly identified in this role in July 1965.[3] This delay suggests the possibility of controversy, perhaps because Khrushchev's use of the post to divide the Central Committee and keep it responsible to him was fresh in the minds of Brezhnev's colleagues. They may have feared that Brezhnev would use it in a similar manner.

Notably, Brezhnev was identified as Bureau Chairman only when he began to vigorously assert himself against Podgorny and Shelepin. The Bureau's political use, however, was shortlived because it was abolished at the Twenty-third Party Congress, a move that was, perhaps, in part designed to check Brezhnev or perhaps was the result of a trade-off for the prestigious title of "General Secretary of the Central Committee" conferred on Brezhnev at the Congress.

Stalin had been the only Party leader to hold the title of General Secretary, yet the title was restored at the Twenty-third Party Congress in 1966. Its restoration, ironically proposed by the Secretary of the Moscow City Party Committee whom Brezhnev would remove a year later for personal criticism, enhanced Brezhnev's authority. It implied that he was on a plane above the other members of the Secretariat, not just first in line.

But the real significance rested in the fact that the Party was singling out an individual leader from the collective leadership. This was demonstrated, and Brezhnev's status and political leverage further improved, by the resurrection of the Party Politburo at the 1966 Congress.

Brezhnev initiated this change himself. On the basis of "a proposal made in many letters from Communists," he "recommended that the Presidium be renamed the Politburo of the C.P.S.U. Central Committee because "For a long time, during V.I. Lenin's lifetime and subsequently, there was a Politburo of the Central Committee and the restoration of the name would more fully express the nature of the activities of our Party's highest political body...."[4]

Thus, by 1966, Brezhnev was already emerging as a single entity. However, his efforts to enhance the standing of the post of General Secretary spurred resistance. Warnings about violating collectivity appeared in the press. A *Pravda* article on July 20, 1966, had Brezhnev in mind when it observed that any individual "regardless of the Party post he occupies" is fallible. The article asserted that "the secretary of a Party committee is *no chief*, he does not have the right to command—he is only the senior person in an organ of collective leadership" (italics supplied).

Lastly, Brezhnev inherited the chairmanship of that executive body in the Politburo responsible for deciding "all questions of military construction and strengthening of the armed forces," the Defense Council. In keeping with the established procedure of empowering the Party chief with supreme responsibility for the armed forces and executive authority over the Council, Brezhnev became the Chairman.

This gave Brezhnev an edge over the other Politburo members in national security policymaking. An examination of the Council's membership reveals why. After Khrushchev's ouster, only Brezhnev, Mikoyan, Kosygin, and possibly Suslov sat on the Council.[5] However, only Brezhnev and Kosygin had extensive expertise in military matters and of the two, Brezhnev's was far greater. He therefore enjoyed a double advantage, which enabled him to push his personal views regarding the country's defense policy.

It wasn't long before Brezhnev moved against the oligarchy itself. Despite the direct and indirect personal advantages derived from occupying the top post in the Party Secretariat, Brezhnev's power in that body appeared to be diluted in October 1964. His initial visible level of activity was low, making his position seem uncertain relative to the other senior secretaries, but particularly Nikolay Podgorny.

Podgorny retained the number two position in the Secretariat after Khrushchev's ouster. His policy outlook, however, which emphasized light and consumer industrial development and a Khrushchev-oriented defense posture, directly conflicted with Brezhnev's policies. Moreover, at the November Party plenum, Podgorny showed his strength when he delivered the speech announcing dissolution of the controversial Party bifurcation scheme.

Brezhnev was bound to show a healthy respect for the political threat that Podgorny, as the Party secretary responsible for Party organization, could pose. Brezhnev viewed Podgorny's presence in the Secretariat as the main obstacle to his own effective exercise of power.

Brezhnev moved quickly to check Podgorny. The Party chief worked behind the scenes to improve his own position and, to ensure more responsive execution of his policies, he exercised his authority to appoint Party functionaries to the staff of the Secretariat. Seizing upon policy issues that would likely rally a broad base of support, Brezhnev sought and won backing for a public confrontation with Podgorny in 1965. Brezhnev's cohorts backed him on this tactic and so did Suslov. Brezhnev probably also solicited and won the direct aid of Aleksandr Shelepin, who undoubtedly anticipated moving into Podorny's number two position in the Secretariat.

Using a line of "guns vs. butter" as the policy issue, the anti-Podgorny campaign became public in February 1965. It was launched by an unsigned lead article in the Central Committee's weekly publication *Ekonomicheskaya Gazeta*,[6] severely criticizing the Party leadership of Podgorny's old bailiwick, Kharkov, for slack economic work. In another article in the same issue, Shcherbitskiy highly praised the economic record of Brezhnev's hometown in an obvious comparison.

It seems that Podgorny had sided with Kosygin against Brezhnev in the cause of a pro-consumer policy course, a more moderate foreign policy line, and continuation of Khrushchev's defense policy. The two articles actually represented the battle between the defense complex, symbolized by Dneprodzerzhinsk on the one hand and the consumer industry, symbolized by Kharkhov, on the other. *Pravda* carried both Mikoyan and Suslov's contribution to the attack in their statements emphasizing "objective realities" that Podgorny had allegedly overlooked.[7]

A second and more serious stage in the campaign commenced in July when Kharkov was cited in a Central Committee decree criticizing Khrushchev's Party admissions policy.[8] Podgorny had headed the Kharkov Party organization during the period under criticism. The exposure of past misconduct in Kharkov was intended to place Podgorny's ability to manage Party organizational matters at the national level into doubt.

Podgorny's protégé, Vitaliy Titov, was also the butt of the criticism and was dismissed as head of the Central Committee Party Organs Department at the September 1965 Party plenum. The following December he was formally removed from the Secretariat. Titov's dismissal may have been the result of Podgorny's own action to save himself. However, it was too late.

At the December 1965 Party plenum Brezhnev edged Podgorny out of the Secretariat and into the lesser post of Chairman of the U.S.S.R. Supreme Soviet Presidium to replace the retiring Mikoyan. This sharply curtailed Podgorny's influence in operational Party matters and effectively eliminated his threat to Brezhnev from an organizational standpoint in the Secretariat.

The December 1965 plenum thus represented a major breakthrough for Brezhnev. Besides Podgorny, Shelepin, who had also mounted a challenge to Brezhnev, was shorn of an important element of his power base at the plenum. This was the first step towards Shelepin's removal from the Secretariat a year and a half later and elimination of him as a constraining factor on Brezhnev's career. In October 1964, however, Brezhnev could scarcely have asked for a closer ally. Shelepin was a conservative whose political outlook in foreign policy and defense matters mirrored Brezhnev's. Brezhnev had supervised his early work, and Shelepin was the former boss of the KGB who helped Brezhnev rally police support for the coup against Khrushchev.

In 1965, however, he became an intriguer of the Beria variety, operating from an unusually large and diversified organizational base which included a deputy chairmanship of the Council of Ministers,

Chairmanship of the U.S.S.R. Party-state Council Committee, seats in the Party Secretariat and Party Presidium (the latter conferred on him at the November 1964 plenum), and authority over the KGB. When Brezhev became Party head, supervisory responsibility in the Secretariat for the Administrative Organs Department was turned over to Shelepin. In short, Shelepin was in an excellent position to impinge on Brezhnev's authority.

Some observers contend that the ex-KGB chief made a bid for even more power in the summer of 1965. The Moscow rumor mill had it that Shelepin, using his organizational base and KGB contacts, made an outright attempt to take command of the Party that year. Mikoyan reportedly started the rumor. Other sources claimed that it originated from Shelepin's cronies high up in the KGB, and still others believed that responsibility rested with the Chinese or with Shelepin himself.

The probability that Shelepin actually tried to grab Brezhnev's job is low. Shelepin was a youthful comer though, and his rapid rise to power, his contacts in the KGB, and his broad base of power, compounded by the much publicized image of Brezhnev (created by the Western press) as an interim leader, had probably prompted such rumors. The rumors also indicated the intensity of the clash with Brezhnev over policy issues.

Debate in the Party leadership in 1965 focused on the economy, defense and the question of Stalin's place in history. Shelepin, riding the wave of anti-Khrushchev reactionism and neo-Stalinism, attacked Brezhnev for inertia in some policy areas and lack of vigor in others. For example, Brezhnev was reluctant to fully dissolve the Party bifurcation scheme. The fact that Podgorny and not Brezhnev addressed the November 1964 Party plenum to announce the reversal of the scheme indicated this reluctance.

Brezhnev also procrastinated on the adoption of policies he had earlier promised to support, and placed himself between the moderates and the neo-Stalinists in the Party on a variety of issues, including Stalinism. However, in the wake of Shelepin's attacks Brezhnev quickly gravitated to the right, devising a strategy to undermine Shelepin's political platform, steal his supporters, and then rally a majority of the Party Presidium against Shelepin in order to cut off his power base.

The latter took the form of a clash between Shelepin's Party-State Control Committee and Brezhnev's Party apparatus. Several articles calling for Committee authority to coordinate the efforts of *all* organizations involved in control activity appeared in the press in the summer of 1965 on Shelepin's behalf. Brezhnev sounded his own battle cry in the R.S.F.S.R. Bureau newspaper *Sovetskaya Rossiya*. On August 4, 1965, the newspaper asserted that Party and state control is an inalienable part of all Party organizational work. There followed more Party attacks on the Committee's independence and accusations of "violations of state discipline and socialist legality" by the Committee.

On August 20, during Shelepin's absence from Moscow, Brezhnev used *Pravda* to attack the Party-State Control Committee in an effort to bring it directly under the direction of the Party, halting its independent status.[9] Regional newspapers and officials followed suit. Kunayev, Brezhnev's cohort in Kazakhstan, became one of the Committee's sharpest critics. Attacks continued until December 6 when the Committee was dismantled on grounds that the Party had determined that "the organs of people's control do not control the work of Party organs."[10]

Brezhnev may have brought even more serious charges against Shelepin stemming from the latter's trip to North Korea in August. According to a Soviet émigré, Shelepin, without prior consultation with the Politburo, flew from Korea to Peking and requested an audience with Mao in hopes of establishing a framework for Soviet-Chinese rapprochement. He failed, but Brezhnev learned of the try through his KGB contacts, and upon Shelepin's return home the Party chief severely reprimanded him for violating the principles of collective leadership.

Thus a combination of charges may have been responsible for stripping Shelepin of his main power base at the December 1965 plenum. Shelepin was also relieved of his deputy premiership, further depleting his power.

Shelepin's subsequent removal from all offices clearly showed Brezhnev's hand at work. The appointment of Kirilenko to the Secretariat in April 1966, resulting from the abolition of the R.S.F.S.R. Bureau, further undermined Shelepin's position in the Secretariat. Kirilenko probably became Brezhnev's second in command at this time, assuming responsibility for supervision of the Central Committee's Party Organs Department. Shelepin continued to supervise the Administrative Organs Department, and thus the KGB for a time, but was soon demoted to overseeing the comparatively unimportant consumer goods industry. Several of his associates were removed from sensitive jobs in the police establishment, and Shelepin's protégé, Semichastny, was removed as KGB head. Finally, in June 1967, Shelepin was removed from the Secretariat.

This event represented a complete victory for Brezhnev in overcoming Shelepin's opposition in the Secretariat. Brezhnev's steady aggrandizement of power from March through December 1965, however frightened some of his colleagues into trying to limit the extent of his December 1965 success over Shelepin. The removal of Titov from the Secretariat and Brezhnev's acquisition of the title of General Secretary bolstered his position to the extent that although there were attempts by some colleagues to restrain any further rise, Brezhnev overcame all resistance.

A requirement for any Soviet Party leader aspiring to rule in his own right is that he exercise effective control over the Central Committee and its apparatus. The Committee was largely Stalin's creation and became his personal fiefdom. Khrushchev tried to achieve the same measure of personal control by his frequent reorganizations and placement of loyal men. His successor's approach has been different.

Brezhnev has combined a successful strategy of expanding the voting membership of the Central Committee, thereby affording himself an opportunity to create an even larger group within the body who are indebted to him for their promotions, while pursuing a policy of member stability and longevity. He has placed loyalists in Central Committee department head positions, while adopting actions and policies benefitting the Party apparatchik; he has given the apparatus greater power in some areas while weakening it to his benefit in others.

At the 1966 Party Congress, Brezhnev personally alluded to Khrushchev's "subjective" methods and reassured the apparatchik of "the Party's pride in its cadres."[11] Thus, from the outset it appeared that Brezhnev would seek to avoid the type of anger that Khrushchev's "voluntarist" and "subjective" reorganizations and interventions provoked among the Party apparatchik and Central Committee members. A low turnover in Central Committee membership under Brezhnev reflects this outlook.

Brezhnev's pledge of confidence in cadres notwithstanding, he did not hesitate to displace personnel in the Central Committee departments with his own men when necessary. In fact, by 1966, he had already presided over a general shakeup, particularly in those departments where Podgorny or Shelepin had held supervisory responsibilities. Between April and December 1965, nine (nearly half) of the Central Committee department heads were replaced. Brezhnev's hand was evident in most cases, with all the crucial posts going to his men.

Fyodor Kulakov was made Agriculture Department head at the November 1964 plenum. His assignment was related to a parallel move by Brezhnev at that time to appoint a new agricultural secretary. Brezhnev succeeded in securing plenum approval for the removal of Polyakov as Party Secretary for Agriculture and head of the Agricultural Department, thereby creating two vacancies in the central apparatus. Brezhnev sought approval for Kulakov to head both positions, but succeeded in getting him into only one.

Ivan Kapitonov is a classic example of a rehabilitated Khrushchev victim who became indebted to Brezhnev. A few years before the 1964 coup, Kapitonov lost his position as head of the Moscow City Party Committee and was given the lesser post of Party Secretary of the Ivanova *oblast* Party organization. But Brezhnev plucked him from Ivanova, made him chief of the R.S.F.S.R. Party Organs Department, and arranged his membership on the R.S.F.S.R. Bureau. Kapitonov's Party organization work and his strong support of Brezhnev's policies, particulary foreign policies, indicates his loyalty and gratitude to Brezhnev for his appointment to the Central Committee department in December 1965.

Two close cohorts were put in command of the departments charged with administering internal Central Committee affairs. Konstantin Chernenko became head of the politically sensitive and strategic General Department in July 1965, and in December Georgiy Pavlov was brought in from the Mari *oblast* to head up the Administration Department. Sergey Trapeznikov, former head of the Modavian Higher Party School in Moldavia, was made Director of the Department of Science and Education in May 1965. Konstantin Rusakov, known to be personally close to Brezhnev, became First Deputy head of the Liaison Department with the Communist Workers' Parties of the Socialist Countries. Vasiliy Shauro, a former associate in Belorussia, was made head of the Cultural Department in November 1964.

Brezhnev may have experienced a setback in November 1966 though, when Mikhail Solomentsev was appointed chief of the Heavy Industry Department. Brezhnev may have mistrusted him since the purge of Kunayev under Khrushchev had resulted in the promotion of Solomentsev to Party Secretary of Kazakhstan. A

month after Solomentsev's appointment as Heavy Industry Department head he was elected to the Secretariat, suggesting that Suslov
and others were attempting to balance Brezhnev's power both in the
Secretariat and in the Central Committee apparatus.

The assignments of cohorts to the apparatus in 1965 gave
Brezhnev essential control of the Central Committee administrative
departments. The number of Brezhnev's appointees increased in subsequent years, frequently at the expense of other Party leaders,
giving Brezhnev a quantitative majority in the Central Committee
departments. In 1968, for example, Brezhnev's grip over the Liaison
Department with the Communist and Workers' Parties of Socialist
Countries was tightened, evidently at Suslov's expense, when
Rusakov replaced Yuriy Andropov as head of the Department.
Rusakov's efforts on behalf of Brezhnev were subsequently rewarded
when he was brought onto Brezhnev's personal staff as a senior foreign
affairs advisor.

A crucial change occurred in 1973 facilitating Brezhnev's at-
tainment of a prominent position in foreign policy. In April of that
year Pyotr Abrasimov, a close friend, was brought back from his
post as Ambassador to France and named head of the Department of
Cadres Abroad (foreign service personnel). The appointments of
Rusakov and Abrasimov represented a watershed in Brezhnev's control of the departments responsible for the implementation of Soviet
foreign policy. Together with Andrey Aleksandrov-Agentov and
Georgiy Tsukanov, both foreign policy specialists on Brezhnev's personal staff, they constitute the main machinery for Brezhnev's foreign
policy role.

Brezhnev also devoted considerable attention to the police
establishment early in his incumbency. His control and influence
within the police had slipped somewhat after Mironov's death and
the assignment of supervisory responsibility for the Administrative
Organs Department to Shelepin after the October coup. Shelepin's
later aspirations demonstrated the necessity for Brezhnev to take
steps to correct this slippage.

The first step was to take KGB supervisory responsibility away
from Shelepin. This was achieved in mid 1966 when Brezhnev
assumed direct responsibility for the KGB. The shift of Vladimir
Laputin from head of the R.S.F.S.R. Bureau's Administrative Organs
Department to deputy chief of the C.P.S.U. Administrative Organs
Department after the Bureau was abolished, strengthened Brezhnev's
position. In addition, Brezhnev had an ally in Nikolay Savinkin, who

had been Mironov's assistant and who functioned as acting head of the Department until his formal appointment as its head in 1968.

In July 1966, Brezhnev sought to recentralize the uniformed police and appoint his own man to direct its activities. The police, decentralized by Khrushchev, were reorganized into a single ministry in July. The appointment of a police chief, however, was delayed until that fall, the reason becoming apparent only after it was announced that Nikolay Shchelokov, the deputy premier of Moldavia and a life-long Brezhnev cohort,* was chosen over Vadim Tikunov. There had been strife over the choice, but Tikunov, a senior policeman with extensive KGB experience who had headed the R.S.F.S.R. Ministry until its incorporation into the new central ministry, was not given the job because he was a Shelepin client.

But the head office of the KGB, some directorates and some lower level commands remained in the hands of men beholden to Shelepin in 1966. Brezhnev wished to move against them but was unable to do so unilaterally; a good reason and Politburo backing were required.

Finding justification did not prove difficult. When Semichastny was removed as KGB head in 1967, the Western press speculated that defection of Stalin's daughter to the West had been the reason. According to media reports Svetlana's defection sufficiently embarrassed Soviet leaders to necessitate a change in the leadership of those organs responsible for preventing such incidents.

The possibility that Brezhnev, working with Tsinev and Tsvigun behind the scenes, made a strong case for "anti-Party" activity on the part of Shelepin's KGB cronies cannot be ruled out either. This would have been sufficient reason for the Politburo to make a change in KGB leadership as well as select a new leader who could be trusted by all. Thus, in May 1967, Semichastny was removed as KGB head and Yuriy Andropov appointed in his place.

The new chief's ties were probably with Suslov, though

In 1938 Shchelokov was Party Secretary of the Dnepropetrovsk Krasnogvardeyskiy rayon. Shortly after Brezhnev became Propaganda Secretary in Dnepropetrovsk, Shchelokov was given the job of Chairman of the Dnepropetrovsk City Soviet and then served in the Red Army during World War II. When Brezhnev became head of the Political Administration of the Carpathian Military District, Shchelokov was secretary of a Party Committee in the district. After the war both he and Brezhnev returned to the Ukraine; Shchelokov became Ukrainian Deputy Minister of local industry, then head of the Heavy Industry Department of the CP (b)U Central Committee. He followed Brezhnev to Moldavia as First Deputy Chairman of the Moldavian Council of Ministers.

Brezhnev had worked with Andropov in the Secretariat where the latter had become a secretary in 1962. This gave Brezhnev ample opportunity to observe him and gauge his performance. Andropov could not have been appointed had Brezhnev disapproved. The change in KGB leadership enhanced Brezhnev's authority over the KGB and his position vis-à-vis Shelepin.

Subsequent personnel changes strengthened Brezhnev's position. This was particularly so with the appointments of such clearly identifiable Brezhnev men as Tsvigun, who became second in command of the KGB in the summer of 1967, and Tsinev and Viktor Chebrikov who became deputy chairmen. Chebrikov's appointment was not announced until October 1969,[12] but he was listed as leaving his post as Party Second Secretary in Dnepropetrovsk in October 1967. That same year Tsinev was promoted to the KGB Second Directorate, which is responsible for Soviet internal security and counterintelligence. He became a KGB Deputy Chairman two years later. At about the same time Vladimir Pirozhkov, who served under Brezhnev in Kazakhstan, was appointed a KGB Deputy Chairman. His election to the R.S.F.S.R. Supreme Soviet in June 1971 revealed his status.

With these appointments, Brezhnev men occupied at least four of the six deputy chairmanships immediately under Andropov, suggesting checks and balances on the police chief and clearly placing control of the KGB at headquarters level in Brezhnev's hands.

The appointments of some Party officials to the highest KGB positions reflected a Brezhnev stated policy goal of strengthening the security organs "with cadres who are politically mature."[13] This implied that the KGB had undertaken "politically immature" actions (i.e., the 1965 rumors about Brezhnev) under Shelepin, making increased Party control necessary. If the move aroused animosity among the KGB professionals it was mollified by giving the KGB increased political power and prestige by electing Andropov a candidate member of the Politburo in 1971,[14] elevating Chebrikov and Tsvigun to candidate status in the Central Committee at the Twenty-fourth Party Congress, and electing Tsinev to the Central Auditing Commission in 1971. Further, Brezhnev gave the KGB greater authority in internal security matters, particularly in activities directed against dissidents. In sum, Brezhnev has given the KGB good reasons to be happy with his leadership and they have responded with their close support.

XXII

Stalin, Agriculture and Defense

The Khrushchev days are over — funny, they
now seem rich in retrospect. — A Soviet citizen.

STALIN WAS A MAJOR SOURCE OF CONFLICT within the Party leadership in 1965. Shelepin and his supporters definitely wanted to change the image of Stalin created under Khrushchev and re-Stalinize in selected areas, and a large number of Party apparatchiks and government officials who were unhappy with de-Stalinization supported him. Brezhnev, however, did not — not fully anyway. Nor did he wish to continue de-Stalinization, which to a large extent had been motivated by Khrushchev's personal considerations and there could be little or no gain for Brezhnev in continuing it.

In 1965, the Party chief therefore instituted a campaign to end de-Stalinization. This provided an alternative to Shelepin's proposals and included the condemnation of "one-sidedness" in the treatment of Party history and "personalities"; the resurrection of selected Stalinist symbols, the rehabilitation of some victims of Khrushchev's anti-Stalin campaigns, and the favorable revision of history of the Stalin era, including that of collectivization, industrialization and Stalin's war role.

Brezhnev was the first to reveal Stalin's war role in a favorable light. At the Twentieth anniversary victory celebrations of World War II Brezhnev proclaimed.

> The German fascist troops had been mobilized, deployed for strike, and moved right up to our borders well ahead of time. Surprise was on the side of the fascists. Our Party and people did not flinch. The State Defense Committee was organized under the leadership of I.V. Stalin ... to guide all operations in organizing the rebuff of the enemy. While the enemy reveled in his temporary successes, the mind and will of the Party and the selfless efforts of the people forged and tempered the invincible steel force that soon became the terror of the fascist invaders.[1]

Brezhnev gave no reasons for the temporary victory of the German forces other than their advance was "well ahead of time" and a "surprise." This implied that an attack had been forecast, but had come before anticipated; yet, according to Brezhnev, there was no

259

panic with the invasion. He did not mention the emergency evacuation of important officials from Moscow, lack of prewar preparations, or Stalin's miscalculations. This was a clear attempt to rehabilitate Stalin's thesis, which attributed all the failures in the initial period of the war to the treacherousness and unexpectedness of the German attack.

The Party chief was also highly instrumental in rewriting much of Stalin's history after Shelepin's defeat in the Party Secretariat, suggesting that Brezhnev was perhaps personally, as well as politically, motivated on at least Stalin's role in the Great Patriotic War. Moreover, Brezhnev directly benefited from the resurrection of such Stalinist symbols as "General Secretary."

The return to orthodoxy was naturally carried over into the cultural sphere. Censorship was tightened and more stringent demands were placed on all spheres of society. According to one Soviet dissident, "Not only in the Politburo, but in tens of thousands of factories, offices, bureaus, educational and research institutes, committees and commissions, the balance has swung sharply toward orthodoxy and a hard line.... It's quite enough to make everyone shrink back into his shell. Everyone knows which way the wind is blowing."[2]

Gory tales about Brezhnev's personal dealings with dissidents began to circulate among the underground. One involved an assassination attempt on him. At a speaking engagement in Leningrad, guards detained two 17-year-old boys who had attempted to sneak through one of the building entrances. One boy was carrying an old briefcase containing two homemade bombs. When interrogated they confessed their intention: "Yes, we wanted to kill Brezhnev. We hate the ugly ape." They had planned to toss the bombs beneath the podium where Brezhnev was to speak. In place of the ceremony an ad hoc tribunal met with Brezhnev presiding. The boys were condemned to death and publicly executed by a firing squad two hours later. The story preceded an actual assassination attempt on Brezhnev by a police guard in January 1969.

Brezhnev became increasingly assertive in establishing the authority of the First Secretary. At the March 1965 Party plenum he introduced a major program for agriculture, thus undoing Khrushchev's administrative changes and clearly putting himself in the forefront of responsiblility for agriculture in the Soviet Union.

Brezhnev, like Khrushchev, made agriculture his personal responsibility and chose the March Party plenum to announce his

"New Deal" for Soviet agriculture.[3] He presented a program of increased capital investment, stable prices for farm produce and financial incentives, all designed to "put a firm economic foundation under agriculture" and stimulate agricultural production. Precise cost accounting in the collective farms was one objective; others were agricultural specialization and greater autonomy for collective farm planning.

In order to ensure the "correct development" of the two types of communal economy, the institution of the collective farm was reaffirmed as playing a vital role in building the material-technical base of Communism. The transformation of collective farms into state farms was to be halted. The Party's obligation was to promote "in every way the development and prosperity of both types of communal farming," but a new collective farm charter would have to be drafted.

Brezhnev presented numerous proposals designed to induce work incentive. A new, more liberal income tax based on net instead of gross farm income was introduced, basic purchase prices for grain crops were raised 50 to 100 percent, and the rules regulating the collective farmers' private plots were relaxed. Firm plans for procurement of produce over a number of years in combination with new purchase prices were to put a firm economic base under the grain economy and end the low profitability of grain production on the collective and state farms.

The Party chief emphasized the need for improving material and technical supplies for farms. He recommended the standardization of parts; adjustments in equipment prices tied to the price level of industrial consumers, creation of mechanized detachments and machine rental, mechanized animal husbandry, and meadow reclamation stations. To solve the problem of electrification a plan for the broad electification of agriculture was to be drafted.

Brezhnev also called for a meeting of the Third All-Union Congress of Collective Farmers for 1966. For unknown reasons the Congress was not held until 1969. When it did meet, it was hardly an historical cornerstone in the lives of collective farmers. The farmers, however, were granted the same social security benefits as regular government employees.

The course of action for agriculture adopted at the March 1965 plenum and subsequently at the 1966 Party Congress were steps in the right direction toward improving this sector of the economy. However, they failed to go far enough in altering the material, legal, social and economic structures of agriculture, which remain the principal causes of Soviet agricultural inefficiency.

In the military realm, Marshal Malinovskiy's support had been important to Brezhnev in the coup against Khrushchev. This support would also be essential in early maneuvering as the Party chief and would remain a necessary condition for retention of power. Therefore, Brezhnev could be expected to defer to the military on at least some critical defense questions raised under Khrushchev. Brezhnev's early statements on defense did, in fact, reflect a discernible pro-Malinovskiy defense line.

It is now clear that Brezhnev's first policy action in the Politburo was not in the sphere of agriculture but in defense, based on immediate political considerations and his own perceptions of the U.S.S.R.'s defense requirements. This explains Brezhnev's determined effort in 1965 — the key preparation year in which major defense planning decisions for the next five years were to be finalized — to push through a defense plan that would alter the existing structure of the Soviet Armed Forces and nearly double the size of the Soviet defense budget.

Strategic considerations and the desire to maneuver on the international scene from a "position of strength" in the post-Khrushchev era prompted Brezhnev to seek a markedly stronger military posture in October 1964. Strategic needs vis-à-vis the People's Republic of China, the need to repair the Soviet position in the political competition with China, and the power struggle with the West were all important considerations. He believed that if the Soviet Union were to pursue its international objectives effectively — some of them likely entailing a sharpening of American-Soviet relations and running the risk of confrontation with the West — the Soviet Union would have to change its strategy of being second-best and acquire a wider range of military options.

These thoughts were expressed in Brezhnev's speech to graduating military cadets on July 3, 1965:

> In some areas abroad they are continuing to raise a hue and cry about the alleged superiority of the United States over the Soviet Union in the field of strategic weapons. This campaign is being pursued not only by the press, but has been actively touted by people occupying high posts in the United States government. This is a routine attempt to revive the long bankrupt policy of nuclear blackmail directed primarily against the Soviet Union and calculated to intimidate the freedom-loving people of our countries.[4]

An additional requirement was the need more firmly to integrate military doctrine and structure of forces with diplomacy. This politico-military orientation could be seen in Brezhnev's first major foreign policy speech, on November 6, 1964. In that important speech he asserted that henceforth the Soviet Union would, in implementing the policy of peaceful coexistence, proceed only on the "basis of the military power of the countries of the socialist camp. We shall maintain our defense potential at the highest possible levels."[5]

This statement must be treated as the baseline for the whole of Brezhnev's foreign policy approach—from declared hostility to the West in the early 1960s to détente a decade later. Its significance rests in the fact that it established a direct link between success or failure in the "struggle" with the West and the Soviet military posture, thereby providing an important rationale for a costly commitment to a variety of military programs that would entail tangible security and diplomatic benefits.

Initially Brezhnev had rough sailing in the Party Presidium. Kosygin was opposed to any alteration of existing defense policy, which presupposed that any war with the West would become nuclear and that such a war was unwinnable because of the destructiveness of nuclear weapons.

Podgorny opposed Brezhnev's defense policy recommendations and on at least two occasions spoke in public forums against them. He was the only Party leader to publicly praise the military budget cut for 1965, which Kosygin had announced in December of the previous year.[6] Decisions for these cuts amounting to 500 million rubles had been made under Khrushchev, and under the new regime represented a "stand pat" position until a majority consensus could be reached on defense expenditures for the 1966-1970 defense plan.

In a speech in Baku in June 1965, Podgorny took the position that "restrictions on consumer welfare and national sacrifices by the population to allow for priority development of heavy industry and strengthening of defense are a *thing of the past.*"[7] He never repeated this after his demotion from the Secretariat. In fact, in a manner typical of the apparatchik maneuvering to improve his relative power, he joined Brezhnev and even began to promote a Brezhnev cult on the basis of the Party chief's personal "contribution to strengthening the country's defense potential."[8]

On Brezhnev's sixtieth birthday in 1966, the Party chief was awarded the Order of Lenin for "strengthening of the country's defense potential," among other things. Podgorny said in his December 19

A vigorous Brezhnev during a visit to Budapest days before his sixtieth birthday, 1966. (World Wide Photos.)

presentation remarks that the Order was specifically awarded "for an exceptionally great contribution to the activity of the Party and state in the restoration of Leninist principles and standards, in switching the economy to scientifically motivated development, in *strengthening the defense potential of the country*, and in implementing major social developments for the good of the people."

Unlike Kosygin and Podgorny, in 1965 Suslov argued that "objective reality" dictated adoption of Brezhnev's ideas.[9] Except for Brezhnev, however, no one made an effort to spell out where he stood on how large the several branches of the armed forces should be and what relative weight and importance they should have.

In each of Brezhnev's five major speeches on defense in 1965,[10] he called for "ceaselessly strengthening" the Soviet Armed Forces and emphasized the need for a combined arms force incorporating a large conventional warfare complement. Thus, Brezhnev publicly identified himself with the combined arms school of Marshal Malinovskiy,[11] which Khrushchev had opposed.

For a time the Party Presidium remained divided on defense policy. However, international tension in Southeast Asia underscored the need for a demonstratively stronger Soviet defense posture. Ironically the United States launched its first air strike over North Vietnam when Kosygin was visiting Hanoi. The American action served Brezhnev's cause.

The decision to go ahead with Brezhnev's defense recommendations was reached by July 1965. He revealed in a speech that month that "economic planning is now taking into account the need to strengthen the country's defense in light of the international situation." He specifically assured the military that the five year plan for 1966-1970 being "worked out" would spare no efforts "to increase the defensive might of the U.S.S.R."

The new emphasis on defense was symbolized in the Party's *Theses* for the fiftieth anniversary of the October Revolution, which prioritized increases in the economic and military might of the country as the main business of the Party. The *Theses* concluded that the past half century had proven that if socialism were to survive, the Soviet Union and other socialist countries would have to maintain the strongest possible military posture as a "real counterweight to the aggressive forces of imperialism." Where Khrushchev in his last years had emphasized the building of Communism at home for which he was accused of neglecting the Party's worldwide revolutionary goals, the fiftieth anniversary *Theses* stressed the indivisibility of the Party's internal aims with its external.[12]

The 1966-1970 Soviet defense budget and all subsequent budgets have reflected this emphasis. Defense spending nearly doubled in the 1966-1970 plan. It rose by about 63 percent in the 1971-1975 period and increased at about the same rate in the Tenth Five Year Defense Plan for 1976-1980. According to Brezhnev, one out of every three rubles in the Soviet Gross National Product is spent on defense today.[13] Over the last half decade the Soviet Union has spent an estimated 50 to 80 percent more on defense than the United States.[14]

Modification of Khrushchev's doctrinal formulations was necessary for the kind of military forces Brezhnev sought in 1965. He responded in two ways. First, he dissociated himself from Khrushchev's optimistic themes of a world decline in the danger of war and the prospect of "removing war from the life of society." Second, he propagated his own doctrine which essentially developed the argument earlier by military strategists that possibilities for a conventional war (fought without nuclear weapons) might be on the increase.[15] He took their arguments a step further by refuting the belief, promoted by Khrushchev, that any future war would automatically become nuclear. Referring to Europe in a speech at Karlovy Vary, Czechoslovakia, in 1967, for example, Brezhnev asserted that if a new war started it "could" become thermonuclear,[16] but need not "inevitably" be nuclear, as Kosygin continued to argue.[17]

Brezhnev's doctrinal formulations involved both a rejection of the notion that a nuclear war would destroy civilization and a retreat from the once rigid Soviet declaratory line that local wars involving major powers would "inevitably" escalate into nuclear war and therefore must be avoided. Hence, encouragement and assistance to national liberation movements could be given in order to demonstrate that the Soviet Union was not, as China claimed, defaulting on its obligations to revolutionary movements.

Khrushchev had cut the budget of the Ground Forces and eliminated it as a separate command of the Armed Forces in September 1964.[18] Brezhnev reinstated the Ground Forces as a separate branch and enhanced its importance by appointing Deputy Minister of Defense Ivan Pavlovskiy as its head. In Brezhnev's speech to military graduates in 1966, he reported that "the Soviet Army is being supplied with the most up-to-date tanks, aviation, artillery and other equipment," indicating major modernization of general purpose ground forces and tactical aviation. Also significant was the fact that the numbers of personnel in uniform rose on an average of 200,000 annually to a total of 4 million soldiers by 1972.

A major upgrading of the Warsaw Pact was also undertaken to comply with Brezhnev's stated objective to "strengthen the might and defense potential of Warsaw Pact member states." This decision had significant political utility. Boosting the Warsaw Pact theater forces with Soviet troops would, in part, deal with the ferment in Eastern Europe and reduce uncertainty about the political disposition of some countries to lend themselves fully to the Warsaw Pact effort. Khrushchev had placed heavy emphasis on East European responsibility for Pact maintenance. Brezhnev emphasized Soviet responsibility.

For the development of weapons for intercontinental conflict, Brezhnev stressed in his 1965 military graduates speech the "special attention being paid to nuclear missile weapons." About 200 second- and third-generation missiles had been deployed in the Soviet Union before Khrushchev's ouster. Significant deployment of intercontinental ballistic and submarine launched ballistic missiles (SLBM) have since taken place. The Soviet Union surpassed the United States in ICBM launchers in 1969 and in SLBM launchers in 1972.[19]

The decision for largescale deployment of the ICBM was probably made before Khrushchev's downfall. It was possibly taken in March 1963 when plans for the last two years of the Seventh Five Year Plan were revised. Khrushchev stated in his memoirs that

> I don't think it was until after my retirement that we completely converted our missile system from launching pads to sunken silos, but I was proud of my role in originating the idea and later seeing that the conversion was begun. The experience of the Caribbean crisis also convinced us that we were right to concentrate on the manufacture of nuclear missiles.[20]

Podgorny and Kosygin may have challenged some of these decisions after Khrushchev fell. But Brezhnev pressed for and won their inclusion in the eighth five year defense plan package. He is the sponsor of all subsequent strategic and related military programs, which include transformation of the Soviet Navy into a force befitting a superpower[21] and unprecedented arms sales to the Third World. He should also be credited with finalizing the decision pending in 1964 for largescale development of antiballistic missile systems. In his July 3, 1965, speech, Brezhnev asserted that "further important headway is being made in developing Soviet means of anti-missile defense."

All of these military programs provide great security benefits and political dividends to the Soviet Union. In 1968, Brezhnev claimed for the first time that "the balance of forces on a worldwide scale continues to tilt in favor of socialism and its allies [because] the might of the socialist camp is now such that the imperialists are afraid of a military rout in case of a head-on clash with the main forces of socialism."[22]

The enchanced importance given to the Soviet Armed Forces has paid off politically for Brezhnev by rallying substantial military support for his leadership. This is not to say that relations have been trouble free. There have been periods of adversity. One instance was the tussle over the selection of a Minister of Defense after Malinovskiy died in 1967. The military promoted Marshal Grechko while at least Podgorny and Kosygin wanted Ustinov, perhaps because they believed that he would bring more effective management to the Ministry of Defense. Brezhnev's position remains clouded but in 1967 relations with Grechko were not as close as they were earlier or came to be.

Relations improved immeasurably in 1968 and 1969 though, in part because of the military's role in Czechoslovakia. Grechko, who had become increasingly involved in military related diplomatic matters, was a principal Soviet actor in the 1968 political crisis in Czechoslovakia. His role and the Politburo's reliance on force to achieve its political objectives in Czechoslovakia enhanced the military's prestige and its influence in policymaking. Such influence first became institutionalized in 1968 when the Ministry of Defense established a direct working relationship — related mainly to problems of disarmament — with the Ministry of Foreign Affairs. Five years later under Brezhnev's personal sponsorship, Grechko was coopted onto the Politburo.

XXIII

Détente: The Policy Instrument

*We make no secret of the fact that we see
détente as the way to create more favorable
conditions for peaceful socialist and communist
construction.* — L.I. Brezhnev, Speech to the
XXV C.P.S.U. Congress, 1976.

EVERY POLITICAL LEADER NEEDS A POLICY designed to capture
the spotlight. Brezhnev chose foreign policy. He began early in October 1964 to return the Party to an orthodox foreign policy line.
Eager to reverse the forces working to fragment the world Communist
movement, he attempted to form a single anti-imperialist front; ver-
bally, the level of hostility against the United States increased. He
took steps to upgrade Soviet support for national liberation
movements around the world and to strengthen bonds with Eastern
Europe and "progressive forces," including an intensified effort to increase Soviet influence through local Communist parties in Europe.
He also attempted to normalize relations with Communist China.

Brezhnev's goals in Europe were to eliminate United States influence and split Western allies in NATO in order to effect erosion of
that organization. He hoped to achieve a German peace treaty
legitimizing Germany's division under international law, thereby
confirming the division of Europe along existing lines, and hopefully
bringing together Eastern and Western Europe into a security sphere
minus American presence or influence. In the realm of Soviet-East
European relations Brezhnev aimed to stabilize the Socialist Com-
monwealth, confirm the leading role of the Soviet Union in it, and
gain Western acceptance of the status quo there.

Brezhnev's European policies found support among all Party
leaders. His orthodox approach particularly pleased the predominantly conservative leadership. But by 1969 the tide was beginning to
shift, especially as Kosygin took the lead in articulating a policy of
reducing tensions with the West. Other signs of political maneuving
began to be manifest too.

In 1969, Shelepin, despite having lost everyting but his Politburo seat two years earlier, been undercut by Brezhnev on the Stalin

question and other issues, and deprived of many followers, mounted
a second challenge to Brezhnev. Using the very tactic that had served
him well in the first challenge, Shelepin adopted the platform of
Brezhnev's critic's so much so that by 1974, it was difficult to
distinguish him from moderates like Kosygin.

Shelepin used facilities at his disposal to undermine Brezhnev's
policies and exploit his weaknesses. He mobilized the All-Union Central Council of Trade Unions as spokesman. A movement to undermine Brezhnev by publishing articles out of step with his policies,
particularly foreign policy, got underway in *Komsomolskaya Pravda*,
whose editor was appointed when Shelepin headed Komsomol,
and *Trud*, the trade union newspaper.

The Komsomol newspaper took a comparatively tolerant
view of dissident Soviet intellectuals, evidently for the purpose of
exposing the harshness of Brezhnev's cultural policies. Shelepin
promoted the idea of Soviet-West European cooperation in general,
and his trade union activities encouraged a positive response to Willy
Brandt's feelers for normalized relations between West Germany and
the U.S.S.R. Moreover, Shelepin, perhaps hoping the political crisis
in Czechoslovakia would backfire on Brezhnev, dissented in the
Politburo's decision to intervene militarily in Czecholsovakia in the
summer of 1968.

Kosygin, and other Party leaders including Suslov, who had
provided some theoretical rationale for a positive response to Brandt,
now also became critical of Brezhnev for lack of direction on key
foreign policy questions. Brezhnev's numerous propaganda campaigns asserting that "American collusion with German revanchism"
threatened a new war in Europe and his limited economic in-
ducements — including construction of a gas pipeline from the Soviet
Union to Western Europe[1] — designed to lure European nations away
from the United States had done little to achieve his earlier declared
Euopean goals. The attempt to normalize relations with China had
also failed, leading the September 1964 C.P.S.U. plenum to conclude
that "normalization was not supported by the Communist Party of
China."[2] Serious fighting between Soviet and Chinese military forces
on the Sino-Soviet border in 1969 further complicated Soviet-
Chinese relations.

Brezhnev's efforts to increase cohesion in the Communist
world had also been frustrated. The postponed Communist Parties'
Conference finally met in June 1969. Brezhnev could not, however,
persuade the conference to condemn the Chinese. In Eastern Europe,

Soviet influence disintegrated as states moderated their policies to accommodate establishment of diplomatic and economic ties with "revanchist" West Germany and other West European states. The Soviet invasion of Czechoslovakia in 1968 provided some answers to the questions posed by the U.S.S.R.'s East European policies, but the "Brezhnev doctrine," while useful in justifying the use of military force to restore Communist authority in Czechoslovakia and strengthen the grip over the satellite state, hardly constituted a basis for a comprehensive foreign policy.

Brezhnev needed to respond to his critics and he needed a new foreign policy strategy. Thus, in the months preceding the Twenty-fourth Party Congress, he gravitated toward the so-called "moderate foreign policy line advocated by Kosygin and Shelepin. By 1971 he had become the standard bearer of a policy of *razryadka* (relaxation of tensions) or *détente* with the West.

The changed course of Soviet foreign policy bore all the earmarks of classic Brezhnev maneuvering. His critics found themselves in the uncomfortable position of seeing policies they had long espoused finally adopted, but with Brezhnev receiving the credit. Shelepin in particular was devastated by this maneuvering. He fell from sixth to fifteenth (last) place in the Politburo listing at the 1971 Party Congress.

To say, however, that Brezhnev's decision to embark on a policy of détente with the West was simply a political response to challenge within the Politburo would be erroneous. It was much more.

The policy was opportunistic. Brezhnev had limited personal knowledge of the United States before 1967, but after the Czech crisis and as the Soviet Union approached strategic parity with its rival superpower, he began to devote considerable attention to future Soviet global prospects. One obvious advantage of being the General Secretary was better and quicker access to foreign policy data and wider contacts which, coupled with his position on the Defense Council, gave Brezhnev the edge over his colleagues in foreign policy formulation.

He crafted a comprehensive détente foreign policy strategy that reflected existing Soviet perceptions of the political, military and economic strengths and weaknesses of the U.S.S.R., its allies and rivals abroad. Brezhnev envisioned two complementary, though seemingly contradictory, lines of attack: normalized state-to-state relations with Soviet rivals and vigorous support of national liberation movements and sympathetic factions and regimes engaged in regional conflicts. The policy he presented to the Politburo and the Central Committee offered fresh opportunities to promote changes in world politics favorable to the U.S.S.R. Détente, it was thought, would limit American interest in collaboration with the People's Republic of China against the Soviet Union.

China loomed large in Brezhnev's considerations. He came to recognize that the ideological struggle with China and the efforts to force Mao back into the fold were driving the Chinese toward accommodation with the Americans. To cease pressuring the Chinese would mean de facto recognition of the rift and perhaps acquiescence in the Chinese claim to be the true interpreters of Marx and Lenin. Yet to increase pressure might enable the United States to secure a diplomatic foothold with China. Brezhnev was persuaded to seek détente in order to keep his options open and be in a better position to handle the China situation.

The creation of a political climate in which economic relations, particularly a flow of Western credits and technology, could flourish provided a second inducement. Economic trade would facilitate growth in the requisite areas of the Soviet economy while allowing defense construction to benefit and to continue at a high rate. Although it was never stated in the Soviet Ninth Five Year Plan, which was published under Brezhnev's signature and emphasized consumer interests, given the state of the economy and the ambitious nature of the plan, there had to be built into it heavy dependence on largescale economic assistance from the West.

Brezhnev convinced his colleagues that détente would lead to the development of precedents and mechanisms for consulting with the United States during crises, thereby reducing the liklihood of war and giving the Soviet Union an opportunity to influence American behavior in response to Soviet activities abroad. At the same time, the Soviet Union would take advantage of a weakening of unity and purpose within the United States and Western Europe to promote Soviet global interests and objectives and help bring to power pro-Soviet governments in Africa and elsewhere in the Third World. Most importantly, détente would help reduce Western military spending.

Brezhnev placed high value on the arms control aspect of détente as a means of assisting Soviet military policy by limiting the response of the West to the growth of Soviet military power. He believed that increased Soviet strength could be achieved through the process of arms negotiations at various levels, ultimately leading to a reduction in Western defense efforts, a weakening of NATO and other military alliances, and a neutralization of those areas of competition where superior Western technology put the Soviet Union at a disadvantage.

Also important was Brezhnev's own personality. He has no less a fascination with foreign affairs than American presidents or European prime ministers. Indeed, his delight with the ceremony, protocol and recognition that accompany diplomacy was evident during his tenure as President. Foremost, of course, is Brezhnev's desire for greatness. History judges political leaders by the success of their foreign policies, and this may very well explain Brezhnev's activities in this sphere.

Because détente would mean a radical departure from his previous cautious and orthodox style of leadership, Brezhnev took care to secure conservative support for, or at the very least to neutralize conservative opposition to, the policy.

To forestall opposition in the Politburo, most notably from Polyanskiy and Shelest, Brezhnev backed a costly agricultural investment program for the Ninth Five Year Plan that they favored. In addition, since Polyanskiy and Kirill Mazurov, Kosygin's deputy, were the two most likely candidates to succeed Kosygin in the Council of Ministers should he step down, a private expression of support for Polyanskiy as the next premier would increase his loyalty to Brezhnev. Kirilenko too, though of conservative bent, realized that his ambitions would also be served by continued support for Brezhnev, while Suslov, despite his tough political outlook, had already expressed support for détente.

To reassure the domestic security forces, relaxation of internal control would not accompany détente as had occurred under Khrushchev. Brezhnev would allow the police to increase pressure on dissident elements within society. Great pains were taken to reassure heavy industry, the defense industry bureaucracies and the military of continued high investment in defense.

Détente, from the military's perspective, was not unwelcome. Military leaders viewed the policy as a means of deflating the resources allocation problem. Not only would the Soviet armed forces be better able to cope with a threat from China in the Far East, but capital equipment and products for agriculture and light industry could be purchased in the West without a substantial reorientation of priorities.[3] With détente, the U.S.S.R. could have both guns and butter.

The Minister of Defense was called on to participate in the Politburo's decision on détente. In May 1970, Andrey Grechko assured the defense bureaucracies and the military that détente would not alter military priorities and that "the country's defenses *will always* be strong and reliable."[4]

Having laid the necessary groundwork and secured the support of the right, Brezhnev chose Willy Brandt's election as the West German Chancellor in 1970 to launch détente. The policy paid immediate dividends. Bilateral negotiations led to the signing of the West German-Soviet Treaty in August 1970 and achievement of one of Brezhnev's principal goals: recognition of postwar borders in Eastern Europe. The treaty in turn opened the door for the signing of a Four-Power Agreement on Berlin in September of the following year.

The latter represented a milestone in resolving East-West contention over Berlin. Among other things, Brezhnev secured implicit recognition of East Berlin as the capital of the German Democratic Republic, agreement on a reduction in the Western military presence in West Berlin, and recognition of that city as outside the "constituency" of the Federal Republic of Germany. At the same time, the city's "ties" to the Federal Republic were recognized and the unimpeded access of civilian traffic to and from West Berlin was guaranteed.

The treaty also cleared the way for extensive economic agreements. Major steps were taken to relieve the pressure on several sectors of the Soviet economy, with trade, technology transfer agreements and longterm industrial cooperation expanded. By 1973, Bonn had become Moscow's largest trading partner in the West.[5]

At times during the West German political debate in 1971, the fate of the treaty appeared uncertain. When the West German parliament affixed its seal of approval to the treaty a year later, dissent from such critics of Brezhnev as Shelest was reduced, making the second step in détente — extension of the policy to the United States — possible.

The forging of détente relations with the United States was conditional upon a successful summit with President Richard Nixon. But Nixon's order on May 8, 1972, to mine Haiphong harbor to stop Soviet ships from delivering war supplies to North Vietnam almost ruined the summit before it began. Shelest's calls to cancel the summit and challenge the blockage resounded in Central Committee headquarters. Brezhnev, however, remained calm and urged his colleagues to do the same. He carried the day. The emergency Politburo meeting called on May 9 decided against a showdown and for a go-ahead with the summit.

The Central Committee's plenary meeting held on May 9, just a few days before Nixon's arrival in Moscow, therefore constituted a significant milestone in lining up support for détente. As Brezhnev told the Twenty-fifth Party Congress in 1976, "The plenary meeting in May 1972 discussed the problems facing us at the ... *crucial moment* in the struggle for détente," and the meeting "set the right course."[6] Brezhnev emerged with support for the Nixon visit, himself firmly committed to the policy of détente.

The subsequent summit projected Brezhnev as the dominant figure in the U.S.S.R. At his presummit meeting with Secretary of State Henry Kissinger he appeared nervous and fidgety. But during the 41-hour and 53-minute session with President Nixon he was a relaxed, self-assured, and volubly demonstrative negotiator. Brezhnev impressed Kissinger as a man of "concrete positions and concete objectives," who excels in "doing things rather than philosophizing about them," an "elemental" and "physical" person who knew what he wanted and how to get it.[7] Brezhnev even showed his humorous side. Once Brezhnev bounded to his feet and started to drive home his point, then suddenly he stopped and muttered: "Ah hell, I'd better sit down, every time I get up, I make a concession."[8]

The summit turned out to be a big success. The lack of a firm trade deal was disappointing, but the Strategic Arms Limitations Talks (SALT) Interim Agreement on Offensive Systems signed by Nixon in Moscow gave the U.S.S.R. the quantitative advantage in strategic weapons. Brezhnev personally was impressive. He was the principal Soviet negotiator and he signed the agreement for the Soviet Union on his own, as General Secretary of the C.P.S.U. Central Committee. This was an unprecedented act since he was not then officially head of state.

In a real sense Brezhnev had accomplished what Khrushchev had sought but failed to do; win recognition of Soviet political-military parity with the United States. The Soviet Union could henceforth expect to be treated as a superpower equal to the United States in the world arena. This constituted a significant political gain, useful in the competition with China and in Soviet political and military endeavors in the Third World.

The SALT Interim Agreement represents the first arms limitations negotiations in which the Soviet military has played a direct and major role. Inclusion of the military in SALT policy-making

Brezhnev (third from left), Alexei Kosygin, and U.S. President Richard Nixon toast the signing of the Interim Agreement on strategic arms limitations, reached at the May 1972 Moscow summit meeting. (World Wide Photos.)

and the cooptation of Marshal Grechko onto the Politburo in 1973 — helped seal military support for détente. To demonstrate this support, just after the summit the Party *aktiv* in every major staff, every group of forces and fleet, and all military districts held meetings to "discuss" the "May Central Committee plenum." Senior military commanders and the chiefs of the corresponding political departments rendered "unanimous" endorsement of détente policies and their author, Brezhnev.[9]

Two more summits were immediately scheduled, one in Bonn in May 1973, the other in Washington the following month. As customary a Party plenum was held before Brezhnev's departure abroad.

The April 1973 C.P.S.U. plenum must go down in history as the most important for détente and for Brezhnev personally. The resolution published after the meeting "wholly and fully" endorsed détente. Even the ouster of Brezhnev's opponents, promotion of his supporters, and endorsement of his policies at this plenum must be viewed in the context of détente successes. Moreover, Brezhnev succeeded in obtaining an unprecedented personal measure of support from his colleagues. The April 1973 plenum, for example, took note of the "great personal contribution of comrade L.I. Brezhnev in resolving the tasks of guaranteeing stable peace in the whole world and reliable security for the Soviet people building communism."[10]

A broad cross-section of the Party and government made an unusual appearance at the plenum in support of détente and Brezhnev. Thus, Brezhnev could say with some honesty when he greeted his German hosts in Bonn a few weeks later that "the policy I am pursuing ... has been unanimously approved by the Central Committee. That means I have 15 million Party members, 32 million Komsomol members and 250 million people of the U.S.S.R. behind me."

This symbolized the euphoria over détente that pervaded the political atmosphere in Moscow and was very much in evidence during Brezhnev's visit with Willy Brandt. Brezhnev, for example, expounded at length on the practicalities of the "unlimited" potential for economic cooperation between West Germany and the Soviet Union.

Indeed, the Bonn trip proved fruitful both politically and economically, but Brezhnev came away personally disappointed. He was not accorded the full head of state honors he had come to expect

Brezhnev and Castro at José Martí Airport, Havana, Cuba, 1974. (World Wide Photos.)

and had received on an earlier trip to France. However, the visit to America the following month buoyed his spirits.

Immediately preceding and during the United States trip the domestic and foreign media focused on Brezhnev the global statesman and policymaker of détente in a campaign to portray Brezhnev's human side. Ever since Russian tanks crushed the liberal Czechoslovak regime Brezhnev had been sensitive about the Western portrayal of him as a kind of beetle-browed villain.

Photographs of Brezhnev sailing his yacht, babysitting his granddaughter and hunting boar, coupled with the numerous short biographies that appeared in Western journals, helped project a new image and build his popularity. Newsweek magazine observed that he "showed a flair for public relations that might have flabbergasted his predecessors." He was presented as "a warm human personality, a man who admits to smoking too much, who has trouble keeping his weight down, and who is not too stuffy to clasp hands with his wife Viktoriya in public or to babysit his grandchild."[11] As one observer put it, "He seems to have found a hidden wellspring of personal diplomatic charm."[12]

In the United States Brezhnev presented himself as "a little like a visiting uncle,"[13] At home his prestige was further enhanced by the favorable publicity the American press gave to him. His visit was a personal success. President Nixon acknowledged Brezhnev's leading position in the U.S.S.R., and he was treated as an equal and shown every mark of cordiality.

The Soviet Union billed the second Brezhnev-Nixon summit "a history making event serving the peaceful interests of the whole world." Some objectives were only partially obtained. Evidently a principal aim had been to convince President Nixon to underwrite a credit arrangement for exploitation of the Siberian gas and oil deposits, giving the Soviet Union the technology to drill these fields and help stave off future energy shortages. But Nixon would only promise to give "serious and sympathetic considerations" to the proposal.[13] The Politburo nevertheless enthusiastically approved the American visit and the Central Committee "highly prized" Brezhnev's personal contribution and "completely and wholly approved the political and practical results of his visit."

However, unexpected problems soon arose. The economic bonanza that Brezhnev expected to reap from the United States failed to materialize in 1974 and wrangling over the Jewish emigration quota requirement contained in the Jackson-Vannik Amendment to the trade agreements signed with the United States soured détente relations. Failure to achieve most favored nation status because of the unacceptable emigration amendment was a disappointment and a source of personal embarrassment for Brezhnev. He displayed his anger at the November 1974 summit by pounding his fist on the table and accusing Henry Kissinger of losing control over Senator Henry Jackson.

Controversy over how to deal with the United States dominated the discussions at the December 1974 Party plenum. At Party plenums held that year in Moldavia, the Ukraine and Kazakhstan, republics run by Brezhnev's strongest supporters, the foreign policy of the "Central Committee, the Politburo and of Brezhnev personally" was approved.[17] According to Grigory Romanov, the Leningrad Party chief, Brezhnev's speech at the December plenum dealt with foreign policy and "outlined *problems* to be solved."

Romanov hinted that Brezhnev may have been willing to settle the Jewish emigration issue. Soviet repudiation of the Soviet-American trade agreements in January 1975 came at a time when Brezhnev, probably, was in the hospital. If this was the case it is possible that his influence was not fully brought to bear. Aleksandr Shelepin's removal at the April 1975 plenum and the declaration in the plenum's resolution that "events have convincingly confirmed the correctness and farsightedness of Brezhnev's peace policy" demonstrated that Brezhnev's authority and prestige remained high, though his American détente policy was stalled.

Alternating periods of cooperation and outright hostility began to characterize relations between the two powers. Brezhnev warmed to the United States at the Conference on Security and Cooperation in Europe held in Helsinki in July 1975. The succesful conclusion of what came to be called the Helsinki Accord realized a basic Brezhnev foreign policy goal and he received extensive publicity and credit for his role in the deliberations which resulted in an agreement between the participating states. Relations soon cooled over interpretation of the Helsinki agreements, however.

In an effort to reap potential economic benefits Brezhnev sought to promote the "Basket Two" provisions of the agreement that provided for increased East-West economic cooperation. The West, however, chose to emphasize the human rights provisions and insisted on strict Soviet compliance as a prerequisite for further discussion on other aspects of the argreement. President Gerald Ford's stand on this reminded Brezhnev of the emigration quota provisions in the Jackson-Vannik Amendment.

Sharing the latest joke with President Ford, Vladivostok, 1974.

At the Seventh Congress of the Polish Worker's Party in December 1975, Brezhnev revealed his irritation with the United States. Stressing the need to view the agreement as "a whole" and not "yield to the temptation to tear individual bits from it that some consider more tactically advantageous to themselves," he sharply rebuked the West for not publicizing the full texts of the agreement, contrasting this with the coverage given to it in the Soviet media. More directly, he charged that immediately after the Helsinki Accord the West undertook a deliberate "disinformation campaign" designed to "incite a retaliatory reaction and poison the atmosphere."[18]

The message of these and other charges leveled by the Soviet leader was that the United States was not living up to the spirit of détente and was reponsible for its stagnation. This widely publicized propaganda theme was designed to put pressure on the United States. In the main it reflected Brezhnev's frustration with the United States administration under President Ford.

Brezhnev anticipated some improvement in Soviet-American relations under Jimmy Carter, but as the new President's foreign and defense policies began to gel the Soviet leader became doubtful, then critical of the new President. He reacted to Carter's human rights campaign, support for a stronger American defense posture and a tougher stand at SALT by publicly accusing the United States of trying to "wreck détente."

Brezhnev also saw in the United States strategic programs approved by President Carter a renewed American willingness to improve its strategic arsenal. A rapid conclusion to a SALT treaty became imperative. In Brezhnev's estimation, failure to reach a new arms limitations agreement soon would fuel anti-Soviet elements abroad and set in motion improved and maybe even new Western strategic programs that could offset or reverse existing Soviet military advantages vis-à-vis the United States and in turn weaken Soviet global strength. He wanted a treaty before the 1972 Interim Agreement expired on October 3, 1977, because he saw SALT as the key to getting détente back on track.

In the subsequent negotiations, however, Brezhnev remained tough on the issues and intransigent on equitable military reduction and deployments. Progress was slow. In February 1978, he launched a new SALT propaganda campaign and threatened serious deterioration in relations with the United States in response to American protests of Soviet military involvement in the Horn of Africa and U.S. attempts to link these activities to the arms talks.

By late summer, President Carter had backed off on some American positions standing in the way of a treaty, making an agreement possible. But the process of finalizing a document was far more tedious than either side expected, and American diplomatic overtures to China late in the year aroused Brezhnev's suspicions. He stalled in order to iron out last minute differences and reassess the intent of American relations with the People's Republic of China. Finally, in the spring of 1979, with Vice Premier Deng Xiaoping's visit to the United States in the background, Brezhnev gave his go-ahead for a SALT agreement. A treaty limiting each side to 2250 long-range missiles and bombers by 1981 was made public in Moscow and Washington on May 11, 1979.

Presidents Carter and Brezhnev met in Vienna the following month to formally sign the document and discuss foreign policy matters of mutual interest. A confident if somewhat less than robust Brezhnev was determined to make a good showing at Vienna for, as Soviet spokesman Leonid Zamyatin noted: "The attention of the entire world is glued on the present summit."[19] Indeed, Vienna afforded the Soviet Union a long awaited opportunity to make political capital out of the publicity generated by the arms control summit.

Brezhnev told the American President, "God will not forgive us if we fail" in our efforts to contain nuclear weapons.[20] Coming from a man whose political creed professes atheism the Soviet leader's appeal to "God" exuded sincerity. Carter could hardly believe his ears. Was Brezhnev trying to exploit the religious proclivity of the American President, or was he actually pondering his own mortality? Carter believed the Soviet leader was sincere in his desire for peace, but would be disappointed later by Brezhnev's insensitivity to any notion of reducing Soviet interference in Africa.

Indeed, in five plenary sessions and one 90-minute private meeting with President Carter, Brezhnev demonstrated his resolve on the issue of Soviet activities in Africa and on other established Soviet foreign policy positions. There was no give and take, and Brezhnev showed no sign of concern over the serious differences that marked the discussions.

Brezhnev acted as though he needed to settle nothing at Vienna but the immediate arms control issue. He grew angry at treaty critics such as Senator Jackson, who promised to fight the treaty, and warned, "Any attempt to rock this elaborate structure ... to substitute any of its elements, to pull it closer to one's own self," would "entail serious, even dangerous consequences for our relations."[22] The

With President Carter at the Vienna summit meeting, 1979. The couch was the same but the world situation was not when Khrushchev and John Kennedy sat here in 1961.

Soviet media echoed Brezhnev by promising a strident arms race and a resumption of the cold war if the United States Senate refused to ratify the treaty.

Brezhnev dominated the Vienna summit and he reveled in the attention. Back home he was again projected as the dominant figure in the U.S.S.R. and as the world's leading statesman. On June 21, 1979, the Politburo met in full session and "wholly and completely approved the activities of the Soviet [Vienna] delegation led by Leonid Brezhnev." The collective body "expressed profound satisfaction with the results achieved at the meeting," and as before plenty of media play was given to the "personal contributions of Leonid Brezhnev in the search for world peace."[23]

In sum, Brezhnev has cleverly exploited opportunities available to him in the realm of foreign policy to establish his preeminence within the Soviet leadership as well as to maximize

Soviet global power. His dominant and personal role in the Party leadership and his prestige at home and abroad originally sprang out of his framing of major policy guidelines in the years 1971 through 1973 and his handling of foreign policy. The so called "Peace Program" he presented to the Twenty-fourth Party Congress in 1971 provided specific Soviet foreign policy goals for enchancement of the Soviet role in the global arena, while détente provided the policy instrument.

Détente has advanced Brezhnev's own political ends because tangible strategic and political dividends for the Soviet Union have come about because of it. Despite the economic disappointments and the erratic nature that characterized relations with the United States after 1974, the policy helped slow the growth of American military power enabling the U.S.S.R. to gain the military advantage. Détente also dampened American political and military resolve abroad, as was first demonstrated by the United States' defeat in Vietnam and the American failure to respond in Angola, despite expanding Soviet pressure. Brezhnev ordered the modernization of Cuba's armed forces, stationed a brigade of Soviet troops on the island, intervened with Castro in Africa and encouraged regional expansion by another proxy, Vietnam, with near impunity. Brezhnev and his colleagues believe that détente, combined with the tremendous growth in Soviet power in the 1970s, actually facilitated a decisive shift in the global relationship between the capitalist and Communist camps in favor of the Soviet Union and its allies. A Soviet diplomat has boldly proclaimed: "The years in which the United States had the say as to what could be done in the world and what could not are past once and for all. *We can no longer tolerate Washington behaving as if it were the umpire of contemporary history.*"[24]

The blatant and massive Soviet invasion of Afghanistan and the installation of a Kremlin controlled Communist regime there in December 1979 demonstrates such unprecedented confidence. It also marks a distinct change in Brezhnev's foreign policy tactics. The use of Soviet troops to counter the threat of a successful Islamic insurgency in Afghanistan as well as to seize a chance to expand Soviet presence in Southwest Asia and the Middle East signals the Kremlin's willingness to employ militant foreign policy tactics in the 1980s that were unthinkable a decade previous. Under Brezhnev, Moscow has employed proxies with increasing success, but this is the first time since World War II that direct military force has been used to seize territory outside Eastern Europe.

Since Brezhnev has invested significant time and sizeable resources into building a military force capable of backing the Kremlin's political claims, Soviet foreign policy in the decade ahead is likely to be characterized by the threat of or direct use of Soviet military force in an effort to reshape the East-West balance yet more drastically. À *propos* are Brezhnev's remarks in a 1973 top secret speech in Prague outlining the rationale behind détente for his East European colleagues in which he predicted that by about 1985 the massive increase in Communist military power would enable the U.S.S.R. and its allies virtually to "dictate the terms of our relationship with any country."[25]

XXIV

The Struggle for Supremacy

*The true Communist is a mixture of a fanatic
and an unrestrained power-holder. Only this
type makes a good Communist. The others are
idealists and careerists.* —Milovan Djilas, *The
New Class.*

BREZHNEV'S STRENGTH IN THE POLITBURO has been achieved
by removals from that body and by adding members on whom
Brezhnev can rely to vote with him on most policies. In almost every
case policy considerations have motivated the Politburo as a whole
to vote out those who failed to conform or obstructed the implementation of "popular" policies, despite the fact that the removals always
strengthened Brezhnev's position and weakened the power of the
remaining members.

The successful manipulation of policies and men in this manner since 1964 constitutes a central feature of Brezhnev's Politburo
tactics. He has filled vacancies where they have been created with his
own candidates and he has expanded the size of the Politburo to accommodate new supporters.

The low degree of turnover in the Politburo from October
1964 to the Twenty-fourth Party Congress reflected Brezhnev's
"stability of cadres" pattern. Before the 1971 Congress, only three full
Politburo members and one candidate left that body. Frol Kozlov
was officially removed at the November 1964 plenum, and Mikoyan
and Shvernik both retired in April 1966. Also in April, Leonid
Yefremov was removed as a candidate member under conditions
suggesting that his dismissal was tied to Brezhnev's maneuvering
against Podgorny.

Brezhnev did not see fit to alter the composition of the Politburo's full membership much during this period because of the enormous attention he had to devote to securing his position in other
critical organs of power. Kirill Mazurov, a Kosygin sponsored addition, was promoted from candidate membership to full membership in 1965, and Arvid Pelshe who has supported Brezhnev on
several matters was added in April 1966. Brezhnev did take some im-

287

portant preliminary steps by bringing Ustinov, Shcherbitskiy and Kunayev in as candidate members in March and December 1965 and April 1966 respectively.

However, at the Twenty-fourth Party Congress Brezhnev demonstrated his determination and ability to improve his Politburo position by the cooptation of Fyodor Kulakov as a full member and the promotion of Shcherbitskiy, Viktor Grishin[1] and Kunayev, expanding the voting membership to 15.

Another Brezhnev sponsored candidate, Boris Ponomarev, was added at the May 1972 Party plenum. Ponomarev's addition at the plenum that finalized plans for the Brezhnev-Nixon summit was a reward for his personal efforts in preparing Brezhnev for the summit. The appointment revealed the role and the importance of this ex-Comintern agent in Soviet foreign policy.

In 1972, a candidate member was dismissed. Vasiliy Mzhavanadze, the former Party First Secretary of Georgia whom Brezhnev had deposed from that post, was formally deprived of his candidate membership at the December plenum. This was done under a cloud of corruption charges stirred up by his successor, local police chief and Brezhnev fanatic Eduard Shevardnadze.

Brezhnev strengthened his Politiburo position most at the April 1973 Party plenum through leadership changes that were almost entirely related to foreign policy and national security matters. The notorious Pyotr Shelest and Gennadiy Voronov were both removed at the plenum. Their positions were taken by KGB chief Andropov and then Minister of Defense Andrey Grechko. Foreign Affairs Minister Andrey Gromyko and Brezhnev's protégé Grigoriy Romanov were also added, the former to full membership, the latter to candidate status.

The Shelest and Voronov removals are classic examples of Brezhnev's maneuvering. The rivalry between Shelest's Ukrainian faction and the Dnepropetrovsk group became exacerbated after October 1964 because of the growing influence of the Dnepropetrovsk group in Moscow, though the infighting temporarily subsided during Brezhnev's clash with Shelepin. By being more amenable to Shelest's politics, Brezhnev apparently succeeded in securing Shelest's support, or neutrality, in the difficult maneuvering against Shelepin. Shelest was intensely conservative and yet intensely Ukrainian and he used Ukrainian nationalism to bolster his position in the Ukraine. He was generally tolerant of Ukrainian nationalist writers and worked toward a policy of limited Ukrainization of the cultural and political spheres in the Ukraine, which smacked of a degree of independence from Moscow.

The calm, however, soon gave way to the storm. A first round was fought in 1969 at the national collective farmer's congress. The details of the tussle are extremely sketchy, but Shelest allegedly accused Brezhnev of reneging on a promise to support an agricultural decentralization scheme. Their differences mounted, resulting in a row at the Twenty-fourth Party Congress where Brezhnev initiated a political break with Shelest.

Shelest's complaint was that the funds allocated for the Donetsk coal industries in the draft Ninth Five Year Plan were insufficient, but obviously there were larger issues regarding the Ukraine involved. Shelest hinted as much when he launched into a speech at the Congress portraying and praising the "monumental role" that the "Ukraine and its people play in the economic and cultural sphere of socialist society."[2] Brezhnev countered by lauding the achievements of Great Russians and their contribution to the building of Communism.[3]

While Brezhnev conducted the chorus of opposition against Shelest, Shcherbitiskiy bided his time. Shcherbitskiy had every reason to turn against Shelest after the 1963 incident in which he lost out to him in the bid for the post of Ukrainian Party head. Shcherbitskiy stepped forward at the Congress and bluntly refuted Shelest's claims. He praised the Dnepropetrovsk group and, condemning Shelest's factionalism, added that "great credit" should go to "those in Moscow who remain undaunted in their concern and work for all the republics."[4] Kunayev and other Brezhnev proxies followed with equally cutting sallies.

Shelest was stunned; though he was reelected to the Politburo he had definitely lost ground. Brezhnev's Dnepropetrovsk cohorts were favored over Shelest's associates in the Central Committee elections, from which both Kunayev and Shcherbitskiy received promotions to full Politburo membership, further strengthening Brezhnev's position in the Politburo. Shcherbitskiy's promotion was an especially sharp blow to Shelest. The promotion clearly showed Brezhnev's hand, since the top governmental (Shcherbitsky was Premier of the Ukraine) and Party (Shelest) officials of the same republic rarely hold full Politburo voting status simultaneously.

Shelest still refused to bow to Brezhnev. Championing conservative ideals, he became Brezhnev's loudest critic, particularly over détente. He actively promoted a sectarian line in the Ukraine and distorted and ignored Politburo policies. He publicly blasted the consumerism aspects of the five year plan, tried to spoil détente by stirring up "imperialist" hatred campaigns, hammered the danger of ideological laxness in Moscow, openly opposed the Strategic Arms Limitations Talks and any kind of negotiation over Berlin, and promoted Ukrainian nationalism.[5]

He was especially bold on the eve of the November 1971 plenum. Shelest either started or responded to rumors that personnel changes would be made at the plenum to further enhance Brezhnev's political strength. Voronov was a likely candidate for removal since his ouster as Premier of the R.S.F.S.R. the previous July disqualified him from continued Politburo membership. Shelest must have been nervous about his own position, thus joining forces against Brezhnev.

Voronov had frustrated Brezhnev on two counts. First, as a ranking member of the R.S.F.S.R. Bureau in 1965, he had blocked the appointment of a new First Deputy for Agriculture of the Bureau following the transfer of Politburo candidate member and Bureau Deputy Chairman Leonid Yefremov to Stavropol. Voronov, as the senior Bureau member, wanted Yefremov's vacant post. Failing in his bid, Voronov rallied enough support to block the appointment of a Brezhnev man, and the seat remained vacant.

Brezhnev was annoyed. Voronov was on very shakey ground when he opposed Brezhnev's agricultural policies. In the spring of 1970 a bitter public debate broke out between Secretary for Agriculture Polyanskiy and Voronov, a quarrel that was carried over into the July plenum. Voronov rallied Shelest and those who would be affected by the proposed resource allocation to challenge Polyanskiy and Brezhnev on this and other aspects of the agricultural program for the Ninth Five Year Plan. This helped delay the Party Congress that year.

Voronov's fortunes, however, dissipated rapidly in late 1970. On his sixtieth birthday he was publicly humiliated by the slight official Party greeting given to him. His persistence in criticizing Brezhnev's agricultural program resulted in his being dropped in Politburo ranking from fifth to fourteenth place at the Twenty-fourth Party Congress. Later tangling with Kirilenko brought the loss of his R.S.F.S.R. premiership in July 1972.

The intrigues of these two most unlikely allies united by the common threat of their removal from the Politburo briefly slowed Brezhnev's momentum and though his policies were endorsed, the Central Committee failed to accord him the usual personal acclaim for détente. Neither Shelest nor Voronov were removed from the Politburo. Of course Brezhnev may have opted not to remove Voronov at this point since his departure might have upset the political balance on détente in the Politburo. But his failure to remove Voronov may have disappointed conservatives like Polyanskiy who had lent their support to détente, and pointed up the limits of Brezhnev's ability to come up with political concessions for allies in return for support of policies.

In a classic move designed to increase his conservative support Brezhnev made a special trip to the conservative stronghold of Leningrad following the November 1971 plenum. There he praised the city's initiative in setting up production associations and for drawing up a comprehensive economic and social plan for the city. He promised to support extension of the concept of integrated planning to other cities.

This was followed by the arrest of numerous Ukrainian intellectuals on charges of nationalist activities. Shelest had long opposed reprisals against Ukrainian dissidents because it would reflect on his leadership. Charges of laxness against Lvov officials appeared in the media, proving particularly embarrassing to Shelest since he had just presented the city with an Order of Lenin. Brezhnev also maneuvered to promote Shelest's rivals in the Ukraine, and finally Brezhnev removed him as the Ukrainian Party chief in 1972.

The elevation of Grechko, Gromyko and Andropov to full Politburo membership at the April 1973 plenum was sponsored by Brezhnev for the purpose of bolstering his Politburo position and enabling him to attain a "personal" majority of voting members in 1973. Brezhnev had taken pains to cultivate good relations with Grechko since 1967. Andropov had obviously performed to Brezhnev's expectations. In his rare speeches, he supported Brezhnev and his "wise and capable" leadership. Likewise, Gromyko publicly praised Brezhnev's foreign policies.

Romanov's elevation to candidate membership at the April 1973 plenum was the direct result of his installation as Vasiliy Tolstikov's successor in Leningrad and as a reward for his success in whipping the defense industry there into shape. In 1970 Brezhnev presided over both Romanov's installation as Leningrad Party Chief and Konstantin Katushev's installation in Gorky. This was the first time since Frol Kozlov's departure in 1963 that Leningrad had held a seat on the Politburo.

Brezhnev's majority after the April 1973 Party plenum was

nevertheless a narrow one. The need to tip the balance further in his favor was driven home by the debate over economic priorities for the Tenth Five Year Plan.

For a time the Politburo was divided over the approach to take for the 1976-1980 economic plan. Brezhnev's position in the Politburo after the December 1974 plenum that approved his recommendations for the Five Year Plan was complicated by his three month absence from public affairs because of illness and the emotional trauma resulting from his mother's death in early January. He was completely out of action from late December to early March, with much of this time spent in the hospital or resting in his dacha at Zavidovo outside Moscow. Kirilenko represented him in the Politburo.

This situation left the "opposition" with a de facto Politburo majority. Only one major policy decision was announced during this period; the renunciation of Soviet obligations under the 1972 U.S.S.R./U.S. Trade Agreement in response to the American legislation setting Jewish emigration quotas. The Politburo's failure to proceed speedily with implementation of Brezhnev's economic plans led to repeated charges by his supporters that the Politburo was trying to avoid or procrastinate on the execution of decisions approved by the December 1974 plenum. Both Pyotr Rodionov, the First Deputy Director of the Central Committee's Institute of Marxism-Leninism, and Shcherbitskiy published criticisms and insisted that the Politburo implement the "course entrusted."[6]

Shcherbitskiy elaborated at length on the "proper" relationship between the Central Committee and the Politburo, using the Ukraine as a model. He obliquely suggested that the Central Committee should not hesitate to criticize those balking in the Politburo and should get rid of the recalcitrant elements in the government economic ministries. Shcherbitskiy repeatedly referred to Brezhnev and he quoted a relevant Brezhnev statement to the effect that "we are going through a most interesting and simultaneously complicated development phase." Rodionov cited the same quotation which seemed to refer to the trouble caused by individual differences over the Five Year Plan and Brezhnev's illness and absence.

An account of a worse case situation that winter was published in July 1976. In an article for the *Washington Post Outlook Magazine*, Boris Rabbot, a former high level Soviet political advisor, asserted that Shelepin had conspired to unseat Brezhnev in December 1974. Trouble for Brezhnev allegedly began when the United States

Congress passed the amendment attaching Jewish emigration quotas to the most favored nation and trade credits agreement negotiated between Brezhnev and Kissinger in 1972. This bargaining over the number of "credits and trade for a fixed number of Jewish bodies" supposedly placed Brezhnev in a vulnerable position, which Shelepin attempted to exploit by showing that détente was bankrupt and by rallying conservatives to defeat Brezhnev. Shelepin argued that a "new course" in Soviet foreign policy was needed and proposed sending "volunteers" to Portugal as Stalin had sent Soviet troops to Spain during the Spanish Civil War. To counter Shelepin, Brezhnev allegedly came up with the compromise idea of using Cuban troops in Angola. Brezhnev's idea was adopted and, having lost his bid for power, Shelepin was dropped from the Politburo at the April 1975 plenum.

Shelepin could have exploited Brezhnev's inactivity during his illness. He may have opposed Brezhnev's 1976-1980 economic plan. What is certain is that Shelepin's removal enabled Brezhnev to further shift Politburo membership in his favor. This, and not an unsuccessful conspiracy, was probably the reason for Shelepin's ouster.

Shelepin had become vulnerable by early 1975 after a sharp political decline in the previous year. In May 1974, he was the only Politburo member to be assigned a different electoral district. Moreover, he was transferred from a city district to a Leningrad rural district in order to enable Romanov, the most junior among the candidate Politburo members, to move up from an *oblast* to a Leningrad city position. In November 1974, Shelepin was conspicuously passed over in the nominations for the traditional October Revolution speech. Moreover, he suffered a serious political backlash as a result of his disastrous visit to Britain at the beginning of April 1975, during which he was pelted with rotten eggs and booed loudly by crowds.

Brezhnev probably used Shelepin's visit to Britain as a pretext to remove his opponent from the Politburo. Shelepin had embarrassed the Soviet Union and undercut his own usefulness as a Trade Union leader at a time when the Soviet Union was trying to strengthen its ties with European trade unions. Moreover, he was weakened at a time when Brezhnev was again in ascendancy. The April plenum "fully approved and supported" Brezhnev's foreign policy course. The failure of Kissinger's Middle East policy, the gains of the Communist Party in Portugal and the collapse of South Vietnam all strengthened Brezhnev's hand.

After Shelepin's dismissal there were only three Politburo members who had openly clashed with Brezhnev. They were Kosygin, Podgorny and Polyanskiy. Polyanskiy was made the scapegoat for the agricultural failures of 1975 and dismissed at the Twenty-fifth Party Congress. The promotions of Romanov and Ustinov to full Politburo membership and the elevation of Geydar Aliyev, the Azerbaydzhan Party Secretary, at the Congress firmed up Brezhnev's Politburo position.

Except for Kosygin, whom he has handled in other ways, Brezhnev has managed to oust all of his opponents from the Politburo with a solid majority vote behind him and without resort to force or the devious illegal means used by Khrushchev and Stalin. (The case of Podgorny is discussed later in this chapter.) One by one each opponent went out without much public fanfare. What is remarkable is that in every case they were phased out cautiously over a long period of time. In this way Brezhnev avoided subjecting the system to sudden shocks. Each removal was preceded by a smooth, but unmistakable, descent for those identified for some time as unlikely to conform to policy positions adopted by the remaining Politburo membership.

Further evidence of Brezhnev's desire to augment his position in the Politburo was provided by the elevation of Konstantin Chernenko and Vasiliy Kuznetsov to candidate status at the October 3, 1977, Party plenum. Chernenko, who became a Party Secretary at the Twenty-fifth Party Congress, was promoted as a highly competent member of the Brezhnev coterie. Kuznetsov's elevation to the Politburo signaled a change within the Ministry of Foreign Affairs since Soviet practice precludes a single ministry from holding two positions on the Politburo. Later in the month Kuznetsov quit his job of 22 years as Gromyko's deputy to fill the newly created post of First Deputy Chairman of the Supreme Soviet Presidium, thereby relieving Brezhnev of some protocol duties as Presidium Chairman.

Fyodor Kulakov's death in July 1978 created two vacancies in the central Party organs, in the Politburo and in the Secretariat, and considerably altered the Party leadership succession picture. Kulakov was a strong potential successor to Brezhnev and his showing, particularly on his sixtieth birthday in February 1978, suggested that he was making progress in the effort to be the leading candidate. Rumors that he was being maneuvered into a position as Party heir started. This made him look ambitious and had got him into serious trouble with Brezhnev.

With his old friend Konstantin Chernenko, March 1979. Was Chernenko being groomed?

The personnel shifts at the Party plenum in December 1978 indicated that Brezhnev continued to dominate the leadership. The plenum was the occasion for the largest turnover of personnel in the Party's leading organs since 1973. Mikhail Gorbachev, the Stavropol *Kray* Party chief and a relative unknown, was appointed to the Party Secretariat to take Kulakov's place as the secretary responsible for agriculture. Nikolay Tikhonov became a candidate Politburo member replacing Kosygin's deputy Kirill Mazurov. Eduard Shevardnadze, the Party Secretary for Georgia and former KGB official, also became a candidate Politburo member.

The most important change was the elevation of Chernenko to Kulakov's vacated Politburo seat. It strengthened Brezhnev even more since Chernenko is now the only Party leader after Kirilenko, Kosygin and Suslov to hold positions in both the Party Secretariat and the Politburo. Chernenko took up the fifth position in the leadership, his protocol ranking confirmed in the U.S.S.R. Supreme Soviet election nominations in January 1979.

That same month, Chernenko, at 68, started to receive prominent public treatment. A trip to Bulgaria with Brezhnev in

Viktoriya Brezhnev watches as Leonid casts his ballot in the Supreme Soviet elections, March 1979.

January was used to boost his image further. In an unprecedented move Bulgarian leader Zhivkov personally went out of his way to single out Chernenko for attention. Similarly, Brezhnev allowed him to share the limelight in reporting on the success of the trip.

In contrast to Chernenko's good fortunes, senior Politburo member Kirilenko suffered a loss of status. In the 1979 round of nominations for the Supreme Soviet, the 72-year-old Kirilenko was accorded the status only of "prominent Party figure." Chernenko was billed as a "prominent Party and state leader." Thus Chernenko's position relative to Kirilenko was changed from one of marked inferiority to one of superiority, probably to counterbalance Kirilenko's power. The departure of Kirilenko's protégé Yakov Ryabov from the Party Secretariat (he was responsible for the defense industry) in February 1979 was another sign of Brezhnev's intention to take Kirilenko down a notch or two. Kirilenko is healthy and though as second in command in the Party he is strategically placed to take over the General Secretary's job, throughout 1978 there were manifest signs of coolness between Brezhnev and Kirilenko.

Brezhnev may be angling to substitute Chernenko for Kirilenko as the deputy Party chief. But Kirilenko still appeared in early 1980 to be in the best position to succeed Brezhnev should the Party chief suddenly die, though Chernenko, as well as Shcherbitskiy and Romanov, could also become major contenders in the Kremlin struggle.

A major concern of Brezhnev's after October 1964 was to check the power of the second pillar of the collective leadership — the government — and establish the primacy of the Party and its chief over the government and its head, Aleksey Kosygin. This was essential for there were wide differences on major policy issues.

Promulgating a Malenkov line in the early months of the new regime, Kosygin foresaw the mutually destructive consequences of nuclear war with the United States and argued against Brezhnev's defense policy. Kosygin placed consumer welfare before defense, and economic reform at home before the revolutionary movement abroad. He saw economic reform combined with détente and trade with the West as a method of resolving domestic resource allocation problems and bolstering the economy. Most of all, he wished to reduce Party interference in the economy, assert governmental authority, and give his ministries and manager a free hand in running the economy.

But Brezhnev asserted Party primacy early in the new regime. Even before 1964 ended, he instructed Party officials to continue "control" of governmental activity.[7] This strong directive was not intended simply to reprimand Kosygin for unilaterally extending the Bolshevika-Mayak economic reform experiment[8] to a large number of other enterprises in the textile field in violation of the principle of collectivity, but was a determined attempt by Brezhnev to limit the government's authority and overshadow Kosygin personally.

At the outset of the regime, responsibility for the economy was evenly divided. Brezhnev took agriculture and Koysgin, industry. However, the media focused on Brezhnev's responsibilities. His March 1965 Party plenum speech on agriculture monopolized the media, receiving immediate and widespread publicity, while Kosygin's important Gosplan speech (to the same plenum), reversing the guidelines for the Eighth Five Year Plan set down by Khrushchev, appeared weeks later and then only in two specialized and limited-circulation journals.[9]

In the field of foreign policy, Kosygin initially captured the limelight, but Brezhnev moved to overshadow him there too. In April 1965, the media gave extensive coverage to Brezhnev's visit to Poland, but ignored Kosygin who had accompanied him. Other snubs followed which spurred a series of exchanges between government and Party-sponsored newspapers in the late spring. *Pravda*, for example, accused Kosygin of promoting Khrushchev's brand of "goulash communism." *Izvestiya*, in turn, hurled cryptic remarks at Brezhnev. It takes more than an engineering degree, *Izvestiya* commented, to run the economy.[10] Ironically, the exchanges aided Shelepin's cause abuilding at the time. The latter may account for the temporary halt in polemics between Brezhnev and Kosygin.

Brezhnev weathered Shelepin's 1965 challenge well and his strengthened position facilitated renewed moves against Kosygin. At the September 1965 plenum Brezhnev lent as much, if not more, weight to the discussion on industrial reform as Kosygin. Although the latter delivered the main report, it was Brezhnev who staked the Party's claim to primacy by placing a number of stringent institutional checks on the government and by centralizing the administrative process which, when combined with the lax implementation of the reform measures, promoted the failure of Kosygin's reforms. Failure of much of the reform allowed Brezhnev to make further inroads into Kosygin's realm with his own economic proposals.

The use of Podgorny and the Supreme Soviet Presidium as proxies to dilute Kosygin's economic authority constitutes an interesting and effective Brezhnev tactic. Even before Brezhnev had firmed up his position in the Secretariat, he began to court Podgorny. On the latter's transfer to the Supreme Soviet, Brezhnev agreed to a proposal to enhance that body's authority over the Council of Ministers through the Supreme Soviet Presidium's permanent commissions.

The proposal, first made by Brezhnev at the Twenty-third Party Congress and later emphasized by Podgorny in his June 1966 election speech and August Supreme Soviet speech, called for expanded authority for the permanent commissions in order to allow formulation of state legislation and closely verify execution of orders by "all state organs." While in the past the commissions had been empowered to check on government ministerial activity, in practice they were bypassed by the Council of Ministers. The proposal was enacted in August 1966 and Party apparatchiks were moved in to staff the commissions and given a tough mandate to deal with Kosygin's ministers.

Brezhnev could thus exercise greater control over the formulation and execution of state legislation without giving Podgorny enough organizational authority to rival his own. The active role of these commissions could be seen by the frequent reports of their activities appearing in the press. *Izvestiya* on February 26, 1966, offered a prime example of their authority in regard to Kosygin when it reported that "several days ago a U.S.S.R. Council of Ministers meeting was held which discussed a draft of a general statute on the U.S.S.R. Ministers worked out by the commissions of the Supreme Soviet Presidium."

Brezhnev continued to play Podgorny against Kosygin. For example, in Brezhnev's 1967 Supreme Soviet election speech, he reported that the Central Committee had decided to enhance the authority of the local *soviets* in dealing with government ministries.[11] This directly supported an appeal for greater local *soviet* authority made by Podgorny only the day before. This line was further promoted by Brezhnev, and in his December 1969 Party plenum speech it was combined with a new drive for rigorous Party control of the economy.

The latter was in evidence in a key change in the *Theses* for the Lenin birthday celebrations published on December 23, 1969. The *Theses* affirmed that the Party "accomplishes its tasks both directly and through the *soviets* [note the order], state bodies and public organizations."[12] This nullified the formula provided by the 1967 October Revolution Anniversary *Theses*. It had stated that the Party's leading role in society is executed "through the system of *state* and public organizations."[13] In line with the 1969 change, a decree issued by the Central Committee in January 1970 required Party committees of the government's economic ministries to keep Party headquarters informed on shortcomings in the work of the ministries.[14]

Brezhnev used the issues of Vietnam and defense initially to beat Kosygin in foreign policy. Between October 1964 and 1967, Brezhnev consistently minimized the prospects for improving relations with the United States, while Kosygin generally promoted a more favorable outlook. The Vietnam War was the central obstacle to Kosygin's foreign policy line.

Even before American bombing of North Vietnam began in February 1965, Brezhnev had stated his readiness to "render the necessary aid" to Hanoi.[15] Kosygin did not endorse such aid, holding out that prospects for negotiating a settlement in Southeast Asia remained good.[16] But when the bombing began, Kosygin lost ground. He was ultimately "persuaded" not only to endorse the aid but to recognize the tenacity of "imperialism" and his own misjudgment. He temporarily backed down, expanded his view on the scope of American "imperialism" and switched to Brezhnev's rationale for strengthening the armed forces. Had he not conformed, his economic reform package might have been defeated.

The question of negotiations with the United States cropped up again in 1966. Kosygin called for discussions on Vietnam in response to new American initiatives. But as before, Brezhnev outmaneuvered him. In Brezhnev's March 1967 election speech, he said that despite American proposals continued bombing had "convinced even the most *naive people* that the American government had deceived the world and its own people when it stated that the United States was striving for a peaceful settlement of the Vietnam issue."[17]

Khrushchev resolved the problem of shared power by purging Malenkov and taking over as head of the government. Brezhnev has handled the problem by eroding Kosygin's authority, transferring much of the power of the Council of Ministers to the Supreme Soviet Presidium, then assuming Podgorny's seat as Chairman of the Presidium. He has never made a direct bid for Kosygin's position in the Council of Ministers.

Rumors of Kosygin's "imminent retirement" in 1970, though, led many Western observers to conclude otherwise. Rumors like this had circulated since 1966 and in each case they were the result of policy clashes with Brezhnev, not maneuvers by the Party chief to grab Kosygin's post. Seldom do rumors of this kind precede high level changes in the Soviet leadership. They do however serve the purpose of factionalism and are frequently promoted by over zealous supporters hoping to move events along. This was the case in 1970.

That year the ever imaginative Moscow rumor mill cranked out notions of all kinds generated by those who would have liked to see Kosygin go and those who feared enhanced power by Brezhnev. Brezhnev's 37-day absence after the December 1969 plenum gave rise to a rumor that he was being investigated on charges by the Central Committee and that *his* fall was imminent. Two other accounts of attacks on Brezhnev were reported; one led by Suslov, Shelepin and Mazurov in the form of a letter addressed to the Central Committee severely criticizing Brezhnev's leadership, and another mounted by Shelepin and Shelest.[18]

The rumors of Kosygin's "retirement" and of Brezhnev's "fall" in early 1970 must be viewed in the context of two separate yet related factors: the poor state of the economy resulting in the unprecedented attack on the government at the December 1969 Party plenum and Brezhnev's very rapid leadership ascendancy on the eve of the 1970 Lenin centenary.

Brezhnev now asserted more forcefully than ever his own and the Party's authority over the economy on the supposition that "the current economic situation does not permit one to be satisfied with old practices — administrative problems are political problems."[19] He crusaded against poor management and disorganized officialdom through increased Party control over the administration of the economy and a "moral stimulants" approach involving "sacrifice," penal measures designed to reinforce work discipline, and other measures to enhance productivity. He effectively ignored Kosygin's 1965 reforms. In the late 1960s and early 1970s, Gosplan officials and management cadres became the frequent target of Brezhnev's attacks. At the December 1969 Party plenum, he labeled them irresponsible." He also attacked "certain" officials in the important Scientific and Technical Committee.

Subsequent personnel changes in those bodies were directly related to Brezhnev's call for greater efficiency in economic management and delivered a sharp personal blow to Kosygin, whose son-in-law Dzermen Gvishiani, for example, was soon "transferred" from his First Deputy slot in the Scientific and Technical Committee to make room for a Brezhnev appointee. Tikhon Sokolov, another Brezhnev cohort, was posted to Gosplan as one of its four First Deputy Chairmen. The heads of government in Kazakhstan, Moldavia, Azerbaydzhan and Latvia and two U.S.S.R. republic ministers were dropped and replaced with Party apparatchiks selected by Brezhnev. Several Party secretaries were dismissed because of poor economic performance.

Kosygin's authority had clearly dwindled. A retreat on some matters of official responsiblity and customary concern was plain in his 1970 Supreme Soviet election speech. Moreover, in that speech he spoke of the 1965 reforms in the past tense. During the Supreme Soviet election campaign in April, Kosygin was simply described as a "Party organizer" and he received fewer election nominations than even Podgorny. His diminished stature was further symbolized by his drop from second to third place in the Politburo ranking below Podgorny at the 1971 Party Congress.

Brezhnev, however, emerged on a significantly higher leadership plateau. The formulation "the Politburo headed by Brezhnev"
was made for the first time in 1970; two volumes of his speeches appeared; a large bust of a younger Brezhnev donning his general's
uniform was prominently featured in an art exhibit at the House of
Art on Kuznetskiy Most Street in Moscow; Brezhnev singly oversaw
the celebrated DVINA military maneuvers in Belorussia and he
presided over purely government meetings in Kosygin's absence.

Kosygin continued to lose ground after the 1971 Party
Congress, giving way to Brezhnev's Party guidance and activism in
economic affairs. Nothing Kosygin and the government did seemed
to satisfy Brezhnev. At the 1973 Party plenum he mounted a sharp
attack on the government for mismanagement of the economy and
asserted "Party" responsiblity for future direction of the economy.
"Leadership of the economy is a Party matter, we must direct the
working people to an active struggle for the implementation of the
five year plan and, above all, for the 1974 plan" he told the plenum,
which "fully" endorsed the view and gave Brezhnev unusual
prominence for his "economic contributions." Instructions were issued
that all Party organizations would be "guided" by Brezhnev's plenum
"speech."[20]

Brezhnev's economic dominance was taken one step further at
the Party plenum held in December 1974. The Central Committee's
decree stated that not only the Party, but all "Soviet, economic and
trade union organizations" (government organs) would be "guided"
by the "instructions of General Secretary L.I. Brezhnev" on the "fundamental questions of social and economic development of our country."[21] This was the first time Brezhnev had issued "instructions" to
the government regarding the economy, which signalled a major personal victory over Kosygin.

A "new" Brezhnev economic line was put forward at the 1974
Council of Ministers session and in a speech in Kishinev a short while
later. The new directions posited a reorientation of investment and a
reversal of earlier economic priorities. In both speeches Brezhnev
called for a retrenchment in the "development" of "new production
capacity" for the upcoming Five Year Plan. But in a speech at Frunze
on November 2, Kosygin insisted that the "main direction" of the
economy is "now to achieve fuller utilization of existing capacities
and the fastest possible development of new production capacities."[22]
The result was a split in the Politburo.

Brezhnev had banked on détente to satisfy a number of the

country's economic needs but the import of Western consumer products, technology and capital goods had been disappointing. By the end of 1974 he realized that some economic readjustment and a modified strategy would have to be adopted in order to continue high defense resource allocation. Thus Brezhnev sought a retrenchment in new production investment, particularly in consumer goods, and reliance on "efficiency" and "quality" for the 1976-1980 period.

Brezhnev carried the day. The published Central Committee resolution called for "new successes in strengthening the might of our homeland."[23] The article also abounded in oblique criticism of Kosygin and his government organs. Neither were given even the slightest credit for overfullfilment of the annual economic plan that year. In fact, it was implied that success had been attained in spite of them. This paralleled an earlier article discussing a parable in which "officials" had neglected to take into account political interests in their economic planning.

At the Twenty-fifth Party Congress Kosygin was obliged to endorse the Brezhnev economic line. Brezhnev blamed him and his subordinates for the country's economic ills. If people were not getting the consumer goods they had been promised, it was because of failures in production. The chief scapegoats were the (remaining) officials of Gosplan — hence more Brezhnev assignments to Gosplan were made in 1976. Brezhnev also pressed the need for further changes in economic management and he insisted on "improvement" of the "whole system of [economic] indicators for ministries, associations and enterprises." Kosygin defended what aspects of his reform remained and obliquely accused Brezhnev of shortcomings in agriculture, which he said had hampered the growth of consumer goods.

Whether these and other problems — particularly the clash over Brezhnev's campaign in late August 1976 to promote an unprecedented and costly winter grain sowing program (Kosygin has always opposed costly investment in agriculture) marking a partial reversal of post-Khrushchev policies — pushed their differences into a showdown before Kosygin fell ill, or were the cause for his prolonged illness and public disappearance from August to October 1976, or heralded a showdown that was averted by his illness, cannot be known for certain. Clearly something happened.

Unlike Brezhnev, Podgorny and Suslov, Kosygin was not treated with a bronze bust erected in his hometown (even though he was entitled to one as the winner of two Hero of Socialist Labor awards) in the summer of 1976. A bust would have been a particulaly nice gesture and a morale booster during his hospitalization. Furthermore, media reports on Kosygin's illness cast doubt on his ability to continue in his post. Brezhnev himself told Averell Harriman that Kosygin "has some sort of heart condition that is giving him trouble."

Brezhnev may have availed himself of Kosygin's forced absence to push through decisions in the Politburo concerning government work: such decisions might have pertained to the Constitution or to economic managment, it is hard to tell. What is certain is that he made certain significant personnel changes, the most important of which was the appointment of Nikolay Tikhonov, another *Dnepropetrovsty*, to the Council of Ministers as Kosygin's First Deputy.

On October 18, 1976, Kosygin reappeared in public for the first time. He, Brezhnev and Podgorny greeted Communist Party leaders at the Moscow airport. This appearance came only three days before the October 27 Supreme Soviet session, which approved the controversial Tenth Five Year Plan, but *Kosygin did not report* on the plan to the Supreme Soviet. Since then, Kosygin's activites have been extemely limited. Kirilenko took over a large portion of his economic responsibilities in 1977. Kosygin in 1979 could be described as a "lame duck" premier.

XXV

The Ascent Complete

*The struggle may be long or short, it may be
compromised and blunted again and again, but
the whole dynamics of dictatorship cries out for
a dictator, autocracy for an autocrat, militar-
ized life for a supreme Commander, infallible
government for an infallible leader, an authori-
tarian setup for an authority, a totalitarian
state for a Duce, Fuhrer, Vozhd.* — Bertram
Wolfe, *An Ideology in Power.*

RUMORS OF BREZHNEV'S "IMPENDING RESIGNATION" domi-
nated the Soviet political scene in the months preceding the Twenty-
fifth Party Congress. Supposedly Brezhnev's health was so bad that he
would announce his retirement at the Congress. In interpreting the
rumors some Western observers concluded that Brezhnev was in
danger of being replaced by hardline anti-détente "hawks" in the
Politburo. Rumors that the KGB's Andropov might replace Brezhnev
reinforced such speculation.

However, Brezhnev's showing at the Party's Congress held in
February 1976 gave lie to these. He was not only in good enough
health to deliver a six hour speech, but his performance was impressive. He said or did nothing to indicate that he contemplated
retirement. Moreover, the Congress exuded more confidence in his
leadership than ever before.

He played the dominant role at the Congress with obvious enthusiasm, monopolizing both the foreign and domestic policy
discussions and occasionally interrupting other participants with
questions, humorous interjections, and elaborations. He focused on
increased Party control over society and continuity of trends at home
and abroad. Stressing his own personal role in foreign policy, he ad-
ministratively undercut Gromyko on topics for which the latter had
been responsible and had addressed at earlier congresses.

Brezhnev's assessment of the U.S.S.R.'s world position was
designed to demonstrate the validity of his policy lines and to justify
their continuation. Confidently evaluating the U.S.S.R.'s inter-

national position in terms of the 1971 "Peace Program," he explained in vivid detail how Soviet-led forces, at the expense of the United States and its "imperialist" allies, had made significant gains. He poked fun at the bourgeoisie who had expected the Soviet Union to end support of revolutionary struggles because of détente. A distinct hardening of the Party line was discernible. Less attention was given to possibilities of compromise and cooperation with either the West or the People's Republic of China.

Leadership changes made at the Congress gave the clearest indication of Brezhnev's political strength. Politburo member Polyanskiy was blamed for the 1975 crop failure and other agricultural problems and dismissed. Grigoriy Romanov was promoted to full Politburo membership after three years as a candidate member. And in an unprecedented move Dimitry Ustinov was elevated to full membership. In each case, the individual was a supporter of both the military establishment and of Brezhnev personally. Ustinov had been elected to the Party Secretariat and made a Presidium candidate member in March 1965, suggesting Brezhnev's very early sponsorship of this representative of the defense establishment.

The content of speeches at the Congress also showed Brezhnev's strength. For their part, the speakers directed more lavish praise toward Brezhnev than at any time in the past. A comparison of these speeches to speeches made at the two previous congresses reveal striking differences in Brezhnev's power position if personal praise is used as a measure. At the 1971 Congress, for example, six out of 16 speeches contained praise, none more than a sentence in length. But at the Twenty-fifth Congress, every speech contained at least one sentence of praise while seven of 60 speeches contained more than 13 lines of praise. Eduard Shevardnadze broke the record with no less than 40 lines devoted to Brezhnev.

Laudatory remarks about Khrushchev at the Twenty-second Party Congress pale in comparison. Moreover, at that congress there were no references to Khrushchev as "heading the Politburo." But at the 1976 Congress the term was used no fewer than 20 times with reference to Brezhnev, and was frequently used by regional congresses and Party *aktivs* after the 1976 Congress.

The "cult of Brezhnev" was enthusiastically propagated throughout the Soviet Union after the delegates returned home. Shevardnadze's statement was typical:

> The Twenty-fifth C.P.S.U. Congress once again convincingly displayed to the entire planet that in the modern world, which is

As "Marshal of the Soviet Union," a promotion of May 1976 rewarding his "development of military science and strategy" and recognizing his "talents as an outstanding organizer of our country's defenses."

full of dialectical contradictions—a complex world with many problems—there is in the international arena no more eminent a political figure and statesman; no more farsighted and wise politician; no more vivid personality for whom people of good will throughout the world harbor such sincere feelings of sympathy and love, gratitude and trust; no other person seen as a more outstanding fighter for peace and universal progress ... and as the outstanding organizer and inspirer of this sacred struggle, than Leonid Ilyich Brezhnev.[1]

These signs of increased power contrasted sharply with the rumors of Brezhnev's resignation. Any judgment about the purpose of those rumors is extremely speculative, but one hypothesis deserves mention. The leadership may have wished to create the impression that Brezhnev's position was unstable as a means of putting pressure on the United States to sign a SALT agreement before the Twenty-fifth Party Congress. When it became clear that no new agreement could be signed in time and with Soviet-American tensions heightened over Angola, it was obvious that Soviet interests would be better served by using the 1976 Congress to project the image of a unified leadership with Brezhnev fully at the helm.

The surprise conferral of "Marshal of the Soviet Union" on Brezhnev in that same year, announced with great fanfare in May,[2] represented yet another enhancement of his public image, if not real power. Though not wholly without precedent — Stalin, Beria, Bulganin and Voroshilov had received the Marshal's star — Brezhnev's "military promotion" was unusual.

What was behind it? Had the Party lost control of the military? Was Brezhnev going to bring it to heel? The evidence does not support this hypothesis. However, the publicity given to Brezhnev did serve to symbolize and emphasize his personal authority over the military. Moreover, as Marshal he would formally outrank the military representatives on the Defense Council. Thus, Brezhnev's ego was served by it. The promotion,[3] combined with the public announcement of his chairmanship of the secret Defense Council,[4] also served nicely to publicly identify him for the first time as the supreme commander-in-chief of the Soviet Armed Forces.

The promotion may have been specifically tailored for this. Sokolovskiy's 1963 edition of *Military Strategy* publicized Khrushchev as Higher Military Council head and Commander-in-Chief during peacetime and war.[5] After Khrushchev's removal nothing was said about who held this position.[6] It was generally understood that during a war the Party chief would assume command of the armed forces, but Grechko operated in this capacity in peacetime.

Grechko had frequently expressed concern over the lack of a definitely constituted high command. But steady progress was made in the 1960s toward expanding the command and control capabilities of the armed forces — especially centralized command at the national level — and Brezhnev's promotion to Marshal in the wake of Grechko's death and the appointment of Ustinov as Minister of

Defense cleared up any uncertainty as to who was the peacetime commander-in-chief. Thus, the promotion capped developments long underway. The October 1977 edition of *Voyennyy Vestnik* specifically designated Brezhnev the "Commander-in-Chief."[7]

The promotion may also have been intended to quiet those in the Party who were concerned over a possible diminution of vigilance due to détente. Three times in Brezhnev's acceptance speech he said he viewed the award "not only as personal recognition, but recognition for the Soviet people's heroism during the Great Patriotic War and their unselfish labor to resurrect the economy and defense after the war." More to the point, "It is," Brezhnev said, "one more reminder of the great, beneficial significance ... of the struggle for stable peace on earth and development of peaceful cooperation among states...."[8] Podgorny carried the theme a step further by observing that the award "will be greeted with great satisfaction in the ranks of the glorious armed forces."[9] Shcherbitskiy went on to add that the promotion was being given in recognition of "the merit of comrade Brezhnev as an *outstanding strategist and organizer of the defense of our country*"[10] (emphasis added).

The wide publicity given to Brezhnev's October 26, 1976 Party plenum speech broke the decade old precedent of generally unpublicized plenary proceedings. This and the leadership changes announced at the conclusion of the two-day plenum again reflected Brezhnev's will. A protégé was added to the Secretariat expanding the number in that body to an even dozen. This was the first time since 1964 that 12 members sat in the Secretariat. The newly elected secretary was Yakov Ryabov, Sverdlovsk *oblast* Party Secretary. A Kirilenko man, he also backed Brezhnev against Podgorny.

Vladimir Karlov, who had replaced Kulakov as head of the Agricultural Department, Yuriy Belyak and Fyodor Morgun, the latter two elevated to Central Committee candidate status at the Twenty-fifth Party Congress, were made full members at the plenum. Both Karlov and Belyak have factional affiliations with Brezhnev. Morgun is another Brezhnev protégé who had marked himself in early September and October by sallies against Podgorny. Morgun's promotion to full membership in the Central Committee so soon after his quarrel with Podgorny demonstrated what little leadership solidarity there really was with the Chairman of the U.S.S.R. Supreme Soviet Presidium.

Great strides were made in the development of the Brezhnev personality cult between the 1971 and 1976 Party Congresses.

Brezhnev was awarded the Lenin Peace Prize and compared to Lenin for "warmth and humanity."[11] Phonograph records of his speeches and a postage stamp commemorating his visit to Cuba were issued. Six collections of his speeches and articles, as well as several volumes of his collected works were published. *Pravda* marked the tenth anniversary of the October 1964 plenum with a long unsigned article emphasizing the development of policies associated with Brezhnev. Shevardnadze even thanked Brezhnev for making possible the October plenum that ousted Khrushchev.[12] Brezhnev was portrayed on stage for the first time in 1975.[13] His wartime contribution received increased publicity and he took the limelight at the World War II victory celebrations in May 1975.

Adulation at the Twenty-fifth Party Congress sparked a new round of unusual personal praise. The earlier themes were given polish and, evidently in preparation for his seventieth birthday, something special was done. On the urban landscape, Brezhnev's beaming countenance was everywhere: in large color photographs and huge portraits painted on walls of buildings and draped across streets. A flood of Brezhnev posters and records of his speeches went on sale in the bookshops. The extension of this grand publicity campaign to Lenin's hometown, and to the Lenin memorial in Ulyanovsk in particular, was the most revealing aspect of the entire buildup. No less than five display cases at the memorial were devoted to Brezhnev—only Suslov and Ponomarev rated their own small displays.

As with Stalin and Khrushchev, Brezhnev reached the apogee of his personality cult on his seventieth birthday. He received intensified media buildup just before the celebrations in December 1976. Kunayev at his own televised award ceremony on October 27 recalled his working relationship with the "outstanding figure of our Party and the Soviet government," and observed that all the achievements of the Soviet people were directly linked to Brezhnev. As Kunayev spoke, the camera focused on Brezhnev, who fought back tears.

In other events, Gustav Husak, the Party chief of the Czechoslovak Communist Party, made a special pilgrimmage to Moscow to present Brezhnev with a medal. This naturally generated more coverage in the media. The first official "short biography" of Brezhnev was published in *Moscow News* and a life documentary was televised. Brezhnev later contracted with the American publishing firm of Simon & Schuster for the publication in the United

States of an official biography written by top Kremlin aides. In all of these Brezhnev was portrayed as an unusually gifted and warm leader responsible for all major policy initiatives in recent years.

Such ideas were expanded and others introduced during the actual birthday celebrations. Foreign Communist leaders sent laudatory congratulations that were published daily in the press. Each emphasized Brezhnev's war role and his role in developing Soviet military power and recognized him as an "outstanding political and state leader."[14] He was presented with state awards from Communist countries and the World Peace Council's Frédéric Joliot-Curie Gold Medal for his contribution to peace through détente.

The press elaborated on Brezhnev as a Marxist-Leninist theoretician.[15] He was portrayed as a "steadfast Leninist and outstanding political and state leader" whose "Leninist wisdom has creatively developed Marxism-Leninism to meet the fundamental requirements of building Communism today."[16]

Considerable emphasis was placed on Brezhnev as an experienced and accomplished military leader. Four of the top military journals[18] took responsibility for this by detailing his activities during the war, his role as chairman of the Defense Council and the reasons for his promotion to marshal. Direct references to Brezhnev as a military leader were new in this round of praise (emphasis added):

> As Chairman of the Defense Council, L.I. Brezhnev devotes his constant attention to strengthening the armed might of the country. Under his *immediate leadership*, decisions are taken on questions of military construction, the strengthening of the power and the combat readiness of the Soviet Armed Forces....
> L.I. Brezhnev systematically meets with the soldiers, addresses graduating classes of military academies, and gives constant attention to the all-round increase in the military preparedness of the community of Socialist states.[18]

The journals departed from their earlier pattern of reticence regarding Brezhnev's promotion to marshal. They attributed the award to Brezhnev's "development of military science and strategy as a whole,"[19] "contributions to strategy and campaign tactics,"[20] and recognition of his "talent as an outstanding strategic organizer of our country's defenses,"[21] and simply his "military talent."[22]

It was entirely logical that the cult should be carried to its pinnacle on his birthday by proclaiming Brezhnev *vozhd*, a title denoting a recognized ideological and political leader, in fact an *incontestable* and *infallible leader*.[23] Brezhnev achieved this status in October when Kirilenko, during his own seventieth birthday celebration, described Brezhnev as *vozhd*.[24] Two days later, Geydar Aliyev praised Brezhnev as "*Vozhd* of our Party and of the Soviet people." Six weeks later it was mentioned again at a plenum of the Central Committee of the Communist Party of Azerbaydzhan. There Aliyev paid tribute to Brezhnev, noting that: "With enormous pride and eternal love, the Soviet people rightly call comrade Brezhnev, who is the great man of our times, *Vozhd* of our Party and of all the peoples in our homeland."[25] And on December 19, Mukhamednazar Gapurov, the Party Secretary of Turkmenistan, also referred to Brezhnev as "The *Vozhd* of our Party."[26]

Notably on the eve of Brezhnev's birthday a "theoretical conference on the outstanding statesman of our time" was held in Alma-Ata under Kunayev's sponsorship.[27] Among the papers presented were "L.I. Brezhnev and the Development of Marxist-Leninist Teachings on the Party," "L.I. Brezhnev on the Party's Economic Strategy," "The Development of the Agrarian Policy of the C.P.S.U. in the Works of L.I. Brezhnev," "L.I. Brezhnev's Great Contribution to the Development of the Economy and Culture of Soviet Kazakhstan," "L.I. Brezhnev and the Problems of Cultural Construction in the Period of Developed Socialism," and "The Outstanding Role of L.I. Brezhnev in Implementing the Program of Peace." It was all very reminiscent of the measures carried out many years earlier to establish Joseph Stalin as luminary of all the sciences. Besides the Conference, Brezhnev was cited several times in the republican press as *Vozhd* during his birthday.

Having ascended to the rank of *vozhd*, Brezhnev was in his best position yet to impose his will. Yet his absence from public view after his birthday gave rise to new rumors of trouble. But events were to prove that he had been neither inactive nor lacked political vitality. In fact, as summer approached, he was on the move again, this time against the third member of the leadership troika, Podgorny.

Relations between Brezhnev and Podgorny had been visibly strained for some time. Numerous factors were responsible. There were differences over détente, for example. But Brezhnev's plan to assume Podgorny's job in the Supreme Soviet was the reason for Podgorny's opposition to the new constitution Brezhnev wanted.

As Chairman of the Subcommittee on State Administration,[28] Podgorny was in a strong position to block Brezhnev's plans. Compromise was reached on some items accounting for some of the imperfections and unfinished form of the Constitution approved in 1977.

But not all differences with Podgorny and other members could be resolved. To expedite drafting of the Constitution in time for presentation to the June convocation of the U.S.S.R. Supreme Soviet, Brezhnev summoned a Consititutional Commission meeting on May 24, 1977, at which he called for and got the Commission reorganized. Podgorny was ousted as the Subcommittee's chairman at this meeting, thus allowing passage of a draft Constitution.

This foreshadowed Podgorny's removal from the Politburo. At the Party plenum held the next day, Brezhnev presented the Draft Constitution. After approving it "in the main," the plenum dismissed Podgorny from the Politburo. Two weeks later, he was relieved of all posts; Brezhnev assumed Podgorny's duties as Chairman of the Supreme Soviet Presidium. On May 27, Brezhnev reported on the Constitution to the Presidium which in turn issued an ukase approving the draft and setting the date of June 4 for its publication.

Brezhnev may have had mixed motives for pressing the constitutional matter in May 1977. Aside from Brezhnev's interest in seeing his own policy preference put in concrete, the move was politically expedient in light of the 18 years the constitution had been in the works and the reports that it would probably be ready by the Twenty-fifth Party Congress. After having been proclaimed *vozhd*, the degree of his infallibility and power was directly measured by whether the constitution that he wanted was approved or not. Despite the compromise nature of the new constitution, it is predominently Brezhnevian and the crown of Brezhnev's career.

The Constitution expands the economic, social and cultural rights of Soviet citizens, but these rights must be exercised so as "not to harm the interests of society." Brezhnev's plenum speech seemed to indicate that the leadership would organize a propaganda campaign around the Constitution with a view toward averting domestic and foreign attention from the crackdown on Soviet dissidents.

The theoretical basis of the new Constitution is as much Khrushchevian as Brezhnevian. The term "state of the whole people" contained in the document was Khrushchev's which Brezhnev discarded in 1964 and took up again only in 1970. The term "developed socialism" (*razvitoy sotsialism*), used to refer to the U.S.S.R.'s present stage of development, is merely a substitution for Khrushchev's earlier term "mature socialism" (*zrely sotsialism*).

At the same time, the Constitution contains changes in institutional relationships that Brezhnev has long pressed for. The "guiding role of the Party" is more explicitly spelled out and given added prominence, reflecting Brezhnev's desire to invigorate the C.P.S.U. and reassert its primacy vis-à-vis the state organs. The powers of the Supreme Soviet Presidium have also been enlarged, which reflects the formal recognition of the actual growth of its power over the past decade. The Supreme Soviet has the power to decide all matters of state, economic, societal, and cultural development and control of the execution of those decisions by the Council of Ministers. Brezhnev's choice of control from the center and strengthened integration of central and republic authorities are emphasized.

The government's ministries are discussed only in general terms instead of being listed individually as in the previous constitution. The omission of details about the composition of the Council of Ministers, while providing no advantage to Brezhnev if he wanted a change in its composition, has removed unnecessary detail from the Constitution and therefore the need for a constitutional amendment whenever a ministry is reconstructed. This will make it easier for him and others long interested in streamlining economic management to effect reorganization of part of the ministerial structure. Authority over the people's control committees is transferred from the Council of Ministers to the Supreme Soviet where, in the hands of a vigorous Presidium chairman, it could be used as a watchdog to pinpoint bureaucratic obstructionalism in policy execution.

The Constitution therefore appears to incorporate some institutional features with potential significance for tackling some fundamental problems in the domestic sphere. Brezhnev now has some of the requisite tools with which to whip the inert government bureaucracy into shape. On July 20, Mikhail Solomentsev, Politburo member and Chairman of the R.S.F.S.R. Council of Ministers, hinted as much when he observed that: "L.I. Brezhnev's combining of work in the highest post of Party and state leadership is expedient" because "it will serve to further elevate the controlling and directing role of the Party and ... will facilitate new achievements in fulfilling the decisions of the Twenty-fifth Party Congress in building communism."[29]

Two distinct features of and notable additions to the Constitution are the special chapters on foreign and defense policy. The fundamental strengthening of the Soviet position in the world makes these appropriate, as does Brezhnev's own desire to identify himself indelibly with the political and military significance of the Soviet Union in the world today. The salient feature of these chapters is their linkage. Not only do the articles on defense follow foreign policy, but their content is consistent and, most importantly, give continuity to the basic linkage of foreign policy with military preparedness established by Brezhnev in 1964.

The foreign policy goals listed are themselves noteworthy for their content and because they bear a distinct Brezhnev imprint. They are virtually identical to objectives presented by Brezhnev at recent Party congresses. Understandably, "peaceful coexistence" as an operative foreign policy strategy is incorporated into the Constitution. As consistent with Soviet theory and practice, it is linked with the goal of strengthening the Soviet Union and the "world socialist system." Moreover, the long held Soviet position that peaceful coexistence is entirely consistent with Soviet support of national liberation movements and "social progress" is now codified. By providing for support of these in the Constitution the Soviet Union and its clients can now claim that the U.S.S.R. not only has a right but a constitutional obligation to assist national liberation struggles and intervene in Third World conflicts on their behalf.

Significant too is the fact that the "Brezhnev Doctrine" is rationalized and legitimized by the Constitution. The latter states that relations with socialist countries should be based on "socialist internationalism" and "comradely mutual aid." This, of course, was the ideological premise used to justify Soviet intervention in Czechoslovakia in 1968. Thus, the Constitution ensures continuation of the basic direction of Soviet-East European relations.

Brezhnev has long argued that "proletarian internationalism" — meaning Soviet hegemony — also be the basis of relations between the "fraternal communist states." In an authoritative article published in the December 1976 issue of *Voprosy Filosofii*, Mikhail Iovchuk, the director of the Party's Academy of Social Sciences and a prominent Party ideologist, praised Brezhnev for his unswerving allegiance to the "Leninist interpretation" of the principle of proletarian internationalism and its defense against all revisionist attempts to reinterpret it. Iovchuk concluded that proletarian internationalism had thus become a principle element of Soviet life and has contributed significantly to cementing the ideological unity of the socialist camp.[30] The recent manifestations of extreme "anticentralism" of the Eurocommunists stands condemned by the article and by the Constitution.

Besides approving the Draft Constitution and ousting Podgorny from his Party and governments posts, the May 1977 plenum appointed Brezhnev Chairman of the Supreme Soviet Presidium. Controversy immediately arose over whether this decision represented a personal honor or an institutional arrangement. Whoever suceeded Brezhnev would obviously benefit by it. It would also serve to protect Brezhnev since it would not allow for relegating him at some later date to a strictly honorary position as President.

Brezhnev clearly interpreted it as an institutional arrangement. Suslov contended that it was not. In Brezhnev's inaugural speech to the Presidium he explicitly observed that the May plenum had decided to "combine the posts of General Secretary of the C.P.S.U. and Chairman of the Supreme Soviet Presidium."[31] However, Suslov, in nominating Brezhnev as the Party's candidate for the Presidency a day earlier, interpreted the plenum's deliberations differently. He explained that the plenum had "decided that comrade Leonid Ilyich Brezhnev, General Secretary of the C.P.S.U., should simultaneously hold the post of Chairman of the Presidium of the U.S.S.R. Supreme Soviet"[32] because it was expedient since he had long been the regime's leading statesman. In other words, Brezhnev was being recognized for a role he had long played—but that was all. Brezhnev, however, contended that the decision had been taken because it related to the reality of the "constant growth of the leading role of the Communist Party." Surpisingly, he, not Suslov, provided the theoretical justification for combining the Party and state posts.

Brezhnev came out ahead in the controversy. Most top leaders spoke on the matter and supported Brezhnev. Moreover, Suslov suffered because of it. During his seventy-fifth birthday celebration the media slighted him by giving only minimal coverage to his theoretical contributions. Attention was given to Brezhnev the theorist instead. Two days before Suslov's birthday, *Pravda* featured a story on the presentation of the Karl Marx gold medal to Brezhnev for his "outstanding contribution ... to Marxist-Leninist theory" and elaboration of the "problems on developing socialism."[33] A long *Pravda* editorial previewing a new collection of Brezhnev's theoretical speeches followed.[34] The lack of focus on Suslov was especially striking in light of publication of his own collected work the previous March. These circumstances suggest that a move was underway to also transfer the mantle of chief theorist from Suslov to Brezhnev.

XXVI
The Struggle in Perspective

If we imagine no worse of them than they of themselves, they may pass for excellent men. — William Shakespeare.

NEARLY SIXTY YEARS HAVE PASSED since Leonid Brezhnev enrolled in Komsomol to escape the myopic existence of Kamenskoye. Beginning with Lenin's NEP he has participated in every major turn, good and bad, in Soviet socialist development.

Looking back over it all, the terrible Bolshevik Revolution, forced collectivization and industrialization, Stalin's blood purges, World War II, breakneck reconstruction, the political in-fighting after Stalin's death, one wonders how Brezhnev lived through it all. How did a man of his humble origins become so inured to death and brutality that he seized the chance to direct the instrument dealing it out?

He survived on the obstacle strewn path to power because he possessed the right mixture of tenacious energy, drive, cunning, discipline, ruthlessness, concealment, a polemic-sharpened intellect and a healthy respect for the Soviet political terrain. But above all Brezhnev had ambition. He was at once a dreamer and a disguised power seeker. He was a Stalinist and he practiced Stalinist methods because it was necessary for survivial and advancement. His early ascent, like Stalin's and Khrushchev's, was not one a scrupulous man could have made.

Khrushchev groomed him well. Brezhnev's style was one of shrewdness in the early years, the very talent Khrushchev sought when he brought Brezhnev to Moscow. Brezhnev was skilled in the art of political maneuvering. He was resilient and patient. No reformist fanatic, he portrayed himself as a safe Party man with practical experience who, though a trifle lackluster, had the requisite drive and leadership ability. In the words of one Soviet official, Brezhnev had proven himself to be a "pragmatist" and a "political engineer."

The fact that Western diplomats did not regard him as a serious contender for Khrushchev's throne suggests that Brezhnev's personal qualities and capabilities were unknown. Even after he

317

captured power, Western observers regarded him as a "reed painted the color of steel," "an unprepossessing mediocre Party caretaker" who would not violate collective leadership. Brezhnev proved them wrong.

Though Brezhnev's style and timing have differed, his political strategy as the Party chief has been the same as his predecessors. Both Stalin and Khrushchev rose to the heights of power through the skillful utilization of organizational opportunities and manipulation of personalities and issues already available or created by them. Brezhnev's de facto organizational advantage as Party head enabled him to aggrandize the power of the secretarial office and influence the Central Commitee, the Party Congresses and other critical institutions of the Party and state while successfully preempting his colleagues' views on many important policy initiatives such as détente.

As far as is known in the West, Brezhnev did not use terror or illegal means to aggrandize power. He was able to move ahead of his colleagues and instinctively exploit the issues and opportunities inherent in his Party position to maneuver against his critics and extend his leading role, particulary in policy formulation. He adhered to the same process of establishing primacy in the Secretariat and control of the central Party apparatus as did his predecessors. At the same time, he consolidated influence in the secret police and the military and established dominance in the Politburo by ousting opponents to establish a personal majority. He controls a majority of the votes in the Politburo and Secretariat and, in addition to his Party and military positions, he has captured high state office.

From the beginning, Brezhnev's Party post placed him in a better position than other Party leaders to manipulate executive Party machinery for personal gain. His methods were dictated by the oligarchical leadership mode established in 1964, an acute awareness of his predecessor's mistakes, and his own personality. This caused him to seek new ways to work through and around the collective leadership.

Brezhnev had to appear not to threaten the oligarchy. He was careful to observe collective protocol. This was true even after he achieved dominance in many critical areas. During the 1974-1975 Supreme Soviet elections, for example, comparable treatment was afforded to all leaders. Photographs of Brezhnev, Kosygin, and Podgorny were placed side by side in *Pravda* and their speeches published on consecutive days. Only on television did Brezhnev receive prominence. The seventieth birthday celebration of Suslov in November 1972, Podgorny in February 1973, and Kosygin in 1974 were standardized, while the presentation of fiftieth anniversary awards in the republics visited by Brezhnev, Kirilenko, Kosygin, Podgorny and Suslov during 1973-1974, were also accorded equal press coverage.

It was Brezhnev who, in his speech to the Twenty-fifth Party Congress, went out of his way to emphasize the importance of collective decision making; of course by this time he had secured a personal voting majority in the Politburo. His speech to the Congress stressed the role of the Politburo in contrast to his earlier emphasis placed on the Central Committee when things were not going well in the Politburo for him.

Brezhnev's methods of conducting business differ from those practiced by Khrushchev. While Khrushchev committed such offenses as "premature conclusions, actions divorced from reality, love of injunctions, and unilateral decisions," Brezhnev has been careful to build Politburo consensus for his authority and policy initiatives. He provided some insight into this process before his 1973 Washington trip when he told Western journalists that "ninety percent of the time we decide [policy matters] by discussion, not by vote. But if discussion fails, we postpone the issue, or set up a small group of members to talk it over further."[1]

Thus, he has shown regard for the niceties of discussion and even compromise. Herein lies the key to Brezhnev's success in maneuvering himself into a position of dominance. When removing critics Brezhnev has sought and secured the same kind of consensus against his opponents. This has relieved him of direct liability for their ouster.

Other major aspects of his style include his general adherence to the "confidence-in-cadres" principle as witnessed by the continuity of Central Committee membership and overall territorial leadership stability since 1964, as well as the cooptation on the Politburo of representatives of institutions with which conflict over policies would most likely arise. The latter has been a major factor in Brezhnev's ascendancy as it has enabled him to keep a better feel on the pulse of these institutions and quickly respond to them.

Though Brezhnev may see himself as still working within the bounds of collective leadership, he did not appear, even in the beginning, to be personally committed to "pure" oligarchy. Despite the unexpected leadership stability and outward unity displayed by the absence of a purge within the Politburo for nearly a decade, Brezhnev has worked steadily to enhance his own power.

His aggrandizement of power in the different arenas of struggle has been extensive. To those who were convinced that no one man in the Soviet Union could again concentrate so much authority in his hands, his ascent has been nothing less than remarkable. In 1964, of course, observers attributed the unlikelihood that Brezhnev would not violate the principle of collective leadership as no small factor in his becoming Party chief. Thus, we may have misunderstood the commitment of the Soviet leaders to oligarchical leadership. The accessions to full power of Lenin, Stalin, Khrushchev and Brezhnev have demonstrated remarkable consistency in the ability of the Party chief to forge ahead and emerge, to varying degress, above his colleagues.

Significantly, on the tenth anniversary of Khrushchev's downfall an unsigned article appeared in *Kommunist* stating "the scientific approach to leadership" (*i.e.*, not collectivity) is the determining "mode of work style." Judging by the homage paid to "the Central Committee Politburo headed by C.P.S.U. General Secretary Comrade L.I. Brezhnev" in that article, it represented an effort to link Brezhnev's personal leadership with the "scientific approach."

One of Brezhnev's cohorts supporting this move was Morgun, who stressed that the "activity of the C.P.S.U. Central Committee [which is headed by Brezhnev] serves as a remarkable *example of revolutionary innovation* and Leninist style of work for the whole Party"[2] (emphasis supplied). *Kommunist Uzbekistan* came right to the point when it stated:

> Collectivity of leadership in no way diminishes the role of the Party leader nor turns him into a mere executor who cannot decide a single question without a conference or a meeting. On the contrary, collectivity, if understood correctly and organized in a business-like manner, assumes a high degree of responsibility and autonomy on the part of the leader in making his own timely decisions on practical questions.[3]

The prime determinant of whether or not the Party chief has attained personal rule is his ability to determine the composition of the Politburo and establish a personal majority in that body to vote with him. Brezhnev's Politburo changes at the April 1973 plenum brought him to the brink of personal rule, but it was not until Shelepin's ouster at the April 1975 plenum that he attained it. Symbolic of that achievement was the publication of a cable from a Belgrade correspondent to *Pravda* on June 19, 1975. The cable, reporting the local publication of Brezhnev's *Selected Works,* noted: "Being C.P.S.U. Central Committee General Secretary ... L.I. Brezhnev directs the C.P.S.U.'s activity toward solving tasks which stand before the U.S.S.R. at the current stage of development."

Podgorny's ouster from the Politburo and Brezhnev's assumption of his post in the Supreme Soviet in 1977, were clear cut manifestations of limited personal rule. This personal rule is generating confidence and satisfaction. Much of the warmth and affection displayed for Brezhnev at the Twenty-fifth Party Congress appeared genuine. Brezhnev was praised for his comradeliness and trust, his "respectful relation to people and the Party" and for providing "a good atmosphere in which to work" and "breathe easy." Shevardnadze even characterized him as one who does not "clothe himself in the mantle of a superman, nor does he try to do everyone's work and thinking for them."[4]

The long years of political struggle at home and aboard have clearly taken their toll on Brezhnev. Ever since his trip to Cuba in January 1974, delayed because of illness, it has become increasingly evident that his health is deteriorating. Going strictly by reports in the Western press, Brezhnev would seem to suffer from every major disease from heart trouble to cancer. In 1974, he underwent surgery for dental and jaw problems and he wears a pacemaker. During a severe bout with influenza in early January 1978, Soviet dissident Roy Medvedev told American jounalists that Brezhnev was "seriously ill." The following spring there were rumors that Brezhnev had suffered a heart attack.

Rumors like these abound in Moscow whenever Brezhnev is absent from public view for any length of time. They personally irritate him and cause him to go to great lengths to disprove them. He officially protested an article on his health in the January 25, 1978 edition of the Yugoslav biweekly *Start* and demanded an apology. He also made at least ten public appearances in late January and February 1978, to show that he was a healthy and confident leader going about the business of running the state. For the first time in months he attended two evening soccer games during that time to convey the impression that he was not only able to carry out his daily duties, but brave the bitter cold to enjoy an evening or two of soccer as well. Similar displays were made in early 1979 when the switch in venue from Washington to Vienna for the American-Soviet summit sparked new rumors that he was really not up to the meeting with President Carter.

President Carter receives the kiss of peace in Vienna, August 1979.
Brezhnev warned that any United States attempt to amend the arms
limitation treaty would result in "serious even dangerous consequences for
our relations." (World Wide Photos.)

Though Brezhnev has tried hard to hide it, in his seventies old
age and poor health have caught up with him. His speech is slurred
and labored. His face is often flushed and puffy and his mouth and
jaw remain contorted from the 1975 operation. He now seldom
displays spontaneous animation at public appearances. Once he was
the life of the party. Today he no longer jumps up from his table to
propose toasts, shake hands, or chat with guests. His fatigue
threshold seems significantly lower. Sometimes he stumbles and loses
his balance and despite heavy television editing his public perform-
ances are shaky.

Foreign leaders who have met him in the late 1970s had mixed
impressions of his fitness. During his trip to France in June 1977,
Brezhnev appeared fatigued and relied heavily on aides and prepared

notes, but he made numerous strong appearances before and after the trip. In West Germany on May 1978, however, he had to be assisted down the steps of his plane, cut back his itinerary, took numerous rest stops and was reportedly accompanied by two special vans carrying heart and lung equipment. President Giscard d'Estaing was disappointed with Brezhnev's brief periods of concentration during the French-Soviet summit in Moscow in April 1979. But before he died, Tito, in his eighties, found Brezhnev vigorous in a visit later that year.

Nearing 75 years of age, time is running out for Brezhnev. But it can be expected that he will hold on to the reins of power as long as it is humanly possible. He is possessive of the power he fought so hard to attain and so long as he is physically able he will stay at the helm of a state whose senior leaders are almost as old or even older than himself—Kosygin, also no longer strong was born in 1904, and Suslov, in 1902 (though he is in better health than Brezhnev).

Brezhnev is suspicious of younger men who would publicly demonstrate their fitness as contenders for his Party crown in the contest for succession that must come. Kulakov fell into the trap and Brezhnev relegated him to the outer limits of the Politburo. Brezhnev probably has not made extensive succession arrangements. However, he has built a powerful personal political machine to which he can delegate responsiblity as his physical and mental capabilities decline and to which he feels that he can entrust his place in Soviet history when the time comes. For now, though, Leonid Ilyich Brezhnev remains the engineer quietly directing the politics of the Kremlin.

Chapter Notes

NOTES TO CHAPTER I

1. The Institute of Marxism-Leninism of the CPSU Central Committee, *Leonid Ilyich Brezhnev: Kratkiy biograficheskiy ocherk* (Moscow: Politizdat, 1974) p. 4. (Hereafter cited as *Ocherk*.)

2. Data on Kamenskoye were derived from numerous sources, including the 1973 interview and letters from Nathan Kruglak, the various Russian and Ukrainian official histories and encyclopedias, particularly the Ukrainian Republic Academy of Sciences, *Istoriya rabitnichogo klasi Ukrainskoy RSR* (Kiev: Naikova Dimka, 1967), I, II; and A. Ya. Pashchenko, et al., *Istoriya mist i sil URSR Dnepropetrovska* (Kiev: Institut Istorii Akademii Nauk URSR, 1969). (Hereafter cited as *Mist i sil Dnepropetrovska*.)

3. Photos of Natalya with the family taken in the 1930s were shown for the first time on Moscow television on the occasion of Brezhnev's seventieth birthday celebration in 1976. See also the *Ocherk*, opposite page 144.

4. "Tomorrow Is Three Suits," *Time*, 21 February 1964.

5. The Academy of Sciences of the USSR, *Leonid I. Brezhnev: Pages from His Life* (New York: Simon & Schuster, 1978), p. 17. (Hereafter cited as *L.I. Brezhnev.*)

6. *Ibid.*, p 20.

7. *Ibid.*

8. "What the Reds Did to the Ukraine," *Current History* (New York Times) vol. 16, no. 14 (1922), p 631.

9. *L.I. Brezhnev*, p 22.

10. General Anton Denikin, *The White Army* (London: Jonathan Cape, 1930), p 292.

11. For an account of Makno's activities see P. Arshinov, *Istoriya Makhnovskogo Dvizheniya 1918-1921* (Berlin, 1923).

12. "The Russian Famine Tragedy," *Current History* (New York Times) vol. 16, no. 1 (April 1922).

13. Nathan Kruglak, interview, 1973.

14. Victor Kravchenko, *I Choose Freedom* (London: Robert Hale, 1947), p23.

NOTES TO CHAPTER II

1. By restoring the profit motive and private trade, in effect Lenin postponed the goals of the revolution.

2. See T.H. Rigby's discussion on selection of personnel in his *Communist Party Membership in the USSR 1917-1967* (Princeton, N.J.: Princeton University Press, 1968) p 456. (Hereafter cited as *Party Membership 1917-1967*.)

3. *Pravda*, April 24, 1974.

4. See Merle Fainsod, *How Russia Is Ruled* (Cambridge, Mass.: Harvard University Press, 1953), pp242-3.

5. *Pravda*, April 24, 1974.

6. *Vlast sovetov*, no. 23, June 6, 1927.

7. B.N. Ponomarev et al., *History of the Communist Party of the Soviet Union*, 2d rev. ed. (Moscow: Foreign Languages Publishing House, n.d.) II, p441. (Hereafter cited as *History of the CPSU.*)

8. *KPSS v rezolyutsiyakh*, (Moscow: Politizdat, 1954), II, pp461, 485; *Bednota*, April 1928 (emphasis supplied).

9. Brezhnev generally prefers to say that his "working life" began in a factory: "I myself had the good fortune to start my working life in a collective at a large factory." From a speech at the Likhachev Automobile Plant on April 30, 1976, cited in "A Short Biography of Leonid Brezhnev," *Soviet News*, December 14, 1976, published by the Press Department of the Soviet Embassy in London.

10. *Leonid Ilyich Brezhnev, General Secretary of the Central Committee of the Communist Party of the Soviet Union: A Short Biography* (Moscow: Novosti Press Agency Publishing House, 1976) p6 (emphasis supplied). (Hereafter cited as *Short Biography.*)

11. N. Mikhaylov, *Soviet Geography: The New Industrial and Economic Distribution of the USSR* (London: Methuen, 1935) pp119, 146-7.

12. Quoted in *Na agrarnom fronte*, no. 8 (1928), p123.

13. *Istoriya Sovetskogo krestyanstva i kolkhoznogo stroitelstva v USSR* (Moscow: Politizdat, 1963), p127.

14. *Shestnadtsataya konferentsiya VKP (b)* (Moscow: Politizdat, 1962), pp276, 277.

15. Brezhnev's promotion to chief of a land team is noted in the *Bolshaya Sovetskaya entsiklopediya-yezhegodnik* (Moscow: Politizdat, 1965), p587.

16. For a translation of Stalin's speech see Joseph Stalin, *Leninism* (London: Allen & Unwin, 1940), II, pp159-60.

17. *Stalin Sochininiya* (Moscow: Politizdat), XII, pp 8, 90; *Shestnadtsataya konferentsiya VKP (b)*, pp76, 322-3, 780.

18. Stephen F. Cohen, *Bukharin and the Bolshevik Revolution: A Political Biography, 1888-1938* (New York: Knopf, 1973), p327.

19. See Rigby, *Party Membership 1917-1967*, p186.

20. The 1927 census added a number of occupations to the "white collar" worker category. Junior technical personnel like Brezhnev were included and generally excluded from membership in the Party. Rigby, *Party Membership 1917-1967*, p 160; F. Risel, "Rost partii za dva goda," in *Partiynoye stroitelstvo*, no. 10 (May 1930), p10.

21. Ponomarev, *History of the CPSU*, pp442-3.

22. *Pobeda oktyabrskoy revolyutsii na Urale i uspekhi sotsialisticheskogo stroitelstva za 50 let Sovetskoy vlast* (Sverdlovsk: Politizdat, 1968), p352 (hereafter cited as *Pobeda oktyabrskoy*); Ponomarev, *History of the CPSU*, p438.

23. *Pobeda oktyabrskoy*, p351.

24. *Ibid.*, p352.

25. *Resheniya partii i pravitelstva po khozyaystvenym voprosom (1917-1967)* (Moscow: Politizdat, 1967), II, pp157-60.

NOTES TO CHAPTER III

1. *Pravda,* June 27, 1930; and *Mist i sil Dnepropetrovska,* pp233-5.
2. *Ocherk,* p7.
3. *Mist i sil Dnepropetrovska,* p234.
4. *L.I. Brezhnev,* p28.
5. *Ibid.,* p29.
6. *Ocherk,* p7.
7. Resolution of the CPC and CC CP(b)U of 15 December 1932, cited in S.O. Pidhainy et al., ed., *Black Deeds of the Kremlin: A White Book,* vol. 2, (Toronto: Ukrainian Association of Victims of Russian Communist Terror, 1955), p455-6. (Hereafter cited as *Black Deeds of the Kremlin.*)
8. *Mist i sil Dnepropetrovska,* p235.
9. Pidhainy, *Black Deeds of the Kremlin,* p594.
10. *Ibid.,* pp72, 73, 676.
11. *Ibid.,* p115.
12. William H. Chamberlin, *Russia's Iron Age* (Boston: Little, Brown, 1934), p89.
13. Edward Crankshaw, *Khrushchev: A Career* (New York: Viking Press, 1966) p81. (Hereafter cited as *Khrushchev.*)
14. Ponomarev, *History of the CPSU,* p487.
15. See *Pravda,* May 27, 1976.
16. *L.I. Brezhnev,* p31 (emphasis supplied).
17. See *Pravda,* January 13 and May 17, 1936.
18. For a detailed discussion of Brezhnev's view of the Stalin era, see Paul J. Murphy's "The Stalin Legacy under Brezhnev," in *World Review,* 13 (March 1974), pp29-41.
19. *Pravda,* November 4, 1967.
20. *Pravda,* November 29, 1969.
21. *Leonid Ilyich Brezhnev: stranitsy zhizni-stranitsy epokhi* (Moscow: Izdatelstvo "Planeta," 1976), p39. (Hereafter cited as *L.I. Brezhnev stranitsy.*)

NOTES TO CHAPTER IV

1. See *Pravda* January 24 and August 23, 1936.
2. Crankshaw, *Khrushchev,* pp114-115.
3. *Bolshivik Ukrainy,* no 7 (1938), p25.
4. *Pravda* March 21, 1939.
5. *Visti,* June 17, 1938.
6. *Pravda,* March 21, 1939.
7. See Robert Sullivant, *Soviet Politics in the Ukraine 1917-1957* (New York: Columbia University Press, 1962), p234.
8. *Industriya,* August 24, 1939.
9. *Industriya,* December 3, 1939.
10. See *Industriya,* July 18, 29; September 20, 21; December 3, 1939.
11. *Industriya,* November 24, 1939.

12.   "Ukaz presidii verkhovnoy radi Ukrainska radyanska sotsialistichna respublika," *Visti rad deputativ trudyashchikh Ukrainska radyanska sotsialistichna respublika,* October 29, 1939. (Transliterated from the Ukrainian.)

13.   *Pravda* February 16, 1940.

14.   Vsesoyuznaya Kommunisticheskaya Partiya (bolshevikov), Tsentralnyy komitet, *Istoriya Vsesoyuznoy kommunisticheskoy partii (bolshevikov): kratkiy kurs,* Moscow, 1938.

NOTES TO CHAPTER V

1.   *Pravda,* February 15, 1956.

2.   See *Dnepropetrovskaya oblast v gody Velikoy Otechestvennoy voyny Sovetskogo Soyuza 1941-1945 gg. (Dnepropetrovsk: Dnepropetrovskoye* Knizhnoye Izdatelstvo, 1962).

3.   Iona Andronov, "Looking Back at the Roads of War," *New Times,* no. 9 (February 1972), p20. (Hereafter cited as "Roads of War.")

4.   *Ibid.*

5.   Konstantin S. Grushevoy, *Togda, v sorok pervom* (Moscow: Voyenizdat, 1974) p. 13. This is an excellent, detailed, and fair account of the Dnepropetrovsk *obkom's* activities in the first year of the war. Unless otherwise indicated, all references to Brezhnev by Grushevoy cited in this chapter are taken from this book. General background data were taken from various sources, including the history of Dnepropetrovsk cited in footnote 3 above.

6.   Grushevoy, *Togda, v sorok pervom.*

7.   *Ibid.,* pp24, 25.

8.   *Ibid.,* p62.

9.   General-Lieutenant Alexander Khmel et al., *Education of the Soviet Soldier (Party-Political Work in the Soviet Armed Forces)* (Moscow: Progress Publishers, 1972), pp7, 8, 25, 26. (Hereafter cited as *Education of the Soviet Soldier.)*

10.   Grushevoy, *Togda, v sorok pervom,* pp62, 65.

11.   B.N. Ponomarev, ed., *History of the Communist Party of the Soviet Union* (Moscow: Foreign Languages Publishing House, 1960), p555. (Hereafter cited as *CPSU History.)*

12.   *Ocherk,* p12.

13.   *Short Biography; Ocherk,* p12; and Andronov, "Roads of War," no. 9, p20.

14.   Grushevoy, *Togda, v sorok pervom,* p87.

15.   Andronov, "Roads of War," no. 9, p20.

16.   *L.I. Brezhnev,* p41.

17.   Andronov, "Roads of War," no. 9, p20.

18.   Grushevoy, *Togda, v sorok pervom,* pp94, 95.

19.   As cited in Andronov, "Roads of War," no. 9, p18.

NOTES TO CHAPTER VI

1.   Khmel, *Education of the Soviet Soldier,* p25.

2. S.M. Klyatskin, *SSSR v Velikoy Otechestvennoy voyne 1941-1945gg* (Moscow: Voyenizdat, 1970), p98. For details of this action and the retreat of the Front eastward documented in a Western source, see Albert Seaton, *The Russo-German War 1941-1945* (London: Barker Ltd., 1971), p148.

3. Grushevoy, *Togda v sorok pervom*, p160.

4. *Pravda*, May 9, 1976.

5. Mikhail Kotov and Vladimir Lyaskovskiy, "V porokhovam dymu," *Ogonek*, no. 20 (May 1972), p11.

6. *Ibid*.

7. As reported in *Pravda*, December 27, 1972.

8. Iona Andronov, "Defender of the Caucasian Black Sea Coast," *New Times*, No. 19 (1971), p8. (Hereafter cited as "Black Sea Coast," no. 19).

9. *Ibid*.

10. Grechko cited in "Black Sea Coast," no. 19, p8.

11. *Ibid.*, p9.

12. For a discussion of the problem see *Krasnaya zvezda*, July 29, 1942. For treatment in Western sources see Alexander Werth, *Russia at War, 1941-1945* (London: Barrie and Rockliff, 1964), pp418-9.

13. This was done in an *ukaze* of the Presidium of the USSR Supreme Soviet on October 9 which did away with the "dual command" of political commissars and officers. See Khmel, *Education of the Soviet Soldier*, p26.

14. *Ocherk*, p17.

15. Andronov, "Roads of War," no. 10, p21.

16. *Ibid*

17. Vladimir Lyaskovskiy, "V te dni," *Ogonek*, no. 38 (September 1973), pp12-5.

18. *Ocherk*, p18.

19. *Ibid.*, Lyaskovskiy,"V te dni," p15; S. Borzenko (correspondent), "Vstrecha odnopolchan," *Ogonek*, no. 24 (June 13, 1970), p5.

20. *Ibid.; Ocherk*, p17.

21. "Outstanding Party and State Figure," *Voyennyy vestnik*, no 12 (1976), translated and published in U.S. Army *Translation, Military Herald*, no. 12, (1976), p1 (Hereafter cited as *Voyennyy vestnik, Translation);* and *Ocherk*, p9.

22. Lyaskovskiy, "V te dni," p14.

23. A. Sofronov, "To, chto nikogda ne zabivaetsya," *Ogonek*, no. 38 (September 14, 1975), p14; *Pravda Vostoka*, May 15, 1975.

24. *Ocherk*, p18.

25. Admiral Kholostyakov cited in Iona Andronov, "The Battle of the Caucasus," *New Times*, no. 38 (1969), pp20-1 (hereafter cited as "Battle of the Caucasus"); Iona Andronov, "Defenders of the Caucasian Black Sea Coast," *New Times*, no. 20 (1971), p20 (hereafter cited as "Black Sea Coast," no 20). For the reference to Gorshkov, see Sergey Borzenko, *Zhizn na voyne* (Moscow: Izdatelstvo "Pravda," 1965), p191.

26. Sofronov, "To, chto nikogda ne zabivaetsya," p4.

27. Leo Heiman, "Military Background of the New Soviet Leaders," *Military Review* (April 1965), pp46-50. (Hereafter cited as "Military Background of Soviet Leaders.") Heiman is described as a foreign press correspondent who was born in

Poland, studied in the Soviet Union, and fought with Soviet partisan forces. He attended Munich University and in 1948 went to Israel, where he served in the army and navy for seven years.

28. A.A. Grechko, "The Liberation of Czechoslovakia," in I.S. Konev et al., *The Great March of Liberation* (Moscow: Progress Publishers, 1972), p150 (hereafter cited as "The Liberation of Czechoslovakia"); *Oni osvobozhdali Zakarpatye*, 2d ed. (Uzhgorod: Karpaty, 1968).

29. Reference is frequently made in Soviet sources to Brezhnev's fighting in Hungary. He did emerge in fighting on the Hungarian-Czech border as well as later on the Polish border. See Grechko, *Cherez Karpaty*, p219.

30. *Krylya rodiny*, July 7, 1975.

31. Lyaskovskiy, "V te dni," pp14-5.

32. Sergey Borzenko, *Zhizn na voyne* (Moscow: Izdatelstvo "Pravda," 1965), p189. This is a collection of essays written by Borzenko during the war when he was a correspondent for the newspaper *Znamya rodiny*.

33. Solovyov, cited in Andronov, "Black Sea Coast," no 20, pp18-19. See also *Krasnaya zvezda*, May 19, 1971; A.A. Grechko, *Battle of the Caucasus* (Moscow: Progress Publishers, 1971), p255; and I.C. Shiyan, *Na maloy zemle* (Moscow: Voyenizdat, 1974), p112.

34. A third version as told by the French journal *Paris Match* (no. 1422) (August 18, 1976), alleges that it was Admiral Gorshkov who rescued Brezhnev.

35. K.S. Moskalenko, *Na yugo-zapadnom napravlenii 1943-1945*, kniga II (Moscow: Izdatelstvo "Nauka," 1973), p221. (Hereafter cited as *Na yugozapadnom*.)

36. Andronov, "Roads of War," no. 10, pp18-9.

37. *Ibid.*

38. *Ibid.*

39. *Ocherk*, p25.

40. L.I. Brezhnev, *Na Leninskim kursom* (Moscow: Politizdat, 1976), p128.

NOTES TO CHAPTER VII

1. *Short Biography*, p1.

2. V.I. Petrikin et al., *Istoriya mist i sil URSR Zakarpatska oblast* (Kiev: Institut Istorii Akademii Nauk, URSR, 1969), pp390-1. (Hereafter cited as *Mist i sil Zakarpatska*.)

3. Iona Andronov, "When Freedom Came to the Czechs and Slovaks," *New Times*, no 43 (October 1971), p21.

4. *L.I. Brezhnev*, p79.

5. As cited in Leland Stone, *Conquest by Terror* (New York: Random House, 1951) pp7-9.

6. *Mist i sil Zakarpatska*, p59 (emphasis supplied.)

7. See F. Nemec and V. Moudry, *The Soviet Seizure of Subcarpathian Ruthenia* (Toronto: William B. Anderson, 1955), pp41-2.

8. *Mist i sil Zakarpatska*, p95-6.

9. *Ibid.*

10. *Ibid.*, p95.

11. See, e.g., *Izvestiya*, November 11, 1944; *Zakarpatska Pravda*, November 13, 1944.

12. Vasyl Markus, *L'Incorporation de l'Ukraine subcarpathique à sovietique, 1944-45* (Louvain, Belgium: Centre Ukrainien d'Etudes, en Belgique, 1956) pp46-7. (Hereafter cited as *L'Incorporation.*)

13. *Ibid.*, p47.

14. *Ocherk*, p23.

15. *Mist i sil Zakarpatska*, p95-6.

16. Andronov, "When Freedom Came to the Czechs and Slovaks," p21.

17. *Ibid.*, p19; Iona Andronov, "When Freedom Came to the Czechs and Slovaks," *New Times*, no. 44 (October 1971), p25.

18. *L.I. Brezhnev*, p88.

19. *Mist i sil Zakarpatska*, p59.

20. *Ibid.*

NOTES TO CHAPTER VIII

1. L.I. Brezhnev, "Vozrozhdeniye," *Novyy mir*, no. 5 (1978), p3. (Hereafter cited as "Vozrozhdeniye.")

2. *Ibid.*

3. *L.I. Brezhnev*, p93.

4. Stalin introducing the first postwar Five Year Plan as cited in Crankshaw, *Khrushchev*, p152.

5. Brezhnev, "Vozrozhdeniye," p5.

6. *Ocherk*, p32.

7. Party archives of the Zaporozhskaya *Obkom* of the Communist Party of the Ukraine, Drawer 102, Inventory 1, File 814, Sheets 125-126, as cited in *Ocherk*, p30-1.

8. Central Party Archives of the Institute of Marxism-Leninism of the CPSU Central Committee, Drawer 17, Inventory 48, File 2151, Sheet 395, as cited in *Ocherk*, p36.

9. *Pravda Ukrainy*, October 5, 1946.

10. *Ibid.*, January 18, 1947.

11. Brezhnev, "Vozrozhdeniye," p15.

12. *Ibid.*, p16 (emphasis supplied).

13. "Brezhnevi Gamble," *Thought* (New Delhi), November 7, 1970, p4.

14. Brezhnev, "Vozrozhdeniye," p7.

15. *Ibid.*, p7.

16. *Ibid.*, p9.

17. *Ocherk, p37.*

18. Brezhnev, *"Vozrozhdeniye," p24.*

19. *Pravda Ukrainy*, October 2, 1947.

20. *Ibid.*, July 6, 1947.

21. *Pravda Ukrainy*, August 1, 1947.

22. *Pravda Ukrainy*, December 7, 1947.

23. These objectives were stated by Brezhnev in retrospect at the *oblast* Party conference in March 1948. See *Pravda Ukrainy* March 3, 1948, and January 14, 1949.

24. *Pravda Ukrainy*, March 3, 1948.

25. *Ibid.*, January 14, 1949.

26. This was true for the Ukraine as a whole. See T.H. Rigby, "Social Orientation of Recruitment and Distribution of CPSU Membership: Recent Trends," *Amercan Slavic and East European Review*, October 1957, pp275-90.

27. *Pravda Ukrainy*, January 29, 1949.

28. *Ibid.*, January 29 and 31, 1950. (Emphasis supplied.)

NOTES TO CHAPTER IX

1. *Pravda Ukrainy*, March 31, 1950.

2. L.I. Brezhnev, "Kritika i samokritika-ispytannyy metod vospitaniya kadrov," *Bolshevik* no. 17 (September 1952). (Hereafter cited as *Bolshevik*, no. 17.)

3. *Sovetskaya Moldaviya*, July 28, 1950.

4. *Ibid.*, September 3, 1950.

5. *Ibid.*, October 14, 1950.

6. D. Tkach, "Politicheskiye doklady mestnykh rukovodyashchikh rabotnikov dlya naseleniya," in *Bolshevik* no. 24 (December 1951), pp64-5. (Hereafter cited as *Bolshevik*, no. 24.) (Emphasis supplied.)

7. *Sovetskaya Moldaviya*, October 14, 1950.

8. *Ibid.*, January 31, 1951.

9. Tkach, *Bolshevik*, no. 24, p69.

10. *Sovetskaya Moldaviya*, September 15, 1952. These changes were based on an article by Stalin entitled "On Questions Concerning the Development of the Moldavian Language, published in *Sovetskaya Moldaviya* in 1952.

11. *Ibid.*

12. *Ibid.*

13. *Ibid.*, April 4, 1951.

14. S.P. Trapeznikov, *Istoriya Moldavskoy SSR* (Moscow: Izdatelstvo "Kartya Moldovenyaske," 1968) p580.

15. A.A. Zavtur and A.M. Lisetskiy, *Profsoyuzy Sovetskoy Moldavii* (Kishinev: Izdatelstvo "Kartya Moldovenyaske," 1975) pp101-2.

16. *Sovetskaya Moldaviya*, April 4, 1951.

17. *Ibid.*, July 15, 1951.

18. *Pravda*, September 13, 1952.

19. *Ibid.*

20. Trapeznikov, *Istoriya Moldovskoy SSR*, p620.

21. *Pravda*, September 2, 1952.

22. Brezhnev, *Bolshevik*, no. 17.

NOTES TO CHAPTER X

1. Crankshaw, *Khrushchev*, pp182-3.

2. Leo Gruilow, ed., *Current Soviet Policies*, Vol. II: *Documentary Record of*

the Twentieth Communist Party Congress and Its Aftermath (New York: Praeger, 1957), pp172-88.

3. The existence of this body was only made known on March 6, 1953. See *Pravda* that date.

4. B.D. Wolfe as cited in W.W. Rostow, *The Dynamics of Soviet Society*, (New York: W.W. Norton, 1967), p231.

5. See *Pravda*, March 17, 1953.

6. *Partiynaya rabota v Sovetskikh Vooruzhennykh Silakh* (Moscow: Voyenizdat, 1972), p67.

7. The transfer from head of the Navy's political administration to deputy head of the MPA should not be seen as a further demotion, rather it reflected the transitory nature of Brezhnev's position. For an opposite view see John Dornberg, *Brezhnev: The Masks of Power* (London: Andre Deutsch, 1974), p123.

8. A.A. Grechko, ed., *Sovetskaya Voyennaya Entsiklopediya* (Moscow: Voyenizdat, 1976), I, p586.

9. Rostow, *The Dynamics of Soviet Society*, p258.

10. See *Sotsialisticheskiy vestnik*, vol. 36, nos. 7-8 (1956), p46; John Fisher, "Easy Chair — Some Guesses about the Next Kremlin Conspiracy," *Harper's Magazine*, 238 (March 1969); Thaddeus Whittlin, *Commissar — The Life and Death of Lavrenty Pavlovich Beria* (New York: Macmillan, 1972), page xxxiii; Victor Alexandrov, *Khrushchev of the Ukraine: A Biography,* (London: Victor Gallancz, 1957), p110-4.

11. John Fisher, "Easy Chair — Some Guesses about the Next Kremlin Conspiracy."

12. Oleg Penkovsky, *The Penkovsky Papers* (New York: Doubleday, 1965) p280.

13. *Krasnaya zvezda*, August 11, 1953.

14. *Ibid.*, August 22 and 23, 1953.

15. *Ibid.*, August 24, 1953.

16. *Ibid.*, September 9, 1953.

17. *Ibid.*, September 14, 1953.

18. See *Pravda*, June 19, 1953.

19. The shift in the importance of the military was apparent by their increased inclusion in the Central Committee elected in October; 14 full and 27 candidate members elected were full generals and marshals.

NOTES TO CHAPTER XI

1. As cited in Alexandrov, *Khrushchev of the Ukraine: A Biography*, p161.

2. L.I. Brezhnev, "Tselina," *Nedelya*, no. 45, (November 6-12, 1978), pp3-13.

3. L.I. Brezhnev, "Iz rechi na sobranii izbirateley Alma-Atinskogo gorodskogo izbiratelnogo okruga," March 11, 1954, in Brezhnev, *Voprosy agrarnoy politiki KPSS i osvoyenye tselinnykh zemel Kazakhstana* (Moscow: Politizdat, 1974), p6 (hereafter cited as *Voprosy agrarnoy*). This book is a collection of Brezhnev's speeches from Kazakhstan, 1954-1956. Unless otherwise indicated, all quotes by Brezhnev cited in this chapter are from this collection of speeches.

4. See the numerous shortcomings related to the Kazakh Party's management of agriculture registered by Brezhnev in his "Itogi yanvarskogo plenuma Tsk KPSS i zadachi respublikanskoy partiynogo aktiva," March 12, 1955, in Brezhnev, *Voprosy agrarnoy*, pp33-46.

5. *Ekonomika selskogo khozyaystva*, no. 3 (1959), p5.

6. *Pravda*, March 27, 1965.

7. The order was signed by Khrushchev and N.A. Bulganin, who succeeded Malenkov as Chairman of the Council of Ministers on March 9, 1955, and published in *Pravda* on March 11, 1955.

8. Speech on February 14, 1956, published in *Pravda*, February 15, 1956.

9. "Iz rechi na XX syezde KPSS February 15, 1956," in Brezhnev, *Voprosy agrarnoy*, p91.

10. *Kazakhstanskaya sovetskaya sotsialisticheskaya respublika* (Alma-Ata: Kazakhskoye Gosudarstvennoye Izdatelstvo, 1960), p173. On October 20, 1956, over 40,000 Party members and collective and state farmers received orders and medals for the 1956 harvest.

Notes to Chapter XII

1. Moscow Domestic Radio Service, January 20, 1957, 0545 GMT, in Foreign Broadcast Information Service Daily Report (Washington, D.C.) [hereafter referred to as *FBIS*], October 23, 1957, page CC12.

2. Professor Hugh Seton-Watson quoted in Rostow, *The Dynamics of Soviet Society*, p212.

3. Penkovsky, *The Penkovsky Papers*, p212.

4. *Krasnaya zvezda*, July 5, 1957. See also *Sovetskaya Rossiya*, Feb. 25, 1959.

5. See *FBIS*, June 3, 1958, page CC6.

6. Michael Lucki reporting in *Trybuna Ludu*, July 7, 1957.

7. See Leo Gruilow, ed., *Current Soviet Policies*, vol. 3: *Documentary Record of the Extraordinary 21st Party Congress of the Soviet Union* (New York: Praeger, 1960), pp181-2.

8. Lucki, *Trybuna Ludu*, July 9, 1957.

9. N. Ignatov, *Izvestiya*, October 25, 1961.

10. Boris N. Ponomarev, *History of the Communist Party of the Soviet Union* (Moscow: Politizdat, 1959), p655.

11. See the *Daily Telegraph* (London), September 11, 1957, citing a Polish source on the proceedings.

12. See Paul J. Murphy, "The Stalin Legacy under Brezhnev," *World Review*, no. 1 (March 1974).

13. While no further action was taken against the group, new charges were added when Marshal Malinovskiy, Zhukov's successor as Minister of Defense following Zhukov's disgrace and dismissal because he refused to comply with Party decisions concerning Party control of the military, inferred that the group, like Zhukov, had had a harmful effect on the development of the Armed Forces.

Notes to Chapter XIII

1. Two other recipients of the award on that occasion were Khrushchev and Dimitry Ustinov, now the Soviet Minister of Defense, for their respective roles in the development of Soviet missile and space programs.

2. Moscow Radio, November 24, 1973, 1600 GMT, transl., pub. in English in *Joint Publications Research Service* (Washington, D.C.), no. 60795 (1973), p21.

3. *Krasnaya zvezda* and *Pravda* October 27, 1971.

4. See Werner Keller, *East Minus West = Zero*, (New York. Putnam, 1961), p326. For a detailed discussion of this period see *Put v kosmos: materialy gazety "Pravda" o trekh Sovetskikh iskustvennykh sputnikakh zemli*, (Moscow: Politizdat, 1958), p238.

5. *Pravda Ukrainy*, January 29, 1959.

6. General of the Army V. Tolubko, "Raketnye voyska strategicheskogo naznacheniya," in *Voyenno-istoricheskiy zhurnal*, no. 10 (1976), pp14-21.

7. Alfred J. Zaehringer, *Soviet Space Technology*, (New York: Harper, 1961) p104-5.

8. P.T. Astashenkov, *Glavnyy konstruktor* (Moscow: Voyenizdat, 1975), pp163-4; and Leonid Vladimirov, *The Russian Space Bluff* (New York: Dial, 1973), p56.

9. B. Pokrovskiy, "Na ispytaniyakh," *Krasnaya zvezda*, December 13, 1976.

Notes to Chapter XIV

1. *Münchner Merkur* (Munich), May 9, 1960.

2. *Ibid.*, and *Suddeutsche Zeitung* (Munich), May 9, 1960. The latter newspaper referred to Brezhnev as "one of the most powerful figures of the Moscow Party machine."

3. Moscow Tass radioteletype in English to Europe, cited in *FBIS*, April 19, 1960, pages BB 32-3; and *Ibid.*, April 22, 1960.

4. As cited in Robert S. Ehlers, ed., *Current Digest of the Soviet Press* (Ohio State Univesity, American Association for the Advancement of Slavic Studies), vol. 12, no. 49 (January 4, 1961).

5. He was particularly vocal in Africa. Unless otherwise indicated all citations in this chapter are from Brezhnev's speeches broadcast or published in the media. They include speeches at the Friendship Rally at Conakry: Moscow in English to Eastern North America, 0100 GMT, 13, February 13, 1961, published in *FBIS*, February 15, 1961, page BB 19; Friendship Rally at Kankan: Moscow Tass, radioteletype in English to Europe, 0619 GMT, Feburary 14, 1961, in *FBIS*, February 15, 1961, page BB 22; speech at Labe: Moscow Tass, radioteletype in English to Europe, 0010 GMT, February 14, 1961, in *FBIS* February 15, 1961, pages BB 23-5; Kankan Rally: Moscow in English to United Kingdom, 1315 GMT, February 15, 1961, in *FBIS*, Feburary 16, 1961, pages BB 27-9; speech at Kissidougou: Moscow Soviet Home Service, 1432 GMT, February 16, 1961, in *FBIS*, February 17, 1961, pages BB 11-6; speech at Winneba: Moscow Tass in English to Europe, 0634 GMT,

February 19, 1961, and Tass in English to Europe, 1341 GMT, February 19, 1961, in *FBIS*, February 20, 1961, pages BB 22-3; dinner speech Ghana: Moscow Home Service, 1310 GMT, February 19, 1961, in *FBIS*, February 20, 1961, pages BB 24-5; Conakry speech, *Pravda*, February 14, 1961; speech at Labe, *Izvestiya*, February 15, 1961; speech at Kankan, *Izvestiya*, February 16, 1961; speech at Winneba, *Izvestiya*, February 19, 1961, *Pravda*, February 20, 1961.

    6. Tashkent in English to India and Pakistan, 1400 GMT, February 14, 1961, in *FBIS*, February 15, 1961, page BB 27.

    7. See Moscow Tass in English to Europe, 0917, February 17, 1961; Moscow Tass in English to the U.K., 1315 GMT, February 17, 1961, in *FBIS*, February 20, 1961, page BB 29; and William Attwood, *The Reds and the Blacks: A Personal Adventure* (London: Hutchinson, 1967) p14.

    8. Moscow in Greek to Greece, 1630 GMT, February 20, 1961, in *FBIS*, February 21, 1961, page BB 17.

    9. Moscow domestic radio service in Russian, 0936 GMT, June 10, 1961, in *FBIS*, June 12, 1961, page BB 33.

NOTES TO CHAPTER XV

    1. *Pravda*, June 10, 1961.

    2. All quotes from Brezhnev's speech at the Soviet-Indonesian friendship rally are from the Moscow domestic radio service report in Russian, 0936 GMT, June 10, 1961, in *FBIS*, June 12, 1961, pages BB 29-45.

    3. *Times of India*, October 4, 1960; *New York Times*, September 3, 1961.

    4. *Foreign Affairs Record*, no. 6 (June 1960).

    5. Broadcast in Hindu, December 18, 1961; also in Tass report in English, December 10, 1961.

    6. Tass dispatch in English from Bombay, 1959 GMT, December 19, 1961, in *FBIS*, December 19, 1961, page BB 13.

    7. The *Statesman*, December 22, 1961.

    8. *Pravda*, February 14, 1963; Moscow domestic radio service in Russian, 1000 GMT, February 18, 1963, in *FBIS* February 18, 1963, page BB 47.

    9. Airport farewell speech, Moscow domestic radio service in Russian, 1430 GMT, February 18, 1963, in *FBIS*, February 19, 1963, page BB 31.

    10. Moscow Tass in English to Europe, 1119 GMT, February 14, 1963, Moscow Tass in English to Europe 1924 GMT, February 15, 1963.

    11. Moscow Radio broadcast in English to Southeast Asia and Australia, 1545 GMT, October 12, 1963.

    12. Moscow Radio broadcast in Bengali to India and Pakistan, 1100 GMT, October 17, 1963, in *FBIS*, October 18, 1963, page BB 22.

    13. Moscow Tass in English to Europe, 1630 GMT, October 17, 1963, in *FBIS*, October 18, 1963, page BB 23.

    14. *Neue Zürcher Zeitung* (Zürich), September 28, 1962.

    15. *Ibid.*

    16. See *Pravda*, September 24, 1962.

    17. Moscow Tass in English to Europe, 1911 GMT, September 27, 1962.

    18. *Neue Zürcher Zeitung*, September 28, 1962.

19. Moscow Tass in English to Europe, 1952 GMT, September 29, 1962.

20. *New York Times*, October 5, 1962; *The Washington Post*, September 30, 1962.

21. *New York Times*, November 22, 1963.

NOTES TO CHAPTER XVI

1. *FBIS*, June 12, 1961, pages BB 29-45.

2. See the joint communiqué published in *Pravda* June 13, 1961.

3. *Soviet News*, no. 4091, August 7, 1959.

4. *New York Times*, June 6, 1961.

5. Robert M. Slusser, *The Berlin Crisis of 1961: Soviet-American Relations and the Struggle for Power in the Kremlin, June through November 1961* (Baltimore: Johns Hopkins Univesity Press, 1973).

6. *Pravda*, June 16, 1961.

7. *Pravda*, September 30, 1961. All quotations from Brezhnev's speech to the Finnish Parliament in this chapter are from this edition of *Pravda*.

8. *Pravda* September 22, 1961.

9. *Ibid.*

10. *New York Times*, September 16, 1961.

11. See articles in *Krasnaya zvezda* beginning on September 13, 1961.

12. *New York Times*, September 4, 1961.

13. All statements attributed to Brezhnev's report to the Twenty-second Party Congress are taken from *Pravda*, and *Izvestiya*, both October 21, 1961.

14. Michel Tatu, *Power in the Kremlin from Khrushchev to Kosygin* (New York: Viking Press, 1969) pp151-7.

15. *Pravda*, October 22, 1961.

NOTES TO CHAPTER XVII

1. *Pravda*, July 17, 1960

2. See *Pravda*, May 22, 1962.

3. See *Pravda*, October 31, 1962.

4. Brezhnev's pre-election speech to the electorate of the Baumanskiy electoral district, entitled "Our Faith in Our Leninist Party Is Boundless," was published in *Vechernaya Moskva*, February 27, 1963.

5. *Pravda*, February 27, 1963.

6. Frank Stevens, "Who Would Succeed Mr. K?" in *US News and World Report*, April 27, 1964, p53.

7. See Carl Linden, *Khrushchev and the Soviet Leadership: 1957-1964* (Baltimore: John Hopkins Press, 1966), p178.

8. *Daily Telegraph* (London), November 12, 1963.

9. Boffa *L'Unita*, March 3, 1963.

10. See *Kazakhstanskaya pravda*, June 25, 1963.

11. *Le Monde*, July 3, 1964.

Notes to Chapter XVIII

1. Various Soviet and standard Western published biographical directories, books and Soviet memoirs, monographs on specific regional parties, all-Union and Union Republic periodicals and newspapers, especially *Pravda Ukrainy*, as well as lists of elected officials to the Party Congresses were used to obtain biographical data in this chapter.

2. For Mironov's biography see the 1965 *Yezhegodnik*, p597.

3. For reports of this kind in the Western press, see *The Christian Science Monitor*, October 17-19,1964, and RRG, "What Happened to Khrushchev?, Part II," *Radio Free Europe Research* October 20, 1964, p31.

Notes to Chapter XIX

1. Brezhnev's speech to the Czech Party Congress cited here and elsewhere is from the broadcast over Czech Domestic Service in Czech, 2032 GMT, December 4, 1962, in *FBIS*, December 6, 1962, page GG 32.

2. Quotations from Brezhnev's supreme Soviet Pre-election speech are from the *Joint Publications Research Service [JPRS]* August 30, 1963, pp3-15.

3. *Pravda* August 10, 1964.

4. *Pravda*, March 27, 1965.

5. See, e.g., Linden, *Khrushchev and the Party Leadership 1957-1964*, p187.

6. Malinovskiy as cited in *FBIS*, May 1, 1964.

7. December Prague speech, *FBIS*, December 6, 1962, page GG 33.

8. East German Domestic Service, cited in *FBIS*, October 12, 1964, pages GG 15-6.

9. Prague Domestic Service in Czech, 0920 GMT, December 12, 1963, in *FBIS*, December 13, 1963, page GG 37.

10. See interview in *Nepszabadsag*, April 4, 1962, and the article "Programma KPSS, voprosy ukrepleniya vooruzhennykh sil SSSR," *Kommunist*, no. 7 (May 1962), pp11-22.

11. Brezhnev's Supreme Soviet Pre-election Speech, 1963.

12. Prague Domestic Service in Czech 0920 GMT, December 12, 1963, in *FBIS*, December 16, 1963.

13. *Pravda*, October 7, 1964; East Berlin Domestic Service in German, 1716 GMT, October 6, 1964.

14. East Berlin Domestic Service in German, 1716 GMT, October 6, 1964.

15. Moscow Domestic Service in Russian, 1800, August 25, 1964, in *FBIS* August 26, 1964.

16. See French and German newspapers and the *London Times*, various reports October 15, 20, 1964.

17. See *Berliner Zeitung* (East Berlin) and other East German newspapers, October 17-18, 1964; *Pravda*, October 19, November 7, December 4, 1964.

Notes to Chapter XX

1. Martin Page, *The Day Khrushchev Fell* (New York: Hawthorn, 1965), p179.

2. *Frankfurter Allegemeine Zeitung*, January 18, 1964.

3. Hannah Arendt, *The Origins of Totalitarianism*, London: Allen & Unwin, 1958), p405.

4. Tatu, *Power in the Kremlin*, p369.

5. *Pravda*, April 17, 1964.

6. John Barron, *KGB* (New York: Readers Digest Press, 1974), p64.

7. Moscow Domestic Radio Service, October 5, 1964, in *FBIS*, October 6, pages BB 16-18.

8. See East Berlin APN Domestic Service in German, 2102 GMT, October 16, 1964, in *FBIS*, October 19, 1964, page BB 15.

9. Podgorny personally had no reason to oppose Khrushchev. His activities after leaving Moscow suggest that he was unaware of the conspiracy. On October 9 he travelled to Kishinev to represent the leadership at the anniversary celebration of the Moldavian Republic. Not only did his speech support Khrushchev fully, but he added a personal note, stating that he had just spoken with Khrushchev by phone and that he brought Khrushchev's personal greetings. If Podgorny had suspected a conspiracy he could have alerted Khrushchev. If, on the other hand, Podgorny was aware of the plot and was covering up, his subsequent behavior and position in the Brezhnev regime suggests that he did not receive his due reward.

10. This account was reported in Page, *The Day Khrushchev Fell*, pp48-9.

11. *Ibid*.

12. *Pravda*, November 7, 1964.

Notes to Chapter XXI

1. *Pravda*, July 17, 1964.

2. *Pravda*, December 20, 1966.

3. Brezhnev was listed as occupying this post in the 1965 edition of the *Yezhegodnik*, "Buro Tsk KPSS po RSFSR," p18.

4. *Pravda* March 31, 1966.

5. Oleg Penkovsky included Suslov as well as Kozlov in his list of members on the Council under Khrushchev — Penkovsky, *The Penkovsky Papers*, p209.

6. See *Ekonomicheskaya gazeta*, no. 8, (February 1965), pp1-2, 4.

7. *Pravda* May 22, 1965.

8. See *Kommunisticheskaya partiya Sovetskogo Soyuza v resolyutsiyakh i reshenyakh syezdov, konferentsiy, plenumov Tsk*, vol. 8, 1959-1965 (Moscow: Politizdat, 1972).

9. *Pravda* August 20, 1965.

10. Brezhnev's report on Party State Control to the Central Committee was cited in *Pravda*, December 7, 1965.

11. *Pravda*, March 30, 1966.

12. *Izvestiya*, October 11, 1969.

13. *Documents and Resolutions (of the) XXVth Congress of the CPSU* (Moscow: Novosti Press Agency, 1976), p85.

14. Andropov was dropped from the Secretariat at this time because it was probably unacceptable for the KGB head to be a member of the body responsible for supervising the KGB.

NOTES TO CHAPTER XXII

1. *Pravda*, May 9, 1965.

2. An Observer, *Message from Moscow* (New York: Vintage Books, 1971), p55.

3. All quotations from Brezhnev's speech to the plenum cited in this chapter are from *Pravda*, March 27, 1965.

4. *Pravda* and *Izvestiya*, July 4, 1965.

5. *Pravda*, November 7, 1964.

6. See *Pravda*, January 10, 1965.

7. *Pravda*, June 5, 1965.

8. For Podgorny's switch to Brezhnev's way of thinking on defense and resources allocation, see Podgorny's June 9, 1966, Supreme Soviet election speech, in *Pravda* August 3, 1966.

9. *Pravda*, May 22, 1965.

10. They were his speeches to the Victory Day anniversary celebration meeting (*Pravda*, May 8, 1965); the Gold Star award to Leningrad (*Pravda*, July 10, 1965); the military academy graduates speech (*Pravda*, July 4, 1965); and *Pravda* September 10, 1965 and *Pravda* October 24, 1965.

11. See articles by General-Major K. Bochkarev and Colonel I. Zakharov, *Krasnaya zvezda*, January 21, 1965; Marshal Zakharov, *Krasnaya zvezda*, February 4, 1965; and General-Colonel Shtemenko, *Nedelya*, no. 6, January 31 and February 6, 1965.

12. *Fiftieth Anniversary of the Great October Socialist Revolution: Theses of the Central Committee of the CPSU* (Moscow: Novosti Press Agency Publishing House, 1967), p61.

13. Jack Anderson, *The Washington Post*, December 12, 1976.

14. See, e.g., Arthur J. Alexander, Abraham S. Becker, and William E. Hoehn, Jr., *The Significance of Divergent US-USSR Military Expenditures* (Santa Monica, Calif: Rand Corp., 1979), pages vii, viii.

15. See V.D. Sokolovskiy and General-Major M. Cherednichenko, *Krasnaya zvezda*, August 28, 1964, and Marshal P.A. Rotmistrov, *Krasnaya zvezda*, December 29, 1964. They were in part responding to the NATO strategy of "flexible response" and planning, which committed a larger portion of resources to capabilities for fighting a conventional war.

16. *Pravda*, April 25, 1967.

17. In his speech to the United Nations General Assembly on June 19, 1967, Kosygin asserted that "nobody doubts" today that should a new world war start, it would "inevitably be a nuclear one." A.N. Kosygin, *Izbrannye rechi i stati* (Moscow: Politizdat, 1974), p.397.

18. S. Lototskiy et al., eds., *The Soviet Army* (Moscow: Progress Publishers, 1971), p339.

19. General George S. Brown, USAF, *United States Military Posture for FY 1979* (Washington, D.C.: Department of Defense, January 1978), p7.

20. *Khrushchev Remembers* (Boston: Little, Brown, 1970).

21. See Paul J. Murphy, ed., *Naval Power in Soviet Policy* (Washington, D.C.: U.S. Gov. Printing Office, 1978).

22. Brezhnev's speech to Fifth Polish Workers Congress, *Pravda*, November 13, 1968. (Emphasis supplied).

Notes to Chapter XXIII

1. *Pravda*, April 25, 1967.

2. *Pravda*, September 30, 1965.

3. See arguments along these lines in *Kommunist vooruzhennykh sil*, no. 16 (August 1970), pp16-22.

4. *Pravda, Izvestiya*, May 9, 1970. (Emphasis supplied.)

5. *Ekonomicheskaya gazeta*, no. 10, May 1973.

6. *Documents and Resolutions [of the] XXVth Congress of the CPSU* , p79. (Emphasis supplied.)

7. Bernard Kalb and Marvin Kalb, *Kissinger* (Boston: Little, Brown, 1974), pp293, 316.

8. "From Russia with Hope," *Newsweek*, June 5, 1972, pp26-32.

9. *Krasnaya zvezda*, June 13-21, 1972.

10. *Pravda*, April 16, 1973

11. "Detente II: A Web of Common Interests" and "The Many Faces of Brezhnev," *Newsweek*, June 25, 1973, pp31-33. For Brezhnev's image, see "And Now, Moscow's Dollar Diplomat" and "Inside Brezhnev's Office," *Time*, June 25, 1973, pp26-32.

12. *Newsweek*, June 25, 1973. This image contrasted sharply to the impression Brezhnev made on President Charles de Gaulle during the French/Soviet summit in Moscow in 1966. President de Gaulle summed up Brezhnev as "a narrowminded cold warrior, who is unaware of the world in which he lives" — *Newsweek*, June 25, 1973, p11.

13. Roy Macartney, "Warm Summit," *Sydney Morning Herald* (Sydney, Australia), June 20, 1973.

14. *Moscow News*, June 31, 1973, p3.

15. For the agreements see *Text of Communique Released at the Conclusion of Visit to U.S. by Leonid Brezhnev* (Washington, D.C.: United States Information Agency, Official Text, June 24, 1973).

16. Tass, January 30, 1974, in *FBIS*, January 30, 1974, page N 5.

17. See *Kazakhstanskaya pravda*, December 26, 1974; *Pravda Ukrainy*, January 16, 1975.

18. Moscow Domestic Radio Service, December 9, 1975 in *FBIS*, December 9, 1975, page D 5.

19. Tass in English, 0804 GMT, June 17, 1979, in *FBIS*, June 18, 1979, page AA 8.

20. For press reporting of the incident, see "The SALT Summit," in *Time* June 25, 1979, p30.

21. *Ibid; Wall Street Journal*, June 19, 1979.

22. Tass in English 2014 GMT, June 17, 1979, in *FBIS*, June 18, 1979, page AA 12.

23. Tass in English, 1716 GMT, June 21, 1979, in *FBIS*, June 23, 1979, page AA 1.

24. *Die Welt* (Bonn), January 14, 1980. (Emphasis supplied.)

25. *The New York Times*, September 17, 1973, *Boston Globe*, February 11, 1977.

Notes to Chapter XXIV

1. Grishin's support of Brezhnev has somewhat varied over time and with the issues. Essentially he is a conservative who follows Brezhnev's leadership and sees eye to eye with him on defense, industrial and foreign policies. Having become a candidate member in 1961, he was already on the Party Presidium when Brezhnev became Party chief. However, he became indebted to Brezhnev on two counts. First, Brezhnev installed him as Moscow Party chief after the dismissal of Nikolay Yegorychev in 1967 for criticizing Brezhnev's handling of the Arab-Israeli crisis. This facilitated Shelepin's reassignment to Grishin's old job as head of the trade unions. Second, it was under Brezhnev's sponsorship that he was elected to the Politburo as a full member in April 1971.

2. See *XXIV syezd kommunisticheskoy partii Sovetskogo Soyuza stenographicheskiy otcheti* (Moscow: Politizdat, 1971), pp149-56.

3. *Ibid.*, pp26-141.

4. *Ibid.*, pp64-73.

5. See *Pravda Ukrainy*, May 19, June 8, September 22, October 29, and November 11, 1971, May 2, 1972.

6. *Pravda*, January 21, 1975; *Partiynaya zhizn*, no. 2, (January 1975), pp8-9.

7. Moscow Domestic Radio Service, December 3, 1964, in *FBIS*, December 4, 1964, page BB 3.

8. In August 1964, Khrushchev approved a Kosygin proposal to implement an industrial planning scheme (based on earlier proposals made by Professor Yevsey Liberman of the University of Khakhov) at the Bolshevik and Mayak textile plants. The scheme was designed to give managers leeway for initiative and at the same time provide incentives for efficient use of the plant to attain maximum production targets. Its salient points were decentralized administration and incentive bonuses made available to management and workers, determined by the rate of profit earned on the total capital invested in the enterprise.

9. They were *Planovoye khozyaystvo* and *Ekonomicheskaya gazeta*. See, e.g., "V gosplane SSSR," *Planovoye khozyaystvo*, April 4, 1965, pp90-1.

10. *Pravda* and *Izvestiya*, May 16-21, 1965.

11. *Pravda*, March 11, 1967.

12. *Pravda*, December 23, 1969.

13. *Pravda* June 25, 1967.

14. "O rabote partkoma ministerstva myasnoy: molochnoy promyshlennost SSSR," *Partiynaya zhizn*, no. 4 (April 1970), pp3-6.

15. Moscow Domestic Radio Service, December 3, 1964, in *FBIS*, December 4, 1964, page BB 3.

16. *Pravda*, December 10, 1964.

17. *Pravda*, March 11, 1967. (Emphasis supplied.)

18. Michel Tatu, "Kremlinology: The 'Mini Crisis' of 1970," *Interplay*, October 1970, pp13-4.

19. *Izvestiya*, April 13, 1970; *Pravda*, January 13, 1970.

20. L.I. Brezhnev, *On Basic Problems of the Economic Policy of the CPSU at the Present Stage* (Moscow: Politizdat, 1975), translated and published in *JPRS*, November 26, 1975.

21. *Pravda*, December 18, 1974.

22. *Pravda*, November 3, 1974.

23. *Pravda*, December 14, 1974.

Notes to Chapter XXV

1. *Zarya vostoka* (Tbilsi), March 17, 1976.

2. *Krasnaya zvezda*, May 9, 1976.

3. Brezhnev was made General of the Army in 1975.

4. *Krasnaya zvezda*, April 7, 1976.

5. V.D. Sokolovskiy, *Soviet Military Strategy*, trans. Harriet Fast Scott (New York: Crane, Russak, 1975), pp344-61.

6. Sokolovskiy skirted the matter in the 1968 edition of his book.

7. *Voyennyy vestnik*, no. 10 (1977), pp9-10.

8. *Pravda*, May 11, 1976.

9. *Ibid*.

10. *Pravda*, May 8, 1976.

11. *Krasnaya zvezda*, September 16, 1973.

12. *Sovetskaya Moldaviya*, October 12, 1975.

13. *Pravda vostoka*, May 15, 1975.

14. See *Pravda*, December 19, 1976.

15. See especially G.L. Smirnov, "XXV syezd KPSS i teoreticheskiye voprosy razvitiya etape kommunisticheskogo stroitelstva," *Voprosy filosofii* no. 12 (1976), pp3-7.

16. *Pravda*, December 19, 1976: *Izvestiya*, December 18, 1976: *Selskaya zhizn*, December 18, 1976, *Za rubezhom*, December 17-23, 1976; V Zhuravlev and B.N. Ponomarev, "For the Sake of Peace and Progress," in *Sotsialisticheskaya industriya*, December 18, 1976, p13.

17. They were *Voyenno-istoricheskiy zhurnal*, *Kommunist vooruzhennykh sil*, *Voyennyy vestnik*, and *Morskoy sbornik*, all December 1976.

18. *Voyenno-istoricheskiy zhurnal*, no. 12 (1976), p10. See also "Velikaya vdokhnovlyayushchaya i organizuyushchaya sila sovetskogo obshchestva," *Kommunist vooruzhennykh sil*, no. 24 (December 1976), p12; Marshal of Aviation A. Pokryshkin, "Oboronnomy obshchestvu — 50 let," *Morskoy sbornik*, no. 12, (1976), p10.

19. *Voyenno-istoricheskiy zhurnal*, no. 12 (1976), p10.

20. "Vydayushchiysya deyatel partii i gosudarstva," *Voyennyy vestnik*, p3.

21. *Morskoy sbornik*, no. 12 (1976), p5.

22. *Kommunist vooruzhennykh sil*, no. 12, p12.

23. See S.I. Ozhegov, *Slovar russkogo vazyka* (Moscow: Politizdat, 1975), p84. The definition of *Vozhd* is given as "1. Generally recognized ideological and political leader. 2. Formerly: military leader, chief."

24. *Pravda*, October 15, 1976.

25. *Bakinskiy rabochiy*, November 1976, pp3-5. (Emphasis supplied.)

26. *Turkmenskaya iskra*, December 14, 1976. (Emphasis supplied.)

27. *Kazakhstanskaya pravda*, December 18, 1976.

28. In *Pravda* on July 17, 1964, Brezhnev was identified as heading the sub-committee, but as he was relieved of his functions as Chairman of the Supreme Soviet Presidium in July 1964, and assumed chairmanship of the Constitutional Commission in October 1964, the committee chairmanship in due course passed on to Podgorny.

29. Speech to the fifth session of the RSFSR Supreme Soviet on July 20, *Sovetskaya Rossiya*, July 21, 1977. In this noteworthy passage, Solomentsev described the advantages of having one person hold the top party and state posts in language that argued for institutionalization of the practice.

30. M.T. Iovchuk, "Internatsionalizm sotsialisticheskoy kultury," *Voprosy filosofii*, December 1976, pp18-9.

31. *Pravda* and *Izvestiya*, June 18, 1977.

32. *Izvestiya*, June 17, 1977.

33. *Pravda*, November 17, 1977.

34. *Pravda*, November 18, 1977.

NOTES TO CHAPTER XXVI

1. "The Many Faces of Brezhnev," *Newsweek*, June 25, 1973, p33.

2. F.T. Morgun, "Utverzhdaem Leninskiy stil partiynoy raboty," *Kommunist Ukrainy*, no. 4 (1975), p17. (Emphasis supplied.)

3. S. Tatybayev and V. Kudryakov, "Leninskiy stil partiynogo rukovodstva," *Kommunist Uzbekistana* (Tashkent).

4. See *Pravda*, February 27, 1976.

Index